United States Edition

2017 Year A

Workbook for Lectors, Gospel Readers, and Proclaimers of the Word®

Marielle Frigge, OSB, PHD

Elaine Park, SSL, STD

Douglas Leal

LTP
LITURGY
TRAINING
PUBLICATIONS

CONTENTS

Liturgy Training Publications, 3949 South Racine Avenue, Chicago, IL 60609, 1-800-933-1800, fax 1-800-933-7094, orders@ltp.org, www.LTP.org.

Cover art: Barbara Simcoe

This book was edited by Lorie Simmons. Christopher Magnus was the production editor, and Luis Leal was the production artist.

Printed in the United States of America.

ISBN: 978-1-61671-283-9
WL17

In accordance with c. 827, permission to publish was granted on April 26, 2016, by Most Reverend Francis J. Kane, DD, Vicar General of the Archdiocese of Chicago. Permission to publish is an official declaration of ecclesiastical authority that the material is free from doctrinal and moral error. No legal responsibility is assumed by the grant of this permission.

(see endnotes on page x)

As a publisher, LTP works toward responsible stewardship of the environment. We printed the text of *Workbook for Lectors, Gospel Readers, and Proclaimers of the Word*®, with soy-based ink on paper certified to the SFI (Sustainable Forestry Initiative®) Certified Fiber

(continues on next page)

Ordinary Time

The Authors

Two Scripture scholars have written the commentaries:

Marielle Frigge, OSB, has taught Scripture and theology for thirty-three years at Mount Marty College in Yankton, South Dakota. Her PHD in theology and education is from Boston College. A Benedictine sister, she now directs ongoing formation for Sacred Heart Monastery and continues teaching in pastoral settings. Her most recent publication is *Beginning Biblical Studies* (Anselm Academic, 2009; revised 2013).

Elaine Park has a licentiate in Sacred Scripture (SSL) from the Pontifical Biblical Institute and a sacred theology doctorate (STD) from the Gregorian University, both in Rome. She has been a professor of biblical studies and academic dean at Mt. Angel Seminary in St. Benedict, Oregon. Currently she is a pastoral associate at Christ the King parish in Milwaukie, Oregon, and frequently gives talks and retreats on biblical topics.

Douglas Leal has written the margin notes. He holds an MA in pastoral ministry from Boston College. He has directed programs in adult faith formation and education for the Archdiocese of Los Angeles, has written, directed, and acted in numerous theater productions, conducts lector training workshops nationwide, and is the author of *Stop Reading and Start Proclaiming!*, available from LTP. Currently he is vice president of mission integration with St. Joseph Health.

(continued from previous page)

Sourcing Standard CERT–0068767, confirming that the paper manufacturer takes a responsible approach to obtaining fiber. The wood pulp that was required in the making of this paper was sourced from sawmill residuals or pulp logs unsuitable for other uses. A thermo mechanical pulp process in manufacturing provides 100% more efficient use of wood fiber than the conventional process.

Additionally, this paper was produced using completely chlorine-free technology. Biomass fuels were used in manufacturing for lower greenhouse gas emissions, and therefore a reduced carbon footprint.

MINISTRY OF THE WORD BASICS

The Word of God in the Liturgy.

The Word of God proclaimed in the Liturgy is a living Word with power to nourish and transform both those who proclaim it and those who hear it. In the words of the Second Vatican Council's *Constitution on Divine Revelation* (*Dei Verbum*), "The Church has always venerated the divine Scriptures just as she venerates the body of the Lord, since, especially in the sacred liturgy, she unceasingly receives and offers to the faithful the bread of life from the table both of God's word and of Christ's body" (DV, 21).

Throughout its history, the Church has affirmed over and over the close tie between the Word proclaimed in the Liturgy and the Word made flesh received in the Eucharist, recognizing both as Christ present to give himself as food. Pope Francis, in his Apostolic Exhortation *Evangelii Gaudium*, writes that the hearts of the faithful who gather on the Lord's Day are nourished both by his Word and by the bread of eternal life (EG, 15). He emphasizes as well that being fed at both tables gives strength for the whole journey: "God's word, listened to and celebrated, above all in the Eucharist, nourishes and inwardly strengthens Christians, enabling them to offer an authentic witness to the Gospel in daily life. . . . The preaching of the word, living and effective, prepares for the reception of the sacrament, and in the sacrament that word attains its maximum efficacy" (EG, 174).

The image of food to refer to God's Word has a strong foundation in the Hebrew Scriptures. Moses tells the people prior to their entering the land, "it is not by bread alone that people live, but by all that comes forth from the mouth of the LORD" (Deuteronomy 8:3). The prophet Jeremiah, commanded to proclaim God's Word, cried out, "When I found your words, I devoured them; your words were my joy, the happiness of my heart" (Jeremiah 15:16). And God later instructed Ezekiel to open his mouth and eat the scroll. Ezekiel recounts the episode: "Feed your stomach and fill your belly with this scroll I am giving you. I ate it, and it was as sweet as honey in my mouth" (Ezekiel 3:1–3). Each of these passages, and many more, highlight God's gift of satisfying our deepest hungers with a Word that is life-giving.

How does this Word of God actually feed us with joy, happiness, sweetness, and an abundance of life? Think of what goes into a lavishly prepared feast that gives delight and nourishment to guests. In the same way, the Word of God proclaimed in the liturgy also requires careful selection and preparation. Those proclaiming the Word are like good chefs who have done everything needed to present a nourishing meal. The Lectionary provides the selection of the food set at the table of the Word. Its

In the beginning was the Word, and the Word was with God, and the Word was God.

design offers a rich variety, much like a well-chosen menu. The variety of fare means that the readings provide, as fully as possible, an overview of the biblical story and its great themes, even when they might not be people's favorite menu items. Although it isn't the role of the reader to make the selection, it is important for those who proclaim to see where particular texts fit into the broad sweep of the biblical story (our salvation history), how it harmonizes with the season or feast we are celebrating, and how it can offer insights for their particular community at this particular moment. Some questions we might ask are: Why was this text selected? How does it relate to the other readings of the day? How does it provide the variety of nourishment essential for a mature faith? Was the passage selected because of the season or feast, or as part of a continuous reading of a book, letter, or Gospel? How do we hear it echoed in the images and words of the prayers, music, liturgical environment, and ritual actions of this specific liturgy?

In addition to being nourishing food, the Word in the liturgy is also a very personal communication from God to his people: **"When the Sacred Scriptures are read in the Church, God himself speaks to his people, and Christ, present in his word, proclaims the Gospel"** (*General Instruction of the Roman Missal*, 29). Proclaimers of the Word, then, lend their voices for this personal communication, preparing themselves with sincere humility, through prayer, study, and practice to faithfully convey to the people what God intends.

Understanding the Word We Proclaim

Preparation for reading at the table of the Word can be just as multifaceted as preparing for a family feast. Consider the story of Philip and the Ethiopian eunuch, in which Philip asked the eunuch who was reading from Isaiah, "Do you understand what you are reading?" (Acts 8:30), a question that we should ask ourselves in preparing for liturgical proclamation. If we who proclaim do not understand our reading, how can we help the assembly understand it? In his Apostolic Exhortation *Verbum Domini*, Pope Benedict XVI commented: "Word and Eucharist are so deeply bound together that we cannot understand one without the other: the word of God sacramentally takes flesh in the event of the Eucharist. The Eucharist opens us to an understanding of Scripture, just as Scripture for its part illumines and explains the mystery of the Eucharist" (VD, 55).

Understanding Word and Sacrament comes partly through research that draws on the wisdom of others, and also through prayer that relies on the inspiration of the Holy Spirit. The wisdom of others may be both from written sources and from discussion and prayer flowing from the readings, perhaps with people from the parish. The biblical texts themselves, as well as prayers used in the liturgy of the day, are rich sources that can prepare one's mind and heart. Such careful reading, research, and prayer comprise the preparation we do in the days prior to our proclamation. Some additional quiet reflection immediately before the celebration of the liturgy is the final preparation.

Good preparation for proclamation aims at unleashing the power of the Word for the whole assembly. As at a festive meal, a hospitable attitude welcomes all who are gathered and also welcomes the Word that will be proclaimed. We taste, we chew, we savor, we digest and absorb the Word so that it becomes a part of us, going forth with the energy of the Holy Spirit. It is most particularly in the liturgy that God's Word becomes bread plentiful enough to feed five thousand and more, becoming an abundant source of nourishment. This is beautifully expressed by St. Ambrose: "This bread which Jesus breaks is, according to the mystery, the Word of God and a teaching about Christ. When this bread is distributed, it multiplies. . . . Jesus gives his words as bread" (*Treatise on Luke's Gospel*, 6:86).

Elaine Park

Proclaiming Effectively: The Art of the Storyteller

Jesus was an excellent storyteller. The evidence of his skill is right there in the Gospels. Everyone was "astonished" at his "gracious words" which had authority and impact (Matthew 7:28; Mark 11:18; Luke 4:22, 32). You don't attract more than five thousand people to a hillside on a hot day if you don't know how to tell a good story! His skills allowed the Word that he preached to touch the hearts and minds of those gathered. Isn't that what we hope to do with our proclamation?

Listen closely to the good storytellers you know. See how the stories they tell appear on their face, are colored by their voice, seem to flow from their whole being. These people are full of energy as they tell their stories; they work to connect with the family or community that listens; they have a desire, a need, to communicate well. We have the same desire to com-

> # This is my commandment: love one another as I love you.

municate that Word of God well, so these same skills will be crucial to our proclamation of the Word. This book is designed to help you develop those skills.

The commentaries on each reading are written by Scripture scholars who share their insights. The margin notes give you advice on proclaiming the readings, helping you incorporate essential skills into your ministry of the Word. Those notes are intended to coach you as you prepare for your proclamation.

Think of them as comments from a guide or mentor, standing alongside you as you practice, throwing out helpful ideas, hints, strategies, questions, cautions, and encouragements.

Preparing the Text

The ministry of a proclaimer is rooted in the text, so begin there. Read the Scripture commentary that accompanies each reading to help you understand what you're proclaiming. No matter how skilled a proclaimer you are, you can't proclaim what you can't understand! It's also helpful to read the passages from your Bible that come before and after the text, so you have a better idea of its context. For the same reason, it's important to read the other readings of the day, including the Responsorial Psalm. As you gain experience you'll also become interested in how your reading relates to the readings of the weeks prior, and following, and to the season as a whole.

Form or Purpose

The margin notes identify the *form* or *purpose* of each reading, which tells us a lot about how best to proclaim it. Different forms require different emphases, and different ways of proclaiming. Those who study Scripture classify texts into many different forms, but for the purposes of proclaiming, we will use three: *narrative*, *didactic*, and *exhortatory*.

A **narrative** text reads like a story, and may include characters, dialogue, a setting, and action. The point of view may be that of the narrator or any character in the story. Scripture is full of narratives—stories about creation, our ancestors in faith, the history of Israel, the life of Jesus, or the ministries of the first Apostles.

When proclaiming a narrative, strive to help your assembly know what's happening in the story. Keep characters distinct. Be clear about shifts in setting. Allow the community to *see* the story unfold as you proclaim. Some stories may be very familiar to your community through years of repetition. Your goal is to bring back a sense of wonder and anticipation to these stories, so they maintain their power to amaze. Avoid *telegraphing*—that is, resist allowing the end of the story to color how you proclaim the entire reading.

A **didactic** text makes a point or teaches something. The author may lay out an argument or make a case to support the point. The letters of Paul contain mostly didactic text, as do some of the history books, prophets, and wisdom books. The texts describing Jesus' teachings in the Gospel accounts are usually didactic. It's important to understand the author's point and the flow of any supporting argument or logic. Your goal is to help your community follow the argument and understand what's being taught.

Exhortatory texts make an urgent appeal to listeners. They may encourage, warn, or challenge, and often include a call to action. In these texts the emotions are heightened and the stakes are high. Sometimes, the exhortation is directed to God, pleading for mercy or justice or praising God's goodness and love. The speaker is sometimes the author; other times God directly addresses the people. They are most often found in the prophets and the epistles, or letters, but there is also exhortatory text in the Gospels, especially John. In an exhortatory text, it's essential to convey the urgency and passion behind the words.

Although most readings are primarily one of these three styles, some may combine styles. The notes will identify places where the style of the reading changes.

Literary Devices

As you study your text, identify any literary devices. The notes will point out some of these. They can reveal much about the meaning of the passage, so pay attention and make a choice about how they will affect your proclamation. The most common devices are *parallelism*, *thought rhyme*, *paradox*, and *repetition*.

Parallelism refers to phrases or sentences that have a similar structure or express a similar idea, as in these examples:

> for he has clothed me with a robe of salvation,
> and wrapped me in a mantle of justice.
> (Isaiah 61:10)

> I will bless those who bless you
> and curse those who curse you. (Genesis 12:3)

> Remain in me, as I remain in you. (John 15:4)

The rhythm of our proclamation—the words we choose to stress—will help the community hear the parallelism in these lines. If we disregard the parallel structure in our proclamation, we will obscure the meaning. Parallelism is one of the most frequently used literary devices in both testaments.

Thought rhyme is a form of parallelism used in Hebrew poetry. Hebrew poets showed their skill not in the cleverness of their rhymes but in their ability to be deeply descriptive of a thing or idea. Consider this passage from Sirach (15:18–20):

> Immense is the wisdom of the Lord;
>   he is mighty in power, and all-seeing.
> The eyes of God are on those who fear him;
>   he understands man's every deed.
> No one does he command to act unjustly,
>   To none does he give license to sin.

Notice that both lines of each couplet say the same thing, but each line says it in a different way. Thought rhyme occurs throughout wisdom literature and the prophets. When proclaiming, use care to keep the two lines together and use emphasis to show the parallelism.

Paradox uses parallelism to express an idea that seems to contradict itself. Jesus often employs paradox to show that the reign of God will turn our expectations upside down:

> Thus, the last will be first, and the first will be last. (Matthew 20:16)

> For every one who exalts himself will be humbled,
> but the one who humbles himself will be exalted. (Luke 14:11)

Again, use the rhythm of your proclamation to make the parallelism evident, with some extra emphasis on the contradictory phrase.

Repetition of the same word or phrase over the course of a reading emphasizes a point. Sometimes a word is doubled ("Amen, amen"). More often, a word, phrase, or idea is repeated a few times throughout a reading. When you proclaim, make each instance distinct, and build your intensity with each repetition.

Tools: Voice and Body

Studying the text is only the beginning of our work as proclaimers. Our ministry has a significant *physical* aspect—it requires the use of our bodies as well as our minds. Simply reading the words clearly from the ambo so they can be heard and understood is not enough for effective proclamation; we must also pay attention to what we are communicating with our tone, pace, volume, eyes, face, even our posture. In fact, those who study communication tell us that we read meaning more from nonverbal cues than from spoken words.

If I were to approach you with a concerned look and say, slowly, in a low tone and with sadness in my voice, "I have some news for you," you'd likely be very worried about this news. But if I were to run up to you excitedly, with eyes shining, energy in my voice, and quickly say, "I have some news for you," you'd probably be eager to hear the news. Notice that the words were exactly the same in both situations, yet the meaning was completely different. The difference was conveyed entirely through nonverbal cues. Nonverbal expression is critical to our ministry; without the right cues the community will never understand what we proclaim. The notes will help you work on this.

Pace refers to the speed of your proclamation—how fast you speak. The most common problem for proclaimers new to the ministry is going too fast to be understood. More important than finding the right pace, however, is making sure to *vary* your pace, since pace gives clues to the *meaning* of a reading. We express joy or anxiety at a faster pace and sorrow or sadness at a slower pace.

Volume pertains both to being heard (loudness or softness) and to *vocal energy* (the direction and strength of your intention to speak). The notes will suggest places where you might raise or lower your volume, but you should still have good vocal energy even when your volume is low. It's also important to

Magnify the LORD with me; let us exalt his name together.

articulate well so you can be clearly understood; the notes will warn you about any tricky phrases that might require extra attention to articulate correctly.

Inflection refers to the pitch or tone of our voice (high or low). It conveys attitude and feeling. The high end of our range of inflection might be used to express intensity and excitement, while the low end could express sadness or contrition. Find places to vary your inflection throughout your proclamation.

The notes will point out words or phrases in danger of being "swallowed"—that is, words which could be mumbled, and thus lost to the assembly. Make sure you articulate these so they are clearly heard.

Pauses are critical cues that allow your listeners to follow the sense of a text, especially one laying out an argument. Pause in order to break up separate thoughts, set apart significant statements, or indicate major shifts of thought. Never pause in the middle of a single thought. Your primary guide for pauses is punctuation. In general, pause and take a full breath at periods, question marks, exclamation points, and sometimes at semicolons and colons. Don't come to a full stop at commas; rather, break your speech briefly (and take a short, catch-up breath if needed).

There should always be a pause at the end of the reading, before you proclaim the closing dialogue ("The Word of the Lord" or "The Gospel of the Lord"). The notes will indicate when a reading might require a longer pause than usual.

Choice Words. Some words in the readings in this book are printed in bold. These are *choice words*. They're the key words that an effective proclaimer will use to convey the meaning, emotion, and intent of the reading. *They are not necessarily meant to be stressed.* Rather, they are flagged to encourage you to make some *choice* about them. They're significant words, so take some time in your preparation to consider how you will proclaim them.

Eye contact with the community is necessary for effective proclamation. You wouldn't trust someone who didn't make eye contact with you while they were speaking; you'd either dismiss or quickly lose interest in what they were saying. Making eye contact with the assembly connects us with them and connects them to the reading more deeply than using our voice alone. This helps the assembly stay with the story and keeps them engaged.

Except in a few instances, the notes don't indicate where you should be making eye contact in your proclamation because you are encouraged to do so *throughout* the text. Experienced proclaimers look down and scan the next part of the text quickly, then look up and proclaim it. They may make eye contact for as much as seventy-five percent of a reading, particularly on the more significant lines. Of course, this takes practice and experience to do well! If you're new to this skill, set modest goals at first, then increase steadily. Your skill with eye contact will grow over time as your confidence as a proclaimer increases.

Whenever you look up, include everyone in the assembly with your glance, looking most often at (or just above) the people farthest away from you. Link your vocal energy to eye contact; that is, direct your voice to where you look. This will help keep your vocal energy up so you can be both seen *and* heard by the whole assembly.

The notes will indicate difficult or awkward phrases which you might want to proclaim looking directly at the text. Apart from these, however, aim to make eye contact with the assembly as much as you comfortably can.

Posture and Facial Expression. Stand at the ambo in a relaxed posture, with your hands on the Lectionary or the ambo. Don't hunch over, hiding your face from the assembly. Share yourself freely.

Your face will communicate much to the assembly about the reading. It will especially tell them that you're proclaiming "Good News"—the meaning of the word "Gospel." When we share Good News from the ambo we should also share our joy—with a *smile* on our face (and in our eyes and voice). Our smile tells the assembly that we proclaim news of joy, love, mercy, forgiveness, and compassion. Without this cue, they may miss it, so allow yourself to smile when it's appropriate to the reading.

Intention

Our *need* to communicate *something in particular* gives our communication urgency and drive. One of the pitfalls of proclamation is that we don't always have a clear reason to communicate, other than "now it's time for the Liturgy of the Word." The result is a reading that's flat and unfocused. For our proclamation to be effective, we have to rediscover our reason to communicate, our *intention*.

The Scripture commentary will help you understand the original purpose for the text—a good starting point for discerning an intention. What does the reading ask your assembly to *do* or to *be* after hearing your proclamation? After all, we are to "be doers of the word and not hearers only" (James 1:22). Choosing an intention like, "This reading gives the origin of Passover" or "This reading tells about the Annunciation" is a weaker choice than "This reading shows that God will set you free" or "This reading urges you to trust God as Mary did." It's an even stronger choice to shorten the intention into a brief command: "Be free!" or "Trust God!"

Focus on an intention every time you proclaim. (The notes will offer suggestions for some of the readings.) An intention helps pull together all the necessary elements of good proclamation because when we have a *need* to communicate, we work hard to use all our skills to make sure our communication is clear. Of course, you are an *instrument* of the Holy Spirit. Your intention helps you focus your proclamation, but the effect of your proclamation on your listeners is always the work of the Holy Spirit, who gives to "each person individually everything that in the proclamation of the word of God is spoken for the good of the whole gathering of the faithful" (Introduction to the Lectionary, 9).

Expressive Proclamation

Although the Liturgy of the Word is not intended to be theatrical, proclamation cannot be effective unless it is expressive. Readers have little time and few words with which to convey the meaning of a Lectionary passage, and the judicious expression of emotion aids that process greatly. We read emotions very quickly. In the example given earlier, you would have determined a great deal of meaning in my approaching you with excitement or with sadness, before I even said, "I have some news for you." Emotion is a powerful nonverbal communicator, and thus a central element in proclamation.

As we prepare our proclamation we need to make choices about expression. Some choices are

The LORD's word is true; all his works are trustworthy.

already evident in the text. If it says Paul is rejoicing, or Jeremiah is grumbling, or God is acting with compassion, then the emotion we need to express is clear. In other cases, we must make our own choice. The notes offer some suggestions. In a narrative, find an emotion or point of view for each character, keeping in mind that these might change during the reading. In an exhortatory text, all the emotions are heightened, so make bold choices and practice conveying them with your voice, eyes, and face. A didactic text might seem emotion*less*, but assuredly there is emotion present. A teaching is usually given out of *love* for the community being taught.

Admittedly, proclaiming expressively can be a challenge. Many people aren't comfortable showing emotions in public. But the Scriptures we proclaim are not sterile, cold stories; they're dynamic and full of passion. If we fail to include emotion in our proclamation, we're leaving out meaning, thus making it even more difficult for our assembly to understand and connect with the Word. Of course, we shouldn't

proclaim with exaggerated emotion so that we draw attention to ourselves and away from the text. Rather we are called to faithfully proclaim the emotion as it is present in the text.

Pray the Text

You may have a favorite method of praying with Scripture; if so, use it with your text. If not, you can read and meditate on your text during prayer. If you proclaim a narrative text, you could imagine yourself in the story as one of the characters or as an onlooker. If you proclaim a didactic or exhortatory text, you could imagine yourself as the original writer of the text, or as one of the first hearers. If your text speaks directly to God, you can use it *as* your prayer. In your prayer you may discern an intention for your text, or certain emotions may arise that you'll want to use in your proclamation. Take note of these or any other insights.

Recognize That the Stakes Are High

Would you work harder to tell someone that they had a loose thread on their shirt or that their hair was on fire? Likely the latter! When the *stakes are high*, all your communication skills are heightened without your even thinking about them. That's why it's important to recognize how significant your ministry is to the community. The Word that you have the privilege of proclaiming is a Word that desperately needs to be heard by your community, and if you don't proclaim it well, an opportunity is lost. Remind yourself of this awesome responsibility each time you proclaim, and you'll be inspired to work hard to help the Word of God come alive for the community.

Douglas Leal

An Option to Consider

The third edition of *The Roman Missal* encourages ministers of the Word to chant the introduction and conclusion to the readings ("A reading from . . . "; "The word of the Lord"). For those parishes wishing to use these chants, they are demonstrated in audio files that may be accessed either through the QR codes given here (with a smartphone) or through the URL indicated beneath the code. This URL is case sensitive, so be careful to distinguish between the letter l (lowercase L) and the numeral 1.

The first QR code contains the tones for the First Reading in both a male and a female voice.

http://bit.ly/l2mjeG

The second QR code contains the tones for the Second Reading in both a male and a female voice.

http://bit.ly/krwEYy

The third QR code contains the simple tone for the Gospel.

http://bit.ly/iZZvSg

The fourth QR code contains the solemn tone for the Gospel.

http://bit.ly/lwf6Hh

A fuller explanation of this new practice, along with musical notation for the chants, is provided in a downloadable PDF file found at http://www.ltp.org/t-productsupplements.aspx. Once you arrive at this web page, scroll until you find the image of the cover of Workbook, click on it, and the PDF file will appear.

Pronunciation Key

bait = bayt	thin = thin
cat = kat	vision = VIZH*n
sang = sang	ship = ship
father = FAH-<u>th</u>er	sir = ser
care = kayr	gloat = gloht
paw = paw	cot = kot
jar = jahr	noise = noyz
easy = EE-zee	poison = POY-z*n
her = her	plow = plow
let = let	although = ahl-<u>TH</u>OH
queen = kween	church = cherch
delude = deh-L<u>OO</u>D	fun = fuhn
when = hwen	fur = fer
ice = īs	flute = fl<u>oo</u>t
if = if	foot = foot
finesse = fih-NES	

Recommended Works

Find a list of recommended reading in a downloadable PDF file at http://www.ltp.org/t-productsupplements.aspx.

Shorter Readings

In the Scripture readings reproduced in this book, shorter readings are indicated by brackets and also by a citation given at the end of the reading.

Endnotes

(continued from page ii)

FIRST SUNDAY OF ADVENT

LECTIONARY #1

READING I   Isaiah 2:1–5

A reading from the Book of the Prophet Isaiah

This is what **Isaiah**, son of Amoz,
    saw concerning **Judah** and **Jerusalem**.
  In **days to come**,
the **mountain** of the LORD's house
    shall be established as the **highest** mountain
    and **raised** above the hills.
All nations shall **stream** toward it;
    many peoples shall come and say:
"**Come**, let us **climb** the LORD's mountain,
    to the house of the God of Jacob,
that he may **instruct** us in his ways,
    and we may **walk** in his paths."
For from **Zion** shall go forth **instruction**,
    and the **word of the Lord** from Jerusalem.
He shall **judge** between the nations,
    and impose terms on many **peoples**.
They shall **beat** their swords into **plowshares**
    and their spears into **pruning hooks**;
one nation shall not **raise** the **sword** against another,
    nor shall they **train** for **war** again.
O house of Jacob, **come**,
    let us **walk** in the **light** of the **Lord**!

An exhortatory reading, announcing Israel's glorious future and the fullness of the reign of God. Keep your emotions and energy up throughout!
Isaiah = ī-ZAY-uh
Amoz = AY-muhz
Judah = JOO-duh

Popular media makes the end times bleak; Isaiah's view is different. Make us know this vision is good news!

Really see the vision unfold before you. Proclaim with emotions that rise up for you as you watch.

The ways of the Lord teach wisdom.

Learning wisdom from the Lord leads to peace.

How does such a peaceful world make you feel? Use that emotion as you proclaim. Let it show on your face and be heard in your voice.

Slight pause before this final invitation; maintain eye contact; use "O" to encourage us and call us to follow you.

READING I   The opening verses of the Book of Isaiah recount the kings who reigned in Judah during Isaiah's time, indicating that the prophet's ministry spanned four decades, ending about 701 BC. Some scholars think it may have been even longer. During this time, Judah repeatedly turned to foreign alliances for protection against the expanding might of Assyria, which led an unsuccessful attack on Jerusalem in 701. The prophet repeatedly called Judah to trust in divine rather than human power, but with little success. Many of Isaiah's prophecies charged the people with infidelity to their covenant with the Lord: they were failing to worship sincerely or insure social justice, and they must repent. Other prophecies spoke of God's coming judgment and future divine rule over God's people and all nations.

Today's First Reading focuses on the second motif. In verses previous to the reading, Isaiah has rebuked the people for numerous transgressions and called them to return to God, their one true source of life. Now he evokes an image of Israel's splendid new future. Nearly identical to a prophecy of Micah (4:1–4), his contemporary, this passage envisions God enthroned in the Jerusalem Temple, drawing together all Israelites into one righteous people. What's more, all nations will finally recognize the Lord as the one true source of life, gathering on Mt. Zion to learn and practice his teaching. When Israel and all the nations walk in the light of God's instruction, they will truly "cease doing evil" and "learn to do good" (Isaiah 1:16).

For meditation and context:

RESPONSORIAL PSALM   Psalm 122:1–2, 3–4, 4–5, 6–7, 8–9

R. Let us go rejoicing to the house of the Lord.

I rejoiced because they said to me,
  "We will go up to the house of the LORD."
And now we have set foot
  within your gates, O Jerusalem.

Jerusalem, built as a city
  with compact unity.
To it the tribes go up,
  the tribes of the LORD.

According to the decree for Israel,
  to give thanks to the name of the LORD.
In it are set up judgment seats,
  seats for the house of David.

Pray for the peace of Jerusalem!
  May those who love you prosper!
May peace be within your walls,
  prosperity in your buildings.

Because of my brothers and friends
  I will say, "Peace be within you!"
Because of the house of the LORD, our God,
  I will pray for your good.

A didactic reading. Avoid admonishing the
assembly for their behavior; rather, encourage
them to be centered in Christ, and to let that
relationship make a real difference in their
lives.

Remind us that we already know what we
are to do.
We are different people than we were
before we encountered Christ; we need
to live differently.
Paul uses light and darkness to differentiate
life with Christ from life without Christ.

Be dismissive with this list, not accusatory.

READING II   Romans 13:11–14

A reading from the Letter of Saint Paul to the Romans

Brothers and sisters:
You **know** the time;
  it is the hour **now** for you to **awake** from sleep.
For our salvation is **nearer** now than when we **first** believed;
  the night is **advanced**, the day is at **hand**.
Let us then **throw off** the works of **darkness**
  and **put on** the armor of **light**;
  let us conduct ourselves properly as in the **day**,
  not in orgies and drunkenness,
  not in promiscuity and lust,
  not in rivalry and jealousy.
But **put on** the Lord Jesus **Christ**,
  and make no **provision** for the desires of the **flesh**.

READING II   Paul composed the Letter to the Romans near the end of his life and it stands as his most systematic writing—more a treatise or essay than a letter. What we hear today appears near the end of this lengthy work. In earlier chapters the Apostle explains his conviction that no one is saved through works of the Law, but rather by God's utterly free, unearned gift of divine love poured out to humankind through Christ. Paul discusses the implications of this gift, instructing his audience about how they are to live their new life "in Christ," a phrase that appears frequently in his writings. Immediately before today's reading, Paul sums up his instructions for Christian living by referring to the Commandment to love one's neighbor as oneself, the command that brings the Law to completion.

Today's Second Reading provides the reason for Christians to live according to this law of love: the final fulfillment of God's plan for salvation is near at hand. In the earliest decades of Christianity, Jesus' followers believed that God's definitive act of salvation began with the ministry, Death, and Resurrection of Christ, and would soon reach culmination with his imminent return. Paul stresses that Christians must now act in accord with the new life already begun in Christ and soon to be completed with his coming in glory. His closing admonition to resist "desires of the flesh" encompasses all that opposes the law of love. Christians must have nothing to do with behaviors common in the Roman world of his day, several of which he names. Those who continue to live in the "spirit," the abiding presence of God's love freely given in Christ (Romans 5:5), will surely live by the divine command of love.

A didactic reading. How does this reading call your assembly to respond? Choose an intention: Listen up! Stay awake! Return to God now! Keep your choice in mind and proclaim with the love of someone who wants the best for your community.

Jesus emphasizes the surprise of the flood more than its punishment.

Proclaim these as normal, everyday activities.

Slight pause as you transition to the coming of the Son of Man.

Don't pause here; the next phrase is the moral of this story

An exhortatory command!

Slight pause before "Be sure of this."

Jesus is not criticizing the master; of course he couldn't know, which is why we must always stay awake.

Proclaim this closing with real love and concern for your community.

GOSPEL　Matthew 24:37–44

A reading from the holy Gospel according to Matthew

Jesus said to his disciples:
"As it was in the days of **Noah**,
　so it will be at the **coming** of the Son of Man.
In those days before the **flood**,
　they were **eating** and **drinking**,
　marrying and **giving** in marriage,
　up to the day that Noah entered the **ark**.
They **did not know** until the flood came and carried them
　　all **away**.
So will it be **also** at the coming of the Son of Man.
Two men will be out in the field;
　one will be **taken**, and one will be **left**.
Two **women** will be grinding at the mill;
　one will be **taken**, and one will be **left**.
Therefore, stay **awake**!
For you **do not know** on which day your Lord will come.
Be sure of **this**: if the master of the house
　had **known** the hour of night when the thief was **coming**,
　he would have stayed **awake**
　and not let his house be broken into.
So too, **you** also must be **prepared**,
　for at an hour you do not **expect**, the Son of Man will **come**."

THE 4 STEPS OF *LECTIO DIVINA* OR PRAYERFUL READING

1. *Lectio:* Read a Scripture passage aloud slowly. Notice what phrase captures your attention and be attentive to its meaning. Silent pause.

2. *Meditatio:* Read the passage aloud slowly again, reflecting on the passage, allowing God to speak to you through it. Silent pause.

3. *Oratio:* Read it aloud slowly a third time, allowing it to be your prayer or response to God's gift of insight to you. Silent pause.

4. *Contemplatio:* Read it aloud slowly a fourth time, now resting in God's word.

GOSPEL This passage appears in what is usually called "Matthew's apocalypse," chapters 24–25 of Matthew's account. Jewish expectation about God's final act of salvation took various forms, but in New Testament times the most common view was apocalyptic. This view envisioned numerous calamities on earth and in the heavens signaling the arrival of the end times, followed by divine judgment to determine who would or would not be part of God's new world. In the earlier part of chapter 24, Matthew reflects several characteristics of apocalyptic thinking. Jesus speaks seated on the Mount of Olives, the place Zechariah 14:4 associates with God's final coming, and warns of impending wars, persecutions, and other earthly calamities, along with cosmic disturbances.

Today's Gospel stresses that the time of God's coming is unknown; therefore believers must always be prepared. As the great flood caught people unawares, the coming of the Son of Man will also arrive in God's own time. Matthew uses the Greek word *parousia*, here translated "coming," which, in Roman society, referred to a ruler's visitation to a city or the arrival of a deity bringing salvation to the people. Christians adapted the word, combining both meanings, to speak of Christ's coming to complete God's final rule, which began in his ministry. For that coming, Christians must always be prepared. M.F.

SECOND SUNDAY OF ADVENT

LECTIONARY #4

READING I Isaiah 11:1–10

A reading from the Book of the Prophet Isaiah

On that day, a shoot shall **sprout** from the stump of **Jesse**,
    and from his **roots** a **bud** shall **blossom**.
The **spirit** of the LORD shall **rest** upon him:
    a spirit of **wisdom** and of **understanding**,
a spirit of **counsel** and of **strength**,
    a spirit of **knowledge** and of **fear** of the **Lord**,
    and his **delight** shall be the fear of the LORD.
Not by **appearance** shall he judge,
    nor by **hearsay** shall he decide,
but he shall judge the poor with **justice**,
    and decide **aright** for the land's afflicted.
He shall **strike** the ruthless with the rod of his mouth,
    and with the breath of his lips he shall **slay** the wicked.
Justice shall be the band around his waist,
    and **faithfulness** a belt upon his hips.
Then the **wolf** shall be a **guest** of the **lamb**,
    and the **leopard** shall lie down with the **kid**;
the **calf** and the young **lion** shall browse **together**,
    with a **little child** to guide them.

An exhortatory reading. Build the intensity of your emotions and energy slowly through this reading as the vision becomes more amazing.

Isaiah = ī-ZAY-uh

Open slowly with "On that day," so the community knows you are relating a vision of the future.

Jesse = JES-ee

Proclaim these lines purposefully; emphasize each gift of the spirit.

These are the qualities of a bad judge; proclaim them with the contempt they deserve.

Change your tone to show how a good judge behaves.

His words are powerful enough to "strike" and "slay." The words you proclaim are just as powerful!

Lavish your praise upon this good judge.

Pause as you shift from the qualities of this person to the world his leadership will bring about. This is a startling vision! Predator and prey will live peacefully together. Take your time as you proclaim this; be sure the wonder and amazement come through in your face and voice.

kid = young goat

READING I Like last Sunday's reading, today's prophecy from Isaiah dates from the second half of the eighth century BC, a period when Judah repeatedly turned to various foreign nations for protection from war and invasion. The people seem to take for granted God's promise that a descendant of King David will rule forever and they no longer fulfil their responsibilities in the covenant made on Mt. Sinai. Their rituals are perfunctory and there is widespread social injustice in the land. Although Isaiah confronts Judah with this reality, he also expresses hope for the coming of a righteous son of David, a king who will fulfill his proper role in leading the people back to faithfulness to God.

Immediately preceding today's reading, Isaiah describes Assyria's relentless invasion from the north, marching on Jerusalem itself, the city of David and place of the Lord's dwelling. The prophet views such events as the Lord's judgment on the people's sinfulness, but in today's reading he also turns to hope for a renewed future. He envisions the coming of a righteous king descended from Jesse's son, David, as God's instrument to establish a future kingdom of peace, justice, and right relationships in all creation.

Such a king would, above all, act in the "spirit of the Lord"; he would possess the gift of wisdom to judge rightly, a wisdom learned by proper reverence for God ("fear of the Lord"). The attributes of this hoped-for king later developed into Christian traditional names for gifts of the Holy Spirit. The prophet continues his portrayal of a kingdom ruled by such a ruler: all that God intended for the covenant people would become reality: the power of evil would be

The **cow** and the **bear** shall be **neighbors**,
    together their young shall rest;
    the **lion** shall **eat hay** like the **ox**.
The **baby** shall play by the **cobra's** den,
    and the **child** lay his hand on the **adder's** lair.
There shall be no **harm** or **ruin** on all my holy mountain;
    for the earth shall be **filled** with knowledge of the LORD,
    as **water** covers the **sea**.
On that day, the **root** of Jesse,
    set up as a **signal** for the nations,
    the Gentiles shall **seek out**,
    for his dwelling shall be **glorious**.

Amazing!

Summarizes the entire vision: there's "no harm or ruin"; all is in relationship with the LORD.

It's "the root of Jesse" that "the Gentiles shall seek out."

Parenthetical; drop your voice slightly.

Who wouldn't seek out such a person?

Grand conclusion; keep your voice up, dropping only slightly at the end.

For meditation and context:

RESPONSORIAL PSALM   Psalm 72:1–2, 7–8, 12–13, 17 (7)

R. Justice shall flourish in his time, and fullness of peace forever.

O God, with your judgment endow the king,
    and with your justice, the king's son;
he shall govern your people with justice
    and your afflicted ones with judgment.

Justice shall flower in his days,
    and profound peace, till the moon be
    no more.
May he rule from sea to sea,
    and from the River to the ends of the earth.

For he shall rescue the poor when he
    cries out,
    and the afflicted when he has no one
    to help him.
He shall have pity for the lowly and the poor;
    the lives of the poor he shall save.

May his name be blessed forever;
    as long as the sun his name shall remain.
In him shall all the tribes of the earth
    be blessed;
    all the nations shall proclaim
    his happiness.

TO KEEP IN MIND
Pay attention to the pace of your reading. Varying the pace gives listeners clues to the meaning of the text. The most common problem for proclaimers new to the ministry is going too fast to be understood.

---

broken, and all things would live in peace and harmony. Former conflict and opposition would be reversed, and all relationships set aright. Centuries after Isaiah, Christians understood his vision of God's ultimate reign over all things through a chosen ruler to be fulfilled in Jesus the Messiah, who proclaimed and inaugurated the Kingdom of God.

READING II The Second Reading comes from the Apostle Paul, writing about thirty years after the Death and Resurrection of Jesus. The earliest generation of Christians firmly believed that through Jesus Christ, God's final rule had already begun on earth, and they expected his imminent return in glory, bringing it to completion. In his Letter to the Romans, Paul elaborates his conviction that God's free gift in Christ has shown that a renewed covenant people in this new age of salvation embraces all people. In his lengthy treatise, Paul clarifies that God's grace through Christ brings the Old Testament Scriptures to their fullness, revealing that the new Israel of the final age expands to include both Jew and non-Jew. Several times the Apostle instructs how all those who enter the new Israel, the Church, through Baptism are to treat one another as members of Christ.

Today's reading appears near the end of Romans, after yet another encouragement to live in the now as Christ did, giving one's entire self for the good of the other. For many Jews, including the Gentiles in the Israel of the final age would have been an agonizing reality, since first century Judaism generally regarded them as unbelievers outside the Law and therefore "impure" people to be avoided. But Paul

A didactic reading. Proclaim with love; inspire the community to respond.

READING II   Romans 15:4–9

A reading from the Letter of Saint Paul to the Romans

Brothers and sisters:
Whatever was written **previously** was written for our **instruction**,
   that by **endurance** and by the **encouragement** of the Scriptures
   we might have **hope**.
May the God of endurance and encouragement
   grant you to think in **harmony** with one another,
   in **keeping** with Christ **Jesus**,
   that with one **accord** you may with one **voice**
   glorify the God and Father of our Lord Jesus Christ.

Welcome one another, then, as Christ welcomed **you**,
   for the **glory** of **God**.
For I say that Christ became a minister of the **circumcised**
   to show God's **truthfulness**,
   to **confirm** the promises of the patriarchs,
   but so that the **Gentiles** might **glorify** God for his **mercy**.
As it is written:
   *Therefore, I will **praise** you among the **Gentiles***
     *and sing **praises** to your name.*

The purpose of your ministry of proclamation: that we might have hope!

Imagine harmony in your community. Proclaim with urgency for what this could bring to everyone.

What difference would this make in your community? Encourage your listeners to create this spirit!
Make each of these reasons distinct.
circumcised = SER-kuhm-sīz*d
patriarchs = PAY-tree-ahrks
This is Paul's most important reason.
Gentiles = JEN-tīls

An exhortatory conclusion! Keep your voice and energy up.

GOSPEL   Matthew 3:1–12

A reading from the holy Gospel according to Matthew

John the **Baptist** appeared, **preaching** in the desert of Judea
   and saying, "**Repent**, for the kingdom of **heaven** is at **hand**!"
It was of **him** that the prophet **Isaiah** had spoken when he said:
   *A voice of one **crying out** in the desert,*
   Prepare *the way of the Lord,*
     *make **straight** his paths.*

A narrative with many exhortatory passages, demanding much energy. Draw the assembly into this story with John's fire and spirit.

Judea = joo-DEE-uh
Give this exhortation volume and energy!

Isaiah = ī-ZAY-uh

Isaiah's prophecy is another exhortation. Keep your energy up.

reiterates that Israel's Scriptures are completed in Christ, and so those who are now one in Christ must think and act as one unified community under God's rule. In this way all can unite in praising the God of Jesus Christ "with one voice." Once again, Paul urges the Roman community to imitate Christ's love for all, which fulfills the Jewish Scriptures, gathering all people into a unity of praise glorifying God's mercy. As he does throughout Romans, Paul invokes those Scriptures to illuminate and confirm his thought: did not the Jewish psalmist sing, "I will praise you among the Gentiles" (Psalm 18:50)?

GOSPEL During Lectionary Year A, the Gospel readings most often come from Matthew, who was most likely a Jewish convert to Christian faith, perhaps even a rabbi. Writing about fifty years after the Death and Resurrection of Jesus, he addresses issues of the day: Jewish Christians puzzled about relationships between their past faith and practice and that of Jesus' followers, including a question also on the minds of Gentile Christians: how could "impure" non-Jews be part of the new Israel in the age of salvation, the Church? Throughout his account, Matthew portrays Jesus as the one who "fulfills" the Old Testament Scriptures, bringing them to their fullest development, and part of that fullness appears in the presence of Gentiles in God's Kingdom. This evangelist presents a Jewish Messiah who fulfills the hopes of Israel by inaugurating the Reign of God as true King of Israel who also brings Gentile believers under his rule of salvation.

Slight pause before describing John; then be deliberate with details.
The specific places aren't as important as the sense that people are coming from everywhere.

Slow down and make clear this is the reason everyone is coming to John.
Pause; the storm is about to begin!
Pharisees = FAYR-uh-seez

Sadducees = SAD-yoo-seez

Short pause before John's condemnation.
"brood of vipers" = young snakes (more dangerous than mature ones)
John really lets them have it! Project his fury.

You can echo their haughty tone.

Time is short, John says!

John's tone becomes more intimate as he describes himself and his ministry.

Raise your energy again and keep it up all the way to the end!

winnowing fan = a tool to separate wheat from chaff (hulls) on a threshing floor

---

John wore clothing made of **camel's hair**
  and had **a leather belt** around his waist.
His food was **locusts** and wild **honey**.
At that time **Jerusalem**, **all** Judea,
  and the **whole** region around the Jordan
  were going **out** to him
  and were being **baptized** by him in the Jordan River
  as they **acknowledged** their sins.

When he **saw** many of the **Pharisees** and **Sadducees**
  coming to his **baptism**, he said to them, "You brood of **vipers**!
Who warned you to **flee** from the coming wrath?
Produce **good fruit** as evidence of your **repentance**.
And do not **presume** to say to yourselves,
  'We have **Abraham** as our father.'
For I **tell** you,
  God can raise up children to Abraham from these **stones**.
Even **now** the **ax** lies at the **root** of the trees.
Therefore every tree that does not bear **good** fruit
  will be **cut** down and **thrown** into the fire.
I am baptizing you with **water**, for **repentance**,
  but the one who is coming **after** me is **mightier** than I.
I am **not worthy** to carry his **sandals**.
He will baptize you with the Holy **Spirit** and **fire**.
His **winnowing fan** is in his hand.
He will **clear** his threshing floor
  and gather his **wheat** into his barn,
  but the **chaff** he will burn with **unquenchable** fire."

In composing his account of the Good News, Matthew uses Mark as a major source, but also feels free to alter or add to Mark in order to address his specific community and their needs. In today's reading we can see that he both relies upon Mark and on his own perspective. As in Mark, John the Baptist appears as a sign that the Kingdom of Heaven draws near. (Like other pious Jews of the time, out of reverence, Matthew avoids using the name of God.) Preaching a baptism of repentance, John appears as a figure of Elijah, described in Malachi 4:23–24 as a signal that God's final rule is close at hand.

Matthew then adds to Mark's account with John's challenge to various Jewish religious leaders. They are not guaranteed a place in the Kingdom of Heaven merely because they are descendants of Abraham; they must live as such to demonstrate genuine repentance. Jewish tradition often used the image of a tree known by its fruit to indicate that action must accompany any ritual of repentance, and repentance called for turning away from sin, toward God. As in Mark, the Baptist makes clear that he himself is not the Messiah, but rather, his messenger; he baptizes with water, but God's Anointed will baptize with divine Spirit. In Greek, *baptizo* means to wash or immerse; thus the Messiah will immerse the baptized in God's own life-giving presence. Matthew's images of harvest were a common symbol of God's final rule and judgment. M.F.

THE IMMACULATE CONCEPTION OF THE BLESSED VIRGIN MARY

LECTIONARY #689

READING I   Genesis 3:9–15, 20

A reading from the Book of Genesis

After the man, **Adam**, had **eaten** of the tree,
    the LORD God **called** to the man and asked him,
        "Where **are** you?"
He answered, "I heard you in the garden;
    but I was **afraid**, because I was **naked**,
    so I **hid** myself."
Then he asked, "Who **told** you that you were naked?
You have **eaten**, then,
    from the tree of which I had **forbidden** you to eat!"
The man replied, "The **woman** whom **you** put here with me—
    she gave me fruit from the tree, and so I **ate** it."
The LORD God then **asked** the woman,
    "**Why** did you do such a thing?"
The woman **answered**, "The serpent **tricked** me into it, so I **ate** it."

A narrative, mostly dialogue. Understand the different intentions and emotions of each character: Adam, Eve, and God.

Start slowly, reminding the assembly where we are in the story.

God begins by asking questions. What response does God really want from Adam and Eve here? What response will your proclamation inspire from your community?

Express Adam's fear in voice and face.

God sees no shame in their nakedness.

Proclaim God's lines with the feeling of betrayal.

Adam shifts blame from himself to Eve to God.

Is she being honest, or evading blame? Let your choice come through in the proclamation.

On this Solemnity of the Immaculate Conception, it must be noted that there is no direct biblical reference to Mary as conceived without original sin, the core belief proclaimed in this feast. However, as early as the second century, some Church Fathers described Mary as "most pure," "innocent one," or "all sinless one." By the twelfth century, a feast of the Immaculate Conception was celebrated all over Europe. In addition, from earliest Christianity Mary was viewed as a model of the ideal Christian and of the Church. Today's readings are best understood in light of centuries of Christian reflection on Mary's character and role in the unfolding of salvation history. Such reflection continuously understood all value and virtue attributed to Mary to flow from her nearness to Christ.

READING I This section of Genesis focuses on fundamental human realities: choice, freedom and its limits, and responsibility. In this creation account, all humankind is represented in the characters of Adam and Eve. The Hebrew word *adam* means "humankind," and, as the author of Genesis later indicates (Genesis 3:20), the name "Eve" signifies "mother of all the living."

Preceding the account in today's First Reading, God told the pair that they were free to eat the fruit of any tree in the garden, except the tree of the knowledge of good and evil. Tested by the serpent, both man and woman succumbed and ate of this very fruit, an action that represents an attempt at divine status. Ancient peoples believed that only deities fully understood the realities of good and evil, a conviction reflected in the serpent's cajoling words to the woman. The serpent assured the

8

Pause before God turns to the serpent; gather your energy before unleashing your anger upon the serpent.
Keep pace and energy up; make eye contact with the assembly.
Make this sound as nasty as it is!

enmity = EN-mih-tee (mutual hatred)

Longer pause to allow the "storm" to subside and God to disappear from the scene.

Naming is an act of love.

This blessing results from an otherwise bad situation: Eve is the mother of us all.

For meditation and context:

TO KEEP IN MIND
A *narrative* has characters, dialogue, a setting, and action. Help your listeners see the story unfold, keep characters distinct, and be clear about shifts in setting.

TO KEEP IN MIND
Exhortatory texts make an urgent appeal to listeners. They may encourage, warn, or challenge, and often include a call to action. You must convey the urgency and passion behind the words.

Then the Lord God said to the **serpent**:
"Because you have done this, you shall be **banned**
from all the animals
and from all the wild creatures;
on your **belly** shall you **crawl**,
and **dirt** shall you **eat**
all the **days** of your life.
I will put **enmity** between you and the woman,
and between **your** offspring and **hers**;
he will strike at your **head**,
while **you** strike at his **heel**."

The man called his wife **Eve**,
because she became the **mother** of **all** the living.

RESPONSORIAL PSALM   Psalm 98:1, 2–3ab, 3cd–4 (1a)

R. Sing to the Lord a new song, for he has done marvelous deeds.

Sing to the Lord a new song,
for he has done wondrous deeds;
His right hand has won victory for him,
his holy arm.

The Lord has made his salvation known:
in the sight of the nations he has revealed
his justice.
He has remembered his kindness and his
faithfulness
toward the house of Israel.

All the ends of the earth have seen
the salvation by our God.
Sing joyfully to the Lord, all you lands;
break into song; sing praise.

---

woman that eating the forbidden fruit would not result in death, as God said, but in becoming "like gods, who know good and evil" (Genesis 3:5; see also 3:22). The creatures intended to be God's image in the world (Genesis 1:27) chose to overreach the divine purpose for humankind. Not content to become the living image of God in creation, they grasped at equality with the divine Creator.

Both man and woman transgressed, for which both bear responsibility and must accept the consequences. God's words to the serpent and to the woman indicate that

temptations to resist the divine purpose will continue to pursue Eve's offspring, "all the living." Her descendants will repeat their parents' choices and actions. The New Testament proclaims that Christ, the Second Adam, fully realized God's purpose for humanity as the true and complete image of God. Through centuries of reflection, the Church came to believe that God anticipated this fullness of the Christ Mystery in his mother Mary, a new Eve. She is mother of all who live a new, redeemed life in her son, the New Adam.

READING II The Letter to the Ephesians presents a Pauline view of the universal Church. Many early manuscripts lack the specific address to Christians "in Ephesus," and the perspective of the letter is much broader than that of a specific local congregation. Therefore, today many scholars conclude that Ephesians is a letter intended to circulate among multiple churches in Asia Minor. Vocabulary and imagery of this message strongly suggest that parts of it are drawn from early hymns and liturgy, as is the case with the first part of today's reading.

An exhortatory reading. Keep energy up; smile so your assembly knows this is good news! There are four main thoughts; pause between them. Keep your voice up at the commas and drop only slightly at the periods.

Ephesians = ee-FEE-zhuhnz

Blessed = BLES-uhd

blessed = blesd

First, Paul praises God.

Second, Paul reminds us we were chosen as children of God.

Third, our choice was God's will. Pause before this line and take time with its complex phrasing.
Drop your voice slightly on this parenthetical phrase.

Fourth, we were chosen to praise God.

No pause between "destined" and "will."

Slow down and speak this final line directly to your assembly with love and joy.

TO KEEP IN MIND
Pause in order to break up separate thoughts, set apart significant statements, or indicate major shifts. Never pause in the middle of a single thought. Your primary guide for pauses is punctuation.

READING II   Ephesians 1:3–6, 11–12

A reading from the Letter of Saint Paul to the Ephesians

Brothers and sisters:
Blessed be the God and Father of our Lord Jesus **Christ**,
   who has **blessed** us in Christ
   with **every** spiritual blessing in the heavens,
   as he **chose** us in him, **before** the foundation of the world,
   to be **holy** and **without blemish** before him.
In **love** he destined us for **adoption** to himself through
   Jesus **Christ**,
   in accord with the favor of his will,
   for the **praise** of the **glory** of his **grace**
   that he granted us in the **beloved**.

In him we were also **chosen**,
   destined in accord with the purpose of the One
   who accomplishes all things according to the intention
   of his **will**,
   so that we might **exist** for the **praise** of his **glory**,
   we who first **hoped** in **Christ**.

Paul's letters usually begin with a customary naming of writer and addressee, followed by a prayer of thanksgiving. Here the author inserts a blessing or praise of God for the divine work of salvation in Christ, emphasizing God's eternal plan and intention to recreate humankind through Christ. The writer particularly gives thanks for God's motive: gracious love, through which God makes believers his children by "adoption" through the saving work of Christ. It is this free, loving action of God that creates and unifies the Church as a community of faith whose very existence has one purpose: "the praise of his glory."

GOSPEL This passage is patterned on a literary form used in both Testaments, a call story. Luke follows the basic outline of a call or commissioning narrative: the presence of God or a divine messenger is made known to someone; the person addressed receives a commission or call; the one called responds, usually offering objections meant to excuse a positive response; the call is repeated, with God's assurance of help in carrying out the divine directive.

Luke's account of the angel Gabriel's visit to Mary differs from that of Matthew in several ways, one of which is his emphasis on Mary rather than on Joseph. By the time Luke wrote his account of the Good News, fifty to sixty years after the Death and Resurrection of Jesus, the mother of Jesus was already thought of as the ideal disciple, receptive to and trusting in God's grace. Describing the angel's greeting to Mary, Luke uses an unusual Greek word, the root of which is *charis*, literally meaning "gift"

A narrative, mostly dialogue. Practice changing emotions noticeably as you switch between the words of Gabriel and Mary.

Don't lose the phrase "sent from God."

No pause after "Joseph."

Proclaim this greeting with much joy.
Proclaim these lines with Mary's fear.

Gabriel isn't a speech maker! He must help Mary understand. Notice how he comforts her.

This is great news!

Four phrases describe the child; make each distinct.

GOSPEL   Luke 1:26–38

A reading from the holy Gospel according to Luke

The angel **Gabriel** was **sent** from God
   to a town of Galilee called **Nazareth**,
   to a **virgin** betrothed to a man named **Joseph**,
   of the house of **David**,
   and the virgin's name was **Mary**.
And coming to her, he said,
   "**Hail**, **full** of **grace**! The **Lord** is with you."
But she was greatly **troubled** at what was said
   and **pondered** what sort of greeting this might be.
Then the angel said to her,
   "**Do not be afraid**, Mary,
   for you have found **favor** with God.
Behold, you will **conceive** in your womb and bear a **son**,
   and you shall name him **Jesus**.
He will be **great** and will be called **Son** of the Most High,
   and the Lord God will give him the **throne** of **David** his **father**,
   and he will **rule** over the house of Jacob **forever**,
   and of his **Kingdom** there will be **no end**." »

TO KEEP IN MIND
Use inflection (the high or low pitch of your voice) to convey attitude and feeling. High pitch expresses intensity and excitement; low pitch expresses sadness, contrition, or solemnity.

---

but most commonly translated into English as "grace" or "favor." Paul in particular stresses that God's redeeming work through Christ is a totally unearned gift to humankind: grace. It seems that Luke, who shares a number of Paul's perspectives, wishes to present Mary as one who has been showered with God's grace, which flowers in her receptive openness to divine action in her. Luke repeats the word *charis* again as the angel assures Mary that she has "found favor with God."

Describing Mary's call to bear the Savior, Luke presents a summary of who this child will be: Jesus, meaning "God saves"; Son of God, Son of David, the one through whom the longed-for final Reign of God will begin. Mary's response to the awe-inspiring commission is less an objection or refusal than a logical question: how is it possible that a virgin will bear a child? Gabriel's response reassures rather than explains: the Holy Spirit, the powerful divine presence within Mary, will bring about what seems humanly impossible. From the beginning of his account of the Good News, Luke stresses the continuing presence and action of the Holy Spirit.

Jesus is conceived in a woman totally receptive to God's Spirit, foreshadowing how that same Spirit will continuously act in Jesus himself as he carries out his own divine commission.

For Mary, the angel's assurance that God's power will be at work in her dissolves any need for explanation. As a faith-filled Jewish woman, Mary accepts that the Word of God carries divine presence and power: "May it be done to me according to your word." Luke expresses Mary's attitude of total surrender to God by using a startling word softened in most translations. In

Switch back to Mary's fear and confusion.

Gabriel comforts again.

Take your time with "Son of God."
Again, news of great joy!

Best news of all! Keep energy up, then pause.

Quiet but confident tone.

Pause after this line to let the significance of Mary's response ring in your assembly's hearts, then conclude with the angel's departure.

But Mary said to the angel,
    "**How** can this be,
    since I have no **relations** with a man?"
And the **angel** said to her in reply,
    "The Holy Spirit will come **upon** you,
    and the power of the Most High will **overshadow** you.
Therefore the child to be born
    will be called **holy**, the Son of **God**.
And behold, **Elizabeth**, your relative,
    has **also** conceived a son in her old **age**,
    and this is the sixth month for her who was called **barren**;
    for **nothing** will be impossible for God."
Mary said, "**Behold**, I am the **handmaid** of the Lord.
May it be **done** to me according to **your** word."
Then the angel **departed** from her.

> **TO KEEP IN MIND**
> In a narrative, find an emotion or point of view for each character, keeping in mind that these might change during the reading.

Mary's self-description as "the handmaid of the Lord," Luke in fact uses the Greek word *doule*, "slave." In the Roman Empire of the time, a servant was a paid employee, while a slave was owned by someone else and received no compensation for doing the owner's bidding. Not only Luke but many other New Testament authors frequently describe Christians as "slaves of Christ"; in this sense, Mary represents the primordial Christian. Describing herself as "slave" of the Lord, she chooses to be "owned" by God, expecting no recompense; she chooses to belong totally to the one whose Word she trusts utterly. M.F.

THIRD SUNDAY OF ADVENT

LECTIONARY #7

READING I   Isaiah 35:1–6a, 10

A reading from the Book of the Prophet Isaiah

> The desert and the parched land will **exult**;
>   the steppe will **rejoice** and **bloom**.
> They will bloom with abundant **flowers**,
>   and rejoice with joyful **song**.
> The **glory** of Lebanon will be given to them,
>   the **splendor** of Carmel and Sharon;
> they will see the **glory** of the Lord,
>   the **splendor** of our God.
> **Strengthen** the hands that are **feeble**,
>   make **firm** the knees that are **weak**,
> say to those whose hearts are **frightened**:
>   Be **strong**, **fear** not!
> **Here** is your God,
>   he comes with **vindication**;
> with divine **recompense**
>   he comes to **save** you.
> Then will the eyes of the **blind** be **opened**,
>   the ears of the **deaf** be **cleared**;
> then will the lame **leap** like a stag,
>   then the tongue of the mute will **sing**. »

An exhortatory reading. Keep your emotions and energy up throughout! Isaiah wants to encourage the people with this good news. Be sure your community knows it's good news from your smile.

Isaiah = ī-ZAY-uh

Rich imagery: The earth itself rejoices.

The land sings!

Carmel =KAHR-m*l

Sharon = SHAYR-uhn

Proclaim as if to someone who really needs a message of hope.

Keep eyes and voice up at the ends of all these lines.

Set this sentence apart by slowing down or pausing slightly before and after.
vindication = clearing from blame
recompense = REK-uhm-pens; compensation for wrongs suffered
We've heard these phrases many times, but proclaim them with the wonder they would have inspired in those who first heard them.

Make "leap" and "sing" sound like what they mean!

READING I   The first section of the Book of Isaiah collects numerous oracles the prophet proclaimed over a span of nearly four decades. As the wayward people repeatedly turned to perfunctory rituals of worship and social injustice, a succession of Judah's kings turned to various foreign nations for protection from invasion and attack. The prophet admonished the people to offer sincere worship, care for the poorest among them, and turn to God rather than foreign nations for their security. But Isaiah's calls to repentance repeatedly fell upon closed ears, and additional oracles fluctuated between warnings of impending destruction and visions of God's ultimate deliverance.

Today's First Reading is one of the hopeful visions. Though it is quite similar to a description of the people's return from Babylonian exile in a later century, the precise occasion of this oracle cannot be determined. The following chapter describes the unsuccessful Assyrian attack on Jerusalem in 701 BC, which the prophet attributed to the Lord's faithful deliverance.

Whatever the occasion, Isaiah expresses certain trust that the God of Israel is a saving God who will, at an unknown future time, bring unimagined new life to his people. The land itself will be renewed with lavish growth, revealing to all the life-giving power of the Lord. Divine deliverance will bring freedom from oppression and captivity at the hands of foreign nations. But God's ultimate saving action will also triumph over the enemies of human wholeness and health. Isaiah proclaims the biblical meaning of "salvation," which encompasses notions of healing, wholeness, and all things set aright,

Speaks hope to your assembly.

Slow down and articulate this last phrase carefully. Don't drop your voice at the end or the words will be lost.

For meditation and context:

> **TO KEEP IN MIND**
> *Repetition* of the same word or phrase over the course of a reading emphasizes a point. Make each instance distinct, and build your intensity with each repetition.

This didactic reading resonates with the "already but not yet" theme of Advent. How do you want your assembly to respond to this message of hope?

"Patient" and "patience" occur four times in the reading; increase significance with each repetition.

Speak this line slowly and with gentle encouragement.

This is good news!

Those whom the LORD has ransomed will **return**
  and enter Zion **singing**,
    crowned with everlasting **joy**;
they will meet with **joy** and **gladness**,
    sorrow and **mourning** will **flee**.

RESPONSORIAL PSALM   Psalm 146:6–7, 8–9, 9–10 (Isaiah 35:4)

R. Lord, come and save us.
or
R. Alleluia.

The LORD God keeps faith forever,
  secures justice for the oppressed,
  gives food to the hungry.
The LORD sets captives free.

The LORD gives sight to the blind;
  the LORD raises up those who were
    bowed down.
The LORD loves the just;
  the LORD protects strangers.

The fatherless and the widow he sustains,
  but the way of the wicked he thwarts.
The LORD shall reign forever;
  your God, O Zion, through all generations.

READING II   James 5:7–10

A reading from the Letter of Saint James

Be **patient**, brothers and sisters,
  until the **coming** of the Lord.
See how the farmer **waits** for the precious fruit of the earth,
  being **patient** with it
  until it receives the early and the late rains.
You **too** must be **patient**.
Make your hearts **firm**,
  because the coming of the Lord is **at hand**.

---

expressed in the defeat of all human affliction, both internal and external.

READING II This text comes from a brief work that belongs to a collection of New Testament writings usually called the "Catholic Letters." Here "catholic" means universal, since despite sometimes designating a particular individual or group, they seem to be addressed to early Christian believers in general. The Letter of James bears a strong Jewish character, focusing primarily upon ethical conduct expected in the concrete lives of faithful individuals and communities.

Today's passage implies part of the reason for careful attention to a life shaped by Christian faith: the return of Christ is imminent, bringing with it final judgment. Rooted in Jewish apocalyptic expectations of God's final act of salvation, the early Church generally believed that the Risen Christ would soon return in full glory, bringing the Kingdom of God to completion. A popular strain of Jewish thinking described God carrying out a last judgment through the Messiah at this time. James stresses that the culmination of God's work of salvation is imminent, thus believers must be both patient and prepared for its coming.

GOSPEL Last Sunday's reading from Matthew introduced John the Baptist's call to repent in order to prepare for the arrival of God's final rule, which he described as "the coming wrath." He indicated awareness that he himself was not the Messiah, but his forerunner. At the time of today's reading, the imprisoned Baptist sends some of his followers to Jesus to inquire if he is the Christ. Matthew implies

Complaining and infighting are wastes of time when we are waiting for the coming of the Lord.

The arrival of the Judge (Jesus) is welcomed, not feared.

Do not **complain**, brothers and sisters, about one another,
　　that you may not be **judged**.
Behold, the **Judge** is standing before the gates.
Take as an example of **hardship** and **patience**, brothers and sisters,
　　the **prophets** who spoke in the name of the Lord.

GOSPEL　Matthew 11:2–11

A reading from the holy Gospel according to Matthew

A narrative reading. Identify each character's intentions and feelings (including the narrator's) and bring them to your proclamation.

Don't lose the phrase "in prison."

John has a genuine question; make sure it sounds like a question.

How might Jesus sound as he recounts his deeds? Humble? Excited? Satisfied? Speak with that emotion, not as if a laundry list. Don't rush; give each line its due.

blessed = BLES-uhd

A brief pause before this line, and a longer pause after it as Jesus' focus shifts from John's disciples to the crowd.

Jesus is using irony to make his point about John.

When John the **Baptist** heard in **prison** of the **works** of the Christ,
　　he **sent** his disciples to Jesus with this **question**,
　　"Are **you** the one who is to come,
　　or should we look for **another**?"
Jesus said to them in reply,
　　"**Go** and tell John what you **hear** and **see**:
　　the blind regain their **sight**,
　　the lame **walk**,
　　lepers are **cleansed**,
　　the deaf **hear**,
　　the dead are **raised**,
　　and the **poor** have the **good news** proclaimed to them.
And **blessed** is the one who takes no **offense** at me."

As they were going off,
　　Jesus began to speak to the crowds about **John**,
　　"**What** did you go out to the desert to **see**?
A **reed** swayed by the wind?
Then **what** did you go out to see?
Someone dressed in fine **clothing**?
Those who wear fine clothing are in royal **palaces**. »

---

that John recognizes a difference in the message of the two men concerning the arrival of the end time. Whereas the Baptist emphasized divine anger and judgment, Jesus' ministry up to this time has embodied healing and mercy. The discrepancy leads John to pose a direct question to Jesus: are you God's Messiah or are you not?

　　As is common in Matthew, Jesus refers to the Old Testament Scriptures for his response, alluding to several passages from the prophet Isaiah that envision future salvation as a time of merciful healing, wholeness, and re-creation of all things. He

then adds a gentle but unmistakable admonition to John, urging him to take "no offense" at Jesus' activity. The Messiah's words seem to insist that human expectations cannot and must not govern God's saving action on behalf of sick and wounded humankind.

　　Despite his mild rebuke of John, Jesus then turns to the crowds to clarify the Baptist's important role in the unfolding of God's plan of salvation. The crowd seems to hold various views of John: is he a reed in the wind, following every self-proclaimed Messiah? Does he come from a royal

house, foretelling a new Son of David? Jesus, however, clarifies the Baptist's true identity and role: he is the prophet-like-Elijah described by Malachi. Many Jews of the time believed that Malachi, who prophesied more than four centuries earlier, was their last prophet. But he had proclaimed that a new and final prophet in the pattern of Elijah would appear as God's messenger to signal the arrival of the age of salvation (Malachi 3:23–24). John, states Jesus, again quoting the sacred writings of Judaism, is that very messenger.

The tone changes: Aha! Here's the real answer!

Then **why** did you go out? To see a **prophet**?
Yes, I tell you, and **more** than a prophet.
This is the one about whom it is written:
   *Behold, I am sending my **messenger** ahead of you;*
    *he will prepare your **way** before you.*

The phrase means "Pay attention!"

Amen, I say to you,
   among those born of **women**
    there has been **none** greater than John the **Baptist**;
    yet the **least** in the kingdom of heaven is **greater** than he."

You're speaking about your assembly; make sure they know the Good News: that in the Kingdom of Heaven they are all greater than John the Baptist!

Still, Jesus contrasts the exalted role of the messenger and the fulfillment of that prophetic message. What is about to be fulfilled, God's final rule over all things, will be far greater than John or his message. Beyond anything John or his contemporaries imagine, the approaching Kingdom of Heaven will be a reign of mercy, justice, and healing for all. M.F.

FOURTH SUNDAY OF ADVENT

LECTIONARY #10

This reading starts as a narrative and ends as an exhortation.

Isaiah = ī-ZAY-uh

Ahaz = AY-haz

God invites Ahaz into friendship, but he has already allied himself with human powers.

He is insincere.

Let Isaiah's weariness be heard in your voice. Heighten your energy through the rest of the reading, an exhortatory prophecy.

The tone shifts here to one of hope; God will take the initiative even when we are unresponsive.

A very slight pause before "Emmanuel"; be careful not to drop your voice.

For meditation and context:

READING I   Isaiah 7:10–14

A reading from the Book of the Prophet Isaiah

The LORD spoke to **Ahaz**, saying:
  Ask for a **sign** from the LORD, your God;
  let it be **deep** as the netherworld, or **high** as the sky!
But Ahaz answered,
  "I will **not** ask! I will not **tempt** the LORD!"
Then **Isaiah** said:
  Listen, **O** house of David!
Is it not **enough** for you to weary **people**,
  must you also weary my **God**?
Therefore the Lord **himself** will give you **this** sign:
  the **virgin** shall **conceive**, and bear a **son**,
  and shall name him **Emmanuel**.

RESPONSORIAL PSALM   Psalm 24:1–2, 3–4, 5–6 (7c, 10b)

R. Let the Lord enter; he is king of glory.

The LORD's are the earth and its fullness;
  the world and those who dwell in it.
For he founded it upon the seas
  and established it upon the rivers.

Who can ascend the mountain of the LORD?
  or who may stand in his holy place?
One whose hands are sinless, whose heart
    is clean,
  who desires not what is vain.

He shall receive a blessing from the LORD,
  a reward from God his savior.
Such is the race that seeks for him,
  that seeks the face of the God of Jacob.

TO KEEP IN MIND
Use inflection (the high or low pitch of your voice) to convey attitude and feeling. High pitch expresses intensity and excitement; low pitch expresses sadness, contrition, or solemnity.

READING I The earlier chapters of Isaiah reflect conditions in Judah during the waning decades of the eighth century BC. The prophet repeatedly confronted kings and people with lapses of faithfulness to their covenant with the Lord. Kings who were called to lead the people in righteousness instead turned to various foreign nations for protection from invasion. Isaiah's pleas for true repentance went unheeded, and so his further oracles warned of impending downfall, followed by God's ever-faithful deliverance.

Several verses preceding today's reading refer to an unsuccessful attack on Jerusalem by a coalition of neighboring kings, angered by King Ahaz's refusal to join their anti-Assyrian alliance. However, the motivation of Judah's king was not faithfulness to the Lord; Ahaz sought to rely instead on the strength of mighty Assyria. His seemingly pious refusal to test the Almighty by asking for a sign, therefore, reflects hypocrisy rather than proper reverence for God. The divine reply to Ahaz and his house clearly recognizes such royal insincerity. Nevertheless, the Lord supplies

a sign that David's line will continue; God's promise to David (2 Samuel 7:12–16) will be fulfilled by the future coming of a new, ideal king to be named Immanuel, "God is with us." As seen in today's Gospel, the Church finds the ultimate significance of this Word of the Lord revealed in the birth of Christ.

READING II As the Church nears the celebration of Jesus' birth, the readings increasingly claim that this event "fulfills" Israel's Scriptures. This view flows from the earliest Christians, immersed in the Jewish perspective that

A didactic reading. In these complex sentences, pause only between thoughts; use the punctuation as your cue, but keep your voice up at the commas and drop only slightly at the periods.

Paul introduces three things: himself, his apostleship, and Jesus Christ as the source of Good News. Keep the three thoughts distinct. Drop your voice slightly on this parenthetical phrase.

These three phrases are one thought. Don't pause between "but" and "dead."

Pause before beginning the second part, in which Paul introduces his mission to the Gentiles.

Proclaim Paul's words as your own: I have been called to proclaim the Gospel to you.

Take your time with this final part; smile, make eye contact, and be sincere as you bless the assembly.

TO KEEP IN MIND
A *didactic* text makes a point or teaches something. Help your assembly to follow the argument and understand what's being taught.

READING II   Romans 1:1–7

A reading from the Letter of Saint Paul to the Romans

Paul, a slave of Christ **Jesus**,
    called to be an **apostle** and set **apart** for the gospel of God,
    which he promised previously through his prophets in the
       holy Scriptures,
the **gospel** about his Son, descended from David according
      to the flesh,
    but established as **Son of God** in **power**
    according to the Spirit of **holiness**
    through resurrection from the dead, Jesus Christ our **Lord**.
Through **him** we have received the grace of **apostleship**,
    to bring about the **obedience** of faith,
    for the sake of his name, among all the **Gentiles**,
    among whom are **you** also, who are called to **belong**
      to Jesus Christ;
    to all the beloved of God in **Rome**, called to be **holy**.
Grace to you and **peace** from **God** our Father
    and the Lord Jesus **Christ**.

God's plan of salvation unfolded in their communal life of relationship with God. As time passed, new events revealed ever-deepening meanings of God's Word, often meanings undreamed in centuries past. The thoroughly Jewish Apostle to the Gentiles speaks from this perspective at the beginning of Romans.

What Paul proclaims to the Church at Rome is the "gospel of God," the good news of salvation through the life, Death, and Resurrection of Christ. By proclaiming that his message fulfills the promise of the Scriptures, the Apostle underscores its authenticity. Jesus is revealed as the long-awaited "Son of David," the ideal ruler who inaugurates God's final reign over all things. In raising Jesus from death, God further reveals Christ as "Son of God" in a new sense; he is not only an earthly king adopted by God (Psalm 2:6–7), but shares the fullness of divine Spirit. Paul announces that this Christ who fulfills Israel's Scriptures called him to proclaim the astonishing message: Jesus, Son of David and Son of God, realizes the hopes of Gentiles as well. All are called to be holy in Christ Jesus, for all are called to belong to him.

GOSPEL | Today's Gospel continues to emphasize the Jewish view of "fulfillment" of God's Word in the Scriptures (see the commentary for Reading II). Matthew's account of the Good News addresses a largely Jewish Christian community that has begun to open itself to Gentiles. This author gives evidence of thorough familiarity with the Old Testament Scriptures, referring to them more often than other evangelists, both directly and indirectly. His infancy narrative begins a pattern to be repeated in following chapters: a particular event occurs so as to "fulfill" the

We've heard this narrative reading many times. Try to recapture all the drama, conflict, and wonder in it, as if the outcome were in doubt until the very end. You're answering an important question: Just where did this amazing man known as Jesus Christ come from?
No need for a long pause here.

The conflict in these lines reflects the conflict in Joseph's heart as he decides what to do.

Express some sadness in your voice at this choice.
"Behold" tells us something amazing is about to happen! Express wonder and awe at the angel's visit.
The angel recognizes that Joseph's fear keeps him from honoring his commitment to Mary.

Speak with boldness and clarity.
"God saves" is the meaning of the name "Jesus."
Pause to let the angel disappear from the scene.

Take your time explaining this.

A satisfying conclusion: Joseph has made the right choice, and the story can continue.

TO KEEP IN MIND
Pray the text, using your favorite method of praying with Scripture.

GOSPEL   Matthew 1:18–24

A reading from the holy Gospel according to Matthew

This is how the **birth** of Jesus Christ came about.
When his mother **Mary** was betrothed to **Joseph**,
  but **before** they lived together,
  she was found **with child** through the Holy **Spirit**.
Joseph her husband, since he was a **righteous** man,
  yet **unwilling** to expose her to shame,
  decided to divorce her **quietly**.
Such was his **intention** when, **behold**,
  the **angel** of the Lord appeared to him in **a dream** and said,
  "Joseph, son of David,
  do not be afraid to take Mary your wife into your home.
For it is through the **Holy Spirit**
  that this child has been **conceived** in her.
She will bear a **son** and you are to **name** him **Jesus**,
  because he will **save** his people from their **sins**."
All this took place to **fulfill** what the Lord had said through
    the prophet:
  *Behold, the **virgin** shall **conceive** and bear a **son**,*
  *and they shall **name** him **Emmanuel**,*
  which means "God is **with** us."
When Joseph awoke,
  he **did** as the angel of the Lord had commanded him
  and **took** his wife into his home.

Scriptures. This does not imply that a long-ago writer had a clear vision of future events. Rather, it demonstrates the Jewish belief that God's Word contains complete meaning from the moment it is uttered, but the full significance of Scripture discloses itself only gradually by reflection upon the unfolding events of salvation history.

Although most English translations speak of the "birth" of Christ in today's passage, here and in his opening verse, Matthew in fact uses the Greek word *genesis*, or "origin." He is concerned less with historical details of Jesus' birth than he is

with the origin of the Christ, for the Christ event has one and only one source: God. Hence Matthew states that Mary has conceived "through the Holy Spirit." By using the word that opens the Greek Old Testament, Matthew may also suggest that with the birth of Jesus, God's act of new creation begins.

The evangelist carefully notes that the righteous man chosen to parent Jesus descended from King David, thus suggesting that Samuel's prophecy is about to be fulfilled in Jesus. Lest the point be missed, he repeats that Mary's child has his true

origin in God and God's plan for salvation; further, the child is to bear the name "Jesus," which means "God saves." The events that have their origin in God reveal the fullness of Isaiah's words. In the child soon to be born, God is with us in an unimaginable way: in the person of a human infant. M.F.

THE NATIVITY OF THE LORD (CHRISTMAS): VIGIL

An exhortatory reading; keep energy up throughout. Last line is key: God rejoices in us! Note the many couplets of thought rhyme: the same idea expressed twice using different images. Keep these couplets together; let their structure dictate your rhythm.
Isaiah = Ī-ZAY-uh
Proclaim as if you had no choice but to proclaim!

Make eye contact throughout the reading. Maintain a sense of urgency: Persuade your assembly of how much God loves them.

God gives Zion a new name. Our name is also powerful: Christians. We are followers of the Christ whose birth we celebrate.

Imagine telling a sufferer that all the bad times are over. How would you look and sound giving that news? How would you feel?

Emphasize the metaphors of marriage in these lines. God wants to be as close to us as a married couple is to each other!

Slow down, smile, and maintain eye contact through this final line.

LECTIONARY #13

READING I Isaiah 62:1–5

A reading from the Book of the Prophet Isaiah

> For Zion's sake I will **not** be silent,
>   for Jerusalem's sake I will **not** be quiet,
> until her vindication **shines** forth like the **dawn**
>   and her **victory** like a burning **torch**.
>
> Nations shall **behold** your vindication,
>   and all the **kings** your **glory**;
> you shall be called by a **new** name
>   pronounced by the mouth of the **Lord**.
> You shall be a glorious **crown** in the hand of the LORD,
>   a **royal** diadem held by your God.
> No more shall people call you "**Forsaken**,"
>   or your land "**Desolate**,"
> but you shall be called "My **Delight**,"
>   and your land "**Espoused**."
> For the LORD **delights** in you
>   and makes your land his **spouse**.
> As a young **man** marries a **virgin**,
>   your **Builder** shall marry **you**;
> and as a bridegroom **rejoices** in his bride
>   so shall your **God** rejoice in **you**.

READING I Appearing near the end of the Book of Isaiah, this reading is generally dated near the time when the Judeans who survived Babylonian captivity were allowed to return to the Promised Land, around 539 BC. The third section of the book, chapters 56–66, turns toward hope for a future fulfillment of what several prophets had promised: a new covenant, a new Israel, a new Jerusalem, even a new creation. As in the past, such hope was rooted entirely in God's faithfulness to the covenant people. They understood themselves as a people punished for numerous infidelities, but never abandoned by the God who delivered them from slavery and established with them an unbreakable covenant relationship. God had restored and renewed them in the past, and could be counted upon to do so again.

The prophet announces that God will not only bring the people back to their land, but also that their reestablishment will astound other nations and kingdoms. The powerful Word of God will bring about what it proclaims: Israel will be "called by a new name, pronounced by the mouth of the Lord." In biblical thought, a name indicated one's very character and identity. Through Isaiah, God promises future renewal of the covenant people at the very core; the names by which Israel was known in exile will be changed by divine action.

The significance of the names used by the prophet must be understood in light of imagery used repeatedly by several important prophets. Before the destruction of both Israelite kingdoms, Israel and Judah, the relationship between God and the covenant people was often likened to a marriage. Hence various prophets described the people's frequent lapses into idolatry or

For meditation and context:

RESPONSORIAL PSALM   Psalm 89:4–5, 16–17, 27, 29 (2a)

R. For ever I will sing the goodness of the Lord.

I have made a covenant with my chosen one,
  I have sworn to David my servant:
forever will I confirm your posterity
  and establish your throne for all
    generations.

Blessed the people who know the joyful
    shout;
  in the light of your countenance, O Lord,
    they walk.
At your name they rejoice all the day,
  and through your justice they are exalted.

He shall say of me, "You are my father,
  my God, the rock, my savior."
Forever I will maintain my kindness
    toward him,
  and my covenant with him stands firm.

A didactic reading. Proclaim it with the love teachers have for their students or parents have for their children.

Antioch = AN-tee-ahk

Pisidia = pih-SID-ee-uh

Don't swallow "synagogue;" Paul is speaking to fellow Jews and doesn't assume everyone knows who Jesus is; neither should you.

He motions for silence.

The "God-fearing" = those attracted to the teachings of Judaism but not interested in converting.

Paul recounts salvation history; Jesus is its culmination.

sojourn = SOH-jern (exile)

The reading skips a few verses (and a few hundred years of history) to get quickly to David. Let that be your emphasis.

Proclaim with God's voice of pleased satisfaction.

READING II   Acts of the Apostles 13:16–17, 22–25

A reading from the Acts of the Apostles

When **Paul** reached **Antioch** in Pisidia and entered the **synagogue**,
  he **stood** up, motioned with his hand, and said,
    "Fellow Israelites and you others who are God-fearing, **listen**.
The God of this people Israel **chose** our **ancestors**
  and **exalted** the people during their sojourn in the land
    of **Egypt**.
With uplifted **arm** he led them **out** of it.
Then he removed Saul and raised up **David** as king;
  of him he **testified**,
    'I have found **David**, son of Jesse, a man after my own **heart**;
    he will carry out my every **wish**.' »

---

other infidelities as adultery, or as seeking divorce from the Lord (Jeremiah 3:6–10). Addressing the northern kingdom as its destruction drew near, Hosea presented God as a husband abandoned by unfaithful Israel who seeks out other lovers; that is, other gods. Like a jilted husband, the Lord vacillates between seeking ways to punish his adulterous wife and ways to win her back. But in the destruction of the second Israelite kingdom, loss of the Promised Land, and return to captivity, the people saw God "divorcing" the people he once called "my beloved" (Jeremiah 11:15).

What Isaiah proclaims in this passage is an unimaginable healing of this seemingly shattered bond. A renewed people of God will no longer be named "Forsaken." (The Hebrew word used here can also mean "divorced.") Rather, the Lord, ever faithful husband, will completely erase Israel's infidelities and treat her as a virgin bride, rejoicing in a relationship not only restored but completely re-created. Even more important than the return to their land and the rebuilding God's Temple in a reconstructed Jerusalem would be the newly created bond of faithful love between God and his people.

READING II This reading is taken from one of several speeches in Acts in which Luke presents Peter or Paul proclaiming the Good News of Jesus as the expected Messiah. While Peter addresses fellow Jews, Paul most often preaches to a larger audience comprising fellow Israelites, non-Jews sympathetic to Judaism ("others who are God-fearing"), and Gentiles. Usually these early proclamations of faith strive to demonstrate that the life, Death, and Resurrection of Christ bring the Old Testament Scriptures and Jewish hopes

Here's Paul's whole point.

Paul is quoting John. Don't let it sound like he's referring to himself.

This ending is slightly awkward since we're left with John's words and not Paul's. Take a longer pause than usual to let the community process this before "The word of the Lord."

From this man's **descendants** God, according to his **promise**,
    has **brought** to Israel a **savior**, **Jesus**.
John **heralded** his coming by proclaiming a baptism of **repentance**
    to all the people of **Israel**;
    and as John was **completing** his course, he would say,
    'What do you suppose that **I am**? I am not **he**.
Behold, one is coming **after** me;
    I am not **worthy** to unfasten the **sandals** of his feet.'"

GOSPEL   Matthew 1:1–25

Two readings in one; the first is didactic, the second narrative.

The steady rhythm conveys a sense of security and comfort; through all these generations, God was preparing the world for Jesus. Let the rhythm come naturally, but notice where it is broken; something significant is being said! Do your best with the pronunciations, but don't lose the easy flow. If you make a mistake, go right back into the rhythm. Use the periods as places to briefly stop, then increase energy as you begin again.

geneology = jee-nee-OL-uh-jee

Abraham = AY-bruh-ham; Isaac = Ī-zik

Judah = JOO-duh

Perez = PAYR-ez; Zerah = ZEE-rah

Only five women are included in this list.

Tamar = TAY-mahr

Hezron = HEZ-ruhn

Ram = ram

Amminadab = uh-MIN-uh-dab

Nashon = NAH-shun

Salmon = SAL-muhn

Boaz = BOH-az

Rahab = RAY-hab

Obed = OH-bed

Jesse = JES-ee

A reading from the holy Gospel according to Matthew

The book of the **genealogy** of Jesus **Christ**,
    the son of **David**, the son of **Abraham**.

Abraham became the father of **Isaac**,
    Isaac the father of **Jacob**,
    Jacob the father of **Judah** and his brothers.
Judah became the father of **Perez** and **Zerah**,
    whose **mother** was **Tamar**.
Perez became the father of **Hezron**,
    Hezron the father of **Ram**,
    Ram the father of **Amminadab**.
Amminadab became the father of **Nahshon**,
    Nahshon the father of **Salmon**,
    Salmon the father of **Boaz**,
    whose **mother** was **Rahab**.
Boaz became the father of **Obed**,
    whose **mother** was **Ruth**.
Obed became the father of **Jesse**,
    Jesse the father of **David** the **king**.

to their fulfillment. Today's Second Reading serves this major purpose.

Paul points to Israel's very beginnings, when God brought an enslaved people through the wilderness to freedom. His reference to King David and his descendants alludes to Jewish hopes that in the age of salvation, God would complete the promise of a righteous descendant of David who would lead a new Israel to fulfill its destiny as a holy people. Paul proclaims that the unfolding story of salvation has been brought to completion through Jesus, Son of David and Savior.

The Responsorial Psalm fills in more of this background to which Paul refers. It sings of God's promise to King David of an everlasting rule. In the perspective of the Old Testament, the human king served as God's representative and so was called to govern like God, with justice. Despite centuries of kingship that so often failed to fulfill this ideal, God's people continued to desire and hope for a future descendant of David who would rule like Israel's true King, the Lord. The psalmist looks forward to a day that Christians believe arrived in the form of a child born in Bethlehem, David's

traditional birthplace. This infant is the true Son of David, who can truly say to God in a way the psalmist cannot have imagined, "You are my father, my God."

GOSPEL Unfortunately, proclamation of Matthew's full genealogy of Jesus often causes restless shifting and dazed countenances in many a congregation. In fact, Matthew carefully constructed the opening of his account of the Good News to signal a number of important characteristics of the child who would bring God's definitive salvation to the

Pause before reciting the next fourteen generations.

Uriah's wife, Bathsheba, is unnamed.

Uriah = yoo-RĪ-uh

Rehoboam = ree-huh-BOH-uhm

Abijah = uh-BĪ-juh

Asaph = AY-saf

Jehoshaphat = jeh-HOH-shuh-fat

Joram = JOHR-uhm

Uzziah = yuh-ZĪ-uh

Jotham = JOH-thuhm

Ahaz = AY-haz

Hezekiah = hez-eh-KĪH-uh

Manasseh = muh-NAS-uh

Amos = AY-m*s

Josiah = joh-SĪ-uh

Jechoniah = jek-oh-NĪ-uh

Pause before reciting the last fourteen generations.

Shealtiel = shee-AL-tee-uhl

Zerubbabel = zuh-ROOB-uh-b*l

Abiud = uh-BĪ-uhd

Eliakim = ee-LĪ-uh-kim

Azor = AY-sohr

Zadok = ZAD-uhk

Achim = AH-kim

Eliud = ee-LĪ-uhd

Eleazar = el-ee-AY-zer

Matthan = MATH-uhn

David became the father of **Solomon**,
  whose **mother** had been the wife of **Uriah**.
Solomon became the father of **Rehoboam**,
  Rehoboam the father of **Abijah**,
  Abijah the father of **Asaph**.
Asaph became the father of **Jehoshaphat**,
  Jehoshaphat the father of **Joram**,
  Joram the father of **Uzziah**.
Uzziah became the father of **Jotham**,
  Jotham the father of **Ahaz**,
  Ahaz the father of **Hezekiah**.
Hezekiah became the father of **Manasseh**,
  Manasseh the father of **Amos**,
  Amos the father of **Josiah**.
Josiah became the father of **Jechoniah** and his brothers
  at the time of the Babylonian **exile**.

After the Babylonian exile,
  Jechoniah became the father of **Shealtiel**,
  Shealtiel the father of **Zerubbabel**,
  Zerubbabel the father of **Abiud**.
Abiud became the father of **Eliakim**,
  Eliakim the father of **Azor**,
  Azor the father of **Zadok**.
Zadok became the father of **Achim**,
  Achim the father of **Eliud**,
  Eliud the father of **Eleazar**.
Eleazar became the father of **Matthan**,
  Matthan the father of **Jacob**,
  Jacob the father of **Joseph**, the husband of **Mary**.
Of her was born **Jesus** who is called the **Christ**.

Thus the total number of **generations**
  from **Abraham** to **David**
  is **fourteen** generations;
  from **David** to the Babylonian **exile**, »

Matthew has gone to great lengths to show the parallelism of generations during each of the great epochs of Jewish history. End with a satisfied tone. "See how everything comes out right!"

world. The evangelist offers not a biological family tree, but a biblical literary form intended to show significant elements of a person's origins. While most English translations call Matthew's beginning a "genealogy," the evangelist uses the Greek word *genesis*, which also means "origins" and recalls the creation account that begins the Old Testament. In his first few words, the author thus indicates that the birth of this infant initiates a new creation story. Through this child, God will bring humankind and all creation to the fullness intended from the beginning.

At the beginning of his genealogy, Matthew establishes that Jesus is thoroughly Jewish—a "son of Abraham"—and a descendant of David. The reference to David carries messianic connotations, since early first-century Judaism held strong hopes that the messiah would appear as a new and righteous king of David's line, a true "son of David." In a carefully constructed pattern of three sets of fourteen generations each, the evangelist then highlights particular ancestors of Jesus. This threefold pattern outlines major segments of Israel's life in covenant with

the Lord: Abraham to David, David to the Babylonian exile, and exile to the Messiah. In Jewish number symbolism, the number fourteen points to the name of David; Matthew thus suggests that God is about to bring Israel's salvation story to completion in this child who will prove to be the true "son of David."

At the beginning of today's Gospel reading, Matthew uses the word *genesis*, indicating that this child's origins provide important clues about who he is and what he will accomplish. Twice Matthew stresses that the birth of Jesus came about

Try to recapture all the drama, conflict, and wonder in the story, as if the outcome were in doubt until the very end. You're answering an important question: where did this amazing Jesus Christ come from?

The conflict in these lines reflects the conflict in Joseph's heart as he decides what to do.

Express sadness in your voice at this choice.

"Behold" tells us something amazing is about to happen! Bring a sense of wonder and awe to your proclamation of the angel's visit.

The angel recognizes that Joseph's fear keeps him from honoring his commitment to Mary.

Speak with boldness and clarity.

"God saves" is the meaning of the name "Jesus." Pause to let the angel disappear from the scene.

Another name for Jesus with another meaning. Take your time with each.

There's a satisfied feel to this conclusion: Joseph has made the right choice.

Let Joseph's love for the child come through as you describe his naming.

> **TO KEEP IN MIND**
> Making eye contact with the assembly connects you with them and connects them to the reading more deeply than using your voice alone. This helps the assembly stay with the story and keeps them engaged.

through God's powerful action in the world, the Holy Spirit. The name "Jesus" begins to unfold his true character and identity, for it means "God saves." Matthew further announces that his Nativity brings to fullness the prophetic word concerning a son to be called "Emmanuel," God's own presence in the world. This child, whose ultimate origin is in God, will carry out God's work; through him the original divine purpose of creation will reach completion. This newborn infant is revealed as a true image of God, a human being in whom "God is with us." M.F.

fourteen generations;
from the Babylonian exile to the **Christ**,
fourteen generations.

[**Now** this is how the **birth** of Jesus Christ came about.
When his mother **Mary** was betrothed to Joseph,
    but before they **lived** together,
    she was found with **child** through the Holy **Spirit**.
Joseph her husband, since he was a **righteous** man,
    yet unwilling to expose her to **shame**,
    decided **to divorce** her **quietly**.
Such was his **intention** when, **behold**,
    the **angel** of the Lord **appeared** to him in a dream and said,
    "**Joseph**, son of **David**,
do not be **afraid** to take Mary your wife into your home.
For it is through the Holy **Spirit**
    that this child has been **conceived** in her.
She will bear a **son** and you are to name him **Jesus**,
    because he will **save** his people from their **sins**."
All this took place to **fulfill**
    what the Lord had said through the **prophet**:
        *Behold, the **virgin** shall **conceive** and bear a **son**,*
            *and they shall name him **Emmanuel**,*
    which means "**God** is **with** us."
When Joseph **awoke**,
    he **did** as the angel of the Lord had **commanded** him
    and **took** his wife into his **home**.
He had no **relations** with her until she bore a **son**,
    and he **named** him Jesus.]

[Shorter: Matthew 1:18–25 (see brackets)]

THE NATIVITY OF THE LORD (CHRISTMAS): NIGHT

LECTIONARY #14

READING I   Isaiah 9:1–6

An exhortatory hymn of praise to God. Keep your pace up (but not too fast). Don't stop at the end of each sense line; let punctuation guide your pauses.
Isaiah = ī-ZAY-uh
Emphasize the contrasts between darkness and light.

Although you're speaking to God, make eye contact with the community.

A triple thought rhyme; intensify with each line.

Midian = MID-ee-uhn

Use quiet tone on images of war. Note that it's tramped (one syllable, meaning marched), not trampled.

The cloak is a gruesome image, but sorrow has turned to joy.

Revive your energy here. This is good news; express that!

Give each name its emphasis.

A reading from the Book of the Prophet Isaiah

The people who walked in **darkness**
    have seen a great **light**;
upon those who dwelt in the land of **gloom**
    a **light** has **shone**.
You have **brought** them abundant **joy**
    and great **rejoicing**,
as they **rejoice** before you as at the **harvest**,
    as people make **merry** when dividing **spoils**.
For the **yoke** that **burdened** them,
    the **pole** on their **shoulder**,
and the **rod** of their **taskmaster**
    you have **smashed**, as on the day of Midian.
For every boot that **tramped** in battle,
    every cloak **rolled** in blood,
    will be **burned** as fuel for **flames**.
For a child is **born** to us, a son is **given** us;
    upon his shoulder **dominion** rests.
They name him **Wonder-Counselor**, **God-Hero**,
    Father-Forever, **Prince** of **Peace**. »

In order to understand the liturgy's use of prophetic books, it is helpful to understand several interpretive approaches used by New Testament writers. Judaism believed that God had implanted the complete divine plan in their sacred texts; the faith community could discover its unfolding meaning by continual reflection. Since the earliest Christians were Jewish, they naturally used familiar methods to illumine the religious meaning of Jesus. New Testament authors wanted to demonstrate his significance for their own particular life circumstances, and so often referred to the Old Testament Scriptures to clarify how Jesus fully reveals their significance. New Testament references to Jesus as "fulfillment" of Israel's Scriptures, as in today's Gospel, need to be understood in this way. While an Old Testament text bears rich meaning in its own context, in light of Jesus, new meanings emerge.

READING I Chapters 6–12 of the Book of Isaiah reflect circumstances of the two decades before the fall of the Kingdom of Israel (721 BC), when the Kingdom of Judah, to the south, was at times also embroiled in clashes with Assyria and some of its neighboring allies. Chapter 9 reflects a time of invasion by the powerful, militaristic empire of Assyria into territory immediately north of the two Israelite kingdoms. Especially in such threatening times, Judah longed for the leadership and protection of a mighty and righteous warrior-king. For God's covenant people, the ideal king was not only a political and military leader, but God's representative who ruled like God, establishing right relationships and seeking the good of all.

His dominion is **vast**
　and forever **peaceful**,
from **David's** throne, and over his **kingdom**,
　which he **confirms** and **sustains**
by **judgment** and **justice**,
　both **now** and **forever**.
The **zeal** of the LORD of hosts will **do** this!

Pause before this final line.

For meditation and context:

RESPONSORIAL PSALM   Psalm 96:1–2, 2–3, 11–12, 13 (Luke 2:11)

R. Today is born our Savior, Christ the Lord.

Sing to the LORD a new song;
　sing to the LORD, all you lands.
Sing to the LORD; bless his name.

Announce his salvation, day after day.
　Tell his glory among the nations;
　among all peoples, his wondrous deeds.

Let the heavens be glad and the earth rejoice;
　let the sea and what fills it resound;
　let the plains be joyful and all that is
　　in them!
Then shall all the trees of the forest exult.

They shall exult before the LORD,
　for he comes;
　for he comes to rule the earth.
He shall rule the world with justice
　and the peoples with his constancy.

> **TO KEEP IN MIND**
>
> In *thought* rhyme, two parallel lines say the same thing, but each in a different way. Use care to keep the two lines together and use emphasis to show the parallelism.

An exhortatory reading, short but very significant. Express to the assembly that this is good news!

Titus = TĪ-tuhs

Proclaim so that the community will live as those who know they are loved.

The reading is only one sentence, but don't rush. Pause at commas and at the end of lines (except where noted), but keep your voice up.

blessed = BLES-uhd

You are praising your community for how well they live!

Don't pause at the end of this line.

Use the eagerness in your voice to convey your community's desire to do good.

READING II   Titus 2:11–14

A reading from the Letter of Saint Paul to Titus

Beloved:
The grace of God has **appeared**, saving **all**
　and training us to **reject** godless ways and **worldly** desires
　and to live **temperately, justly,** and **devoutly** in this age,
　as we **await** the blessed **hope,**
　the **appearance** of the **glory** of our great **God**
　and **savior** Jesus **Christ,**
　who gave himself for us to **deliver** us from all lawlessness
　and to **cleanse** for himself a people as his **own,**
eager to do what is **good.**

While Israel had its own succession of kings, the kings of Judah descended from David. Today's First Reading expresses Judah's hope that a true Son of David would soon appear. Such a king would not only bring military victory and protection from foreign powers; he would embody the ideal of Israelite kingship. The expected "child" of Isaiah 7:14, a sign that God was truly present among the people of Judah in dangerous times, is described in Isaiah 9 as the fullness of that ideal. Like God, he would be completely dedicated to the people's welfare, ruling his people wisely and bringing peace to the entire kingdom. The prophet envisions a longed-for Son of David ruling with "justice and judgment." The Hebrew words used here describe one who is truly righteous and who actively labors to bring about right relationships among the people, supporting sincere worship of God and social justice throughout the kingdom.

READING II   The brief letter of Titus, along with the two attributed to Timothy, form a group usually called the "Pastoral Letters." While scholars debate their authorship and dating, these writings give insight into emerging concerns and structures in the early Church. Matters discussed often include elements of Christian living in the midst of opposing cultures and values, distribution of and qualifications for various ministries, and proper church structures.

In one of the shortest of New Testament writings, Titus primarily deals with Christian conduct. In today's reading, the author roots his admonitions in what God has done for us in Jesus Christ. Like Paul, Titus stresses that the Christ event is God's gracious gift, initiated solely by divine

A narrative reading, perhaps best proclaimed simply, as if a bedtime story. What effect do you want this story to have on the assembly? Keep that intention in mind as you proclaim.

Caesar = SEE-zer; Augustus = aw-GUHS-tuhs

Careful not to swallow "enrolled." It refers to the census, but that might not be clear to the community.

Quirinius = kwih-RIN-ee-uhs

Emphasize "city of David." Judea = joo-dee-uh; Bethlehem = BETH-luh-hem

Drop your voice slightly on this parenthetical phrase.

Begin to slow down from here to "inn."

Proclaim with the tenderness of a mother caring for her newborn.

Proclaim this as a simple fact without "comment."

Pause as the scene shifts to the shepherds, then pick up your pace again.

Bring a feeling of wonder and surprise to the angel's appearance. This is not an everyday occurrence; it shouldn't sound like one!

You've been selected to deliver good news that will bring great joy tonight, so let your feeling come through in the words of the angel!

TO KEEP IN MIND
In a narrative, find an emotion or point of view for each character, keeping in mind that these might change during the reading.

GOSPEL   Luke 2:1–14

A reading from the holy Gospel according to Luke

In those days a **decree** went out from **Caesar Augustus**
   that the **whole** world should be **enrolled**.
This was the **first** enrollment,
   when Quirinius was governor of Syria.
So **all** went to be enrolled, **each** to his own town.
And **Joseph** too went up from **Galilee** from the town of
      Nazareth
   to Judea, to the **city of** David that is called Bethlehem,
   because he was of the house and family of David,
   to be enrolled with **Mary**, his betrothed, who was with **child**.
While they were there,
   the **time** came for her to have her **child**,
   and she **gave birth** to her firstborn **son**.
She **wrapped** him in swaddling clothes and **laid** him in a **manger**,
   because there was no **room** for them in the **inn**.

Now there were **shepherds** in that region living in the **fields**
   and keeping the night watch over their **flock**.
The **angel** of the Lord **appeared** to them
   and the **glory** of the Lord **shone** around them,
   and they were **struck** with great **fear**.
The angel said to them,
   "Do **not** be **afraid**;
   for **behold**, I **proclaim** to you good **news** of great **joy**
   that will be for **all** the people.
For **today** in the city of **David**
   a **savior** has been **born** for you who is **Christ** and **Lord**.
And **this** will be a **sign** for you:
   you will find an **infant** wrapped in **swaddling** clothes
   and lying in a **manger**." »

---

love. Like Paul and many early Christians, he also seems to expect an imminent return of Christ in full glory. Emphasizing the self-gift of Christ to and for us, Titus encourages his hearers to live as a community saved by divine gift, eagerly responding to that gift by conduct befitting all who belong to God.

GOSPEL | Of the four canonical Gospel accounts, only Matthew and Luke begin with an account of Jesus' birth. Unlike modern western culture, people in the biblical world did not think in terms of human growth and development; what a person was at birth represented what he or she would be throughout life. Thus an infancy narrative served to depict a person's enduring character and role in the world; accuracy of historical detail was not the primary concern.

Scholars generally agree that this evangelist was a Greek-speaking Gentile convert to Christianity, addressing an audience of similar background. These same scholars differ, however, in describing how Luke viewed the relationship between Christian living and daily realities of imperial Rome.

Some see him attempting to show that Christians offer no threat to Roman authorities and the two groups can peaceably coexist. Others believe that Luke sometimes emphasizes ways in which Christian faith and Roman rule prove to be incompatible.

This evangelist is the only one to place Jesus on the world stage of his time, locating the Savior's birth in the reign of Caesar Augustus and naming Quirinius, the Syrian governor. Luke describes a required "enrollment" as the reason for Joseph and Mary's journey to Bethlehem. No historical record of such a decree at this specific time has

Quicken your energy with "suddenly." Amazement has been taken to a whole new level!

1Although this is the last line, keep your voice and energy up throughout. Then pause before "The word of the Lord"

TO KEEP IN MIND
Proclamation cannot be effective unless it is expressive. As you prepare your proclamation, make choices about emotions. Some choices are already evident in the text.

And **suddenly** there was a **multitude** of the heavenly host with
the angel,
praising God and saying:
"**Glory** to God in the **highest**
and on **earth peace** to those on whom his **favor** rests."

---

been found, though a census did occur at some point under Quirinius. The writer most likely uses such an event in order to locate Jesus' birth in Bethlehem, indicating the fulfillment of Micah 5:1, which states that the expected messiah-king will arise from this traditional birthplace of King David.

Luke includes several details that underscore Jesus' outreach to the poor, as well as his true identity as Savior, Lord, and bringer of peace. The infant who comes to serve the poor and outcast is laid in a feeding trough for animals. Because Luke mentions the manger repeatedly, some scholars

believe that he intends to foreshadow the ministry of Jesus that so often took place at a meal. Eventually, Jesus will give his own life as nourishment for the new life of all humankind.

Again emphasizing Jesus' ministry to the poor and marginalized, Luke presents a startling scene: the first to receive the Good News of dawning salvation is a group of shepherds, generally despised and avoided by other Jews as unclean sinners. The angelic proclamation not only challenges Jewish religious assumptions, but contradicts the imperial cult. Caesar

Augustus was proclaimed in the empire as divine Lord, savior of the people, and bringer of peaceful order in the empire. No, proclaims Luke: not the Roman emperor, but the infant lying in a feeding trough is the true Savior and royal Son of God who establishes peace on earth. M.F.

THE NATIVITY OF THE LORD (CHRISTMAS): DAWN

LECTIONARY #15

An exhortatory reading; it's short, but don't rush it. Isaiah is calling the people to hope in a God who will restore Zion to its former glory. Proclaim this as if to someone you know who needs to hear a message of hope.

Isaiah = ī-ZAY-uh
Keep your voice and energy up throughout!

Announce his coming as if you were on a watchtower, alerting the whole city that you've spotted him from a long way off.

recompense = REK-uhm-pens (compensation for wrongs suffered)
Smile with your face, eyes, and voice so your community knows this is good news!
Make sure "Frequented" (FREE-kwen-t*d) sounds like a proper name; it will not be a word the community expects here.

For meditation and context:

TO KEEP IN MIND
Exhortatory texts make an urgent appeal to listeners. They may encourage, warn, or challenge, and often include a call to action. You must convey the urgency and passion behind the words.

READING I Isaiah 62:11–12

A reading from the Book of the Prophet Isaiah

> **See**, the **Lord proclaims**
>   to the **ends** of the **earth**:
> say to daughter **Zion**,
>   your savio**r comes**!
> Here is his **reward** with him,
>   his **recompense** before him.
> They shall be called the **holy** people,
>   the **redeemed** of the LORD,
> and you shall be called "**Frequented**,"
>   a city that is **not forsaken**.

RESPONSORIAL PSALM Psalm 97:1, 6, 11–12

R. A light will shine on us this day: the Lord is born for us.

The LORD is king; let the earth rejoice;
    let the many isles be glad.
The heavens proclaim his justice,
    and all peoples see his glory.

Light dawns for the just;
    and gladness, for the upright of heart.
Be glad in the LORD, you just,
    and give thanks to his holy name.

READING I This passage comes from the last segment of the longest book of prophecy in the Old Testament. Most biblical scholars believe that chapters 56–66 of Isaiah date from the time of the end of Babylonian exile, around 539 BC. After the loss of land, nationhood, kingdom, and kingship, after more than a half-century of captivity in a foreign empire, prophetic promises of hope for restoration began to be realized. Today's reading closes chapter 62, which exults in God's renewal of covenant love with Israel. With the restoration of this bond, the vision of earlier prophets who spoke of a future new Jerusalem became possible. Immediately before today's reading, the prophet boldly speaks of "watchmen" who serve to remind the Lord (incessantly!) of prophetic promises to rebuild Judah's capital city. Jerusalem was the home of kings in David's line and of the Temple, both visible signs of God dwelling in the midst of the covenant people.

Through Isaiah, God proclaims to Zion (a frequent synonym for Jerusalem) that now is the moment of her savior's coming. The root of the Hebrew word here translated "savior" carries a range of meanings, including salvation, deliverance, rescue, safety, wellbeing, healing, and wholeness. The announcement that God is coming to save Jerusalem thus carries multiple layers of meaning. The rebuilding of the city of Jerusalem implies restoring Davidic kingship and building a new dwelling place for God in Israel's midst; by extension, it points to a renewed covenant relationship. New names for the people and their capital city signify new character and identity. The prophet Hosea, speaking to the Kingdom of Israel before its destruction, was told to give his children names that symbolized

A didactic reading, but it still requires energy and enthusiasm. It's one sentence with three main thoughts as noted. Keep the phrases together, and pause a little more than usual at the commas.

Titus = Tī-tuhs

First thought: When the kindness . . . his mercy.

Drop your voice slightly on this parenthetical phrase.

Second thought: he saved us . . . our savior. Make "bath of rebirth and renewal" one phrase; it refers to Baptism.
Let the word "richly" sound like what it means.

Third thought: so that we . . . eternal life. Slight pause after grace.

Slow down and let the gift of our inheritance really sink in.

> **TO KEEP IN MIND**
> Pause in order to break up separate thoughts, set apart significant statements, or indicate major shifts. Never pause in the middle of a single thought. Your primary guide for pauses is punctuation.

READING II   Titus 3:4–7

A reading from the Letter of Saint Paul to Titus

Beloved:
When the **kindness** and generous **love**
    of God our savior **appeared**,
not because of any righteous deeds we had done
    but because of his **mercy**,
he **saved** us through the **bath** of **rebirth**
    and **renewal** by the Holy **Spirit**,
whom he richly **poured** out on us
    through Jesus Christ our **savior**,
so that we might be **justified** by his grace
    and become **heirs** in **hope** of eternal **life**.

God's view of the people at that time, names like "without compassion" and "not my people." But with a new act of divine salvation, the Lord's people will be called "the holy people, the redeemed of the Lord." By the power of Israel's Redeemer, Jerusalem, once known as a desolate heap of ruins, will also receive a new name, a new identity, from its saving God.

READING II Like the other two "Pastoral Letters," 1 and 2 Timothy, Titus generally focuses on Christian behavior (especially in contrast to prevailing mores), and on ministries and order in the Church. All of these, however, flow from and build upon the saving action of God in Jesus Christ. In this reading, the author presents a masterful summation of core Christian faith in the first century. He stresses the origin of human salvation in God's gracious love, given as completely unearned gift, repeating the important point that we are made whole by divine grace (*grace* translates Greek *charis*, which literally means "gift"). This gift of "generous love" was poured out through Christ, received in Baptism, and continues to renew believers through the indwelling presence of the Holy Spirit.

GOSPEL This passage continues Luke's account of the angelic announcement of the Savior's birth to the most improbable hearers: lowly shepherds, who were usually avoided and despised as ritually impure sinners. The shepherds may also serve as a reminder of King David's humble origins, but they surely underscore one of Luke's favored emphases, Jesus' preference for sinners and outcasts. Shepherds they may be, but they

A narrative reading concluding the Christmas story; it assumes the assembly knows the story up to this point, and they probably do, but your tone will have to remind them that this is a story of joy and excitement.

Start slowly, to let the community catch up to where we are in the story.

Proclaim with the eager enthusiasm of those about to leave their flocks (their entire livelihood!) unguarded to check out this amazing thing.

Don't let it sound like Mary and Joseph are in the manger! Pause after "manger" to let the scene settle.

manger = MAYN-jer

You also should be amazed as you proclaim!

Pause before and after these lines about Mary; proclaim them with the reflective tone Mary assumes.

Use the words "glorifying and praising God" to do just that!

There's a tone of satisfaction to Luke's words here: you can trust what you've been told.

TO KEEP IN MIND
Pay attention to the pace of your reading. Varying the pace gives listeners clues to the meaning of the text. The most common problem for proclaimers new to the ministry is going too fast to be understood.

GOSPEL   Luke 2:15–20

A reading from the holy Gospel according to Luke

When the **angels** went away from them to heaven,
    the **shepherds** said to one another,
    "Let us **go**, then, to Bethlehem
    to **see** this thing that has taken place,
    which the Lord has made **known** to us."
So they went in **haste** and found **Mary** and **Joseph**,
    and the **infant** lying in the manger.
When they **saw** this,
    they made known the message
    that had been **told** them about this child.
All who heard it were **amazed**
    by what had been told them by the shepherds.
And Mary **kept** all these things,
    reflecting on them in her **heart**.
Then the shepherds returned,
    glorifying and **praising** God
    for **all** they had **heard** and **seen**,
    just as it had been told to them.

---

immediately respond to God's Word proclaimed by heavenly messengers. Hurrying toward the Savior, they find him "lying in the manger." For the third time in his infancy narrative, the evangelist points out the manger. By so doing, he indicates that this poor and humble child will also be food for all who hunger for God's deliverance, nourishing first those most in need. Throughout his Gospel account, Luke unfolds much of the meaning of Jesus and of his ministry in the context of a meal; the manger may well foreshadow many ways in

which Jesus will feed the poor, outcasts, sinners, and the marginalized.

In an interesting turn of events, the shepherds act as witnesses to God's revelation, telling the angelic message to Mary and Joseph; their testimony confirms and expands what Gabriel earlier announced to Mary about her child (Luke 1:31–33). Both Mary and the shepherds model a proper response to God's Word of salvation through this newborn child. Mary keeps turning over these words and events in her heart; she seems aware that the full meaning of divine revelation takes place only

gradually and with reflection. The shepherds display a response to the Good News that Luke often depicts; they give joyful praise and thanks to God, the sole source of salvation. M.F.

THE NATIVITY OF THE LORD (CHRISTMAS): DAY

An exhortatory reading of joyous news! Be sure to smile with your face, eyes, and voice so your assembly knows it's good news.

Isaiah = ī-ZAY-uh

Today you are the one who brings glad tidings!

Four similar actions, but make each one distinct.

Practice a few different ways of proclaiming "Your God is King" until you've captured all its inherent conviction and exhilaration.

With the word "Hark" stop and listen for yourself. Then hear the news from the sentinels and relay it to the assembly.

Convince the community that breaking out in song is the only appropriate response to this news!

Don't gloss over "O;" fill it with emotion.

Reassure your community—all will be well with the Lord.

Rolling up one's sleeves is a sign of strength and commitment to the task.

A grand, sweeping conclusion. Proclaim slowly and with amazement, satisfaction, joy, pride, or an appropriate emotion of your choice.

LECTIONARY #16

READING I   Isaiah 52:7–10

A reading from the Book of the Prophet Isaiah

How **beautiful** upon the mountains
    are the feet of him who brings **glad** tidings,
announcing **peace**, bearing **good** news,
    announcing **salvation**, and saying to Zion,
"Your **God** is **King**!"

Hark! Your sentinels raise a **cry**,
    together they **shout** for joy,
for they **see** directly, before their eyes,
    the LORD **restoring** Zion.
Break out together in **song**,
    O ruins of Jerusalem!
For the LORD **comforts** his people,
    he **redeems** Jerusalem.
The LORD has **bared** his holy arm
    in the sight of all the **nations**;
all the ends of the earth will **behold**
    the **salvation** of our **God**.

READING I   Commentators usually divide the lengthy book of Isaiah in three sections, each reflecting a different time in the history of God's people. Today's reading is part of the second segment (Isaiah 50–55) often called "the book of consolation." The context for these chapters appears to be the later part of Babylonian captivity, a time of increasing hope and assurance of return to the Promised Land. The destruction of the Kingdom of Judah and its city, Jerusalem, with its magnificent Temple of the Lord was a devastating event that called into question not only Israel's future but its very identity as God's people. Several prophets, however, continued to proclaim a renewal of the people that went beyond returning to the city. God's new future would be more resplendent than anything that came before; all that had been destroyed would be created anew with divine glory.

In this reading, Isaiah imagines the day of deliverance as it draws near; a divine herald announces the arrival of peace and salvation, with God once again ruling in a new Jerusalem as Israel's true King. The Hebrew words translated here as "peace" and "salvation" are laden with significance. "Peace" means much more than the absence of war, and "salvation" is not limited to heavenly reward. Together, these two terms embrace multiple meanings, including deliverance, rescue, security, wellbeing, health, wholeness, and completeness—all beginning in the present world. Similarly, the Hebrew word translated "redeems" derives from ancient tribal culture, in which the clan's "redeemer" was designated to restore to the family persons or property that had been captured. The prophet envisions Israel's God

For meditation and context:

A didactic reading, showing the unique status of Jesus as Son of God. What does the reading call your community to do after hearing this? Make that the reason you proclaim, and keep that intention uppermost in your mind.

God spoke once through words and actions; now, words and actions are one in Jesus.

Increase your energy as you begin each of the three clauses that describe the Son: "whom he . . . ," "who is . . . ," "who sustains . . . "
refulgence = ree-FUHL-j*nts (radiance or brilliance)
You might show disdain for the "lowly" position of the angels, since Jesus' position is "far superior." The community knows the answers to these rhetorical questions. It's as if you're sharing an inside joke: Can you imagine anyone thinking they're as special as Jesus?
This is the right relationship between Jesus and the angels, and God sees to it.

RESPONSORIAL PSALM   Psalm 98:1, 2–3, 3–4, 5–6 (3c)

R. All the ends of the earth have seen the saving power of God.

Sing to the LORD a new song,
for he has done wondrous deeds;
his right hand has won victory for him,
his holy arm.

The LORD has made his salvation known:
in the sight of the nations he has revealed
his justice.
He has remembered his kindness
and his faithfulness
toward the house of Israel.

All the ends of the earth have seen
the salvation by our God.
Sing joyfully to the LORD, all you lands;
break into song; sing praise.

Sing praise to the LORD with the harp,
with the harp and melodious song.
With trumpets and the sound of the horn
sing joyfully before the King, the LORD.

READING II   Hebrews 1:1–6

A reading from the Letter to the Hebrews

Brothers and sisters:
In times **past**, God spoke in **partial** and **various** ways
    to our ancestors through the **prophets**;
    in these **last** days, he has **spoken** to us through the **Son**,
    whom he made **heir** of all things
    and through whom he created the **universe**,
    who is the **refulgence** of his **glory**, the very **imprint** of his **being**,
    and who **sustains** all things by his mighty **word**.
    When he had accomplished **purification** from sins,
    he took his seat at the **right** hand of the Majesty on **high**,
    as **far** superior to the angels
    as the **name** he has inherited is more excellent than **theirs**.

For to **which** of the angels did God ever **say**:
    You *are my* **son***; this day I have* **begotten** *you?*
Or again:
    I will be a **father** *to him, and he shall be a* **son** *to me?*
And **again**, when he leads the **firstborn** into the world, he says:
    Let **all** *the* **angels** *of God* **worship** *him.*

---

and King acting as redeemer, freeing her from captivity and restoring her as members of God's family.

READING II   Both the authorship and dating of this letter are much debated, but clearly the writer is very familiar with the Old Testament, and addresses "the Hebrews." Like the evangelist, John, the author of Hebrews begins with a poetic introduction presenting Christ as the culmination of God's revelation: God's own Word in a human person, Jesus. Both writers draw upon the Old Testament

personification of divine Wisdom, which in the early New Testament period was virtually equivalent to God's self-revealing Word. Both authors allude to Old Testament wisdom texts that describe the Wisdom or Word of God as coming from the mouth of God, existing with God from the beginning, assisting in the work of creation, and radiating the glory of God in the world (Sirach 24:3; Proverbs 8:22–31; Wisdom 10:1–2; Wisdom 7:25–26).

The writer of Hebrews notes that in times past, partial revelation of God's Word came to Israel, particularly through the

prophets. But in Jesus Christ, that self-revealing Word appears in all its fullness: the Son is "the very imprint" of God's being. The Greek word used here is *charakter*, which originally meant an engraving tool, later a die or mold, still later a stamp for marking a seal or coin; in each case, a reality stood behind the image produced. Finally the term pointed to an exact impression or reproduction that also reveals inner character. In short, the writer indicates that anyone who wishes to know the very character of God has only to turn to the Son. The image of "Son" also points to an exact

An exhortatory reading, which might be best proclaimed with an increasingly quiet intensity rather than exuberant energy—although either could work.

Look carefully at the words in bold. The key to this reading is how you proclaim these operative words. You need to make an intentional choice about what you do with them.

Emphasize the images of life, light, and darkness.

Drop your voice slightly as you describe John in these lines.

Raise your voice again as you return to Jesus.

Don't overemphasize the aspects of rejection. Keep it simple, in line with the rest of the reading.

You are describing us: children of God, born of God.

GOSPEL   John 1:1–18

A reading from the holy Gospel according to John

[In the **beginning** was the **Word**,
    and the **Word** was **with** God,
    and the Word **was** God.
He was in the beginning **with** God.
All things came to be **through** him,
    and without him **nothing** came to be.
What came to be through him was **life**,
    and this life was the **light** of the human race;
the light **shines** in the **darkness**,
    and the darkness has not **overcome** it.]
A man named **John** was sent from **God**.
He came for testimony, to **testify** to the light,
    so that all might **believe** through him.
He was **not** the light,
    but came to testify **to** the light.
[The **true** light, which enlightens **everyone**,
    was coming into the world.
He was **in** the world,
    and the world came to **be** through him,
    but the world did not **know** him.
He came to what was his **own**,
    but his own people did not accept him.

But to those who **did** accept him
    he gave **power** to become **children** of **God**,
    to those who **believe** in his name,
    who were born not by **natural** generation
    nor by human **choice nor** by a **man's** decision
    but of **God**.

representation of the "Father," because in Jewish culture a son could stand in the place of his father to communicate or to carry out a task. When a son thus represented the father, it was as if the father himself were present, speaking and acting.

In his Death and Resurrection, Jesus, exact representation and actual presence of God, is higher or greater than any other divine being. Many followers of Judaism believed in the existence of divine beings other than the Lord, though none were ever on a par with him. Indicating that they were in some sense divine, angels were some-times called "sons of God." Using several Old Testament references, the author of Hebrews takes pains to insist that "the Son," the exact representation of God, ranks high above any and all other "sons of God."

GOSPEL   The import of John's prologue is similar to that of the Second Reading, though he has his unique perspective. John's poetic prologue, both introduction to and summary of his account of the Good News, most likely makes use of an already-existing Christological hymn. It is evident that he intersperses material concerning John the Baptist, but whether and how he might have edited the hymn otherwise cannot be determined precisely. Two interjections concerning John the Baptist emphasize that he functions as witness, giving testimony to "the light" that is Christ; in no way is he himself the one who reveals God. Many scholars think that John inserted this material to counteract claims that the Baptist, not Jesus, was the expected Messiah. This and other themes introduced in the prologue are repeated by John in subsequent chapters.

The climax of the reading—God chooses to take on "flesh," all the messiness of being human. Yet the statement is simple and elegant. Try proclaiming slowly, with a quiet wonder in your voice and face.

You can pick up your pace and energy again here.

Careful with this awkward construction.

Pause briefly to indicate the end of John's quote.

The grace of the new covenant builds on the grace of the old.

The Good News of today is that the birth of Jesus reveals the unseen God to us all!

TO KEEP IN MIND
Always pause at the end of the reading, before you proclaim the closing dialogue ("The Word of the Lord" or "The Gospel of the Lord").

And the **Word** became **flesh**
   and made his **dwelling** among us,
   and we **saw** his glory,
   the glory as of the Father's only **Son**,
   full of **grace** and **truth**.]
John testified to him and **cried** out, saying,
   "**This** was he of whom I said,
   'The one who is coming **after** me ranks **ahead** of me
   because he existed **before** me.'"
From his **fullness** we have all received,
   grace in place of **grace**,
   because while the **law** was given through **Moses**,
   grace and **truth** came through Jesus **Christ**.
No one has ever **seen** God.
The only **Son, God**, who is at the Father's **side**,
   has **revealed** him.

[Shorter: John 1:1–5, 9–14 (see brackets)]

Like the author of Hebrews (see the commentary for Reading II), John draws upon Old Testament references to the Wisdom or Word of God to interpret Jesus to a late first-century audience. More than any other evangelist, John focuses on the identity of Jesus; for him, that identity is the divine Word totally united to full humanity, embodying and so revealing God in the world.

Opening the prologue, John uses the very same words that begin the Greek Old Testament, signaling a new creation begun in Christ. Existing with God from the beginning, assisting God in creation, and radiating divine being into the world all recall the personification of the divine Wisdom or Word in the Old Testament. Still, John forewarns, not all adherents to that testament will accept Jesus; those who do will enjoy a filial relationship to God like that of the Word.

This Word of God, John graphically insists, "was made flesh"; the Greek word *sarx*, usually translated "flesh," means the entire human person in all its weakness and mortality. Precisely by taking on all that is human, including suffering and death, the Word reveals God and makes God present. Here John signals his interpretation of Jesus' Passion: it is the potent revelation of God's own life and love poured out for us (John 15:13; 10:1–18). This is the "fullness we have all received" through the divine Word made flesh. M.F.

MARY, THE HOLY MOTHER OF GOD

An exhortatory reading, all good news, so be sure to smile with your voice, eyes, and face as you proclaim.

God invites the Israelites to request a blessing at any time and for any reason. Let this feeling of generosity come through in your proclamation.

Bless your assembly as you proclaim this age-old, well-known formula.

There are three parts to the blessing; make them distinct.

Pause after the blessing to let it really sink in.

For meditation and context:

TO KEEP IN MIND
A *didactic* text makes a point or teaches something. Help your assembly to follow the **argument** and understand what's being taught.

LECTIONARY #18

READING I   Numbers 6:22–27

A reading from the Book of Numbers

The LORD said to **Moses**:
  "Speak to Aaron and his sons and **tell** them:
  This is how you shall **bless** the Israelites.
Say to them:
  The LORD **bless** you and **keep** you!
  The LORD let his face **shine** upon
    you, and be **gracious** to you!
  The LORD look upon you **kindly** and
    give you **peace**!
So shall they invoke my **name** upon the Israelites,
  and I will **bless** them."

RESPONSORIAL PSALM   Psalm 67:2–3, 5, 6, 8 (2a)

R. May God bless us in his mercy.

May God have pity on us and bless us;
  may he let his face shine upon us.
So may your way be known upon earth;
  among all nations, your salvation.

May the nations be glad and exult
  because you rule the peoples in equity;
  the nations on the earth you guide.

May the peoples praise you, O God;
  may all the peoples praise you!
May God bless us,
  and may all the ends of the earth
    fear him!

READING I The fourth book of the Pentateuch, Numbers, continues the great story of the Exodus journey, and comes after Leviticus, which details God's teaching given to the covenant people at Mount Sinai. Numbers, so called because it includes two accounts of "numbering" the Hebrew tribes, is very loosely organized. It gathers various laws and ritual practices that actually developed in later centuries with stories of clashes with other tribes during the wilderness journey. As the book opens, the escaped Hebrews prepare to move forward in their desert passage, and the author reviews various rules and practices that deal with maintaining the purity of the community dedicated to the Lord.

Today's First Reading appears as an insertion into this elusive story line. It is a passage commonly called "the priestly blessing," which was to be pronounced at the end of an act of ritual worship. In the Old Testament, a blessing is understood to transmit some kind of beneficial power, often the power to give or sustain life, to the person or community that receives it. The Lord is the sole source of the blessing and its power, and the blessing becomes effective when pronounced and accompanied by some act that confirms the blessing. Because the ultimate cause of a blessing is God, it is permanent and forever effective. In this passage the act of blessing includes invoking God's name upon the people. In ancient Israel, a person's name expressed and in some sense contained and conveyed his or her character, and so the name of God often represents the actual powerful presence of God. When God's name is invoked over the people, the divine source of every blessing is called

A didactic reading that reminds us that we are all sons and daughters of God.

Galatians = guh-LAY-shuhnz

Emphasize the contrast between being a slave under the Law and being an adopted heir in freedom.

Make sure the assembly knows that this adoption is good news!

Even better, here is proof!

A cry of love and trust. Make each name distinct. Abba = AH-bah

Imagine bringing someone the news that, unknown to them, they're actually royalty!

A narrative reading; watch the scene unfold in your imagination as you proclaim. As you watch, bring the emotions that arise to your proclamation.

The reading picks up in the middle of the story, and assumes that most of the community knows what came before. Start slowly and distinctly to allow everyone to "catch up."

You also should be amazed as you proclaim!

Pause before and after these lines about Mary, and proclaim them with the reflective tone Mary assumes.

READING II   Galatians 4:4–7

A reading from the Letter of Saint Paul to the Galatians

Brothers and sisters:
When the fullness of time had come, God sent his **Son**,
    born of a **woman**, born under the **law**,
    to **ransom** those under the law,
    so that we might receive **adoption** as sons.
As **proof** that you are sons,
    God sent the **Spirit** of his Son into our **hearts**,
    crying out, "**Abba, Father!**"
So you are no longer a slave but a **son**,
    and if a son then also an **heir**, through God.

GOSPEL   Luke 2:16–21

A reading from the holy Gospel according to Luke

The shepherds went in **haste** to Bethlehem and found **Mary**
    and **Joseph**,
    and the **infant** lying in the manger.
When they **saw** this,
    they made known the message
    that had been **told** them about this child.
All who heard it were **amazed**
    by what had been told them by the shepherds.
And Mary **kept** all these things,
    reflecting on them in her **heart**. »

upon to bestow positive power upon them in the immediate future of their desert journey and in their entire life as God's people.

READING II Paul wrote Galatians perhaps twenty-five years after the Death and Resurrection of Jesus. In this still very new Christian movement, varying and sometimes conflicting interpretations of Christ and what God accomplished through him were circulating. Paul's major purpose in this letter is to defend and clarify his views of Christ in the face of those who had opposed his preaching. Two

points of disagreement were prominent: human salvation through the Law or through grace in Christ, and whether Gentiles could be part of the new Israel of the last days, inaugurated through Christ.

Paul upholds both the divinity and humanity of Jesus the Christ: "God sent his Son, born of a woman." The Messiah came to free those bound by the Law of Moses and offer a relationship to God like his own. The language of "ransom" here can be misleading; the word used more properly means "redeemed." This terminology of redemption is rooted in ancient Israelite

tribal culture in which each family had a designated "redeemer" whose role was to restore to the family anything or anyone taken from it. At times such restoration might require paying a ransom. Paul is primarily concerned with the idea that through Christ, believers are adopted into God's own family as sons and daughters. As proof of this filial relationship, he points out that Christians participate in the Spirit, the powerful presence of the crucified and resurrected Christ, and so with Christ, they can address God as he did: "Abba, Father." Further, the adopted sons and daughters of

Use the words "glorifying and praising God" to do just that!

A longer pause as the scene shifts.

circumcision = ser-kuhm-SI-zhuhn

At the conclusion of this story, Luke reminds us of how it all began with the Annunciation, as if to say, "See, everything has turned out right!"

TO KEEP IN MIND

You can't proclaim what you don't understand. Read the Scripture passage and its commentary in *Workbook*. Then read it from your Bible, including what comes before and after it so that you understand the context.

Then the shepherds returned,
    glorifying and **praising** God
    for **all** they had **heard** and **seen**,
    just as it had been told to them.

When eight days were completed for his **circumcision**,
    he was named **Jesus**, the name given him by the **angel**
    before he was **conceived** in the womb.

God then also share in Christ's inheritance: fullness of life of the final age of salvation.

 GOSPEL Today's Gospel begins by drawing to a close Luke's account of the shepherds' response to the angelic message of a Savior's birth in Bethlehem. As he often does, Luke stresses joyful response to the Good News, and the shepherds immediately seek out the infant Jesus, telling Mary and Joseph of the heavenly revelation they have received. Mary responds like a woman immersed in her Jewish people's understanding of God's Word; it is to be accepted even if it cannot be understood in the moment. Then slowly, with time and reflection, the full meaning of God's Word can reach its full significance.

Mary surrendered to Gabriel's incomprehensible message in this way, and now she receives confirmation of his words from a most unlikely source: a band of shepherds, people despised as unclean sinners. Still, she continues to hold all these words in her heart. Trusting even when she cannot yet fully know, she names her son Jesus, which means "God saves." In time, the meaning of that powerful name, the character of her son as the one in whom God acts to save all humankind, will be revealed to her. For their part, the shepherds continue to rejoice, praising God. Luke thus raises up a theme he will repeat often: God has come in Jesus to save, turning first of all to the lowly, the poor, the outcast, and the despised, including women and sinners. M.F.

THE EPIPHANY OF THE LORD

LECTIONARY #20

READING I Isaiah 60:1–6

A reading from the Book of the Prophet Isaiah

An exhortatory reading, with heightened emotions. Imagine speaking to someone whose life has been full of darkness and struggle. You are announcing that the bad times are over. You are persuading this person to rejoice.

Isaiah = ī-ZAY-uh

A very strong opening. Be vigorous as you proclaim this Good News! Contrast the images of light and dark in these lines.

> **Rise up** in **splendor**, Jerusalem! Your **light** has come,
>   the **glory** of the Lord **shines** upon you.
> **See**, darkness **covers** the earth,
>   and thick clouds **cover** the peoples;
> but upon **you** the LORD **shines**,
>   and **over** you appears his **glory**.
> Nations shall walk by your **light**,
>   and kings by your shining **radiance**.

They are so full of the light of the Lord that other nations are naturally attracted to them.

> **Raise** your eyes and **look** about;
>   they all **gather** and **come** to you:
> your **sons** come from **afar**,
>   and your **daughters** in the arms of their **nurses**.

You're telling someone whose eyes have been downcast that they can now look up, and they will see what the Lord has done!

A tender image; you can soften here.

Renew your energy and really see this rich (literally!) vision unfold before you. Rejoice with the listener at their salvation.

Be amazed at the outpouring of wealth and treasure.

> **Then** you shall be **radiant** at what you see,
>   your heart shall **throb** and **overflow**,
> for the **riches** of the sea shall be **emptied** out before you,
>   the **wealth** of nations shall be **brought** to you.

dromedaries = single-humped camels; Midian = MID-ee-uhn; Ephah = EE-fuh

Sheba = SHEE-buh

> **Caravans** of camels shall fill you,
>   dromedaries from Midian and Ephah;
> all from **Sheba** shall come
>   bearing **gold** and **frankincense**,
>   and proclaiming the **praises** of the LORD.

Pause after you finish to let the image really sink in.

READING I Today the Church celebrates the manifestation of Christ to all the world, beginning with a reading that overflows with light, brightness, radiance, and glory. This passage comes from the last section of Isaiah (chapters 56–66), most likely written about the time of Judah's release from Babylonian captivity and their return to the Promised Land, around 586 BC. The prophet looks forward to the fulfillment of divine promises to re-create the covenant people, the city of Zion, and God's dwelling place among them. Repeatedly, Isaiah stresses that God's act of restoration will be witnessed by foreign nations, who will thus recognize the saving work of the Lord.

Twice in the first two verses of today's reading, Isaiah uses the Hebrew word *kabod*, translated "glory." This significant term indicates an outward manifestation of divine presence, at times nearly equivalent to God himself. The earlier prophet Ezekiel, a Jerusalem priest deported to Babylon among the first wave of exiles, saw a vision of the glory of the Lord leaving the Temple (Ezekiel 10), a certain sign that Judah's final desolation had begun, because without God's saving presence, the city and its people lay completely vulnerable to enemy attack. But Isaiah now announces that not only will the Lord's people return to their land, but more importantly, the "glory" of God will again dwell in their midst in a new Temple, in a new Jerusalem. The prophet further proclaims that the radiance of the Lord's saving act will be the marvel of other nations and their rulers. A defeated and scattered people will again be gathered together in the Promised Land, drawing those from foreign lands to praise the God of Israel.

For meditation and context:

TO KEEP IN MIND
Use inflection (the high or low pitch of your voice) to convey attitude and feeling. High pitch expresses intensity and excitement; low pitch expresses sadness, contrition, or solemnity.

RESPONSORIAL PSALM   Psalm 72:1–2, 7–8, 10–11, 12–13 (11)

R. Lord, every nation on earth will adore you.

O God, with your judgment endow the king,
    and with your justice, the king's son;
he shall govern your people with justice
    and your afflicted ones with judgment.

Justice shall flower in his days,
    and profound peace, till the moon
    be no more.
May he rule from sea to sea,
    and from the River to the ends of the earth.

The kings of Tarshish and the Isles shall
        offer gifts;
    the kings of Arabia and Seba shall
        bring tribute.
All kings shall pay him homage,
    all nations shall serve him.

For he shall rescue the poor when he cries out,
    and the afflicted when he has no one to
        help him.
He shall have pity for the lowly and the poor;
    the lives of the poor he shall save.

A didactic reading, in which Paul shares the Good News that the whole world, Jews and Gentiles, shares in the promise of Jesus.

Paul lays a foundation of credibility before making his point.

Be sure you know the "mystery" he's referring to: that we are all members of the body of Christ.

This is the point, give it importance, and smile with your voice, eyes, and face.

gospel = good news!

READING II   Ephesians 3:2–3a, 5–6

A reading from the Letter of Saint Paul to the Ephesians

Brothers and sisters:
You have heard of the stewardship of God's **grace**
    that was given to me for **your** benefit,
    namely, that the **mystery** was made known to me
        by **revelation**.
It was not made known to people in **other** generations
    as it has **now** been revealed
    to his holy **apostles** and **prophets** by the **Spirit**:
    that the **Gentiles** are **coheirs**, members of the **same** body,
    and **copartners** in the **promise** in Christ Jesus through
        the **gospel**.

READING II Though commonly called "Ephesians," important early manuscripts of this Pauline letter do not carry that designation. Because the letter does not focus on a specific community, but on unity of the entire Church, many scholars believe that it was written for circulation among a number of local churches in Asia Minor. It is uncertain whether Paul himself authored the letter, but it clearly expresses the perspective of Paul, apostle to the Gentiles. Here the writer stresses that the Israel of the new age of salvation expands to embrace both Jews and Gentiles. This insight, a gift of grace for the good of the entire Church, reveals the "mystery" of the Gospel of Christ. In New Testament usage, the Greek word *mysterion* points to much more than something difficult to understand. The "mystery" encompasses God's plan of salvation, ultimately revealed through Jesus Christ. The author emphasizes several times that this mystery cannot be perceived by human effort, but only by means of divine revelation. In this passage, Ephesians strongly emphasizes that God's plan reaches completion in the form of one united Body of Christ on earth, one redeemed community in which Jews and Gentiles equally participate in the culmination of God's plan for human salvation.

GOSPEL Matthew, a Jew who came to faith in Jesus as Messiah, addressed a primarily Jewish Christian community that also seemed open to a Gentile mission. Some scholars believe that by the time Matthew composed his narrative, about AD 85, his community already included some Gentile members. Given the context, this evangelist must simultaneously deal

A narrative reading, with multiple characters and settings. Know each character's feelings and use them in your proclamation. Pause between the many scenes to help the assembly follow the story.

Judea = joo-DEE-uh; joo-DAY-uh

Herod = HAYR-uhd.

Behold = something amazing is about to happen!
Convey the excitement in the voices of the magi.

homage = HOM-ij

Pause before switching to Herod.

Proclaim these lines with Herod's anxiety.

Let the prophet's joy come through in your voice.

Be sure you emphasize "by no means."

Pause again as Herod returns to the magi. Bring an air of conspiracy to his voice, as he tries to hide his actions from the people.

Although we know Herod is insincere, don't make him sound so. He would be very good at hiding it!

GOSPEL   Matthew 2:1–12

A reading from the holy Gospel according to Matthew

When **Jesus** was born in **Bethlehem** of **Judea**,
    in the **days** of King Herod,
    behold, **magi** from the **east** arrived in Jerusalem, saying,
    "**Where** is the newborn **king** of the **Jews**?
We saw his **star** at its rising
    and have come to do him **homage**."
When King Herod heard this,
    he was greatly **troubled**,
    and **all Jerusalem** with him.
Assembling all the chief priests and the scribes of the people,
    he **inquired** of them **where** the Christ was to be born.
They said to him, "In **Bethlehem** of **Judea**,
    for thus it has been written through the prophet:
        And **you**, **Bethlehem**, *land of* **Judah**,
            are **by no means** *least among the rulers of Judah;*
        since from **you** *shall come a* **ruler**,
            who is to **shepherd** *my people* **Israel**."
Then Herod called the magi **secretly**
    and **ascertained** from them the time of the star's appearance.
He **sent** them to Bethlehem and said,
    "**Go** and search **diligently** for the child.
When you have **found** him, bring me **word**,
    that I **too** may go and do him **homage**."
After their audience with the king they **set out**. »

with the varied concerns of his audience. Jewish Christians came to believe that Jesus was the promised Messiah through whom God inaugurated the final age of salvation. However, many Jews had not expected that the new Israel of the final age could include Gentiles; Jewish purity laws of the first century prohibited all contact with non-Jews.

But the Apostle Paul had passionately proclaimed that God's plan of salvation, fulfilled in Christ, offered God's gracious love to all, Gentile as well as Jew. Though by the time of Matthew's writing many Gentiles

had come to faith in Christ, tensions and questions remained. How could Jewish Christians fully accept those they once avoided as impure? How could Gentile Christians be fully persuaded that a religious movement so firmly rooted in Judaism would truly include and integrate them? And what, precisely, was the relation between the Old Testament Scriptures and the Christ who fulfilled them? Attempting to address such varied concerns, Matthew frequently uses quotations or allusions to the Old Testament to illustrate for his audience how Jesus "fulfills" or

brings them to completion. This technique is particularly evident in his infancy narrative.

While many have debated the exact character of the magi, what is more important is that they come "from the east," indicating that they are Gentiles. In Matthew, these foreigners are the first to pay homage to the infant "king of the Jews." Like most in the ancient world, the magi believed that the appearance of a great star signaled a ruler's birth; the evangelist also calls to mind Balaam's oracle that "a star shall advance from Jacob" (Numbers 24:17). Providing a reason for the child's

Pause before this line as the scene shifts.

You, too, should be overjoyed as you proclaim this meeting!

prostrated = PROS-trayt*d

Slight pause after "homage."

List the gifts slowly, with a sense of grandeur, then pause to let the scene settle.

Don't make too much of this dream, lest the story end with a focus on Herod rather than the encounter with Jesus.

And **behold**, the star that they had seen at its rising
    preceded them,
  until it came and stopped over the **place** where the **child** was.
They were **overjoyed** at seeing the star,
  and on entering the house
    they **saw** the child with Mary his mother.
They **prostrated** themselves and did him **homage**.
Then they opened their **treasures**
  and offered him gifts of **gold**, **frankincense**, and **myrrh**.
And having been warned in a **dream** not to return to Herod,
  they **departed** for their country by another **way**.

THE 4 STEPS OF *LECTIO DIVINA* OR PRAYERFUL READING

1. *Lectio:* Read a Scripture passage aloud slowly. Notice what phrase captures your attention and be attentive to its meaning. Silent pause.

2. *Meditatio:* Read the passage aloud slowly again, reflecting on the passage, allowing God to speak to you through it. Silent pause.

3. *Oratio:* Read it aloud slowly a third time, allowing it to be your prayer or response to God's gift of insight to you. Silent pause.

4. *Contemplatio:* Read it aloud slowly a fourth time, now resting in God's word.

---

birth in tiny Bethlehem, Matthew quotes Micah 5:2, which states that Israel's messianic ruler will come from this town of King David's birth. Reference to one who will "shepherd" Israel may further allude to the shepherd-king, David, and to Ezekiel 34:15, in which God promises that in the coming age of salvation, "I myself will pasture my sheep." In a few sentences, Matthew indicates that from his birth, Jesus fulfills the Old Testament Scriptures, and that this completion of God's plan of salvation embraces all humankind, Jew and Gentile alike.

King Herod's pious instruction to the magi is in fact a ruse to discover the child so that Herod can destroy him. Appointed by Rome to rule the province of Judea, Herod was given the honorific title, "King of the Jews," and he was ruthless toward any possible rival. The guiding star leads the magi to the infant and his mother, and these Gentile travelers from afar prostrate themselves before the true King of the Jews, Jesus the Messiah. Warned in a dream to ignore Herod's request, the magi foil his plan. Matthew makes apparent that God, not Rome, has designated Israel's true

Messiah-King, and that although he first appears among the Jews, Gentiles also welcome the revelation of their true ruler. M.F.

SECOND SUNDAY IN ORDINARY TIME

LECTIONARY #64

READING I   Isaiah 49:3, 5–6

A reading from the Book of the Prophet Isaiah

The Lord said to me: You are my **servant**,
　Israel, through whom I show my **glory**.
Now the Lord has **spoken**
　who **formed** me as his servant from the **womb**,
that Jacob may be brought **back** to him
　and Israel **gathered** to him;
and I am made **glorious** in the sight of the Lord,
　and my God is now my **strength**!
It is too little, the Lord says, for you to be my **servant**,
　to raise up the tribes of **Jacob**,
　and restore the survivors of **Israel**;
I will make you a **light** to the **nations**,
　that my **salvation** may reach to the **ends** of the **earth**.

An exhortatory reading, addressed originally to the nation of Israel and now to your assembly. Keep in your mind the effect the reading has had on you and could have on your listeners.

Isaiah = Ī-ZAY-uh

Let your community hear the love of the Lord throughout this proclamation.

Like Isaiah, you too have been chosen to convey God's love to your community! Let your joy be heard.

These are tender images, like lost children being restored to their families.

Your glory comes from the work you've been commissioned to do.

But wait, there's more! God has a still bigger purpose in mind for you and your community! Drop your intensity on these lines to show the "smallness" of this work.

Here is the climax. Speak these lines slowly and with great joy: you and your community have been chosen to bring light to the whole world!

READING I Today's passage from Isaiah is one of four poems that describe the mission of an unnamed Servant of the Lord. Most likely dating from a time near the end of the Babylonian captivity, the figure of the Servant appears as God's obedient instrument in the people's restoration. As in today's reading, in some texts the prophet describes the Servant as the community of Israel, elsewhere as an individual. Most likely, Isaiah intends the Servant to present an ideal: the person or people that truly serves God in response to the divine call, listening and responding

despite the cost, empowered by God's own "spirit" (see Isaiah 42:1).

Today's First Reading addresses a chastened community that no longer exists as a political entity or power, but as a captive people far from their homeland. If they are to be truly restored, they must live out their true calling: to reveal the glory of the Lord as true servants who wholeheartedly worship the Holy One of Israel alone. (It is worth noting that one Hebrew word means both "to serve" and "to worship.") This is God's original purpose for calling the Israelites into covenant, the Lord's intention

"from the womb." The people were chosen for a mission: to make the one God known to all peoples by worshipping the Lord alone. Isaiah calls the exiled people to return, not only to their land, but to their first and lasting call: to serve and worship the one God who called them and wishes to grace all peoples with salvation through their witness.

READING II The Second Reading today might be dismissed as a simple opening greeting to the Christian community at Corinth. But while the Apostle

For meditation and context:

A didactic reading from the opening of Paul's letter. Make sure to express Paul's love for this community.
Corinthians = kohr-IN-thee-uhnz

The structure is: "From Paul and Sosthenes to the church in Corinth, blessings!" Drop your voice slightly on the additional parenthetical phrases so the structure remains clear.

Sosthenes = SOS-thuh-neez
Don't swallow "brother."
Pause slightly before you name the addressee.
Keep your voice up at the end of this line to connect it with the greeting that follows.
Proclaim this greeting slowly, prayerfully, and with love.

RESPONSORIAL PSALM Psalm 40:2, 4, 7–8, 8–9, 10 (8a, 9a)

R. Here am I, Lord; I come to do your will.

I have waited, waited for the LORD,
  and he stooped toward me and heard
  my cry.
And he put a new song into my mouth,
  a hymn to our God.

Sacrifice or offering you wished not,
  but ears open to obedience you gave me.
Holocausts or sin-offerings you sought not;
  then said I, "Behold I come."

"In the written scroll it is prescribed for me,
to do your will, O my God, is my delight,
  and your law is within my heart!"

I announced your justice in the vast assembly;
  I did not restrain my lips, as you,
  O LORD, know.

READING II   1 Corinthians 1:1–3

A reading from the first Letter of Saint Paul to the Corinthians

Paul, called to be an **apostle** of Christ Jesus by the will of **God**,
  and **Sosthenes** our brother,
  to the church of God that is in **Corinth**,
  to you who have been **sanctified** in Christ Jesus,
    called to be **holy**,
  with all those **everywhere** who call upon the **name** of our
    Lord Jesus Christ, **their** Lord and **ours**.
Grace to you and **peace** from God our **Father**
  and the **Lord** Jesus **Christ**.

Paul does use a conventional Greek form to open his letter, he makes several adaptations that serve important purposes. The usual form included naming writer and recipient, and offering good wishes. With a few additions and wordplay, Paul expands the greeting to express his faith in Christ and to preview several matters he will discuss in the rest of his letter. His additions signal several matters of importance addressed in readings of the next six Sunday Masses.

Paul addresses his hearers specifically as the *ekklesia* (church) of God in Corinth.

This word primarily indicates an assembly, a community of believers. Word has reached Paul that there have been factions in the Corinthian church, factions that he will later address quite sternly. Here, he indicates why such divisions are unworthy of any group that bears the name *ekklesia*: its members have been made holy in Christ and are indeed called to be holy. The Greek term here translated "sanctified" and "holy" most fundamentally means to be called or set apart by God, for God. The call comes from God, the Father of Christ and of those who believe in him. By grace, all

Christians have received the gift of God's saving love; one Father, one call, and one gift of God must be the fount and goal of their life together. Paul ends his greeting by wishing his hearers "grace" and "peace from God our Father and the Lord Jesus Christ," reminding them of both source and aim of their oneness as a genuine "church."

GOSPEL Last Sunday the Church celebrated the great Solemnity of the Epiphany, marking the revelation of Christ to all peoples. The Gospel reading for that day presented the infant Jesus made

An exhortatory reading. There is great joy in John's words.

Start slowly; make clear who is where and who is speaking.

What if Jesus were standing in the back of your assembly? How would you help people recognize him? Bring that energy to your proclamation.

Articulate this line carefully.

How might John have felt when he saw this? Awestruck? Excited? Relieved? Bring that emotion to his telling.

John contrasts his baptism with water to Jesus who will baptize with the Holy Spirit.

There's a sense of satisfaction that John's work has been accomplished and done well.

TO KEEP IN MIND

Exhortatory texts make an urgent appeal to listeners. They may encourage, warn, or challenge, and often include a call to action. You must convey the urgency and passion behind the words.

GOSPEL   John 1:29–34

A reading from the holy Gospel according to John

John the **Baptist** saw **Jesus** coming toward him and said,
  "**Behold**, the **Lamb** of **God**, who takes away the **sin**
    of the world.
He is the one of whom I said,
  'A man is coming **after** me who ranks **ahead** of me
  because he existed **before** me.'
I did not **know** him,
  but the **reason** why I came baptizing with **water**
  was that he might be made **known** to Israel."
John testified **further**, saying,
  "I saw the **Spirit** come down like a **dove** from **heaven**
  and **remain** upon him.
I did not **know** him,
  but the one who **sent** me to baptize with water **told** me,
  'On whomever you see the **Spirit** come down and **remain**,
  he is the one who will **baptize** with the Holy **Spirit**.'
Now I have **seen** and **testified** that he is the **Son** of **God**."

---

known to Gentile magi; today multiple meanings of Christ are made known to Jesus' Jewish contemporaries. Two major characteristics of the evangelist John appear in this passage: his insistence on Jesus' primacy over the Baptist, and his penchant for using multiple names, titles, or descriptors of Jesus in one brief event.

The Fourth Gospel was completed near the end of the first century and expresses a faith understanding of Christ that developed over decades. John is far more concerned with the present reality of the Risen Christ than in specific historical details. It seems that some of John's contemporaries regarded the Baptist, not Jesus, as the Messiah. Both in response to this view and in portraying the Risen Christ of glory, John carefully constructs this scene.

The Baptist himself states clearly and emphatically that Jesus "ranks ahead of me"; he adds that his own sole purpose in baptizing is to make Jesus, his identity and role "known to Israel." Jesus is the Lamb of God, the new Passover bringing new deliverance to God's people. Further, he acts in God's Spirit, like the Servant of the Lord (see Reading I); he not only bears the Spirit, but will "baptize" believers in that same Spirit. The Greek word here translated "baptize" also means to wash or immerse; Jesus, the Risen Christ, immerses believers in divine presence. Finally, Jesus is Son of God, the divine Word incarnate (John 1:14–15). M.F.

THIRD SUNDAY
IN ORDINARY TIME

LECTIONARY #67

READING I   Isaiah 8:23—9:3

A reading from the Book of the Prophet Isaiah

First the Lord **degraded** the land of Zebulun
and the land of Naphtali;
but in the **end** he has **glorified** the seaward road,
the land west of the **Jordan**,
the District of the **Gentiles**.

Anguish has taken **wing**, **dispelled** is darkness:
for there is no **gloom** where but **now** there was **distress**.
The people who walked in **darkness**
have seen a great **light**;
upon those who dwelt in the land of **gloom**
a **light** has shone.
You have brought them abundant **joy**
and **great** rejoicing,
as they **rejoice** before you as at the harvest,
as people make **merry** when dividing **spoils**.
For the yoke that burdened them,
the **pole** on their **shoulder**,
and the **rod** of their **taskmaster**
you have **smashed**, as on the **day** of **Midian**.

This exhortatory reading praises our faithful God who brings us out of darkness. Proclaim as if to a specific person you know who needs a message of freedom and hope.

Isaiah = ī-ZAY-uh

Slight pause after "First." Contrast "degraded" with "glorified."

3. Zebulun = ZEB-yoo-luhn

4. Naphtali = NAF-tuh-lī

The rest of the reading is good news! Don't give emphasis to the words of darkness, lest they take over the reading. Rather, stress that the darkness is over.

An awkward construction, meaning "gloom and distress are now gone from where they once were."

Stress contrasts between darkness and light.

Although you're speaking to God, make eye contact with the community.

A triple thought rhyme; intensify with each line.

Let smashed sound like what it means, then pause slightly before the final phrase.

Midian = MID-ee-uhn

READING I This passage from the prophet Isaiah includes the end of one chapter and the beginning of another, and there is a clear shift in focus from one to the other. It dates from the time of the Syro-Ephraimite War, roughly a decade before the final fall of the Northern Kingdom of Israel (also called Ephraim) to Assyria in 721 BC. The great Assyrian empire to the north of the Israelite kingdoms relentlessly marched southward, expanding their ever-widening rule. Isaiah repeatedly exhorted God's people to cease seeking alliances with foreign nations for protection from invasion; rather, they must ally themselves with the Lord alone. One such plea precedes today's reading.

The opening verse of today's First Reading is unusually obscure, but seems to indicate the prophet's hope for a shift in Judah's fortunes. The land belonging to the tribes of Zebulun and Naphthali, the northernmost part of Israel, was first seized by the advancing Assyrians. Though part of the Northern Kingdom, this area was inhabited by a significant number of non-Israelites, considered pagans. But the prophet immediately follows this reference to Assyrian conquest with hope for the future in beautiful poetic images of light and joy. In the verse following today's reading, Isaiah describes a future king of Judah who will never waver in his reliance on the Holy One of Israel. This ruler to come will be a true Son of David, completely reliant on the Lord, rather than foreign rulers, for protection from enemies. When such a king appears, darkness will give way to divine light, the gloom of foreign oppression to the joy of freedom that only God can bring.

The prophet is so confident in the Word of the Lord that he speaks of such a

For meditation and context:

TO KEEP IN MIND
Words in bold are significant words about which you must make a choice to help their meaning stand out. You may (or may not) choose to stress them.

An exhortatory reading. Bring Paul's sense of urgency to your proclamation; speak to your whole assembly out of love and urge everyone to reconcile.

Corinthians = kohr-IN-thee-uhnz

What is Paul's emotion on hearing these reports? Let it come through in your proclamation.

Chloe = KLOH-ee

Apollos = uh-POL-uhs

Cephas = SEE-fuhs

These three questions mock the attitude Paul criticizes. Let intensity build on each line.

Contrast human wisdom with the person of Christ.

RESPONSORIAL PSALM   Psalm 27:1, 4, 13–14 (1a)

R. The Lord is my light and my salvation.

The LORD is my light and my salvation;
 whom should I fear?
The LORD is my life's refuge;
 of whom should I be afraid?

One thing I ask of the LORD;
 this I seek:
to dwell in the house of the LORD
 all the days of my life,
that I may gaze on the loveliness of the LORD
 and contemplate his temple.

I believe that I shall see the bounty
 of the LORD
 in the land of the living.
Wait for the LORD with courage;
 be stouthearted, and wait for the LORD.

READING II   1 Corinthians 1:10–13, 17

A reading from the first Letter of Saint Paul to the Corinthians

I **urge** you, brothers and sisters, in the name of our
 Lord Jesus **Christ**,
 that all of you **agree** in what you say,
 and that there be no **divisions** among you,
 but that you be united in the same **mind** and in the
 same **purpose**.
For it has been **reported** to me about you, my brothers and sisters,
 by **Chloe's** people, that there are **rivalries** among you.
I mean that each of you is saying,
 "I belong to **Paul**," or "I belong to **Apollos**,"
 or "I belong to **Cephas**," or "I belong to **Christ**."
Is Christ **divided**?
Was **Paul** crucified for you?
Or were you baptized in the **name** of Paul?
For Christ did not send me to **baptize** but to preach the **gospel**,
 and not with the **wisdom** of human **eloquence**,
 so that the **cross** of Christ might not be **emptied** of its **meaning**.

dramatic change of fortune as already accomplished. In later centuries, the Christian community understood Isaiah's vision of a coming descendant of David in light of Jesus, one who fully completed the people's longing for a king who would rule with God's own righteousness.

READING II Almost immediately after the usual greeting and thanksgiving of his letter, Paul directly addresses one of the difficulties in the Corinthian community. He established this church about AD 51, but several years later received reports of factionalism, openly immoral behavior, and aberrations even in the celebration of the Lord's Supper at Corinth. The problem of divisions within the church, to which he will return later in this letter, is one of Paul's major concerns. Based on messages he has received, it seems that some members of the church aligned themselves exclusively with a particular teacher or preacher of the Good News. But the Apostle insists that Christians belong to no one but Christ. Teachers, whether Cephas (Peter), Apollos, or Paul, proclaim the Gospel, but Christ himself *is* the Good News.

As for those in the Corinthian church who claim allegiance to the one who baptized them, Paul stresses that he was not sent to baptize, but to preach the Gospel, and at the heart of that Good News stands, not human wisdom, but the Cross of Christ. Later in his letter, the Apostle will emphasize Christ's Death as the total gift of his entire life, given for all. All who belong to this Christ are therefore called to imitate him, united in the same kind of self-giving to and for one another.

A narrative reading; in fact, the longer version is actually two narratives. See the story unfold before you as you proclaim.

Don't swallow "arrested."

Capernaum = kuh-PER-nee-*m or kuh-PER-nay-*m or kuh-PER-n*m

Zebulun = ZEB-yoo-luhn; Naphtali = NAF-tuh-lī

Proclaim this prophecy with real joy!

Contrast these images of light and dark.

Slight pause after concluding the prophecy.

Speak Jesus' exhortation with energy and vigor! It summarizes all of Jesus' preaching.

Longer pause as the scene shifts and the second narrative begins.

Make this sound like a warm invitation rather than a demand.

"At once" is surprising. Don't gloss over it.

GOSPEL   Matthew 4:12–23

A reading from the holy Gospel according to Matthew

[When **Jesus** heard that **John** had been **arrested**,
    he withdrew to **Galilee**.
He left **Nazareth** and went to live in **Capernaum** by the sea,
    in the region of **Zebulun** and **Naphtali**,
    that what had been said through **Isaiah** the prophet
    might be **fulfilled**:
*Land of **Zebulun** and land of **Naphtali**,*
    the way to the sea, beyond the Jordan,
        ***Galilee** of the **Gentiles**,*
    *the people who sit in **darkness** have seen a great **light**,*
    *on those dwelling in a land **overshadowed** by **death***
        ***light** has arisen.*
From **that** time on, Jesus began to **preach** and say,
    "**Repent**, for the kingdom of heaven is at **hand**."]

As he was walking by the Sea of **Galilee**, he saw two **brothers**,
    Simon who is called **Peter**, and his brother **Andrew**,
    casting a **net** into the sea; they were **fishermen**.
He **said** to them,
    "Come **after** me, and I will make you fishers of **men**."
At once they **left** their nets and **followed** him.
He walked along from there and saw two **other** brothers,
    James, the son of Zebedee, and his brother **John**.
They were in a **boat**, with their father Zebedee, mending
        their **nets**.

GOSPEL   With today's Gospel reading, Matthew (most likely a Jewish convert to faith in Jesus the Messiah) opens the curtain on Jesus' public ministry in Galilee. At that time, both Judaism and the new Christian movement were experiencing considerable growing pains. For their part, adherents to Judaism struggled to discern which of various interpretations of the Law were most authentic, while followers of Christ, although comprised mainly of Jews at the beginning, found increasing numbers of non-Jews (Gentiles) in their midst. Today's Scriptures reflect both aspects of the evangelist's context.

Previous to this passage, John the Baptist had called the people to repentance, claiming that God's final rule was drawing near. Jesus will proclaim what appears as the same message, yet his emphasis differs considerably from that of John. The Baptizer seems to call the people to repent, to completely change their lives, so that God's Kingdom can come in fullness. Jesus, in contrast, approaches those whom many Jews regarded as outside of God's offer of salvation, announcing its arrival among them. It is as if Jesus proclaims, "God is already drawing near to you; now you are able to repent, to turn your lives around."

Quoting Isaiah (see Reading I), Matthew emphasizes that Jesus first takes up residence in the part of Galilee known for its large Gentile population. Without asking their conversion to Judaism, he announces that "the kingdom of heaven is at hand." (Like all pious Jews of the time, Matthew avoids using the name of the Lord, considered too holy to pronounce.) The evangelist thus demonstrates that

Again, "immediately" is a surprising response.

What emotion arises for you as you think of Jesus doing all this good work? Bring that feeling to your proclamation.

> **TO KEEP IN MIND**
> Making eye contact with the assembly connects you with them and connects them to the reading more deeply than using your voice alone. This helps the assembly stay with the story and keeps them engaged.

He **called** them, and immediately they **left** their boat
and their **father**
and **followed** him.
He went around all of **Galilee**,
teaching in their synagogues, proclaiming the **gospel**
of the **kingdom**,
and **curing** every **disease** and **illness** among the people.

[Shorter: Matthew 4:12–17 (see brackets)]

Jesus himself embodies the authentic interpretation of Judaism's Sacred Scriptures: by his word and action, they are "fulfilled" or completed. But Jesus brings the Law and the Prophets to fullness in an astounding way: he not only includes Gentiles in God's Kingdom, he proclaims it to them before approaching fellow Jews. While Matthew does not indicate a Gentile response here, he has already suggested it by describing Gentiles, magi from the east, as the first to pay homage to the infant Jewish Messiah (Matthew 2:11).

At this point Matthew changes scenes, and Jesus turns to some of his Jewish neighbors in Capernaum. He approaches first one pair of fisherman brothers, then another, inviting them to "Come after me." The Greek phrase indicates a call to follow Jesus as disciples. Such behavior completely reversed Jewish tradition, in which would-be disciples pursued a rabbi; it was unheard of for a teacher to seek out disciples. It is not the first nor last time Matthew will present Jesus as a teacher who reinterprets the teachings and practices of Judaism.

Hearers of this Gospel account are not told whether Peter, Andrew, James, and John are aware of Jesus' words and actions in the previous scene. Matthew's audience, however, has witnessed Jesus' outreach to Gentiles, and his claim that in so doing he fulfills the Old Testament Scriptures. Jesus himself is already "fishing" for all people, making no distinctions. M.F.

FOURTH SUNDAY IN ORDINARY TIME

An exhortatory reading; encouraging the assembly to remain faithful and extolling those who do. It starts with Zephaniah's words, then switches to God's. How might God sound when describing such a faithful community?

Zephaniah = zef-uh NĪ-uh

Open strongly, with urgency, appealing to all to respond.

Set the two statements apart with pauses before and after each.

Emphasize the shelter over the anger.

Pause here as you shift from the prophet's words to God's words.

Proclaim these lines as if describing someone who is a model of discipleship for you—who challenges and encourages you to live your own discipleship more faithfully.

Heighten this second half of the thought rhyme.

Peace comes when we live out of our true identity as children of God.

LECTIONARY #70

READING I   Zephaniah 2:3; 3:12–13

A reading from the Book of the Prophet Zephaniah

Seek the LORD, all you **humble** of the **earth**,
    who have **observed** his **law**;
seek **justice**, seek **humility**;
    perhaps you may be **sheltered**
    on the **day** of the LORD's **anger**.

But **I** will **leave** as a **remnant** in your **midst**
    a people **humble** and **lowly**,
who shall take **refuge** in the **name** of the LORD:
    the **remnant** of **Israel**.
They shall **do** no **wrong**
    and **speak** no **lies**;
nor shall there be **found** in their **mouths**
    a deceitful **tongue**;
they shall **pasture** and **couch** their **flocks**
    with **none** to **disturb** them.

READING I | The opening verse of the Book of Zephaniah locates it during the reign of King Josiah of Judah (640–609 BC). One of few righteous Israelite kings, Josiah attempted to reform Judah's regression into idolatry and its choice to depend upon foreign alliances (rather than trusting in the Lord). In this time of religious degradation, the prophet proclaims both reproach and promise. Much of this short prophecy warns of the impending Day of the Lord, which Zephaniah envisions as a day of desolation, a time of divine judgment on the covenant people for infidelity to their covenant promises.

Today's First Reading, however, addresses those who have faithfully served the Lord by worship of God alone, in their rituals and in daily life. This reading is taken from two different chapters; the opening lines address the faithful in Judah, while the remaining lines appear after a lengthy description of God's wrath poured out on both Judah and other nations. After this harrowing account of God's judgment, Zephaniah describes God's promise to the faithful remnant. On the Day of the Lord, they will be judged as humble, without deceit, and steadfastly reliant upon God; hence they will enjoy protection and rest from that day's distress.

READING II | Last Sunday's passage from First Corinthians briefly noted the importance of the Cross of Christ. In today's Second Reading, Paul grapples with those who cannot or will not see God's wisdom in a crucified Savior. Because Corinth was a large, cosmopolitan port city of its day, members of the church there had been exposed to many of the

For meditation and context:

TO KEEP IN MIND

In *thought* rhyme, two parallel lines say the same thing, but each in a different way. Use care to keep the two lines together and use emphasis to show the parallelism.

A didactic reading, reminding us that God's plans and values are not the same as ours. Emphasize the contrasts throughout: wise vs. foolish, weak vs. strong, something vs. nothing.

Corinthians = kohr-IN-thee-uhnz

Appeal directly to the assembly.

You're probably describing most assemblies.

Relish revealing God's surprising plan to your assembly, as if letting them in on a secret. Build your intensity with each phrase.

Slow down on this climatic phrase.

Make each gift of Christ's incarnation distinct and better than the last.

RESPONSORIAL PSALM   Psalm 146:6–7, 8–9, 9–10 (Matthew 5:3)

R. Blessed are the poor in spirit; the kingdom of heaven is theirs! or Alleluia.

The LORD keeps faith forever,
    secures justice for the oppressed,
gives food to the hungry.
    The LORD sets captives free.

The LORD gives sight to the blind;
    the LORD raises up those who were
        bowed down.
The LORD loves the just;
    the LORD protects strangers.

The fatherless and the widow the LORD
    sustains,
    but the way of the wicked he thwarts.
The LORD shall reign forever;
    your God, O Zion, through all
        generations.

READING II   1 Corinthians 1:26–31

A reading from the first Letter of Saint Paul to the Corinthians

Consider your **own calling**, brothers and sisters.
Not many of you were **wise** by human standards,
    not many were **powerful**,
    not many were of **noble birth**.
Rather, God chose the **foolish** of the world to shame the **wise**,
    and God chose the **weak** of the world to shame the **strong**,
    and God chose the **lowly** and **despised** of the world,
    those who count for **nothing**,
    to reduce to **nothing** those who are **something**,
    so that **no** human being might boast before God.
It is due to **him** that you are **in** Christ Jesus,
    who became for us **wisdom** from God,
    as well as **righteousness**, **sanctification**, and **redemption**,
    so that, as it is written,
    "Whoever **boasts**, should boast in the **Lord**."

---

varied religions and philosophies that circulated among them. Paul, Jewish Apostle to the Gentiles, must attempt to present Jewish views of wisdom to those influenced by Greek philosophy. While philosophy relied on human reason and abstract propositions, Jewish wisdom saw God as the sole source of concrete, embodied wisdom.

To make his point, Paul asks community members to consider their own experience. They are all redeemed, made whole, and justified in Christ, but not because of any merit of their own. God reversed the status quo of human wisdom, which placed

great value on power and rank resulting from accidents of birth. Instead, divine wisdom bestowed transformed life in Christ on "the lowly and despised" to emphasize redemption as sheer gift, unearned and unmerited in every way. Christ himself embodies God's wisdom, incomprehensible to human logic or reason. By his passage through the Cross to glory, Christ "became for us" divine wisdom and the source of human salvation.

GOSPEL | In the chapter preceding today's Gospel reading,

Matthew presents Jesus beginning his mission: proclaiming in word and deed that God's final rule over all things is inaugurated in his ministry and his person. Aware of the increasing presence of Gentile converts in the Church, the evangelist stresses that Jesus brings his ministry to both Jew and Gentile. Today's reading begins what is commonly called the "Sermon on the Mount," the first of five sections of extended teaching of Jesus, whom Matthew portrays as true Teacher and interpreter of the Law of Moses. Like the instruction given through Moses, Jesus'

An exhortatory teaching of Jesus. It's likely well-known to your hearers. The key to keeping it fresh is not to make it about Jesus teaching the crowd, but about Jesus teaching your assembly through you. Don't let the rhythm lull you into a sleepy, sing-song reading. Make each verse distinct, as if each were a new idea, building up to a complete picture of the community of the faithful.
Blessed = BLES-uhd

The surprise in these verses is that the poor, the mourners, the meek, etc., are blessed, whereas most people would consider them cursed.

Remember, make this about your assembly. Speak directly to the merciful, the clean of heart, the peacemakers in your community.

Note the switch from "blessed are they" to "blessed are you."

Another surprise: we should rejoice when we're persecuted!

Slow down on the final line.

> **TO KEEP IN MIND**
> *Repetition* of the same word or phrase over the course of a reading emphasizes a point. Make each instance distinct, and build your intensity with each repetition.

GOSPEL Matthew 5:1–12a

A reading from the holy Gospel according to Matthew

When **Jesus** saw the **crowds**, he went up the **mountain**,
  and after he had sat **down**, his disciples came to him.
He began to **teach** them, saying:
  "**Blessed** are the poor in **spirit**,
    for theirs is the kingdom of **heaven**.
  Blessed are they who **mourn**,
    for they will be **comforted**.
  Blessed are the **meek**,
    for they will **inherit** the **land**.
  Blessed are they who **hunger** and **thirst** for **righteousness**,
    for they will be **satisfied**.
  Blessed are the **merciful**,
    for they will be **shown mercy**.
  Blessed are the **clean** of **heart**,
    for they will **see God**.
  Blessed are the **peacemakers**,
    for they will be called **children** of **God**.
  Blessed are they who are **persecuted**
    for the sake of **righteousness**,
    for theirs is the kingdom of **heaven**.
  Blessed are **you** when they **insult** you and **persecute** you
    and utter every kind of **evil** against you **falsely**
      because of **me**.
  Rejoice and be **glad**,
    for your **reward** will be **great** in heaven."

teaching is given on a mountain; in being seated, he takes the position of a Jewish rabbi and specifically addresses disciples, not the crowds.

Jesus the Teacher uses a literary form familiar in the Bible; a person or persons is declared "blessed" (happy, to be envied), followed by a reason for enjoying God's goodness. Matthew may be alluding to Isaiah 61:1–4, where the prophet looks forward to God's coming act of salvation. Jesus does also; the Kingdom of Heaven will reverse the fortunes of the lowly, the poor, and the grieving. Twice Jesus highlights

righteousness, a major theme of the Sermon on the Mount. This Old Testament notion is often summarized as *right relationships*, including human relations with God, other people, and the material world.

Jesus hints at what will later become explicit in his teaching; he retains what is of value in the Law of Moses, but expands it with his own depth of meaning. Not only will outward situations of hunger, thirst, and persecution be altered in God's reign, as Isaiah envisioned. Those who suffer these things with proper intention, pursuing the righteousness proposed by God and

revealed through Jesus, will enjoy the fullness of divine blessing. The final beatitude again stresses Jesus' focus on interior motivation. There is no inherent blessing in suffering persecution, but those willing to endure mistreatment because of faithfulness to Jesus' teaching will be greatly rewarded "in heaven." This phrase, and also "kingdom of heaven," as substitutes for the name of God, were not uttered by reverent Jews of Matthew's time. M.F.

FIFTH SUNDAY IN ORDINARY TIME

LECTIONARY #73

READING I   Isaiah 58:7–10

A reading from the Book of the Prophet Isaiah

Thus says the LORD:
 Share your bread with the hungry,
  shelter the oppressed and the homeless;
 clothe the naked when you see them,
  and do not turn your back on your **own**.
 Then your **light** shall **break forth** like the **dawn**,
  and your **wound** shall quickly be **healed**;
 your **vindication** shall go before you,
  and the **glory** of the LORD shall be your **rear guard**.
 Then you shall **call**, and the LORD will **answer**;
  you shall **cry** for help, and he will say: Here I **am**!
 If you **remove** from your midst
  oppression, false accusation and malicious speech;
 if you **bestow** your bread on the hungry
  and **satisfy** the afflicted;
 then **light** shall **rise** for you in the darkness,
  and the **gloom** shall become for you like **midday**.

Margin notes (left column):

An exhortatory reading. Take note of the "if . . . then" structure of this reading.

Isaiah = ī-ZAY-uh

Although they don't start with "if," these are the "if" statements connected to the two "then" statements below. Make these sound like invitations rather than commands.

Let your energy rise here. This is good news, so smile with your voice, eyes, and face.

vindication = clearing from blame

Slight pause after "call," to raise anticipation for the Lord's answer.

You don't need to "cry" but let the phrase sound like a plea, and let God's response resound with love.

These "if" statements shouldn't sound like you're telling a child "if you behave, you'll get rewarded." Rather, encourage your community to become who they are called to be.
See the light rise over your assembly as you proclaim.

 Today's First Reading is part of an oracle that belongs to the third and last section of the Book of Isaiah. The later chapters (56–66) of this prophetic book reflect a very significant time in the history of God's people: the end of their long Babylonian captivity and the opportunity of a new beginning. The prophecies in these closing chapters include words of hope and comfort, reminders of lapses that led to the downfall, and exhortations to a more faithful living of covenant promises.

Today's passage belongs to this last category. The chapter begins with God urging the returned and chastened people to be aware of their past insincerity. While they meticulously carried out various rituals of praise and repentance, these rites were, in fact, empty gestures. Through Isaiah, God emphasizes that religious words and gestures must signal deeper, broader realities. What truly fulfills the Lord's call and command is concrete action on behalf of the needy, poor, and oppressed. Ritual words and actions must be embodied in deeds of righteousness. When ritual

becomes reality, then and only then will Israel's true renewal begin. Then will the strained relationships between the people and their God be healed; then the Lord's people will come into the light, and reflect divine glory to all nations.

READING II   Today's Scripture from Paul is the fourth of seven readings from First Corinthians. A close reading can uncover several of Paul's major themes in today's brief passage. Some of the Apostle's key convictions are mentioned very briefly or merely suggested, but they

For meditation and context:

RESPONSORIAL PSALM   Psalm 112:4–5, 6–7, 8–9 (4a)

R. The just man is a light in darkness to the upright.
or
R. Alleluia.

Light shines through the darkness for the
    upright;
  he is gracious and merciful and just.
Well for the man who is gracious and lends,
  who conducts his affairs with justice.

He shall never be moved;
  the just one shall be in everlasting
    remembrance.
An evil report he shall not fear;
  his heart is firm, trusting in the LORD.

His heart is steadfast; he shall not fear.
  Lavishly he gives to the poor;
his justice shall endure forever;
  his horn shall be exalted in glory.

TO KEEP IN MIND
Use inflection (the high or low pitch
of your voice) to convey attitude
and feeling. High pitch expresses
intensity and excitement; low pitch
expresses sadness, contrition, or
solemnity.

READING II   1 Corinthians 2:1–5

A reading from the first Letter of Saint Paul to the Corinthians

When I **came** to you, brothers and sisters,
    proclaiming the **mystery** of God,
      I did not come with sublimity of words or of **wisdom**.
For I resolved to **know nothing** while I was with you
      except Jesus Christ, and him **crucified**.
I came to you in **weakness** and **fear** and much **trembling**,
    and my message and my proclamation
    were not with persuasive words of **wisdom**,
    but with a demonstration of **Spirit** and **power**,
    so that your faith might rest **not** on human wisdom
    but on the **power** of **God**.

A didactic reading, in which Paul reminds
the community that our faith is centered on
a person, and not wisdom or knowledge.
Imagine your assembly's renewed
relationship with Christ as you proclaim.

Corinthians = kohr-IN-thee-uhnz

Emphasize the contrasts Paul makes
between wisdom (which he considers
worthless) and the mystery of God, who is
Jesus Christ.

Paul exaggerates for emphasis, maybe even
making a little joke: his only knowledge of
value is of Christ.

This could apply to us readers! We can
proclaim this honestly—it's the person of
Jesus, not the messenger—that you want our
assembly to hear.

Again, contrast wisdom with the Spirit and
power of God.

---

are important Pauline motifs nonetheless.
Paul's correspondence with the church at
Corinth addresses a community that had
been exposed to numerous influences circulating in this large, cosmopolitan port
city. Though the Apostle to the Gentiles
spent about two and a half years preaching
and teaching Christ to this urban church,
entrenched habits of thought and action
remained or returned all too soon. The
imperial culture in general valued power,
wealth, and status, while various Greek philosophies exalted knowledge acquired by
use of human reason. Among such realities,

Paul preached the wisdom of a Redeemer
who died on a cross—the shameful instrument of public execution imposed upon
revolutionaries and slaves.

Paul's message offers not human, but
divine wisdom: the "mystery" of God. With
this term (Greek *mysterion*), the Apostle
signifies the divine plan of salvation, which
confounds all knowledge of the philoso-
pher. Christ crucified is exalted by the
power of God—the same power that
underlies Paul's preaching. The Apostle's
own weakness mirrors that of Christ; his
proclamation can bring people to faith, not

because of the speaker's persuasiveness,
but because God freely bestows it. This is
one of Paul's central convictions: redemption in Christ results not from any human
action but from divine graciousness—more
powerful than all human effort.

GOSPEL   Matthew's account of the
Good News frequently
presents Jesus as teacher; in this Gospel
reading he continues the Sermon on the
Mount, begun last Sunday. Like other
Jewish rabbis, Jesus makes liberal use of
metaphors to teach. In this passage, he

An exhortatory reading, in which Jesus encourages us to remain faithful to our identity as disciples, and to live out that identity with boldness. Be sure you proclaim with boldness as well!

Notice the phrase is "you are," not "you might be" or "you can be." Smile as you praise your assembly with this good news.

This is not "punishment" for the salt; it's simply lost its essence and is useless.

Again, "you are."

Really encourage your community, like a coach might encourage their team before a game or a teacher might encourage their students.

GOSPEL   Matthew 5:13–16

A reading from the holy Gospel according to Matthew

Jesus said to his disciples:
    "**You** are the **salt** of the earth.
But if salt **loses** its taste, with **what** can it be seasoned?
It is **no longer** good for **anything**
    but to be **thrown** out and trampled underfoot.
You are the **light** of the world.
A city set on a **mountain** cannot be hidden.
Nor do they light a **lamp** and then put it **under** a bushel basket;
    it is set on a **lampstand**,
    where it gives **light** to all in the house.
Just so, **your** light must **shine** before others,
    that they may **see** your good deeds
    and **glorify** your heavenly Father."

THE 4 STEPS OF *LECTIO DIVINA* OR PRAYERFUL READING

1. *Lectio:* Read a Scripture passage aloud slowly. Notice what phrase captures your attention and be attentive to its meaning. Silent pause.

2. *Meditatio:* Read the passage aloud slowly again, reflecting on the passage, allowing God to speak to you through it. Silent pause.

3. *Oratio:* Read it aloud slowly a third time, allowing it to be your prayer or response to God's gift of insight to you. Silent pause.

4. *Contemplatio:* Read it aloud slowly a fourth time, now resting in God's word.

---

specifically addresses his disciples, a fact emphasized by repeated use of "you" and "your." And like prophets before him, Jesus will demand not just words but actions (see Reading I). Today's text follows immediately upon the Beatitudes, which call Jesus' followers to act according to his view of righteousness. To hear Jesus' teaching and fail to act upon it is worthless, like salt that has lost its flavor.

In the ancient world, salt was used both to season and to preserve food. Salt cannot, in fact, lose these qualities, but in Judaism salt could become unclean and therefore become useless. In describing the fate of such worthless salt, Matthew employs common imagery for God's judgment. He thus implies that followers who have heard Jesus' way of righteousness but fail to walk in that path are in fact useless as his disciples.

Jesus' second metaphor recalls Isaiah's message in the First Reading: people who in fact live according to divine teaching thereby give glory to God. For Matthew, the full meaning of divine instruction concerning righteous attitudes and behavior, which was begun in the Law of Moses, is revealed in Jesus. With the last line of today's Scripture, the evangelist foreshadows important lessons that Jesus repeatedly emphasizes in the Sermon on the Mount. To be effective, words must always be accompanied by deeds; good actions must always spring from proper intentions; and righteous acts are not done to exalt the one who performs them, but to "glorify your heavenly Father." M.F.

SIXTH SUNDAY
IN ORDINARY TIME

An exhortatory reading; keep energy up throughout and keep the couplets of thought rhyme together, using their rhythm in your proclamation.

Sirach = Sĭ-ruhk; SEER-ak

The first half of the reading stresses our free will and choice. Note the thought rhyme here: to keep the Commandments is to trust in God, knowing that he gave them for our happiness and peace.
These four lines compose one couplet; keep them all together.

Pause as the reading shifts to praise God's wisdom.

If we listen to how God has called us to live, we will not sin.

LECTIONARY #76

READING I   Sirach 15:15–20

A reading from the Book of Sirach

If you **choose** you can keep the commandments, they will
   save you;
   if you **trust** in God, you too shall **live**;
he has set before you **fire** and **water**;
   to whichever you **choose**, stretch forth your hand.
Before man are **life** and **death**, **good** and **evil**,
   whichever he **chooses** shall be **given** him.
Immense is the wisdom of the LORD;
   he is **mighty** in power, and all-**seeing**.
The **eyes of God** are on those who fear him;
   he **understands** man's every deed.
No one does he command to act **unjustly**,
   to **none** does he give license to sin.

For meditation and context:

RESPONSORIAL PSALM   Psalm 119:1–2, 4–5, 17–18, 33–34 (1b)

R. Blessed are they who follow the law of the Lord!

Blessed are they whose way is blameless,
   who walk in the law of the LORD.
Blessed are they who observe his decrees,
   who seek him with all their heart.

You have commanded that your precepts
   be diligently kept.
Oh, that I might be firm in the ways
   of keeping your statutes!

Be good to your servant, that I may live
   and keep your words.
Open my eyes, that I may consider
   the wonders of your law.

Instruct me, O LORD, in the way
   of your statutes,
   that I may exactly observe them.
Give me discernment, that I may observe
   your law
   and keep it with all my heart.

TO KEEP IN MIND
In *thought* rhyme, two parallel lines say the same thing, but each in a different way. Use care to keep the two lines together and use emphasis to show the parallelism.

READING I Originally written in Hebrew about 200 BC, the Book of Sirach was translated into Greek perhaps a century later. The author, a sage living in Jerusalem, displays great love for the Law of Moses, the Temple, and its worship. In the opening verse of the book, he announces the prevailing perspective of the wise in Judaism: all wisdom comes from God and thus endures forever. For God's people, the gift of wisdom was practical knowledge of how to live well in all relationships, learned from generations of experience and reflection on life with God and one another. As is common in Old Testament wisdom literature, numerous maxims are grouped according to topics such as the Law, friendship, family relations, education, worship, and other aspects of community life.

The First Reading focuses on human choice in following the commands of God's Law. By this time in Israel's history, exposure to various cultures, especially that of the Greeks, led to much more emphasis on individual responsibility than in earlier centuries. The author presents the reality of free will in various ways, repeating the importance and the consequences of each choice. Trustful following of divine commands brings life, while disobedience earns death; whatever one chooses "shall be given." The sage underscores that God, source of all wisdom, observes all human actions. Further, divine teaching always intends the human good of acting justly, promoting right relationship among all things.

A didactic reading. Paul contrasts worldly wisdom with God's wisdom, through which we have access to God. Read the Second Readings from the past few Sundays to learn how Paul has set up his argument thus far.

Corinthians = kohr-IN-thee-uhnz

Drop your voice slightly on this two-line phrase.

God's wisdom is vastly different from human wisdom. God's wisdom is relationship with Christ.

No one could know the amazing plan God had in store for us: to send his Son so we could have life in him!

Be eager to share this amazing secret with your community: Since we dwell in the Spirit, we have access to the depths of God! Smile and maintain eye contact as you share this good news!

READING II   1 Corinthians 2:6–10

A reading from the first Letter of Saint Paul to the Corinthians

Brothers and sisters:
We speak a **wisdom** to those who are **mature**,
   not a wisdom of **this** age,
   nor of the rulers of this age who are passing away.
Rather, we speak **God's** wisdom, **mysterious**, **hidden**,
   which God predetermined before the ages for our **glory**,
   and which **none** of the rulers of this age knew;
   or, if they **had** known it,
   they would not have **crucified** the Lord of glory.
But as it is written:
   What eye *has not* ***seen****, and* ear *has not* ***heard****,*
      and what has not ***entered*** *the human* ***heart****,*
      what God has ***prepared*** *for those who* ***love*** *him,*
   this *God has* ***revealed*** *to* ***us*** *through the Spirit.*

For the Spirit scrutinizes **everything**, even the **depths** of **God**.

A didactic reading; note the "you have heard . . . but I say" structure, where Jesus introduces a new standard higher than the old. Proclaim with love for the assembly; avoid a chiding tone. Rather, encourage all to live out of their true identity in God.

Jesus does not supersede the Law; rather the Law is the foundation upon which Jesus will build the Kingdom.

"Amen, I say to you" is a way of saying, "Listen up!"

GOSPEL   Matthew 5:17–37

A reading from the holy Gospel according to Matthew

[**Jesus** said to his disciples:]
   "Do not **think** that I have come to **abolish** the law
      or the prophets.
I have come not to **abolish** but to **fulfill**.
Amen, I say to you, until heaven and earth pass away,
      not the smallest **letter** or the smallest **part** of a letter
      will pass from the law,
      until **all things** have taken place. »

READING II Last Sunday's passage from Paul acknowledged that the wisdom of the Gospel he proclaims certainly does not appear wise to his hearers. Not only does the Apostle lack the philosophical knowledge considered wise by this Gentile church; he even claims that a crucified Redeemer reveals God's wisdom!

   In today's Second Reading, Paul clearly acknowledges that his proclamation contradicts the wisdom of his contemporary time and mentality. But that is because his message originates not from human reason but from the eternal, hidden plan of God.

So impenetrable is divine wisdom that "rulers of this age" did not and could not know it; what God intended for humankind can be grasped only through divine disclosure. But what the plan of salvation intended for all men and women now stands revealed in the crucified "Lord of glory." God's "glory," the perceptible manifestation of the divine character and presence, appears in the Risen Christ. Such is the wisdom "God has prepared for those who love him": God's character and plan are revealed in Christ's passage through the humiliation and agony of the Cross to Resurrection.

GOSPEL Today's Gospel reading begins with one of Matthew's primary Christological views: as a true Son of Abraham (Matthew 1:1), Jesus does not abolish the Law and Scriptures of Judaism, but brings them to completion. Since Matthew's community comprised mostly Jewish converts to faith in Christ, Jesus' relation to the Law of Moses was a matter of great importance. Continuing the Sermon on the Mount begun two weeks ago, today's Scripture also continues to present Jesus as a teacher true to Jewish tradition, which emphasized the importance of action. The

This would have shocked Jesus' disciples.
Pause; Jesus has set up the problem.
The rest of the teaching tells us how to achieve righteousness.

Pause before beginning this teaching.

Anger and insults are just as damaging as physical harm, a message we still need to hear today!

Raqa = RAH-kah (an insult; exact meaning uncertain)

Sanhedrin = san-HEE-druhn

Gehenna = geh-HEN-nah

Approaching the altar should make us consider any relationships that need healing.

God desires reconciliation more than offerings.

Any dispute, no matter how justified it seems, has negative consequences.

So why risk it? Better to nip anger and conflict in the bud before they lead to this.

Pause before beginning this next teaching.

Therefore, whoever **breaks** one of the **least** of these commandments
and teaches **others** to do so
will be called **least** in the kingdom of heaven.
But whoever **obeys** and **teaches** these commandments
will be called **greatest** in the kingdom of heaven.
[**I tell** you, unless your righteousness **surpasses**
that of the scribes and Pharisees,
you will **not** enter the kingdom of heaven.

"You have heard that it was said to your ancestors,
You shall not **kill***; and whoever kills will be liable to* **judgment***.*
But **I** say to you,
whoever is **angry** with his brother
will be liable to judgment;]
and whoever says to his brother, '**Raqa**,'
will be answerable to the Sanhedrin;
and whoever says, 'You **fool**,'
will be liable to fiery Gehenna.
Therefore, if you bring your **gift** to the altar,
and there recall that your brother
has anything **against** you,
leave your gift there at the altar,
go first and be **reconciled** with your brother,
and **then** come and offer your gift.
Settle with your opponent quickly while on the way to court.
Otherwise your opponent will hand you over to the **judge**,
and the judge will hand you over to the **guard**,
and you will be thrown into **prison**.
Amen, I say to you,
you will not be released until you have paid the **last penny**.

["You have heard that it was said,
You shall not commit **adultery***.*

Old Testament Scriptures constantly insist that the Law must not be simply taught and heard; above all, it must direct one's behavior in all aspects of life.

After reassuring his audience that Jesus is a genuine Jewish teacher, faithful to its perspectives and emphases, Matthew shifts his focus. Having emphasized that Jesus does not obliterate the Law, the evangelist expounds how, on the other hand, he does bring it to its fullest development. Jesus' view of righteousness, right relationships according to God's teaching, exceeds that of scribes and Pharisees, and

it is his interpretation of the Law that rules in the Kingdom of Heaven. Disciples who participate in God's final rule, inaugurated in Jesus, must live by Jesus' teaching.

What follows includes the first four of six antithetical statements, contrasting the prevailing understanding of the Law ("You have heard") with that of Jesus ("But I say to you"). The first contrast reinterprets the command against murder. For Jesus, the prohibition certainly stands, but his view of right relationships probes before and beneath such a heinous act. Long before the loss of control that leads to killing

another person, perceptions and attitudes toward the other must be uncovered, dissipated, and transformed. Jesus' teaching on offering ritual worship would surely bring gasps from any observant Jew. It would be unthinkable to excuse oneself from participating in the all-important offering of sacrifice, by means of which God and the people were united. But Jesus insists that damaged or broken relationship with other members of the community prevents such union, and so reconciliation with a brother or sister must come first, as the beginning of true worship.

If we don't entertain the idea of sin, we will stay away from trouble.

Jesus is using hyperbole to stress the teaching. This is exhortatory: keep your energy up. His advice is to avoid any cause for sin before it gets us into trouble.

But **I** say to you,
    everyone who **looks** at a woman with lust
    has **already** committed adultery with her in his **heart**.]
If your right **eye** causes you to **sin**,
    tear it out and **throw** it away.
It is **better** for you to lose one of your members
    than to have your whole body thrown into Gehenna.
And if your right **hand** causes you to **sin**,
    cut it off and **throw** it away.
It is **better** for you to lose one of your members
    than to have your whole body go into Gehenna.

Pause and let your energy calm a bit before moving onto the next teaching.

Note it's the husband who is the focus of this teaching.

To provide for herself and any children, a divorced woman would have to marry again.

"It was **also** said,
    *Whoever **divorces** his* wife *must give her a* bill *of divorce.*
But **I** say to you,
    whoever **divorces** his wife—unless the marriage is unlawful—
    causes her to commit **adultery**,
    and whoever **marries** a divorced woman commits adultery.

Pause before beginning this final teaching.

A disciple should be honest and trustworthy without needing to make an oath.

["Again you have heard that it was said to your ancestors,
    *Do not take a **false** oath,*
    *but make **good** to the Lord all that you **vow**.*
But **I** say to you, do not swear **at all**;
    not by **heaven**, for it is God's throne;
    nor by the **earth**, for it is his footstool;
    nor by **Jerusalem**, for it is the city of the great King.
Do not swear by your **head**,
    for you cannot make a single hair white or black.
Let your '**Yes**' mean 'Yes,' and your '**No**' mean '**No**.'
Anything **more** is from the **evil** one."]

[Shorter: Matthew 5:20–22a, 27–28, 33–34a, 37 (see brackets)]

Jesus continues emphasizing the primacy of inward attitudes in his instruction on the commandment against adultery. What leads to such an act begins in the heart, understood as the core of a person and the source of decision and action; Jesus' command thus prohibits entertaining lustful desires. The proverbs that call for excising body parts that seem the source of sin are not meant literally. They are concrete examples insisting that whatever leads to sin, no matter how cherished, must be surrendered.

Regarding divorce, Jesus upholds a much higher ideal than found in the Mosaic Law. Some rabbinic schools of thought allowed a man to divorce his wife for minimal reasons, including lack of cooking skills. But Jesus allows divorce for only one condition: if the marriage is "unlawful." The Greek word *porneia* used here can have various meanings, but many scholars believe it designates a marriage that oversteps the command against marriage within certain degrees of kinship (Leviticus 18:6–18). Such a marriage was considered incestuous and therefore unlawful. (See also Matthew 19:1–9.)

Jesus' prohibition against all oaths is somewhat obscure and has received various interpretations. One view holds that since an oath called upon God to verify the truth of one's claim, the act could be viewed as an attempt to control God. More important than the negative order is the positive command to speak the truth to one another in a simple, straightforward manner. M.F.

SEVENTH SUNDAY IN ORDINARY TIME

LECTIONARY #79

A short but important exhortatory reading. God lays down the centerpiece of the Law: love and do not hate.

Leviticus = lih-VIT-ih-kuhs

Speak out of love to anyone listening who may have forgotten their true identity—created in the image of God, created as holy. Be who you are.

These are all worthless actions, wastes of time and energy; dismiss them as such. They're not consistent with our identity as children of God.

Pause, slow down, and maintain eye contact through this climactic point.

This is the "sign-off" to the message: This is essential; take it to heart.

For meditation and context:

TO KEEP IN MIND
Pay attention to the pace of your reading. Varying the pace gives listeners clues to the meaning of the text. The most common problem for proclaimers new to the ministry is going too fast to be understood.

READING I   Leviticus 19:1–2, 17–18

A reading from the Book of Leviticus

The LORD said to **Moses**,
   "Speak to the whole Israelite community and **tell** them:
   Be holy, for **I**, the LORD, your God, **am holy**.

"You shall not bear **hatred** for your brother or sister in your heart.
Though you may have to **reprove** your fellow citizen,
   do not incur **sin** because of him.
Take no **revenge** and cherish no **grudge** against any of your people.
You shall **love** your **neighbor** as **yourself**.
I am the LORD."

RESPONSORIAL PSALM   Psalm 103:1–2, 3–4, 8, 10, 12–13 (8a)

R. The Lord is kind and merciful.

Bless the LORD, O my soul;
   and all my being, bless his holy name.
Bless the LORD, O my soul,
   and forget not all his benefits.

He pardons all your iniquities,
   heals all your ills.
He redeems your life from destruction,
   crowns you with kindness and compassion.

Merciful and gracious is the LORD,
   slow to anger and abounding in kindness.
Not according to our sins does he deal
   with us,
   nor does he requite us according
   to our crimes.

As far as the east is from the west,
   so far has he put our transgressions
   from us.
As a father has compassion on his children,
   so the LORD has compassion on those who
   fear him.

READING I The Book of Leviticus, which contains some of the most ancient material in the Old Testament, includes numerous commands concerning ritual worship, rules for moral conduct, and penalties for various sins. All these instructions rooted in the Ten Commandments developed over centuries; they were gathered into their present form after the Jews were released from Babylonian captivity and attempted to renew themselves as God's covenant people.

In today's First Reading, Moses makes a statement repeated elsewhere: just as Israel's God is holy ("set apart" or "other"), so the community chosen for special relationship with God is to be holy. The elect community must be recognized for a way of life set apart from that of surrounding peoples and nations. The reason for several commands in this passage appears at its end; those who belong to the Lord are commanded to love each other as they love themselves. Such love naturally forbids inner hatred of another, thoughts or actions of vengeance, and grudges. However, authentic love of neighbor might call for fraternal correction when necessary. In Leviticus, these instructions are addressed specifically to the people of Israel; in Matthew, Jesus will expand the love command to include all, even enemies.

READING II Today's passage from First Corinthians returns to several issues raised by Paul earlier in his letter and noted in previous Sunday readings. Paul was concerned that the church in Corinth had divided into factions who allied themselves with a particular minister of the Gospel; he was also dismayed that the community was valuing human wisdom

An exhortatory reading, describing some extraordinary benefits of life in the Spirit. Proclaim as if you had exciting good news to share.

Corinthians = kohr-IN-thee-uhns

That God dwells within them might be a new or forgotten learning for some. Remind them of their true identity.

Relying on God instead of human wisdom might make one a fool in the world's eyes, but wise in God's eyes. Contrast "wisdom" and "foolishness" in these lines.

Can you sense satisfaction in Paul's quotes about how God brings down the vain? Slow down and set them apart as quotes, let that satisfaction come through.

This is an amazing statement.

List these things with increasing intensity, but keep moving.

Apollos = uh-POL-uhs; Cephas = SEE-fuhs

Now, slow down, pausing after each comma, and make the progression from "you" to "God" very clear.

> **TO KEEP IN MIND**
> *Exhortatory* texts make an urgent appeal to listeners. They may encourage, warn, or challenge, and often include a call to action. You must convey the urgency and passion behind the words.

READING II   1 Corinthians 3:16–23

A reading from the first Letter of Saint Paul to the Corinthians

Brothers and sisters:
Do you not **know** that you are the **temple** of **God**,
    and that the Spirit of God **dwells** in you?
If anyone **destroys** God's temple, God will destroy that **person**;
    for the temple of God, which you **are**, is **holy**.

Let no one **deceive** himself.
If any one among you considers himself **wise** in this age,
    let him become a **fool**, so as to **become** wise.
For the **wisdom** of this world is **foolishness** in the eyes of God,
    for it is written:
    *God catches the wise in their own **ruses**,*
and again:
    The Lord knows the thoughts of the wise,
        *that they are **vain**.*
So let no one **boast** about human beings, for everything **belongs**
        to you,
    Paul or Apollos or Cephas,
    or the world or life or death,
    or the present or the future:
    all belong to **you**, and you to **Christ**, and Christ to **God**.

over God's wisdom, revealed in Christ. Like the Church in every age, members struggled against powerful influences of their contemporary culture, which was clearly stratified and which prized human reason.

The Apostle never tires of reminding Christians that by God's gift they have been recreated in the Holy Spirit. The Church as a whole and each local church is now "the temple of God," the precise place where God dwells and is to be encountered. As God is holy (set apart), so also this new temple must be set apart from the prevailing culture, its values, and its "wisdom."

Contrasting worldly and divine wisdom, Paul quotes Psalm 94:11 to support his claim that in comparison to God's wisdom, the sages of this world are like a mere wisp of air. The wise ones of Corinth might divide themselves into followers of this or that human thinker or leader. But such divisions have no place among those who bear the name of Christ. They have equally received all things through Christ, to whom they now belong, and through him they also belong to the all-holy, all-wise God.

> **GOSPEL**   Today's Gospel Reading continues the Sermon on the Mount, specifically including the last two of six antithetical statements begun last Sunday. Matthew presents Jesus as the true interpreter of the Law Moses received on Sinai by contrasting one of its teachings ("You have heard") with his own instruction ("But I say to you"). It is important to recall that in beginning his instruction to the disciples, Jesus reassures them that he does not intend to abolish, but to fulfill, Jewish Law and Scriptures.

A didactic reading, continuing the "You have heard . . . But I say" sayings from last week. Bring a sense of urgency to this reading. You are calling your assembly to a very high standard of behavior.

This saying is still used today to justify some horrific behavior.

These are radical statements, and would have sounded so to the disciples. Familiarity has dulled their impact on us. Try to give them the power they had at their first proclamation.

These are new standards Jesus is introducing. Make sure your community understands clearly what's being asked of them by taking your time and stressing the response Jesus is demanding.

Pause before this next teaching.

More radical statements that would have shocked Jesus' listeners. They shouldn't sound like greeting-card niceties.

You do these things because that's the way God does things, and you're created in the image of God.

The standard most people live by—love your friends and hate your enemies—is worthless.

Pause, then proclaim this final line deliberately, and let it really sink in.

GOSPEL   Matthew 5:38–48

A reading from the holy Gospel according to Matthew

Jesus said to his disciples:
  "You have heard that it was said,
  *An **eye** for an **eye** and a **tooth** for a **tooth**.*
But **I** say to you, offer **no** resistance to one who is evil.
When someone **strikes** you on your right cheek,
  turn the other one as well.
If anyone wants to go to law with you over your **tunic**,
  hand over your **cloak** as well.
Should anyone press you into service for **one** mile,
  go for **two** miles.
Give to the one who **asks** of you,
  and do not turn your back on one who wants to **borrow**.

"You have heard that it was said,
  *You shall **love** your neighbor and **hate** your enemy.*
But **I** say to you, **love** your enemies
  and **pray** for those who persecute you,
  that you may be **children** of your heavenly Father,
  for he makes his sun rise on the bad **and** the good,
  and causes rain to fall on the just **and** the unjust.
For if you love those who love **you**, what **recompense** will
    you have?
Do not the **tax collectors** do the same?
And if you greet your brothers **only**,
  what is **unusual** about that?
Do not the **pagans** do the same?
So **be perfect**, just as your heavenly Father is perfect."

Both pairings of old and new teachings call Jesus' followers to place no limits on love of the other, regardless of anyone's behavior or seeming worthiness. He first quotes Exodus 21:24, a command of the Law originally meant to curb unlimited retaliation, which was common in the time of Moses. For those who live according to the teaching of Jesus and share in the Kingdom of Heaven, there must be no retaliation at all for injury or offense. Instead, one must replace offense with kindness. Jesus' instruction seems to apply even to the hated Romans, who claimed the right to seize the goods of native peoples or compel them into the service of the empire.

This point leads to one of the most difficult of Jesus' commands: to love not only neighbors, as the Law requires (Leviticus 19:18), but to love and do good even to enemies. The reason for such behavior echoes a repeated teaching of the Old Testament: the pattern for righteous behavior among God's people is God's own way of acting. Besides, even tax collectors and Gentiles ("pagans"), regarded as ritually impure in Jewish belief, show goodwill to one another. For Jesus' disciples, the standard of righteousness is much greater; it is no less than imitation of God. The word *teleios*, translated "perfect," does not demand moral faultlessness, impossible for humans. The term most likely alludes to Deuteronomy 18:13, in which Moses calls the people to be completely devoted to (*teleios*) following divine instruction. Jesus will use the same word later in response to one who inquires what he must do to have eternal life (Matthew 19:16). M.F.

EIGHTH SUNDAY IN ORDINARY TIME

A short but very powerful exhortatory reading with intense emotional content. As with any short reading, take your time and let the feelings come through to your listeners.

Isaiah = Ī-ZAY-uh

These lines must carry the feeling of complete abandonment, or the whole reading will lose its impact.
Pause before switching to God's response and let love, care, and tenderness come through in your voice.
Slow down on this last and most important line.

For meditation and context:

TO KEEP IN MIND
Proclamation cannot be effective unless it is expressive. As you prepare your proclamation, make choices about emotions. Some choices are already evident in the text.

LECTIONARY #82

READING I   Isaiah 49:14–15

A reading from the Book of the Prophet Isaiah

Zion said, "The LORD has **forsaken** me;
  my Lord has **forgotten** me."
Can a **mother** forget her infant,
  be without **tenderness** for the child of her womb?
Even should **she** forget,
  I will **never** forget you.

RESPONSORIAL PSALM   Psalm 62:2–3, 6–7, 8–9 (6a)

R. Rest in God alone, my soul.

Only in God is my soul at rest;
  from him comes my salvation.
He only is my rock and my salvation,
  my stronghold; I shall not be disturbed
  at all.

Only in God be at rest, my soul,
  for from him comes my hope.
He only is my rock and my salvation,
  my stronghold; I shall not be disturbed.

With God is my safety and my glory,
  he is the rock of my strength; my refuge is
  in God.
Trust in him at all times, O my people!
  Pour out your hearts before him.

READING I   In one of the tenderest proclamations of divine love in the entire Old Testament, Isaiah offers comfort to a defeated people who remain in captivity. Today's brief reading appears in the section of this prophetic work that is commonly called "the book of consolation." Chapters 40–55 contain oracles that most likely date from near the end of Babylonian exile in 539 BC. At this point, the exiles of Judah would have endured about a half-century of captivity, far from the Promised Land. Some might have questioned: "Will we ever

return? Will God ever restore us as the elect, covenant people?"

Today's Scripture is placed at the heart of a chapter that promises return to the land and both physical and spiritual rebuilding. The reason for this saving act lies precisely in God's maternal, tender love for the chosen though sinful people. In the verse immediately before today's reading, and in the reading itself, we find the Hebrew word *racham* to describe God's "mercy" and "tenderness." This term, from the root *rechem*, womb, expresses the love of a woman for the child she has carried,

birthed, and raised. In the Old Testament, it is often used to express undeserved, yet deeply felt love. Through Isaiah, the Lord reassures the elect but errant people: even if a woman could forget the "child of her womb," I, your God, "will never forget you."

READING II   Today's Second Reading concludes Paul's discussion on the proper role of God's ministers and how members of the Corinthian church should regard them. As in previous Sunday readings, the Apostle has condemned factions formed by groups aligning themselves

A didactic reading challenging us to put aside judgment. Some among your listeners need this message; proclaim so as to help them hear it.

Corinthians = kohr-IN-thee-uhnz

Paul is setting up his argument: Although servants should be trustworthy, it's not up to us to judge their trustworthiness.

Throw away this line to show how little Paul's concern is.

A little surprising! Many of us suffer from self-criticism.

Paul doesn't judge himself, but he's still quick to point out that he doesn't know of anything he's done wrong.

Pause before this final point, and slow down from here to the end.
We can't judge others because we can never know the real motives behind their actions.

"Everyone" is a surprise. Don't swallow it. After a reading about judgment, this is good news!

An exhortatory reading, sharing the good news that God will provide all that we really need. Proclaim as if to someone you know who needs encouragement to trust in God.

Jesus is stating the obvious.

mammon = wealth; the word will be unfamiliar to some, but the rest of the reading will make it clear.

Don't be too dismissive of these needs. Desiring food and clothes isn't sinful; they're just not worth the worry compared to what we should really desire.

READING II   1 Corinthians 4:1–5

A reading from the first Letter of Saint Paul to the Corinthians

Brothers and sisters:
Thus should one regard us: as **servants** of Christ
   and **stewards** of the mysteries of God.
Now it is of course required of stewards
   that they be found **trustworthy**.
It does not concern me in the **least**
   that I be **judged** by you or any **human** tribunal;
   I do not even pass judgment on **myself**;
   I am not conscious of anything **against** me,
   but I do not thereby stand **acquitted**;
   the one who judges me is the **Lord**.
Therefore **do not** make any judgment before the appointed time,
   until the Lord comes,
   for he will bring to **light** what is hidden in **darkness**
   and will manifest the **motives** of our hearts,
   and then **everyone** will receive **praise** from God.

GOSPEL   Matthew 6:24–34

A reading from the holy Gospel according to Matthew

Jesus said to his **disciples**:
   "No one can serve **two** masters.
He will either **hate** one and **love** the other,
   or be **devoted** to one and **despise** the other.
You cannot serve **God** and **mammon**.

"Therefore I tell you, **do not worry** about your **life**,
   what you will eat or drink,
   or about your **body**, what you will wear.

---

with one or another minister of the Gospel. Such attitudes and actions reflect merely human values, unbefitting a church that views itself as God's temple and a community that belongs to God in Christ.

If the Corinthian church members understand themselves according to God's wisdom, they will accept Paul's description of ministers of the Good News: servants and stewards. True pastors are not themselves the message; they are called to preserve and to serve God's plan as revealed in Christ, and so must be completely trustworthy. Undisturbed by human judgment of

himself or his proclamation, Paul is concerned only about the judgment of Christ. He shares the early Church's expectation of an imminent return of the Risen Lord, bringing the final age to completion. In the fullness of time, faithful servants will receive God's just reward.

GOSPEL   In the opening verse of today's Gospel passage, Jesus echoes divine instruction from Deuteronomy 6:5: those who belong to God's people must love the Lord with their whole being. A divided heart is not a heart

that belongs to God. The verb here translated "serve" implies the service of a slave, and in imperial Rome, slaves belonged wholly to their masters. Jesus does not despise money as such; rather, he teaches that anyone enslaved to wealth cannot belong to God wholeheartedly.

In the remainder of this reading, Matthew continues the Sermon on the Mount—Jesus' teaching that fulfills or brings to full growth the Law of Moses. The beginning and end of this section sound a repeated message about priorities, acting as bookends. What lies between contains

What is Jesus' emotion as he describes the boundless, providential love of God? Joy, excitement, compassion? Bring the emotion you choose to your proclamation.

Of course you are!

Of course you can't!

A new thought; separate it from the previous lines about food.

Drop your voice slightly on this parenthetical phrase.

Have some fun with these questions (as Jesus did) and emphasize the useless anxiety in them.
God affirms that these needs are good, but not worth the worry.
Here is the key. Be eager to share it with your assembly.

That is to say, "today has enough troubles of its own." Jesus affirms a truth we all know—life is difficult. This shouldn't sound like a dire warning, but more like, "You know what I'm talking about, right?"

TO KEEP IN MIND
What does the reading ask your assembly to do or to be after hearing your proclamation? Focus on an intention every time you proclaim.

Is not **life** more than food and the **body** more than clothing?
Look at the **birds** in the sky;
    they do not **sow** or **reap**, they gather **nothing** into barns,
    yet your heavenly Father **feeds** them.
Are not you more **important** than they?
Can any of you by worrying add a single **moment**
    to your life-span?
Why are you **anxious** about clothes?
Learn from the way the wild **flowers** grow.
They do not work or spin.
But I tell you that **not even** Solomon in all his **splendor**
    was clothed like one of **them**.
If God so **clothes** the grass of the field,
    which grows **today** and is thrown into the oven **tomorrow**,
    will he not much **more** provide for **you**, **O** you of little faith?
So **do not worry** and say, 'What are we to eat?'
    or 'What are we to drink?' or 'What are we to wear?'
All these things the **pagans** seek.
Your heavenly Father **knows** that you need them all.
But seek **first** the kingdom of God and his righteousness,
    and **all** these things will be **given** you besides.
Do not worry about **tomorrow**; tomorrow will take care of **itself**.
Sufficient for a day is its **own** evil."

Jesus' further teaching about the conduct of those who follow God wholeheartedly and so share in the Kingdom of Heaven. Too much concern for oneself and one's own life can distract from devotion to God as the supreme value. (The word *psyche*, translated "life," can also mean the "self" or "inner being.")

Jesus takes note of typical human concerns, thus recognizing them as real needs: food, drink, and clothing. But again, the important question is one of priorities. The word here translated "anxious" can include a sense of preoccupation with certain things. While physical sustenance and proper clothing are genuine needs, those who love God above all have faith in divine providence. The One who graciously clothes even wild flowers in magnificent raiment can surely be trusted to provide for all human needs. Excessive concern with physical necessities thus implies lack of trust in God.

Jesus' admonition to "seek first the kingdom of God and his righteousness" forms the core of today's Gospel passage. At the beginning of the Sermon on the Mount, Jesus repeatedly speaks of righteousness befitting those who live fully under God's final rule. The notion of righteousness, moral conduct according to divine teaching, embraces all relationships: with God, others, and material things. While the importance of righteousness permeates the Old Testament, Jesus insists that the dawning Kingdom calls for something greater than righteous external behavior. It desires hearts purified by the God whom one freely chooses to love before all else. M.F.

ASH WEDNESDAY

LECTIONARY #219

READING I Joel 2:12–18

A reading from the Book of the Prophet Joel

Even **now**, says the LORD,
    return to me with your **whole heart**,
    with fasting, and weeping, and mourning;
Rend your **hearts**, not your garments,
    and **return** to the LORD, your God.
For **gracious** and **merciful** is he,
    slow to anger, **rich** in kindness,
    and **relenting** in punishment.
Perhaps he will **again** relent
    and leave behind him a **blessing**,
Offerings and **libations**
    for the LORD, your God.

Blow the **trumpet** in Zion!
    proclaim a fast,
    call an assembly;
Gather the people,
    notify the congregation;
Assemble the elders,
    gather the children
    and the **infants** at the breast;
Let the **bridegroom quit** his room
    and the **bride** her chamber.

An exhortatory reading that mixes good news with challenge. Desire is the key to this reading. How will you express both the Lord's desire for us to repent and our desire for God?

Joel = JOH-*l

Start with strength. It's not too late! Let your assembly hear God yearning for them!

rend = tear

Tearing of one's garments showed grief and sorrow. God desires an open heart more than showy signs.

This is good news. How does it feel to know God waits with open arms, ready to bless us despite our mistakes? Bring that emotion to this proclamation.

Linger over these phrases describing the great mercy of God.

Spoken with gratitude for God's mercy!

Pause slightly after this line.

Now, pick up your pace and keep your voice and energy up as you issue these calls. They should sound like calls to action and not a "to-do" list.

The assembly should know by your attitude that this is urgent!

This is serious business!

READING I Although the Book of Joel lacks a clear historical reference, internal clues indicate 450–400 BC as a likely time for this prophecy. The exiles of Judah had returned; Jerusalem and the Temple had been rebuilt, but within about a century after the Lord's restoration, former lapses reappeared: priestly corruption, social injustice, and lax observance of the Torah. The Old Testament books of Nehemiah and Ezra speak of their attempts at religious reform, probably near the time of Joel's prophecy. Although these reformers called for public recommitment to the way of life described in God's Torah, response was sometimes tepid at best.

At the time of Joel's prophecy in today's reading, scant winter rain, extreme summer heat, and locust plagues threatened Judah's grain fields, orchards, and vineyards. For the prophet, this agricultural disaster represented the voice of the Lord, calling the people to return to living according to their covenant commitment. In the Old Testament, "return" normally translates the Hebrew *shuv*, which literally means "to turn." Most often used to indicate a plea for true repentance or conversion, *shuv* calls for a complete reversal of attitude and behavior. The prophets often express the meaning of "turn/return" as a dual action: both turning away from evil and returning to the good. Since in biblical times the heart represented the core of a human being, Joel demands that Judah's return to covenant faithfulness must originate in the heart. He emphasizes his point again by proclaiming that the ritual action of tearing garments, an outward sign of repentance, remains meaningless without tearing open one's heart to God.

Careful not to swallow "weep."

Now the pleading comes from the people. You are voicing the assembly's desire for God. Fill the word "O" with this desire.

No pause at this comma.

Take a long pause before revealing the Lord's response, and proclaim it gently, with tenderness and love.

For meditation and context:

Between the porch and the altar
    let the **priests**, the ministers of the LORD, **weep**,
And say, "**Spare**, **O** LORD, your people,
    and make not your heritage a **reproach**,
    with the nations ruling over them!
Why should they say among the peoples,
    '**Where** is their God?' "

Then the LORD was **stirred** to concern for his land
    and took **pity** on his people.

RESPONSORIAL PSALM   Psalm 51:3–4, 5–6ab, 12–13, 14 and 17 (3a)

R. Be merciful, O Lord, for we have sinned.

Have mercy on me, O God, in your goodness;
    in the greatness of your compassion wipe
      out my offense.
Thoroughly wash me from my guilt
    and of my sin cleanse me.

For I acknowledge my offense,
    and my sin is before me always:
"Against you only have I sinned,
    and done what is evil in your sight."

A clean heart create for me, O God,
    and a steadfast spirit renew within me.
Cast me not out from your presence,
    and your Holy Spirit take not from me.

Give me back the joy of your salvation,
    and a willing spirit sustain in me.
O Lord, open my lips,
    and my mouth shall proclaim your praise.

TO KEEP IN MIND

Exhortatory texts make an urgent appeal to listeners. They may encourage, warn, or challenge, and often include a call to action. You must convey the urgency and passion behind the words.

An exhortatory reading, with a sense of urgency. Be an agent of reconciliation through your proclamation.

Corinthians = kohr-IN-thee-uhnz

God is appealing through you; increase intensity on "appeal" or "implore."

This is Christ's appeal you bring.

Here is the point of the whole passage: speak deliberately and with intensity, then pause to let it sink in.

READING II   2 Corinthians 5:20—6:2

A reading from the second Letter of Saint Paul to the Corinthians

Brothers and sisters:
We are **ambassadors** for **Christ**,
    as if God were **appealing** through us.
We **implore** you on behalf of Christ,
    be **reconciled** to God.
For our sake he made him to **be** sin who did not **know** sin,
    so that we might become the **righteousness** of God in him. ≫

Using familiar Old Testament language, Joel reminds the people that when they repent sincerely, God always responds with gracious mercy and steadfast love. But as the Responsorial Psalm indicates, genuine recognition and admission of sin and guilt must accompany gestures of repentance. Then, all the people must turn to fasting, prayer, and offering sincere sacrifice. The prophet stresses that all are called to repent—young and old, priest and people—and no other activity is more important. Joel ends his call to "turn" with a direct appeal to the Lord: if not for the people's true repentance, at least spare them for the sake of your own good name! If Israel truly belongs to God, then let God demonstrate that reality to other nations by sparing the Chosen People from disaster.

READING II Second Corinthians is Paul's most personal letter, in which he passionately speaks of both the Good News of God in Christ and his own ministry of that Gospel, with its joys and sorrows. He uses "we" to refer to himself, possibly including his coministers of the Gospel. Immediately before today's reading, Paul speaks of human re-creation and reconciliation with God, brought about through the Death and Resurrection of Christ. Those who are united to Christ are then called to carry on his work of reconciliation, so that God continues this saving work through Christian believers.

Paul continues to emphasize that God's work in Christ can and must continue through the Church, with Christian believers as conduits of ongoing reconciliation. Seeking to communicate the mystery of Christ, Paul uses a difficult and much-discussed statement. He describes Christ as

Working **together**, then,
　　we **appeal** to you **not** to receive the grace of God in **vain**.
For he **says**:

> In an **acceptable** time I **heard** you,
> 　　and on the day of **salvation** I **helped** you.

Behold, **now** is a very acceptable time;
　　behold, **now** is the day of **salvation**.

GOSPEL   Matthew 6:1–6, 16–18

A reading from the holy Gospel according to Matthew

Jesus said to his disciples:
　　"Take **care** not to perform righteous deeds
　　in order that people may **see** them;
　　otherwise, you will have no **recompense** from your
　　　　heavenly Father.
When you give **alms**,
　　do not blow a **trumpet** before you,
　　as the **hypocrites** do in the synagogues and in the streets
　　to win the praise of **others**.
Amen, I say to you,
　　they have **received** their reward.
But when **you** give alms,
　　do not let your left hand **know** what your right is **doing**,
　　so that **your** almsgiving may be **secret**.
And your Father who **sees** in secret will **repay** you.

　　"When you **pray**,
　　do not be like the **hypocrites**,
　　who **love** to stand and pray in the synagogues and on street
　　　　corners
　　so that **others** may see them.

Margin notes (left column):

"Together" refers to Paul, Timothy, and Christ.

It would be a tragedy to receive God's grace and not respond to it.

Capture the tenderness in God's response.

Paul could not be clearer. The time is now!

A didactic reading; proclaim it with love and a desire to help your assembly get the most out of Lent. It concerns the three Lenten practices: almsgiving, prayer, and fasting. Note Jesus' emphasis is not on what you do, but how you do it.

This is the point of the whole passage.

Pause before the teaching on almsgiving.

Jesus is using hyperbole with some humor.

Contrast being seen by others (useless) with being seen by the Father.

And what a small reward it is!

Don't scold; rather, teach out of love. Jesus suggests a better way, which pleases God more.

Pause again before this teaching on prayer.

"made . . . to be sin" so that believers might "become the righteousness of God." Many scholars view this as Paul's way of saying that as Christ took on full humanity, humankind, transformed in Christ, becomes who Christ is: the "righteousness of God" incarnate. By living in communities of reconciliation, the Church embodies the God revealed in Christ. The Apostle urges the church at Corinth, which had struggled with various divisions, to waste no time in responding to God's gift of reconciliation. Referring to Isaiah, Paul indicates that the salvation the prophet proclaimed to God's

people of old has now arrived in Christ; the time to accept and respond to that grace is also now.

GOSPEL　Today's Gospel reading appears in the Sermon on the Mount, three chapters (5–7) that form the first of Jesus' five teaching discourses in Matthew. Because Matthew's community comprises mostly Jewish Christians, near the beginning of this section Jesus stresses that he does not intend to abolish the Law, but to bring it to completion. Matthew thus reassures his hearers that

their former way of life is not obliterated, but reaches full development through Jesus, the Messiah who inaugurates God's final rule. More than any other, this evangelist presents Jesus as teacher and true interpreter of God's instruction given through Moses. The Torah or Law given on Mount Sinai taught a way of righteousness: right relationships among God, human beings, and created things. In the Kingdom of God, righteousness as taught by Jesus is "greater" in that truly righteous acts must spring from internal conversion of mind and heart (see Matthew 5:17–20).

It is the secrets of your heart that the Father wants you to share.

Pause before this final teaching on fasting. This behavior is not only hypocritical but somewhat ridiculous!

Given this teaching, there's some irony in leaving the Mass with ashes on our foreheads. But the point is that outward signs of repentance are worthless without an inward change of heart.

Amen, I say to you,
    they have **received** their reward.
But when **you** pray, go to your **inner** room,
    close the door, and pray to your Father in **secret**.
And your Father who **sees** in secret will **repay** you.

"When you **fast**,
    do not look **gloomy** like the hypocrites.
They neglect their appearance,
    so that they may appear to **others** to be fasting.
Amen, I say to you, they have **received** their reward.
But when **you** fast,
    anoint your head and **wash** your face,
    so that you may **not** appear to be fasting,
    except to your Father who is **hidden**.
And your Father who **sees** what is hidden will **repay** you."

THE 4 STEPS OF *LECTIO DIVINA* OR PRAYERFUL READING

1. *Lectio:* Read a Scripture passage aloud slowly. Notice what phrase captures your attention and be attentive to its meaning. Silent pause.

2. *Meditatio:* Read the passage aloud slowly again, reflecting on the passage, allowing God to speak to you through it. Silent pause.

3. *Oratio:* Read it aloud slowly a third time, allowing it to be your prayer or response to God's gift of insight to you. Silent pause.

4. *Contemplatio:* Read it aloud slowly a fourth time, now resting in God's word.

In today's passage from the Sermon on the Mount, Jesus focuses on Judaism's three major spiritual disciplines: almsgiving, prayer, and fasting. These practices, especially associated with times of repentance (see Reading I), continued in the Christian community. Almsgiving, usually in the form of aid to the needy, was meant to arise from righteousness, which understood wealth as God's gift to be shared with the poor who also had a claim on divine bounty. Prayer, in both individual and communal forms, constituted proper response to divine initiative in rescuing and forming God's people. Judaism practiced fasting, a common religious observance in the ancient world, especially at times of mourning and repentance.

In his teaching on each of these spiritual disciplines, Jesus repeatedly counsels his followers to purify their inner intentions and motivations. He warns his disciples against performing good actions as "hypocrites." (The Greek word *hypocrites* originally described an actor, and so came to designate someone who pretended to be who he or she was not.) True righteousness, Jesus insists, arises from inner conversion; no one should perform religious practices in order to convince people (oneself included) of a genuine right relationship to God, others, and material things. Under God's final rule, authentic righteousness springs from a transformed heart, a heart responding to God. M.F.

FIRST SUNDAY
OF LENT

A narrative reading telling a very familiar story. Don't make the whole reading sound ominous. Rather, emphasize God's goodness and care for humans in the first half, and let the story of the serpent and woman unfold naturally, keeping the result in doubt until the end.

Let God's tender love for humanity echo in your proclamation.

Like any loving parent, God provides generously.

Smile as you relate the wonders of this place.

Pause before beginning. Contrast the serpent's cunning with the woman's honesty.

Note that God made the serpent!

The serpent knows the answer to this question, so why does it ask? To gain the woman's trust? To trip her up? To sow seeds of doubt? Let your choice inform your proclamation.

She responds simply, with the facts.

Make sure the serpent seems genuinely concerned for the man and woman. That's its cunning, and the attraction of all temptations!

Take your time with this explanation. The serpent wants to be sure the woman understands.

LECTIONARY #22

READING I   Genesis 2:7–9; 3:1–7

A reading from the Book of Genesis

The LORD God formed **man** out of the **clay** of the ground
 and **blew** into his nostrils the **breath of life**,
 and so man became a **living being**.

Then the LORD God planted a **garden** in Eden, in the east,
 and placed there the **man** whom he had formed.
Out of the ground the LORD God made various **trees** grow
 that were **delightful** to look at and good for **food**,
 with the **tree of life** in the middle of the garden
 and the tree of the **knowledge** of **good** and **evil**.

Now the **serpent** was the most **cunning** of all the animals
 that the LORD God had **made**.
The serpent asked the **woman**,
 "Did God **really** tell you not to eat
 from any of the trees in the garden?"
The woman answered the serpent:
 "We **may** eat of the fruit of the trees in the garden;
 it is only about the fruit of the tree
 in the **middle** of the garden that God said,
 'You shall not **eat** it or even **touch** it, lest you **die**.'"
But the serpent said to the woman:
 "You certainly will **not die**!
No, God knows well that the moment you eat of it

READING I At the beginning of Lent, the Scripture readings focus on the continuous human struggle to become the living image of God, as the Creator intended from the beginning. As is evident today, during Lent the Church also celebrates the complete fulfillment of God's purpose in Christ, the New Adam.

Today's First Reading belongs to the second account of the creation of human beings in the Book of Genesis. In the first story, the divine plan and purpose is clear: God formed humankind in the divine image (Genesis 1:27; the Hebrew word *adam* used

here means "humankind"). In the language of symbol and metaphor, the second narrative depicts the fundamental sin of the human race: not content to serve as the image of God, the human creature reaches beyond its limits to seize equality with God.

The well-known story of man and woman in the garden unfolds, but its full meaning is less familiar. In the preceding chapter, God entrusted cultivation and care of the garden to the human creature. The fruits of all the trees but one were freely available for food; only one was forbidden: the tree of the knowledge of good and evil.

This limitation clearly served to protect humankind, for "when you eat from it you shall die" (Genesis 2:17). In ancient Hebrew thought, sin and death were inextricably intertwined, for both brought separation from God. (The expectation of an afterlife did not emerge in Judaism until near the end of the Old Testament period.)

In today's First Reading, we can discern the symbolic meaning of the tree of the knowledge of good and evil—and the command to avoid it. Like some neighboring peoples, Israel believed that only divine beings truly know what is good and bad.

Give the sense that the woman is deliberating, looking at the tree. Her perceptions are reasonable. This could happen to any of us!

Slight pause after "So." State these actions simply, without comment.

Pause before "then"; the assembly will know what's coming. Now, finally, let your own sadness, grief, disappointment, or other feeling come through and comment on their action.

They can no longer be open, honest, and naked before each other and God.

For meditation and context:

TO KEEP IN MIND
A *narrative* has characters, dialogue, a setting, and action. Help your listeners see the story unfold, keep characters distinct, and be clear about shifts in setting.

A didactic reading which at first glance seems complex, but its structure is simple. Paul repeatedly contrasts two persons (Adam and Christ), their actions (sin and redemption), and the results of those actions (death and life). Keep single thoughts together without pauses; only pause between thoughts. Use the notes and punctuation as your guide.

Paul starts by explaining how Adam's sin brought death to all.

Sin was in the world even before Moses received the Law that defined sin.

---

your eyes will be **opened** and you will be **like gods**
who **know** what is good and what is evil."
The woman **saw** that the tree was **good** for **food**,
   pleasing to the eyes, and **desirable** for gaining wisdom.
So she took some of its fruit and **ate** it;
   and she also **gave** some to her husband, who was with her,
   and **he** ate it.
Then the eyes of both of them were **opened**,
   and they realized that they were **naked**;
   so they **sewed** fig leaves together
   and made **loincloths** for themselves.

RESPONSORIAL PSALM   Psalm 51:3–4, 5–6, 12–13, 17 (3a)

R. **Be merciful, O Lord, for we have sinned.**

Have mercy on me, O God, in your goodness;
   in the greatness of your compassion wipe
      out my offense.
Thoroughly wash me from my guilt
   and of my sin cleanse me.

For I acknowledge my offense,
   and my sin is before me always:
"Against you only have I sinned,
   and done what is evil in your sight."

A clean heart create for me, O God,
   and a steadfast spirit renew within me.
Cast me not out from your presence,
   and your Holy Spirit take not from me.

Give me back the joy of your salvation,
   and a willing spirit sustain in me.
O Lord, open my lips,
   and my mouth shall proclaim your praise.

READING II   Romans 5:12–19

A reading from the Letter of Saint Paul to the Romans

[Brothers and sisters:
Through **one** man **sin** entered the world,
   and through sin, **death**,
   and thus death came to **all** men, inasmuch as **all** sinned]—
   for up to the time of the law, sin was in the world,
   though sin is not **accounted** when there is no law. »

The tree thus symbolizes divine status. The narrative makes clear that the human creature is very aware of God's command and its purpose, for the woman repeats both to the cunning serpent.

The deceitful serpent replies with partial truth: if you reach out to grasp for yourself the knowledge of good and evil, "you will be like gods." The serpent's untruth appears in denying the further consequence: sin and death, which bring separation from God. The woman succumbs, and sin quickly spreads. She offers fruit of the tree of knowledge of good and evil to her

husband, who repeats the disastrous choice, "and he ate it." Soon both experience the consequences of their choice: once completely free, open, and vulnerable to God, now they begin to hide themselves from the divine presence.

The author thus illustrates foundational human sin: resisting the divine plan and purpose: to become the living image of God on earth. Instead, human beings, male and female, strive to place themselves on the same level as God. Such overreach leads to humankind's estrangement from

God and, ultimately, to alienation from its divinely intended purpose.

READING II   Today's Second Reading requires the background of the First Reading, since Paul uses a Jewish mode of interpretation called typology. In this interpretive mode, present persons and events are most clearly understood in light of previous Scriptures. An earlier text offers a "type" or embryonic form that illuminates the meaning of some person, event, and/or situation in the present. In various letters, as in today's Second Reading, Paul

Now Paul tells the good news! Set this statement apart.

The remainder of the reading alternates bad news with good news.

Pause briefly, raise your energy, and smile each time you mention the good news that Christ's gift is much greater than Adam's transgression. Keep these three lines together.

Good news! Christ's gift is greater, and so are the consequences for us—grace and life.

Good news!

Don't pause at the end of this line.

Good news! Keep these three lines together.

Longer pause before the conclusion.

Good news!

Good news!

But **death** reigned from **Adam** to **Moses**,
    even over those who did **not** sin
    after the pattern of the trespass of Adam,
    who is the **type** of the one who was to come.

But the **gift** is not like the **transgression**.
For if by the transgression of the **one**, the **many** died,
    how much **more** did the **grace** of God
    and the gracious **gift** of the one man Jesus **Christ**
    overflow for the **many**.
And the gift is not like the **result** of the one who sinned.
For after **one** sin there was the **judgment** that brought
        condemnation;
    but the **gift**, after **many** transgressions, brought **acquittal**.
[For **if**, by the transgression of the **one**,
    death came to reign through that one,
    how much **more** will those who receive the abundance
        of **grace**
    and of the gift of **justification**
    come to **reign** in life through the one Jesus **Christ**.
In conclusion, just as through one **transgression**
    condemnation came upon **all**,
    so, through one **righteous** act,
    acquittal and **life** came to **all**.
For just as through the **disobedience** of the one man
    the many were made **sinners**,
    so, through the **obedience** of the one,
    the many will be made **righteous**.]

[Shorter: Romans 5:12, 17–19 (see brackets)]

invokes what is commonly called "Second (or New) Adam" typology. While the First Adam (who represents humankind created in the image of God) failed to fulfill this divine purpose, Christ, through his Passion and Resurrection, fully realizes God's intention for humanity. He is an icon of God: self-giving love poured out for the salvation and re-creation of all (see Philippians 2:5–11). Christ is thus the Second Adam, the beginning of humanity as true image of God, who overcomes the powers of sin and death.

Paul presents "one man," the First Adam, as a figure who represents all of humankind—who resists or fails to realize our purpose as image of God. The Apostle first recalls the pattern unfolded in the long story of the First Adam, in whom sin leads to the all-pervasive rule of death. But this man is a type of the Second Adam, Jesus Christ, who embodies and so reveals God as overflowing, gracious gift of freedom from sin. The First Adam's transgression brought death, but the Second Adam brings the gifts of justification and fullness of life in God.

Paul sums up his point: the one transgression—that of the First Adam—brought the death-dealing "condemnation" of alienation from God and from humankind's intended identity. But one righteous act—the Second Adam's obedient response to God—begins a new pattern. Through Christ, humankind can truly become the creature God intended from the beginning: the divine image, in right relationship to God.

A narrative. Explore the intentions and emotions of both Satan and Jesus. What do each want, and how do they go about getting it? Build the conflict in each encounter—the devil becomes more insistent; Jesus becomes stronger in his response.

Note that it's the Spirit's initiative that brings about this scene.

Put Jesus' own tiredness in this line.
Articulate "tempter" carefully.

There might be a casualness in this first temptation: "What's wrong with eating if you're hungry?"

Jesus' hunger goes deeper than food.

Pause as the scene shifts.
holy city = Jerusalem

parapet = PAYR-uh-puht

There's a smugness to the devil's use of Scripture: "I can quote Scripture for my purposes, too!"

"Don't you trust God?"

Heighten Jesus' response.

GOSPEL   Matthew 4:1–11

A reading from the holy Gospel according to Matthew

At that time Jesus was led by the **Spirit** into the desert
  to be **tempted** by the devil.
He **fasted** for forty days and forty nights,
  and afterwards he was **hungry**.
The **tempter** approached and said to him,
  "**If** you are the **Son** of **God**,
  command that these **stones** become loaves of **bread**."
He said in reply,
  "It is written:
One does not **live** on bread **alone**,
  but on every **word** that comes forth
  from the mouth of **God**."

Then the devil took him to the **holy city**,
  and made him stand on the **parapet** of the temple,
  and said to him, "If you **are** the Son of God, **throw**
  yourself down.
For it is written:
He will command his **angels** concerning you
  and with their **hands** they will **support** you,
lest you **dash** your **foot** against a **stone**."
Jesus answered him,
  "Again it is **written**,
You shall **not** put the Lord, your God, to the **test**." »

GOSPEL On this First Sunday of Lent, the Church provides a model for approaching this sacred season in Jesus himself. Matthew portrays a man who, like all human beings, was tested to discover if he trusts in God above all or relies on his own power in responding to the lure of sin. Consistently eager to demonstrate that Jesus fulfills the Old Testament Scriptures, this evangelist expands Mark's account of Jesus' testing by the Spirit at the outset of his public ministry (Mark 1:12–13). The earlier evangelist simply notes the fact of Jesus' testing and implies the outcome by noting that angels ministered to him. Matthew magnifies the significance of this testing with a triple temptation, each of which Jesus rejects with a quotation from the Old Testament. As Israel of old was tested again and again on its long desert journey from slavery to new life, so is Jesus, the beginning of the New Israel, the Church, repeatedly tested. But unlike ancient Israel, which repeatedly grumbled against or even turned away from the Lord, Jesus steadfastly turns to God and his Word in Scripture.

In beginning his account of the Good News, Matthew identifies Jesus as (among other things) the Son of God. It is important to note that in the first century this title did not yet carry the weight of a claim that he is the Second Person of the Trinity; the Christian community did not fully clarify and articulate this dogma for several centuries. In the time of Jesus, "Son of God" could include several meanings, including a claim to be "like God"; to have a special relationship with God; to be the chosen Messiah; to be a righteous, obedient person; or to be divine in some undefined sense.

Pause as the scene shifts again.

Make this sound like a very attractive offer.

Pause before this line. Here's the kicker.

Jesus is done arguing! Now he musters all his energy to dismiss the devil. Quicken your pace and heighten your energy.

Pause after the devil's departure.

Let the tenderness of this scene come through in your voice and face.

> TO KEEP IN MIND
> In a narrative, find an emotion or point of view for each character, keeping in mind that these might change during the reading.

> TO KEEP IN MIND
> You can't proclaim what you don't understand. Read the Scripture passage and its commentary in *Workbook*. Then read it from your Bible, including what comes before and after it so that you understand the context.

Then the devil took him up to a very **high** mountain,
　　and showed him **all** the kingdoms of the world in their
　　　　magnificence,
　　and he said to him, "All these I shall **give** to you,
　　if you will **prostrate** yourself and worship **me**."
At this, Jesus said to him,
　　"**Get away**, Satan!
It is written:
　　*The Lord, your **God**, shall you **worship***
　　　　*and him **alone** shall you **serve**."*

Then the devil **left** him and, **behold**,
　　angels came and **ministered** to him.

With a repeated "If you are the Son of God," the Devil twice urges Jesus to demonstrate that he does in fact enjoy special status and power because of his singular relationship to God. Jesus responds with quotations from Deuteronomy and Psalm 91 to assert that he trusts in God above all, not in himself or his unique relation to God. With each unsuccessful attempt to lead Jesus to rely on himself rather than upon God, the Devil grows bolder. First he uses his own words to tempt Jesus to a show of power. When Jesus resists with a quotation from Deuteronomy, the Devil slyly supports his next temptation with his own reference to Scripture, to God's special protection of the faithful one (Psalm 91:11–12). But Jesus responds with another quotation: "You shall not put the Lord, your God, to the test." He implies the meaning of the following verse as well, a call to continually walk the path of God's commands.

Failing to use Scripture itself to trap Jesus, the Devil mounts an utterly bold, direct assault, offering to give him all worldly kingdoms and their glory. At this absurd claim to possess what belongs to God alone, Jesus banishes the tempter by invoking the instruction given to Israel of old, the command to worship none but the Lord (Deuteronomy 6:13). Unlike Israel of old, Jesus, steadfastly recognizes that there is no other god, nothing and no one to equal the God of Israel, the One who sent him and One he serves.

Jesus is thus both model for, and beginning of, the New Israel, the Church, in its observance of Lent and in its entire individual and communal life. M.F.

SECOND SUNDAY OF LENT

LECTIONARY #25

READING I   Genesis 12:1–4a

A reading from the Book of Genesis

The LORD said to **Abram**:
  "**Go forth** from the land of your **kinsfolk**
  and from your **father's** house to a land that **I** will show you.

    "**I** will make of you a **great** nation,
      and I will **bless** you;
    I will make your name **great**,
      so that **you** will be a blessing.
    I will **bless** those who **bless** you
      and **curse** those who **curse** you.
    All the communities of the earth
      shall find **blessing** in you."

Abram **went** as the LORD directed him.

An exhortatory reading bookended by a brief narrative.

Abram = AY-br*m

Abram is asked to go from the known to the unknown. His complete trust in God is what makes him our ancestor in faith.

Savor the opportunity to share this amazing news. Take your time with it. How would God sound as he shares the plans for Abram?

We are all still blessed by Abram's act of faith.

A long pause to let this blessing settle.

TO KEEP IN MIND

Making eye contact with the assembly connects you with them and connects them to the reading more deeply than using your voice alone. This helps the assembly stay with the story and keeps them engaged.

READING I With today's First Reading, the Book of Genesis begins a lengthy series of episodes concerning Abram, considered the father of God's people and supreme model of faith. In Genesis 17:5, God changes Abram's name to Abraham. These are simply two forms of the same name, meaning "the father is exalted." However, in biblical thought a new name signifies a change in one's identity, character, or role. Abram is renamed when God assures him that the promises made in today's Scripture will be fulfilled.

As the narrative begins, God invites Abram to an extreme act of trust. To ancient tribal people, kinship relationships held paramount significance; one would lay down life itself for any blood relative in one's clan. Thus the call to leave his kinsfolk implied a sacrifice of tremendous importance. In biblical call stories, however, divine reassurance usually follows God's commission. The Lord asks a great deal of Abram, but promises vastly more, promising that he will become the father of a great nation, a people in whom all humankind will be blessed.

The terminology of bless and blessing in this passage is very important, as it is throughout the Bible, appearing about six hundred times in the Old Testament. The Hebrew word conveys a sense of God supplying strength to do what lies beyond human capacity. In blessing Abram, the Lord assures him that divine power will supply what human weakness cannot accomplish. God's willingness to bless someone springs from covenant loyalty and fidelity; the divine blessing thus hints at the future of the "great nation" descended from Abram: they will become

TO KEEP IN MIND
Words in bold are significant words about which you must make a choice to help their meaning stand out. You may (or may not) choose to stress them.

RESPONSORIAL PSALM   Psalm 33:4–5, 18–19, 20, 22 (22)

R. Lord, let your mercy be on us, as we place our trust in you.

Upright is the word of the LORD,
    and all his works are trustworthy.
He loves justice and right;
    of the kindness of the LORD the earth
        is full.

See, the eyes of the LORD are upon those
        who fear him,
    upon those who hope for his kindness,
to deliver them from death
    and preserve them in spite of famine.

Our soul waits for the LORD,
    who is our help and our shield.
May your kindness, O LORD, be upon us
    who have put our hope in you.

An exhortatory reading, which builds in intensity as it goes, encouraging those who are struggling. Pause only at punctuation.
Note and practice exactly where you'll take a breath.
Let your love for your assembly come through on this line.
Proclaim as if encouraging someone who needs strength to rely on God.
This is why we can rely on God.
Try to keep these three lines together (from "not" to "began"), with no pauses. Our own efforts are weak, but not God's!
God always planned to save us through grace.
Keep your voice up on "began" to connect to the next line. Take a breath at the comma.
Raise your energy; this is even better news: the grace once hidden is now evident in Christ.
The best news of all: life conquers death! Any hardship is bearable if we know that light and life will win in the end.

READING II   2 Timothy 1:8b–10

A reading from the second Letter of Saint Paul to Timothy

Beloved:
Bear your share of hardship for the gospel
    with the **strength** that comes from **God**.

He **saved** us and **called** us to a holy life,
    not according to **our works**
    but according to his **own design**
    and the grace **bestowed** on us in Christ Jesus **before** time began,
    but **now** made manifest
    through the **appearance** of our **savior** Christ Jesus,
    who **destroyed** death and brought **life** and **immortality**
    to **light** through the gospel.

the people chosen for covenant relationship with God. In trusting faith, relying on God's blessing alone, "Abram went as the Lord directed him."

READING II   Today's brief Second Reading comes from Second Timothy, one of the three letters usually called the Pastoral Epistles: First and Second Timothy and Titus. Though attributed to Paul, today they are generally believed to date from the early second century, written by an unknown disciple of Paul or a Pauline school.

These three writings are so named because they address practical matters of life in early Christian communities facing adversity, false teachers, and the opposing values of the prevailing culture. The author of the Pastorals repeatedly reminds Christians of God's gracious gifts, received through Christ. It is because of, and in the strength of, such gifts that Jesus' followers are called to live as faithful disciples in the midst of hardships. Then, as now, those created anew in Christ are thereby called to give daily living witness to God's saving action in Christ.

GOSPEL   Each year on the Second Sunday of Lent, the Church presents a narrative of Jesus' Transfiguration. Matthew, Mark, and Luke all include this account, though with subtle differences, because each addresses a particular community in specific circumstances. Matthew, most likely a Jew who came to faith in Jesus as Messiah, writes for a Christian community with similar background, though it probably had begun to include Gentiles. Consequently, Matthew's hearers seemed to be struggling with various questions about the continuity

GOSPEL   Matthew 17:1–9

A reading from the holy Gospel according to Matthew

Jesus **took** Peter, James, and John his brother,
 and led them up a **high mountain** by themselves.
And he was **transfigured** before them;
 his face **shone** like the sun
 and his clothes became **white** as **light**.
And **behold**, **Moses** and **Elijah** appeared to them,
 conversing with him.
Then **Peter** said to Jesus in reply,
 "Lord, it is **good** that we are here.
If you wish, I will make three **tents** here,
 one for **you**, one for **Moses**, and one for **Elijah**."
While he was still **speaking**, **behold**,
 a bright cloud cast a **shadow** over them,
 then from the cloud came a **voice** that said,
 "**This** is my **beloved** Son, with whom I am **well pleased**;
 listen to him."
When the disciples **heard** this, they fell prostrate
 and were **very** much afraid.
But Jesus came and **touched** them, saying,
 "**Rise**, and do not be **afraid**."
And when the disciples raised their **eyes**,
 they saw **no one** else but Jesus alone.

As they were coming **down** from the mountain,
 Jesus **charged** them,
 "Do not tell the vision to **anyone**
 until the Son of Man has been **raised** from the dead."

A narrative reading. There's a lot going on here. Varying your pace will convey the shifts in energy and help your community follow the events.

This happens suddenly.

An amazing scene; take time describing it.

Moses = MOH-ziz; MOH-zis
Elijah = ee-LĪ-juh

Let the scene settle for a moment before moving on.

Peter's excitement overflows! Quicken your pace and heighten your energy.

Don't swallow "tents."

Slow down at "behold."

The scene gets even more amazing!

Make this sound like a loving parent, not a stern commander.

Quicken your pace to convey the disciples' fear.

Slow down and convey Jesus' gentleness as you proclaim both his actions and words.

There's a firmness to Jesus' words. This is not for everyone to know right now.

---

or discontinuity between Jesus and the Judaism of their birth. Accordingly, this evangelist frequently strives to show that Jesus "fulfills" or brings to completion the Old Testament Scriptures. His treatment of the Transfiguration emphasizes the revelation of God in Jesus, who both epitomizes and transcends all previous disclosure of God in Israel's history and Scriptures.

Previous to today's Gospel reading, Jesus had presented major points of his teaching on a mountain, a setting that recalls God's gift of the Torah to Moses on Mount Sinai. Matthew thus portrays Jesus as true interpreter of the Law of Moses. In today's account of Jesus' Transfiguration, Matthew depicts Jesus as the one who fulfills the Law and the Prophets, symbolized by the figures of Moses, the Lawgiver, and Elijah, prominent among the great prophets of Israel. These figures appear with Jesus, but fade into the background after the revelation of divine presence in Jesus.

The "bright cloud" reminds us of the guiding presence of God as a pillar of cloud in Israel's desert journey. God's voice from the cloud describes Jesus as "beloved Son," recalling the divine voice heard at Jesus' baptism. But here Matthew also refers to the Suffering Servant, "in whom I am well pleased" (Isaiah 42:1). God's voice adds the command to "listen to him." In the Old Testament, to hear and obey God's Word was the identifying mark of a genuine response to God. In the Transfiguration of Jesus, God calls all to listen to his Son's teaching, in the words he speaks and in the self-giving death he will embrace. M.F.

THIRD SUNDAY
OF LENT

LECTIONARY #28

READING I   Exodus 17:3–7

A reading from the Book of Exodus

In those days, in their **thirst** for water,
    the people **grumbled** against Moses,
    saying, "**Why** did you ever make us leave Egypt?
Was it just to have us **die** here of thirst
    with our children and our livestock?"
So Moses **cried out** to the LORD,
    "What shall I **do** with this people?
A little more and they will **stone** me!"
The LORD **answered** Moses,
    "Go over there in front of the people,
    along with some of the elders of Israel,
    holding in your hand, as you go,
    the **staff** with which you struck the **river**.
I will be **standing** there in front of you on the **rock** in Horeb.
Strike the rock, and the water will **flow** from it
    for the people to **drink**."
This Moses **did**, in the presence of the elders of Israel.
The place was called **Massah** and **Meribah**,
    because the Israelites **quarreled** there
    and **tested** the LORD, saying,
    "Is the LORD in our **midst** or **not**?"

Conversations which form a narrative. Give each speaker (the people, Moses, God) a distinct emotion. Look at "grumbled," "cried out," and the simple "answered" for clues. Express the feelings in narrative lines as well as dialogue.

Exodus = EK-suh-duhs; Moses = MOH-zis

The word "grumbled" sounds like what it means.

Proclaim as if one person speaks for all. Are they furious? Annoyed? Terrified? Anxious? Choose and proclaim from that perspective.

Pause before introducing Moses' response.

Moses has reached his limit!

Speak Moses' words with a sense of desperation and fear.

Pause again before introducing God's response

God's answer is as calm as Moses' plea is anxious. "Don't worry; I've got this!"

Horeb = HOHR-eb

Pause again.

The story ends here. Pause before giving the origin of the place names.

Massah = MAS-uh

Meribah = MAYR-ih-bah

Again, proclaim with the emotion of the people.

READING I The theme of water, with various literal and symbolic meanings, flows through many parts of both Old and New Testaments. Anyone who has spent even a little time in the lands of the Bible quickly comes to appreciate the importance of this precious substance in places that might receive an annual inch or two of rain—or none. Without water, living creatures simply cannot survive, but this is especially true in a land of few shade trees and generally cloudless skies, conditions that quicken the loss of what little water might be available.

In the First Reading, this daily, concrete reality confronts the Hebrews fleeing Egypt. Burning thirst leads them to protest against Moses, and indirectly against God, early in their long desert journey. Desperate for water, they seem to prefer the slavery of Egypt to their current plight. In the previous chapter, the people grumbled about lack of food, which the Lord soon provided in the form of quail and manna. Now they seem to have quickly forgotten God's faithful care, complaining anew, so that Moses in turn complains to God about the people he is called to lead.

Again the Lord responds with the faithful love, soon to be made explicit in the Covenant with Israel. God commands Moses to strike the rock of Mount Horeb (an alternate name for Sinai), assuring him that water will gush forth to satisfy the people's thirst. It is abundantly clear that God, not Moses, is the source of life-saving water, for the Lord is "standing there in front of [him] on the rock in Horeb." The life-giving Word of the Lord that created all things will surely continue to give life to those who will soon be formed into the

For meditation and context:

TO KEEP IN MIND

Proclamation cannot be effective unless it is expressive. As you prepare your proclamation, make choices about emotions. Some choices are already evident in the text.

An exhortatory reading. Resist the temptation to rush to the final passage about Christ's death. Emphasize the progression Paul sets up in the first part: faith leads to peace which leads to grace which leads to hope which leads to love. Only then does the final point make sense.

You're telling the community what they already have through their faith.

Good news!

Linger over this phrase describing God's overflowing love!

"Ungodly" is a surprise; don't swallow it.

This is an aside; pick up the pace a bit.

Don't stress "proves," as if God's love needs proof; here, it simply means "shows."

God's gift of love is free, for sinner and saint alike. This is indeed good news.

RESPONSORIAL PSALM   Psalm 95:1–2, 6–7, 8–9 (8)

R. If today you hear his voice, harden not your hearts.

Come, let us sing joyfully to the LORD;
    let us acclaim the Rock of our salvation.
Let us come into his presence with
        thanksgiving;
    let us joyfully sing psalms to him.

Come, let us bow down in worship;
    let us kneel before the LORD who made us.
For he is our God,
    and we are the people he shepherds,
        the flock he guides.

Oh, that today you would hear his voice:
    "Harden not your hearts as at Meribah,
        as in the day of Massah in the desert,
where your fathers tempted me;
    they tested me though they had seen
        my works."

READING II   Romans 5:1–2, 5–8

A reading from the Letter of Saint Paul to the Romans

Brothers and sisters:
Since we have been justified by **faith**,
    we have **peace** with God through our Lord Jesus **Christ**,
    through whom we have gained **access** by faith
    to this **grace** in which we stand,
    and we boast in **hope** of the **glory** of God.

And hope does not **disappoint**,
    because the love of God has been **poured** out into our hearts
    through the Holy Spirit who has been **given** to us.
For **Christ**, while we were still **helpless**,
    died at the appointed time for the **ungodly**.
Indeed, only with difficulty does one die for a **just** person,
    though perhaps for a **good** person one might even find courage
        to die.
But God proves his **love** for us
    in that while we were **still** sinners Christ died for us.

---

covenant people of God (Genesis 1:3–24; Exodus 19:3–8).

The end of today's reading underscores that God chooses Israel out of freely-given divine love, not because of the people's merit. The names Massah and Meribah mean "the place of testing" and "the place of quarreling." As her journey with the Lord continues through the centuries, Israel will continue to try God's patience and argue against God's plan. But the Lord will never cease to offer life-giving waters of grace to his people.

READING II In his Letter to the Romans, written near the end of Paul's life, the Apostle presents his most developed thought on the meaning and effects of the Good News of Jesus Christ. He had been a member of the Pharisee party of Judaism, zealously following the Law of Moses as the supreme mode of pleasing God and finding salvation. But his encounter with the Risen Christ transformed Saul, persecutor of Christians, into Paul, Apostle to the Gentiles (Acts 26:1–23, Galatians 1:11–22). The heart of the Gospel he proclaimed was the Good News that

through Christ, God offers transformed life as a free, unearned gift to all.

One is justified, placed in right relationship with God and with all things, by divine grace, not because of any human accomplishment, however righteous. (The Greek word *charis,* used often by Paul, literally means "gift" but is translated in most English Bibles as "grace.") For Paul, faith involves accepting and responding to God's gift precisely as gift, surrendering all thought of justifying oneself by human effort: one is "not justified by works of the

What makes a narrative interesting is the "character arc"—how a character changes significantly over the course of the story. The woman has a great character arc: She grows from skeptic to inquirer to disciple. Make strong choices about the woman's feelings so that the change is evident.

Samaria = suh-MAYR-ee-uh

Sychar = Sī-kahr

Let some tiredness come through in your voice.

Slight pause to let the scene settle.

How would Jesus sound? Remember his tiredness.

Drop your voice slightly on this aside.

Samaritan = suh-MAYR-uh-tuhn

She is unafraid to challenge Jesus.

Drop your voice again; another aside.

Jesus is not chastising the woman. How could she have known? He appreciates the opportunity to teach. (Later, he says that this ministry nourishes him.)

Let her sarcasm come through.

cistern = SIS-tern

That this well was built by Jacob is a source of pride for the town.

Use care with this sentence's construction: Water taken in becomes a self-sustaining source of water.

GOSPEL John 4:5–42

A reading from the holy Gospel according to John

[Jesus came to a town of **Samaria** called Sychar,
  near the plot of land that **Jacob** had given to his son Joseph.
Jacob's **well** was there.
Jesus, **tired** from his journey, sat down there at the **well**.
It was about **noon**.

A **woman** of Samaria came to draw **water**.
Jesus said to her,
  "Give me a **drink**."
His disciples had gone into the town to buy food.
The Samaritan woman said to him,
  "How can **you**, a **Jew**, ask me, a Samaritan **woman**, for a **drink**?"
—For Jews use nothing in common with Samaritans.—
Jesus answered and said to her,
  "If you **knew** the gift of God
  and **who** is saying to you, 'Give me a drink,'
  you would have asked **him**
  and he would have given you **living** water."
The woman said to him,
  "Sir, you do not even have a **bucket** and the cistern is **deep**;
  where then can you **get** this living water?
Are you **greater** than our father **Jacob**,
  who **gave** us this cistern and drank from it **himself**
  with his children and his flocks?"
Jesus answered and said to her,
  "Everyone who drinks **this** water will be **thirsty** again;
  but whoever drinks the water **I** shall give will **never** thirst;
  the water I shall give will become in him
  a **spring** of water **welling** up to eternal **life**."

law but through faith in Jesus Christ" (Galatians 2:16).

In today's Second Reading, Paul again emphasizes this central conviction. Faith in Christ offers "hope of the glory of God." What is the "glory of God"? "Glory" indicates a manifestation of God's essential character. The true character of God as gracious love poured out for the good of all has been revealed in the Death and Resurrection of Christ. Not only did Christ give up his life so that human beings could be raised to new life with him in the Spirit; he died for sinful humankind, who had in no

way earned or deserved such a gift. For Paul, this gift of unmerited, transforming love is the self-revealing "glory" of God and the Good News of Jesus Christ.

GOSPEL Today's Gospel account abounds with themes and literary techniques common in the fourth Gospel. From beginning to end, this evangelist proclaims that Jesus comes to bring fullness of life, life in God (Greek zóé, distinct from bíos, physical life) (John 1:3, 20:31). John includes several accounts in which a person who engages with Jesus

experiences growing insight into his identity, expressed in various titles. When understanding opens into believing in Jesus, the person is thereby impelled to bring others to encounter him. John often uses terms with layers of meaning, and frequently Jesus must broaden the understanding of someone who takes his words at face value.

As the scene opens, it's clear that water as a biblical symbol of life will be central (see Reading I), because Jesus sits down next to a well. His request for a drink breaches social and religious custom, since

Is the woman sincere, or still a little sarcastic? Perhaps she's intrigued by this man and starting to wonder who he might be. Express the choice in your delivery.

Give the woman a moment before introducing her response.

What is the woman feeling? Shame? Anger? Sadness?

Jesus states the truth simply.

"Good for you for telling the truth!"

She acknowledges Jesus as a prophet, but immediately challenges him again.

Soon, distinctions like Jew and Samaritan will be meaningless.

The woman said to him,
  "Sir, **give** me this water, so that I may not be **thirsty**
  or have to **keep** coming here to draw water."]

Jesus said to her,
  "**Go** call your **husband** and come back."
The woman answered and said to him,
  "I do not **have** a husband."
Jesus answered her,
  "You are **right** in saying, 'I do not have a husband.'
For you have had **five** husbands,
  and the one you have now is **not** your husband.
What you have said is **true**."
The woman said to him,
  "Sir, [I can see that you are a **prophet**.
Our ancestors worshiped on this **mountain**;
  but you people say that the place to worship is in **Jerusalem**."
Jesus said to her,
  "Believe me, woman, the **hour** is coming
  when you will worship the Father
  neither on this **mountain** nor in **Jerusalem**.
You people worship what you do **not** understand;
  we worship what we **understand**,
  because **salvation** is from the **Jews**.
But the **hour** is coming, and is now **here**,
  when **true** worshipers will worship the Father in **Spirit**
    and **truth**;
  and indeed the Father **seeks** such people to worship him.
God is **Spirit**, and those who **worship** him
  must worship in **Spirit** and **truth**." »

Jews and Samaritans generally took pains to avoid each other. In her brusque reply, the woman of Samaria addresses Jesus as "a Jew," perhaps with a curl of her lip. His response includes two phrases, "gift of God" and "living water," used in Judaism to refer to the Torah; John thus suggests that Jesus himself will be the new Torah of the new order dawning in his person.

Addressing Jesus more respectfully, using the title "Sir," the woman assumes a literal meaning of "living water,"—flowing as opposed to stagnant water. But Jesus refers to water that gives not only biological life,

but fullness of life in God. Some translations render the woman's second or third use of the title *kýrios* as "Lord" (the Greek word can signify either meaning), indicating her expanding understanding of the one conversing with her. Her growing insight next leads her to consider Jesus a prophet, one who speaks for God. But she is still unaware that Jesus not only speaks the Word of God, he *is* God's self-revealing Word "made flesh" (John 1:1, 14).

The woman then speaks of the Temple in Jerusalem and Samaria's rival temple, one of the contentious issues dividing two

related peoples. But Jesus suggests a claim that John later makes explicit: soon God's presence will not be confined to any physical location, because God is present in the person of Jesus. In the age of salvation, people will worship in "Spirit and truth"; "truth" points to Jesus himself, and when his work is accomplished, he will send the Spirit, "living water" (John 7:37–39). The woman's reference to a coming Messiah indicates a belief that Jews and Samaritans shared, hope for a long-anticipated deliverer, an Anointed One whom Samaritans called the "restorer."

Notice that Jesus has said nothing about the Messiah. Why does the woman bring up the subject? Does she, a Samaritan woman, suspect Jesus might be the Christ? Could she be hoping he will confirm her suspicion? Let that come through in your proclamation. A long pause here; the woman is awed into silence.

Emphasize "woman" as the source of the disciples' amazement.
The disciples are so confused by Jesus' actions they don't know what to say.
Proclaim her actions with excitement; she leaves in such haste she abandons her jar.

Speak this directly to your assembly; encourage them with the woman's amazement.
The disciples are really concerned about Jesus (perhaps because of his seemingly strange behavior?).
His ministry—such as this conversation with the woman—sustains him.

Drop your volume as if the disciples are whispering to each other.

Jesus tries to refocus the disciples on ministering to the community.

Speak these lines with some urgency.

The woman said to him,
    "I know that the **Messiah** is coming, the one called the
        Christ;
    when he **comes**, he will tell us **everything**."
Jesus said to her,
    "**I** am **he**, the one **speaking** with you."]

At that moment his disciples **returned**,
    and were **amazed** that he was talking with a **woman**,
    but still no one said, "What are you **looking** for?"
    or "Why are you **talking** with her?"
The woman **left** her water jar
    and went into the town and said to the people,
    "Come **see** a man who told me everything I have done.
Could he possibly be the **Christ**?"
They went out of the town and **came** to him.
Meanwhile, the disciples **urged** him, "Rabbi, **eat**."
But he said to them,
    "I have **food** to eat of which you do not **know**."
So the disciples said to one another,
    "Could **someone** have brought him something to eat?"
Jesus said to them,
    "My **food** is to do the **will** of the one who sent me
    and to **finish** his work.
Do you not say, 'In four months the **harvest** will be here'?
I tell you, look up and see the fields **ripe** for the harvest.
The reaper is **already** receiving payment
    and gathering crops for eternal **life**,
    so that the **sower** and **reaper** can **rejoice** together.
For here the saying is verified that 'One **sows** and another **reaps**.'

Jesus confirms that he is indeed the Messiah, making the only direct affirmation of this identity in the entire fourth Gospel to the woman of Samaria. Through the words of a woman despised by Jews, John has proclaimed Jesus to be Jew, sir, Lord, prophet, living Temple of God, truth, source of living water, and Messiah. In his manner of expressing Messiah, John also could be suggesting the fullness of Jesus' identity with the Greek phrase *egó eimi*, which can simply mean "I am [the one]." However, the Greek Old Testament used these words to translate the revealed name of God, "I AM."

Perhaps the evangelist also suggests the uniqueness of Jesus, proclaimed at the beginning of the Fourth Gospel: God speaking the fullness of divine identity and character in the humanity of Jesus.

As the disciples return to the scene, the woman, who has allowed herself to truly encounter Jesus, accepts her mission, bringing others to the Word made flesh. At the very least, she suggests to the towns-people that he may be the expected Messiah. The disciples, for their part, return to the mundane, addressing Jesus simply as "Rabbi" and inquiring about his need for

physical food. Jesus turns the conversation to harvest and reaping, common symbols for the expected final age of salvation. As he attempts to refocus the disciples on his true task, "to do the will of the one who sent me," the woman comes to understand herself as one sent by virtue of her expanded insight into Jesus. As he is sent by God, anyone who truly engages with Jesus is sent to bring others to their own encounter with him.

At first, the woman's word of witness to Jesus brings some of her townspeople to begin to believe. Throughout his account,

Pause

Speak the line with the woman's excitement.

Here is the point of the whole story. Maintain eye contact with the community and speak slowly and deliberately.

I sent you to reap what you have not **worked** for;
  others have done the work,
  and you are sharing the **fruits** of their work."

[Many of the **Samaritans** of that town began to **believe** in him]
  because of the word of the **woman** who testified,
  "He told me everything I have done."
[When the Samaritans **came** to him,
  they invited him to **stay** with them;
  and he stayed there two days.
Many **more** began to believe in him because of his **word**,
  and they said to the woman,
  "We no longer believe because of **your** word;
  for we have heard for **ourselves**,
  and we know that this is **truly** the savior of the world."]

[Shorter: John 4:5–15, 19b–26, 39a, 40–42 (see brackets)]

TO KEEP IN MIND
Use inflection (the high or low pitch of your voice) to convey attitude and feeling. High pitch expresses intensity and excitement; low pitch expresses sadness, contrition, or solemnity.

John frequently indicates that faith in Jesus grows in levels of commitment. The initial stage of faith consists in openness to truly experience Jesus, and the woman's neighbors already demonstrate such nascent belief. John uses the Greek word for "believe" nearly one hundred times, always as a verb. For this evangelist, faith must be active, a mutual indwelling in Jesus born of knowledge, insight, and ultimately love, that takes shape in active discipleship of witness. John uses the Greek word *menó*, "to stay, remain, abide," to indicate this loving union of the believer and Jesus. It is this term he uses for the townspeople's invitation to Jesus "to stay" with them. As a result, many people began to "believe in" Jesus "because of [his] word," John's phrase for deeper faith—believing born of personal relationship.

At this point, the Samaritan woman has fulfilled her mission of leading others to encounter Jesus, and they attest that they now believe in him no longer based on her witness, but on their own experience. Though Jews do not consider them part of God's covenant people, these Samaritans perceive God's unlimited desire to save all people through Jesus, and so they proclaim him "Savior of the world." M.F.

FOURTH SUNDAY OF LENT

LECTIONARY #31

A narrative which teaches us something about "seeing." God, Samuel, and Jesse see a person's worthiness to be "anointed" very differently. Let their unique perspectives come through in your proclamation.

Samuel = SAM-yoo-uhl

We jump right into the action. God is decisive.

Jesse = JES-ee

Why doesn't God simply tell Samuel which son is chosen? Does God want Samuel to learn something too?
Eliab = ee-Lī-uhb

Samuel is confident that he knows what God wants.

The moral of this story. Speak these lines slowly and deliberately.

Now Samuel understands.

Samuel has an idea!

Jesse is a bit incredulous. "David couldn't possibly be the one!"

READING I 1 Samuel 16:1b, 6–7, 10–13a

A reading from the first Book of Samuel

The LORD said to **Samuel**:
  "Fill your horn with **oil**, and be on your **way**.
I am sending you to **Jesse** of **Bethlehem**,
  for I have chosen my **king** from among his sons."

As Jesse and his sons came to the **sacrifice**,
  Samuel looked at **Eliab** and thought,
  "**Surely** the LORD's anointed is **here** before him."
But the LORD said to Samuel:
  "Do not judge from his **appearance** or from his lofty **stature**,
  because I have **rejected** him.
Not as **man** sees does **God** see,
  because man sees the **appearance**
  but the LORD looks into the **heart**."
In the same way Jesse presented **seven** sons before Samuel,
  but Samuel said to Jesse,
  "The LORD has not chosen any one of these."
Then Samuel asked Jesse,
  "Are these **all** the sons you have?"
Jesse replied,
  "There is still the **youngest**, who is tending the sheep."
Samuel said to Jesse,
  "**Send** for him;
  we will not begin the sacrificial banquet until he **arrives** here."

READING I In describing the Lord's choice of David as King of Israel, today's First Reading raises up a familiar theme of the Scriptures: God neither judges nor acts according to human standards. In the preceding chapter, the Lord rejected Saul, the first king to rule a united Israelite kingdom, because of his disobedience. Samuel, the prophet who had anointed him as ruler according to God's Word, mourned the divine judgment on Saul.

As today's First Reading opens, God calls the prophet to cease grieving over Saul and directs him to find the one chosen to succeed the deposed king. As commanded, Samuel seeks out Jesse of Bethlehem, for God has selected one of his seven sons as the next king of Israel. Beginning with his eldest, Jesse presents six sons to the prophet, who determines that God has chosen none of them. Divine standards take no note of appearance or status, but seek to test the heart. In biblical thought, the heart represents the core of a human being, the place where one meets God, the source of decision and action. Since Israel understood the Lord as her true sovereign, an ideal human king was expected to serve as God's representative.

Having determined that God has chosen none of Jesse's elder sons to rule Israel, the prophet inquires if there are any others. Apparently judging that the youngest, still a shepherd youth, could not possibly be God's choice, Jesse has not even presented him to the prophet. Samuel, however, underscores that God's judgment does not employ human standards. As soon as Jesse brings forth the young shepherd, Samuel declares him the Lord's elect, immediately anointing him king. At

Ruddy means having a healthy, reddish complexion.

Think of the most beautiful person you know, and see them before you as you describe David.

There's an eagerness in God's command.

You can use the word "rushed" to sound a bit like wind.

Jesse sent and had the young man **brought** to them.
He was **ruddy**, a youth **handsome** to behold
    and making a **splendid** appearance.
The Lord said,
    "There—**anoint** him, for **this** is the one!"
Then Samuel, with the horn of **oil** in hand,
    anointed David in the presence of his brothers;
    and from that day on, the **spirit** of the Lord **rushed**
        upon David.

For meditation and context:

TO KEEP IN MIND

Exhortatory texts make an urgent appeal to listeners. They may encourage, warn, or challenge, and often include a call to action. You must convey the urgency and passion behind the words.

RESPONSORIAL PSALM   Psalm 23:1–3a, 3b–4, 5, 6 (1)

R. The Lord is my shepherd; there is nothing I shall want.

The Lord is my shepherd; I shall not want.
    In verdant pastures he gives me repose;
beside restful waters he leads me;
    he refreshes my soul.

He guides me in right paths
    for his name's sake.
Even though I walk in the dark valley
    I fear no evil; for you are at my side
with your rod and your staff
    that give me courage.

You spread the table before me
    in the sight of my foes;
you anoint my head with oil;
    my cup overflows.

Only goodness and kindness follow me
    all the days of my life;
and I shall dwell in the house of the Lord
    for years to come.

An exhortatory reading, encouraging us to live as "children of light." Have strong opinions about the value of light versus dark, and let your attitude toward each come through as you proclaim.

Ephesians = ee-FEE-shuhnz

Good news! Smile with your voice, eyes, and face.

READING II   Ephesians 5:8–14

A reading from the Letter of Saint Paul to the Ephesians

Brothers and sisters:
You were once **darkness**,
    but now you are **light** in the Lord.
Live as children of light,
    for light produces every kind of **goodness**
        and **righteousness** and **truth**.
Try to learn what is **pleasing** to the Lord. »

---

the same moment, David receives the powerful divine presence, the Spirit of God, thus emphasizing another common biblical motif: anyone given a task by God also receives continuing divine power to carry it out.

READING II   As a whole, the Letter to the Ephesians focuses on the universal Church and its unity in Christ. For various reasons, many suggest that rather than a personal letter to a local community, this work is a circular letter written by a later follower of Paul, intended for the

entire Church. (Some early manuscripts lack the address to the church "in Ephesus.") The great theme of the letter is the unity of Christians: the Church, including Jews and non-Jews alike, is one body; all are members of Christ through Baptism, living in the one Spirit. The writer urges all members of the Church to live in daily awareness of their unity with Christ and one another, guided by divine Spirit.

Like several other New Testament writers, the author of Ephesians compares life with or without Christ to living in darkness or in the light. Unlike many people

today, ancient peoples were very aware that without adequate light, one can see little or nothing. For those dependent upon daylight or the limited light of oil lamps or candles, the symbolism was powerful. The newly baptized received a lighted candle, reminding them of their commitment to see all things in the light of Christ. Thus the author urges all the baptized to be united in rejecting all that is not of Christ and so belongs to darkness. Instead, those who are one with Christ and his Body on earth, the Church, must live as those who walk in the light of the Risen One. The brief phrase

Be dismissive of these "fruitless" works.

Any part of our lives we try to keep secret needs to be healed in the light.

Take your time with this final quote, and let the community see your joy in this promise.

Take no part in the fruitless works of **darkness**;
　rather **expose** them, for it is shameful even to mention
　the things done by them in **secret**;
　but everything exposed by the light becomes **visible**,
　for everything that becomes visible is **light**.
Therefore, it says:
　"**Awake**, O sleeper,
　and **arise** from the dead,
　and Christ will give you **light**."

GOSPEL   John 9:1–41

A reading from the holy Gospel according to John

A narrative with many characters, much action, and multiple scene changes. Vary your pace, inflection, and volume in this long reading. Know each character's intention and emotion so you can keep your assembly engaged.
Don't swallow "blind from birth."

#1

[As Jesus passed by he saw a man **blind** from birth.]
His disciples asked him,
　"Rabbi, who **sinned**, this man or his parents,
　that he was born **blind**?"
Jesus answered,
　"Neither **he nor** his parents sinned;
　it is so that the works of God might be made **visible**
　　through him.
We have to do the works of the one who sent me while it is **day**.
Night is coming when no one can work.
While I am in the world, I am the **light** of the world."
When he had said this, [he **spat** on the ground
　and made **clay** with the **saliva**,
　and **smeared** the clay on his eyes, and said to him,
　"Go **wash** in the Pool of Siloam"—which means Sent—.
So he went and washed, and came back able to **see**.

His neighbors and those who had seen him earlier
　　as a **beggar** said,
"Isn't this the one who used to sit and **beg**?"

Rabbi = RAB-ī

This traditional teaching—that blindness is punishment for sin—bothers the disciples.

Following Jesus enables one to see rightly.
Take your time describing Jesus' action, and don't be afraid of its earthiness. Use the words "spat" and "smeared" to give it energy.
saliva = suh-LĪ-vuh

#2

Siloam = sih-LOH-uhm
Drop your voice slightly on the parenthetical phrase.
Bring the man's amazement to this line.

Give this exchange a lot of energy; the dissention caused by Jesus' healing begins here. Make sure the different voices in these few lines sound distinct.

"Awake, O sleeper . . . and Christ will give you light" probably derives from an early hymn, possibly one used in baptismal liturgy. Today, the Church addresses all the baptized of this age, still issuing a call to the one Body of Christ to live daily in his new life and light.

GOSPEL Completed near the end of the first century, John's Gospel account reflects religious tensions of that time. The Jewish people were struggling to determine the parameters of authentic Judaism in the midst of various approaches to interpreting the Law and the Prophets. To some Jews, those who proclaimed Jesus as the ultimate fulfillment of Judaism were deluded or heretical. John's repeated negative reference to "the Jews" does not reject the entire Jewish people, but points to those of his time who strongly opposed or rejected belief in Jesus. Among those Jews who rejected Christian faith were the Pharisees, portrayed in a negative light in today's reading.

In his narrative, John includes several incidents in which a person who engages with Jesus experiences growing insight into his identity, expressed in various titles. When initial openness opens into believing in Jesus, the person is thereby impelled to bring others to encounter him. The fourth evangelist strongly emphasizes believing in Jesus; he uses the word ninety-eight times, always as a verb. John also shows a penchant for terms with layers of meaning, and frequently Jesus must broaden the understanding of someone who takes his words at face value.

In the preceding chapter, "the Jews" have intensified their opposition to Jesus and reject several of his claims, including

Some said, "It **is**,"
    but others said, "No, he just **looks** like him."
He said, "I **am**."]
So they said to him, "**How** were your eyes opened?"
He replied,
    "The man called **Jesus** made clay and **anointed** my eyes
    and told me, 'Go to Siloam and **wash**.'
So I went there and washed and was able to **see**."
And they said to him, "Where **is** he?"
He said, "I don't **know**."

#3

[They brought the one who was once blind to the **Pharisees**.
Now Jesus had made clay and opened his eyes on a **sabbath**.
So then the Pharisees **also** asked him how he was able to see.
He said to them,
    "He put **clay** on my eyes, and I **washed**, and now I can **see**."
So some of the Pharisees said,
    "This man is **not** from God,
    because he does not keep the **sabbath**."
But others said,
    "How can a **sinful** man do such signs?"
And there was a **division** among them.
So they said to the blind man **again**,
    "What do **you** have to say about him,
    since he opened your eyes?"
He said, "He is a **prophet**."]

#4

Now the Jews did not **believe**   *Who is Blind?*
    that he had been blind and gained his sight
    until they summoned the **parents** of the one who had gained
        his sight.
They asked them,
    "Is this your son, who you **say** was born blind?
How does he now **see**?"
His parents answered and said,
    "We **know** that this is our son and that he was born **blind**. ❯❯

Pick up the pace and let the man's natural excitement at being healed come through in his words.

The man's responses are simple and honest.

Pause before this scene shift.

Don't swallow "sabbath."

Keep the energy up as the arguing continues, and make sure it sounds like arguing.

Pause here to let his statement settle.

Proclaim these lines with the suspicion of the Pharisees.

Imagine the fright of his parents being brought before the Pharisees and risking expulsion. The stakes are high! Proclaim their lines with anxiety and a desire to get this over with quickly!

that he is the light of the world (John 8:12). In today's Gospel, John employs several approaches outlined above to illustrate both increasing refusal to actually experience Jesus and a flowering of faith in those truly open to encounter him. The evangelist contrasts these two attitudes and their results—in the Pharisees and the blind man: those who refuse the Light of the World sink more deeply into darkness, while the blind man, illumined by Christ, comes to see clearly—and believes.

John develops the contrasting approaches to Jesus in three stages, inter-weaving the blind man's expanding insight and deepening faith (the writer often uses "seeing" as a near equivalent of "believing"). As the narrative begins, Jesus repeats the claim that he is the Light of the World, and sets aside the common Jewish belief that sin accounts for lack of bodily wholeness. After covering the man's eyes with clay, Jesus instructs him to "wash in the pool of Siloam." Noting the meaning of "Siloam," John invokes a favored reference to Jesus: the one sent from God to reveal God. The man, open to what his encounter with Jesus might reveal, attests to the result of obeying him; he is "able to see." Because Jesus made a clay paste on the Sabbath, the Pharisees conclude that he has broken the Law forbidding work on this day, proving that Jesus is "a sinner." They refuse to believe both the man's testimony and his actual experience.

The Pharisees launch a second interrogation; they repeat their interpretation of the Law, insisting that as a sinner, Jesus could not have been God's instrument of healing. In contrast to their repeated "We know," the man states that he does "not know" if Jesus is a sinner, and returns to his

Proclaim these lines with the same anxiety as the parents' response, as if they were speaking their thoughts.

We do **not** know how he sees now,
    nor do we know **who** opened his eyes.
Ask **him**, he is of age;
    he can speak for **himself**."
His parents said this because they were **afraid** of the Jews,
    for the Jews had already agreed
    that if anyone **acknowledged** him as the **Christ**,
    he would be **expelled** from the synagogue.
For this reason his parents said,
    "He is of **age**; question **him**."

#5

So a **second** time they called the man who had been blind
    and said to him, "Give God the praise!

Notice the play on who "knows" what. The Pharisees are sure about their judgments.

We **know** that this man is a sinner."
He replied,
    "If he is a sinner, **I** do not know.

The man refuses to conjecture about another person's heart.

One thing I **do** know is that I was **blind** and now I **see**."
So they said to him,

Be insistent! This doesn't make any sense to the Pharisees. It must be a trick!

    "**What** did he do to you?
    How did he open your eyes?"
He answered them,
    "I told you **already** and you did not listen.
Why do you want to hear it **again**?
Do **you** want to become his disciples, **too**?"

With some sarcasm.
The man has made fun of them and now the Pharisees are really angry!

They **ridiculed** him and said,
    "**You** are that man's disciple;
    we are disciples of **Moses**!

Again, note the play on who thinks they know and who really knows.

We know that God spoke to **Moses**,
    but we do not know where this one is from."
The man answered and said to them,

To the man it's perfectly clear where Jesus is from, and he can't understand the Pharisees' inability to see.

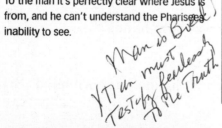

    "This is what is so **amazing**,
    that you do not know where he is from, yet he **opened** my **eyes**.
We know that God does not listen to **sinners**,
    but if one is **devout** and does his **will**, he **listens** to him.
It is **unheard** of that anyone **ever** opened the eyes of a person
    born **blind**.

experience of healing by Jesus. Yet again the Pharisees demand a description of what happened, and the man protests their failure to listen. (Jesus' Jewish hearers would certainly note this allusion to the primary requirement of a true Israelite, to listen to God's Word; see Deuteronomy 6:4.) The man wonders aloud if the Pharisees want to hear of his encounter with Jesus again so that they also might become disciples. They scoff at him, again asserting what they are certain they "know": both Jesus and the man who now "sees" him are rejected as sinners. John notes that the

Pharisees ejected the man from the Temple. This detail likely reflects the author's situation, since there is some evidence that Jews who proclaimed faith in Jesus were, at least in some instances, expelled from Temple worship.

Jesus now returns, and the third scene portrays the healed man's burgeoning insight and faith. Jesus asks the now-seeing man if he believes in the Son of Man, a messianic figure in some Jewish literature. With an outburst of complete openness to what Jesus might reveal, the man asks "Who is he, sir, that I may believe in him?"

Here John uses the Greek word *kýrios*, which can mean both "Sir" and "Lord" as a divine title. Jesus' response suggests that the second interpretation is most apt. John's Greek has Jesus respond to the man's question with "The one speaking with you is he." The author uses the same verb as in Jesus' well-known "I AM" statements; while Greek *egō eimi* could simply mean "I am he," the Greek Old Testament used it to translate the revealed name of God, I AM.

The man now truly sees who stands before him; coming to full faith, he ad-

If this man were **not** from God,
he would not be able to do **anything**."
[They answered and said to him,
"**You** were born totally in **sin**,
and are you trying to teach **us**?"
Then they **threw** him out.

When Jesus heard that they had thrown him out,
he found him and said, "Do you **believe** in the Son of Man?"
He answered and said,
"Who **is** he, sir, that I may believe in him?"
Jesus said to him,
"You have **seen** him,
and the one speaking with you is **he**."
He said,
"I **do** believe, Lord," and he worshiped him.]
Then Jesus said,
"I came into this world for judgment,
so that those who do **not** see **might** see,
and those who **do** see might become **blind**."

Some of the Pharisees who were with him heard this
and said to him, "Surely **we** are not also blind, **are** we?"
Jesus said to them,
"If you *were open to new ideas* **were** blind, you would have no **sin**;
but now you are saying, 'We **see**,' so your sin **remains**."
Obstinate in their incorrect Belief
[Shorter: John 9:1, 6–9, 13–17, 34–38 (see brackets)]

This is too much! This is the high point of the Pharisees' anger.

Describe this action with their outrage.   *# 6*

Expelled, he is again an outcast. Jesus comes to invite him into the community of the Reign of God.

Drop your volume a bit as if this were an intimate conversation between the two.

Not seeing rightly is not a sin if you acknowledge that your sight is imperfect. But when you think your way of seeing is the only right way, then your sin remains.

#7

> **TO KEEP IN MIND**
> In a narrative, find an emotion or point of view for each character, keeping in mind that these might change during the reading.

---

dresses Jesus as Lord (*kýrios*), bowing down in worship. The verb used here appears often in the Old Testament to describe bending low in the divine presence. The man born blind has progressed from seeing "the man called Jesus" to full insight into him as one in whom God is fully present, the one sent to reveal God in the flesh. At Jesus' statement of purpose, the Pharisees note his implication of judgment. They protest that he cannot possibly be suggesting that they, learned in the Law and meticulous in its observance, are blind!

Jesus answers with multilayered meaning characteristic of John. If the Pharisees were, like the man, born without sight, they would be free of sin. But they obstinately refuse to allow an encounter with Jesus to reveal anything of his person and work, and so they "remain" in sin. Here John uses the verb *menó,* which he usually employs to describe his indwelling union with those who come to faith born of intimate relationship with him. But by their chosen blindness, the Pharisees remain one with sin. M.F.

FIFTH SUNDAY OF LENT

An exhortatory reading, which should be proclaimed with great intensity and love. God's promise of restoration is good news.

Ezekiel = ee-ZEE-kee-uhl

Fill these lines (and especially the word "O") with God's love for the people: "I can't wait to bring you life!"

This shouldn't sound like, "Then you'll be sorry!" Rather, "Then you'll know how much I love you!"

The second time this phrase appears; look directly at the assembly as you express God's love and longing for his people.

These lines restate the same ideas as above; slow down to let them sink in more deeply.

What does God sound like as he makes these promises?

Pause.

Take significant pauses at each comma; slow down on "I will do it," and proclaim with steadfast assurance.

For meditation and context:

LECTIONARY #34

READING I   Ezekiel 37:12–14

A reading from the Book of the Prophet Ezekiel

Thus says the Lord God:
   O my people, I will **open** your graves
   and have you **rise** from them,
   and bring you **back** to the land of **Israel**.
Then you shall **know** that I am the **Lord**,
   when I **open** your graves and have you **rise** from them,
   O my **people**!
I will put my **spirit** in you that you may **live**,
   and I will settle you upon your **land**;
   thus you shall **know** that I am the Lord.
I have **promised**, and I will **do** it, says the Lord.

RESPONSORIAL PSALM   Psalm 130:1–2, 3–4, 5–6, 7–8 (7)

R. With the Lord there is mercy and fullness of redemption.

Out of the depths I cry to you, O Lord;
   Lord, hear my voice!
Let your ears be attentive
   to my voice in supplication.

If you, O Lord, mark iniquities,
   Lord, who can stand?
But with you is forgiveness,
   that you may be revered.

I trust in the Lord;
   my soul trusts in his word.
More than sentinels wait for the dawn,
   let Israel wait for the Lord.

For with the Lord is kindness
   and with him is plenteous redemption;
and he will redeem Israel
   from all their iniquities.

READING I   Ezekiel was a priest of the Jerusalem Temple who also served as prophet among the earliest Judean captives taken to Babylon. By the time of today's prophecy, the kingdom was near its end, for the capital city of Jerusalem already lay in ruins. In the land of exile, the prophet attempts to awaken the captive people to the true causes of their catastrophe, above all their repeated refusal to hear and obey God's teaching through the Law and a long succession of prophets. In the chapter preceding this reading, God announced through Ezekiel

that in the future, the exiles will return to their land. That divine restoration will come about, however, not for their sake, but so that other nations will realize that the Lord is, indeed, sovereign over all things. The covenant people repeatedly failed to make God known to other peoples and nations by their worship and way of life; but in days to come, the Lord's own saving act will reveal his true character to all.

Today's passage is part of Ezekiel's vision of scattered dry bones reconnected and enlivened by divine power, the "spirit" of God. Twice the captives are addressed

as "my people," a two-edged sword reminding them of both their failure to act as God's covenant people and the Lord's promise to re-create them as such. Only the power that first brought all creation into being can bring about this new creation: the Spirit of God. In the Book of Genesis, the Hebrew word *rūah,* which can mean wind, breath, or spirit, describes the creation of all things by divine power (Genesis 1:1–2). Translated "spirit" in today's reading, *rūah* signifies the powerful life-giving presence of God at work, bringing about divine purposes. Even the people's

Make sure you understand Paul's reasoning in this didactic reading; keep separate thoughts separate by pausing at the periods. Note the contrast Paul sets up between flesh/body and spirit, between death and life.

Those still bound to sin are "in the flesh." Remind your assembly that they are not in the flesh.

This actually means "since Christ is in you."

Use a dismissive tone in this parenthetical phrase: Don't worry about the sinful body.

Keep the pace up from here to the end, pausing briefly at commas, so as not to lose the train of thought.
The same spirit brings the same Resurrection.

The body is not evil! It will be redeemed as well and come to life.

READING II   Romans 8:8–11

A reading from the Letter of Saint Paul to the Romans

Brothers and sisters:
Those who are in the **flesh** cannot please God.
But **you** are **not** in the flesh;
    on the **contrary**, you are in the **spirit**,
    if only the Spirit of God **dwells** in you.
Whoever does not have the Spirit of **Christ** does not **belong**
      to him.
But if Christ is **in** you,
    although the body is **dead** because of **sin**,
    the spirit is **alive** because of **righteousness**.
If the Spirit of the one who raised Jesus from the dead **dwells**
     in you,
    the One who raised Christ from the dead
    will give **life** to your mortal **bodies** also,
    through his Spirit **dwelling** in you.

repeated sin cannot frustrate the divine plan, which always seeks fullness of life. When God restores the Israelites as a people and returns them to the Promised Land, not only foreign nations but the Lord's own people will know once again the one, true source of life, the God who fulfills promises.

READING II   Written near the end of Paul's life, the Letter to the Romans contains the Apostle's mature thought, some of which can be difficult to translate adequately. Today's Second Reading includes an aspect of Paul's own

attempt to present his native Hebrew thinking in the Greek language. Translated into English, the results can mislead, and often enough have resulted in misunderstanding. Some schools of first century Greek philosophy viewed a human being as a duality, composed of body and soul. On the other hand, ancient Hebrew thought understood the human person as an indivisible unity, though different words were employed to describe a whole human being from various perspectives.

    To clarify the difference between a person oriented toward Christ and a person

without Christ, Paul employed a variety of Greek terms, including *sarx,* usually rendered in English as "flesh." In English, this word usually signifies only the physical reality of a human being, or even suggests the notion of "sins of the flesh." But for Paul, someone "in the flesh" usually refers to a person who is not turned toward Christ, while someone living "in the spirit" indicates a person enlivened by the indwelling presence or "spirit" of the Risen Christ. (The earliest generations of Christians did not yet draw clear distinctions of "persons" of the Trinity, a dogma

A narrative in which all the emotions are heightened. We know this story, but don't telegraph the ending. Rather, keep the emotions authentic to what is happening at each point in the story. Don't be timid.

Lazarus = LAZ-uh-ruhs

Bethany = BETH-uh-nee

"You remember Mary, don't you?"

Jesus has complete confidence that, whatever happens, God will be glorified. His disciples aren't so sure.

Again, it's Jesus' trust in God that allows him to delay his departure.

Rabbi = RAB-ī

Make sure the disciples' anxiety and concern come through.

Jesus remains calm and confident.

GOSPEL　John 11:1–45

A reading from the holy Gospel according to John

Now a man was **ill**, **Lazarus** from Bethany,
　　the village of **Mary** and her sister **Martha**.
Mary was the one who had **anointed** the Lord with perfumed oil
　　and dried his feet with her **hair**;
　　it was her **brother** Lazarus who was ill.
So [the sisters sent word to Jesus saying,
　　"Master, the one you **love** is ill."
When Jesus heard this he said,
　　"This illness is not to end in **death**,
　　but is for the glory of **God**,
　　that the Son of God may be **glorified** through it."
Now Jesus **loved** Martha and her sister and Lazarus.
So when he heard that he was ill,
　　he **remained** for two days in the place where he was.
Then after this he said to his disciples,
　　"Let us go back to **Judea**."]
The disciples said to him,
　　"Rabbi, the Jews were just trying to **stone** you,
　　and you want to go **back** there?"
Jesus answered,
　　"Are there not twelve hours in a **day**?
If one walks during the **day**, he does not **stumble**,
　　because he sees the **light** of this world.
But if one walks at **night**, he **stumbles**,
　　because the light is not **in** him."
He said this, and then told them,
　　"Our friend Lazarus is **asleep**,
　　but I am going to **awaken** him."

---

that would take several centuries to clearly articulate). These aspects of Paul's thought underlie today's reading.

In the verses preceding this reading, the Apostle notes that "the flesh" orients a person toward death, but "the spirit" directs one toward life—the life of God. Paul then asserts that the baptized are not "in the flesh" but share in the life of Christ's Spirit, by which they belong to Christ (see also Romans 13:11–14). Because the baptized belong to Christ, even physical death cannot deprive them of divine life, which has no end. As he often does, Paul points out that Christians are formed in the pattern of Christ's passage through self-giving death to greater life. As God's Spirit raised the Lord Jesus from death, so also his followers are raised from death through the indwelling divine Spirit.

GOSPEL As with most passages from the fourth Gospel, today's reading must be understood in light of John's unique view of Jesus presented in the prologue, as well as his key terminology and perspectives. The evangelist's prologue serves as a kind of summary-introduction to his proclamation of the Good News, which focuses on the identity of Jesus more than the other three Gospel accounts. At the outset, John proclaims that in the fullness of his humanity, Jesus makes present the "glory" or very character of God, for the divine Word is "made flesh" in the concrete person of Jesus. Those who accept and respond to the divine Word made flesh can share in his filial oneness with God; some, however, will not accept the incarnate Word (John 1:1–18).

Throughout his narrative, John reiterates that Jesus is sent from God precisely

"Good, then we don't have to go to Bethany!"

Didymus = DID-uh-muhs (meaning twin)
Thomas recognizes that Jesus has a connection with God that gives him confidence and peace, even unto death, and he wants it too! But this statement is really for us. Use eye contact to invite listeners into this intimate relationship with God.
Bethany = BETH-uh-nee

What is Martha feeling toward Jesus? Don't deny her a very human response.

She catches herself, and affirms her trust in Jesus and God.

This statement shouldn't sound grandiose. Jesus is having a very intimate conversation with a grieving friend, trying to console her.

So the disciples said to him,
    "Master, if he is asleep, he will be **saved**."
But Jesus was talking about his **death**,
    while **they** thought that he meant ordinary sleep.
So then Jesus said to them clearly,
    "Lazarus has **died**.
And I am glad for you that I was not there,
    that you may **believe**.
Let us **go** to him."
So **Thomas**, called **Didymus**, said to his fellow disciples,
    "Let us **also** go to **die** with him."

[When Jesus arrived, he found that Lazarus
    had already been in the tomb for **four** days.]
Now Bethany was near **Jerusalem**, only about two miles away.
And many of the Jews had come to Martha and Mary
    to comfort them about their brother.
[When Martha heard that **Jesus** was coming,
    she went to **meet** him;
    but **Mary** sat at home.
Martha said to Jesus,
    "Lord, if you had **been** here,
    my brother would **not** have died.
But even **now** I know that whatever you ask of God,
    God will **give** you."
Jesus said to her,
    "Your brother will **rise**."
Martha said to him,
    "I **know** he will rise,
    in the **resurrection** on the last day."
Jesus told her,
    "I am the **resurrection** and the **life**;
    whoever **believes** in me, even if he **dies**, will **live**,
    and everyone who **lives** and **believes** in me will **never** die. »

to reveal God, but that some people open themselves to the revelation, while others remain closed. Those willing to perceive divine reality in the humanity of Jesus can come to believe and so live in his light, while those who close their eyes and ears to it will not believe and so remain in darkness. John presents a series of "signs" or revelatory encounters with Jesus, which people respond to with various levels of believing or rejection. These different responses to Jesus most likely reflect the author's own situation near the end of the first century. Judaism was struggling to

define itself in the face of various interpretations of the Law and the Prophets, and some Jews perceived the Christian movement to be one among other Jewish sects that needed to be corrected or wholly rejected. Proponents of authentic Judaism who viewed the Christian movement as unacceptable inspired John's generic term, "the Jews," a kind of aggregate character representing Jewish opposition to Jesus in John's own context.

The raising of Lazarus is the last of John's signs and one that elicits faith even from many of "the Jews," thus escalating

plans to kill Jesus (John 11:45–53). Though Lazarus and his sisters, Mary and Martha of Bethany, are presented as intimates of Jesus, he does not hurry immediately to his sick friend when he learns that Lazarus is ill. Instead, Jesus announces the true purpose of this sign: "for the glory of God," that is, to provide a tangible manifestation of the true character and action of God, who always wills fullness of life for humankind. The disciples' caution about returning to a place where his life was threatened leads Jesus to contrast those who choose darkness and those who see "the light of

Do **you** believe this?"
She said to him, "Yes, Lord.
I have come to believe that you are the **Christ**, the Son of God,
   the one who is coming into the world."]

There's excitement mixed in her grief.

When she had said this,
   she went and called her sister Mary secretly, saying,
    "The teacher is here and is **asking** for you."
As soon as she heard this,
   she rose **quickly** and **went** to him.

Keep the scene moving; no need to linger on these details.

For Jesus had not yet come into the village,
   but was still where Martha had met him.
So when the Jews who were with her in the house comforting her
   saw Mary get up quickly and go out,
   they **followed** her,
   presuming that she was going to the tomb to **weep** there.

Mary makes the same statement as Martha. Is she expressing her anger, her trust, or a little of both?

When Mary came to where Jesus was and **saw** him,
   she **fell** at his feet and said to him,
   "Lord, if you had **been** here,
   my brother would not have **died**."

The human Jesus is clearly overwhelmed by the very human emotions around him.

When Jesus saw her **weeping** and the Jews who had come with her weeping,
   [he became **perturbed** and deeply **troubled**, and said,
   "**Where** have you laid him?"

perturbed = per-TERBD (agitated and upset)

Let Jesus' grief come through as you describe his emotions.
Articulate this short line carefully and with all of Jesus' sadness. Pause before and after.

They said to him, "Sir, come and **see**."
And Jesus **wept**.
So the Jews said, "See how he **loved** him."
But some of them said,

Is the crowd angry too? Disappointed?

   "Could not the one who **opened** the **eyes** of the blind man
   have **done** something so that this man would not have **died**?"

Note Jesus is still upset.

So Jesus, perturbed **again**, came to the **tomb**.
It was a cave, and a **stone** lay across it.
Jesus said, "**Take away** the stone."

---

this world," Jesus (see John 8:12). In answer to the disciples' misunderstanding, Jesus then clarifies again the purpose of this and every sign: "that you may believe."

To emphasize that Lazarus is certainly dead when Jesus finally arrives, John indicates that the dead man has been entombed for four days. Some rabbis taught that the life force hovered about the dead for up to four days, after which decay would surely set in. Jesus' final sign before his own execution will demonstrate divine power over certain death, revealed and acting in Jesus. Martha, running to meet

Jesus, chides him for his tardiness, but still expresses her belief that God is truly present and at work in him: "whatever you ask . . . God will give you." Further exchange develops John's point that God has completely overcome the evil of death through the Death and Resurrection of Jesus, who is in his person the fullness of life that God wishes to share with humankind. For those who believe in Jesus, he is their "resurrection and life." (John uses Greek *zóé* rather than *bíos*; which refers to physical life, while *zóé* means fullness of life in God.)

Responding to Jesus' question, Martha proclaims and expands upon statements of faith uttered by Peter in Mark and Matthew (Mark 8:29; Matthew 16:16). She recognizes him as Messiah/Christ and Son of God, the one sent to reveal the Father, thus repeating what John has affirmed about Jesus' identity throughout the Fourth Gospel.

At this point the narrative turns to Mary, who expresses her belief that Jesus could have prevented her brother's death, and John once more reminds his hearers of the true purpose of this sign. It is not to avert a death, but to reveal that God

Pour all of Jesus' emotion into this prayer: He's seen two close friends in grief; he himself is agitated and sad; and, on top of it all, it seems the crowd still doesn't believe he was sent by God.

You needn't shout but you must raise your volume here.

Slow down on this conclusion.

Martha, the dead man's sister, said to him,
  "Lord, by **now** there will be a stench;
  he has been dead for four **days**."
Jesus said to her,
  "Did I not tell you that if you **believe**
  you will see the **glory** of God?"
So they took **away** the stone.
And Jesus raised his eyes and said,
  "**Father**, I **thank** you for **hearing** me.
I know that you **always** hear me;
  but because of the **crowd** here I have said this,
  that they may **believe** that you **sent** me."
And when he had said this,
  he **cried** out in a **loud voice**,
  "**Lazarus**, come **out**!"
The dead man came **out**,
  tied hand and foot with burial bands,
  and his face was **wrapped** in a cloth.
So Jesus said to them,
  "**Untie** him and let him **go**."

Now many of the Jews who had come to Mary
  and **seen** what he had done began to **believe** in him.]

[Shorter: John 11:3–7, 17, 20–27, 33b–45 (see brackets)]

TO KEEP IN MIND
In a narrative, find an emotion or point of view for each character, keeping in mind that these might change during the reading.

conquers death itself, and does so through his powerful Word, made flesh in Jesus. The evangelist again stresses that a choice confronts those who encounter Jesus: to believe in him, or to reject him. Some still question, asking if one who healed a blind man could not have prevented this death; they still do not comprehend the true intent of the sign unfolding before them. After reminding his hearers that Lazarus has been dead for four full days, John again focuses on this purpose: to elicit belief that the glory of God is manifest in Jesus, who in his person and action reveals God's character as life-giving love that overcomes death itself.

Jesus prays to the Father for Lazarus' release from death, fully confident of his sonship, repeating the reason for God's response: "that they may believe that you sent me." At the word of the Word made flesh, the dead man emerges from the tomb, bearing his burial wrappings. As a result of this sign, even "many of the Jews . . . began to believe in him." M.F.

PALM SUNDAY OF THE PASSION OF THE LORD

LECTIONARY #37

GOSPEL AT THE PROCESSION   Matthew 21:1–11

A reading from the holy Gospel according to Matthew

When Jesus and the disciples drew near **Jerusalem**
   and came to Bethphage on the Mount of **Olives**,
   Jesus sent two disciples, saying to them,
   "**Go** into the village opposite you,
   and immediately you will find an **ass** tethered,
   and a **colt** with her.
Untie them and **bring** them here to me.
And if anyone should say anything to you, reply,
   'The **master** has **need** of them.'
Then he will send them at **once**."
This happened so that what had been spoken through the prophet
   might be **fulfilled**:
   Say to daughter **Zion**,
   "**Behold**, *your* **king** *comes to you*,
      meek *and riding on an* **ass**,
      and on a **colt**, *the foal of a beast of burden.*"
The disciples **went** and **did** as Jesus had ordered them.
They brought the ass and the colt and laid their **cloaks** over them,
   and he **sat** upon them.
The very large **crowd** spread their **cloaks** on the road,
   while others cut **branches** from the trees
   and **strewed** them on the road.

A narrative with much action. See it unfold before you as you proclaim.

Don't swallow "Jerusalem."
Bethphage = BETH-fuh-jee

The disciples are no doubt very nervous about getting so close to Jerusalem. Jesus calmly gives them a specific task and lets them know that everything will unfold as it is meant to.

"Don't worry about anything. All will be well."

A prophecy fulfilled is a cause for rejoicing.

Proclaim as if you see the king arriving from far away. The king's arrival is good news for the assembly. Use the word "Behold" to express that joy.

foal = fohl

The happiness of the crowd expresses excitement and confers honor on Jesus. It's a festival atmosphere.

blessed = BLES-uhd

strewed = strood (scattered or spread)

PROCESSION GOSPEL During Lectionary Year A, a majority of Gospel readings are drawn from Matthew, who was most likely a Jewish convert to Christian faith, perhaps even a rabbi. Writing about fifty years after the Death and Resurrection of Jesus, this evangelist seems very aware of a significant issue of the day: Jewish Christians struggled to discern proper relationships between their past faith and practice and that of Jesus' followers. Are the Law and the Prophets completely set aside? Or does Jesus provide their full and accurate inter-

pretation? Attempting to demonstrate both continuity and discontinuity between the Old Testament Scriptures and Jesus, Matthew portrays Jesus as the one who "fulfills" the Old Testament Scriptures, bringing them to their fullest development, thus completing God's plan of salvation.

In composing his account of the Good News, Matthew uses Mark as a major source, but alters or adds to Mark in order to address his specific community and their needs. Writing for a predominantly Jewish Christian community, the author employs modes of interpreting the Old Testament

used in Judaism for several centuries. By directly quoting or alluding to previous Scriptures, Matthew draws out their meaning for the present moment. This approach was firmly rooted in the Jewish belief that God had implanted all necessary meaning in the Scriptures from their beginning. By reflecting upon their new life experiences in light of their sacred writings, the covenant people could gradually uncover the full meaning of the Scriptures, discovering fresh insights at significant moments in their continuing relationship with God. In his account of the Good News, Matthew often

The crowds preceding him and those following
    kept **crying** out and saying:
       "**Hosanna** to the Son of David;
         blessed is he who comes in the name of the Lord;
       hosanna in the **highest**."
And when he **entered** Jerusalem
    the whole city was **shaken** and asked, "Who **is** this?"
And the crowds replied,
    "This is Jesus the **prophet**, from Nazareth in Galilee."

Proclaim these lines with joy.

Hosanna = hoh-ZAH-nah

Heighten this last acclamation.

Residents of an occupied city would be wary of angering the occupiers. Proclaim as if the crowd speaks with one voice.

READING I   Isaiah 50:4–7

A reading from the Book of the Prophet Isaiah

The Lord **God** has **given** me
    a **well**-trained **tongue**,
that I might know how to speak to the **weary**
    a word that will **rouse** them.
Morning after **morning**
    he opens my **ear** that I may **hear**;
and I have not **rebelled**,
    have **not** turned back.
I gave my **back** to those who **beat** me,
    my **cheeks** to those who plucked my **beard**;
my **face** I did not **shield**
    from **buffets** and **spitting**.

The Lord G O D is my **help**,
    therefore I am not **disgraced**;
I have set my face like **flint**,
    knowing that I shall **not** be put to **shame**.

An exhortatory reading; the prophet affirms his strength through adversity and his unwavering trust in God.

Isaiah = Ī-ZAY-uh

Proclaim this phrase slowly and distinctly, with a "well-trained tongue."

Speak to the weary in your assembly with tenderness.

Imagine and express how this intimate relationship with God might feel.

"I've done what I was asked to do."

How does the prophet feel about the abuse he's suffered? In the context of this reading, it's unlikely that he's angry. He stands his ground, doesn't submit but also doesn't fight back.

buffets = BUF-its (slaps)

"No human insults can hurt me."

Raise your face to the community, and proclaim confidently—with God, nothing can harm you.

---

signals this Jewish method of interpretation by stating that a particular thing happened "so that the Scriptures might be fulfilled."

In today's Reading at the Procession with Palms, Jesus approaches Jerusalem by way of the Mount of Olives and asks two disciples to bring a donkey with its foal. With these two details, the evangelist signals that what is about to happen points to the fulfillment of prophecy and of Israel's greatest hope. Zechariah proclaimed that at the culmination of God's plan, the Lord would stand upon the Mount of Olives, and God's Anointed, as humble king and savior,

would arrive "riding on a donkey" (Zechariah 14:4; 9:9). Jesus instructs the disciples charged with bringing the animals that if anyone questions them, they are simply to reply that the "master" needs them. Matthew uses the word kýrios, which can also mean "lord," used often as a title of authority and divinity. Matthew, Mark, and Luke all include an account of this triumphal entry into Jerusalem, but only Matthew explicitly quotes Zechariah, noting that his words are now "fulfilled" in Jesus.

As Jesus enters the City of David, the crowds pay him homage according to

custom, spreading their cloaks and palm branches before him. Matthew again underscores that this act signifies the arrival of God's chosen Messiah, an expected new Son of David who would restore people, nation, and kingship under his righteous rule. They cry out the words of Psalm 118, part of a thanksgiving liturgy that accompanied a victory procession of Israel's king and people to the Temple of their God, shouting "Hosanna," which means "Lord, grant salvation!"

To the ruling power of Rome, Jesus' actions and the people's response signaled

For meditation and context:

TO KEEP IN MIND
Making eye contact with the assembly connects you with them and connects them to the reading more deeply than using your voice alone. This helps the assembly stay with the story and keeps them engaged.

An exhortatory hymn with a strong start, diminishing to a quiet middle, then rising again to the great proclamation at the end. Use pacing and volume to signal changes in intensity.

Philippians = fih-LIP-ee-uhnz

There's no warm up: We jump right in, so make eye contact with the community right from beginning.

Now begin to diminish your energy slightly.

Quiet intensity here. Drop volume and pace, but don't lose contact with the assembly.

Pause before this line.

Gradually pick up pace and energy from here to the end. It's one long sentence; pause only at the commas.

Keep building your energy.

RESPONSORIAL PSALM   Psalm 22:8–9, 17–18, 19–20, 23–24 (2a)

R. My God, my God, why have you abandoned me?

All who see me scoff at me;
  they mock me with parted lips, they wag their heads:
"He relied on the LORD; let him deliver him,
  let him rescue him, if he loves him."

Indeed, many dogs surround me,
  a pack of evildoers closes in upon me;
they have pierced my hands and my feet;
  I can count all my bones.

They divide my garments among them,
  and for my vesture they cast lots.
But you, O LORD, be not far from me;
  O my help, hasten to aid me.

I will proclaim your name to my brethren;
  in the midst of the assembly I will praise you:
"You who fear the LORD, praise him;
  all you descendants of Jacob, give glory to him;
  revere him, all you descendants of Israel!"

READING II   Philippians 2:6–11

A reading from the Letter of Saint Paul to the Philippians

Christ **Jesus**, though he was in the form of **God**,
  did not regard **equality** with God
  something to be **grasped**.
Rather, he **emptied** himself,
  taking the form of a **slave**,
  coming in **human** likeness;
  and found human in **appearance**,
  he **humbled** himself,
  becoming **obedient** to the point of **death**,
  even death on a **cross**.
Because of this, God greatly **exalted** him
  and **bestowed** on him the **name**
  which is **above** every name,
  that at the name of **Jesus**
  every knee should **bend**,

---

a highly volatile situation: a man whom Jewish crowds hailed as king and liberator, entering Jerusalem as multitudes gathered to celebrate the feast of Passover, God's deliverance from oppression. The empire would soon move to eliminate this latest challenge to its absolute rule. But Matthew focuses on proclaiming the religious meaning of this event: the one whom Rome will soon crucify as a threat to its supremacy is, in fact, Israel's chosen Messiah, inaugurating the Lord's final rule as humble servant, not as dominating force.

READING I   Today's passage from Isaiah is the third of four poems commonly called the "Servant Songs." The prophet variously describes the unnamed "Servant of the Lord," sometimes named the "Suffering Servant," as both individual and corporate figure. Many scholars believe the servant represents an ideal image that embodies what is expected of those in covenant with the Lord: to hear and obey God's Word. Numerous prophets lamented the people's repeated failures to do so, and Isaiah looks forward to a time when God's intent for the Chosen People will reach completion.

The Servant of the Lord appears as a figure chosen and sent by God, filled with divine spirit in order to accomplish God's saving purpose. In the prophet's portrayal, however, the servant sometimes suffers rejection, mental and physical abuse, and even death in carrying out God's commission. Ultimately, the servant is vindicated as one through whom the divine purposes are accomplished. After the Death and Resurrection of Jesus, Christians

of those in **heaven** and on **earth** and **under** the earth,
and every tongue **confess** that
Jesus Christ is **Lord**,
to the **glory** of God the **Father**.

GOSPEL   Matthew 26:14—27:66

The Passion of our Lord Jesus Christ according to Matthew

One of the **Twelve**, who was called **Judas Iscariot**,
    went to the chief **priests** and said,
    "What are you willing to **give** me
    if I hand him **over** to you?"
They paid him thirty pieces of **silver**,
    and from that time on he looked for **an opportunity**
        to hand him over.

On the first day of the Feast of Unleavened Bread,
    the disciples approached Jesus and said,
    "Where do you want us to **prepare**
    for you to eat the **Passover**?"
He said,
    "**Go** into the city to a certain man and tell him,
    'The teacher says, "My appointed **time** draws near;
    in **your** house I shall celebrate the **Passover** with
        my **disciples**."'"
The disciples then **did** as Jesus had ordered,
    and prepared the Passover. »

Margin notes (left column):

Keep your energy up; slow down just a bit and proclaim this final line deliberately and with great joy.

A familiar narrative. Don't saturate everything with sadness and solemnity. Attend also to anxiety, anguish, quiet, compassion, loneliness, violence, fear, confusion, tenderness, and much more. Give each moment its due, and stay focused on telling a story. Determine the intentions of each character.

What is Judas' intention? Keep it in mind as you proclaim.

How does Judas feel as he goes to the chief priests?

Pause before the shift in scene.

As in the Gospel at the Procession, Jesus gives the disciples a task to help calm their anxiety about the danger that surrounds them.

Pause.

Bottom commentary (three columns):

understood Jesus as the final embodiment of the prophet's "Servant of the Lord."

In today's First Reading, God gives the servant both words to proclaim God's message to the people and the skill to do so: "a well-trained tongue." Several characteristics mark the servant as a true member of God's people. In ancient Israel, having an "open ear" was one way to describe an ideal slave or servant; a slave's pierced ear indicated that necessary quality. In other words, a true servant of God is one who continually hears and responds to the divine voice. The prophets often described

the people's sinfulness as rebellion against God and his Torah, but the servant is free of such attitudes or actions. Though the servant suffers contemptuous treatment such as plucking of the beard and spitting, he places total trust in the One who gives him a mission for salvation, "knowing" that he will ultimately enjoy God's vindication.

READING II   The Second Reading, incorporated into Philippians about thirty years after the Death and Resurrection of Jesus, was most likely an already-existing hymn, and so it expresses

very early understandings of the mystery of Christ. At the time of this letter, Paul is in prison, perhaps even facing death for preaching Jesus as Messiah. He exhorts the Philippian church, and perhaps himself, to follow the example of Jesus' passage through death to greater life.

Some scholars believe that this hymn reflects an interpretation of Christ that Paul elsewhere describes as the Second Adam, or New Adam. This understanding uses typology, a Jewish mode of interpreting Scripture in which an earlier figure appears as a "type" or foreshadowing that aids

This would be a comfortable and familiar situation to Jesus and his disciples, eating together and celebrating a festival.

The comment comes from out of the blue.

The disciples are distressed. How would that sound?

Be careful not to make Judas' denial sound disingenuous.

There are four actions here; make each one distinct.

Take your time; Jesus knows the disciples will have some difficulty understanding this.

There is some sadness in Jesus' recognition that he will not share a meal with his disciples in this way again.

A moment of joy.

When it was **evening**,
    he **reclined** at table with the Twelve.
And while they were **eating**, he said,
    "**Amen**, I say to you, one of you will **betray** me."
Deeply **distressed** at this,
    they began to say to him one after another,
    "Surely it is not **I**, Lord?"
He said in reply,
    "He who has dipped his hand into the dish with me
    is the one who will **betray** me.
The Son of Man indeed **goes**, as it is written of him,
    but **woe** to that man by whom the Son of Man is **betrayed**.
It would be **better** for that man if he had never been born."
Then Judas, his **betrayer**, said in reply,
    "Surely it is not **I**, Rabbi?"
He answered, "**You** have said so."

While they were eating,
    Jesus **took** bread, said the **blessing**,
    broke it, and **giving** it to his disciples said,
    "**Take** and **eat**; this is my **body**."
Then he took a **cup**, gave **thanks**, and **gave** it to them, saying,
    "**Drink** from it, all of you,
    for this is my **blood** of the covenant,
    which will be **shed** on behalf of **many**
    for the **forgiveness** of sins.
I tell you, from now on I shall not **drink** this fruit of the vine
    until the day when I drink it with you **new**
    in the **kingdom** of my Father."
Then, after singing a **hymn**,
    they went out to the Mount of **Olives**.

understanding a person or event of the present time. As used by Christian writers, the earlier type could serve as a contrast to the present, or as an incomplete version of someone or something that now fully reveals or embodies God's original intention. In the beginning, God created the human race to be an image, an exact representation of the Creator (the Hebrew word *ādām* normally means "humankind"). However, the First Adam never fully realized this divine purpose. Not content to be an image God, the human creature attempted to seize divine status itself (see Genesis 3:22). In the life, Death, and Resurrection of Christ, however, God's purpose for humanity reaches completion: Jesus Christ is the Second Adam, the beginning or "first fruits" of new humanity as the perfect Image of God.

The hymn Paul uses follows the outline of this typology. The man Jesus, like every human being, bore the "form of God," but unlike the First Adam, did not grasp at equality with God. Instead, in humble obedience and self-giving love, he "emptied himself" of life itself, serving God's purpose like a slave. Precisely because of this, God raised him up to the status of "Lord." In the Roman world, it was common to acclaim the divinity and authority of the ruling Caesar with shouts of "Caesar is Lord!" For Paul and for the Church, only the self-emptying, exalted Jesus Christ merits such praise, which ultimately glorifies God.

GOSPEL With the Passion narratives, it is particularly important to recall that each evangelist writes for a specific community in particular historical circumstances. As a result, each account carefully selects from available oral and

Jesus shows compassion, assuring his friends that though they might momentarily abandon him, he will not abandon them.

Peter shouldn't sound like a braggart, but someone with great self-confidence.

Jesus knows well how weak the human person can be.

Jesus' emotions are stated plainly: sorrow and distress. Make sure these emotions are quite evident in your proclamation of this section.

Jesus is experiencing real pain.

prostrate = PROS-trayt (face down on the ground)

Based on Jesus' emotions already described, we know these are not just pious words. It should sound like Jesus is sincerely asking to let this pass.

Ultimately, Jesus trusts in God; but since he will return to this same prayer two more times, this first expression can be a little tentative.

Then Jesus said to them,
  "This night **all** of you will have your faith in me **shaken**,
  for it is written:
    *I will strike the **shepherd**,*
      *and the **sheep** of the flock will be **dispersed***;
  but after I have been **raised** up,
  I shall go **before** you to **Galilee**."
Peter said to him in reply,
  "Though **all** may have their faith in you shaken,
  mine will **never** be."
Jesus said to him,
  "**Amen**, I say to you,
  this **very** night before the cock crows,
  you will **deny** me three times."
Peter said to him,
  "Even though I should have to **die** with you,
  I will **not** deny you."
And all the disciples spoke **likewise**.

Then Jesus came with them to a place called Gethsemane,
  and he said to his disciples,
  "Sit here while I go over there and **pray**."
He took along Peter and the two sons of Zebedee,
  and began to feel **sorrow** and **distress**.
Then he said to them,
  "My soul is sorrowful even to **death**.
Remain here and keep **watch** with me."
He advanced a little and fell prostrate in **prayer**, saying,
  "My Father, if it is possible,
  let this cup **pass** from me;
  yet, not as **I** will, but as **you** will."
When he returned to his disciples he found them **asleep**. ❯❯

written sources both his content and particular modes of presenting the Good News (see Reading at Procession). Matthew's audience, mostly Jews who had come to faith in Jesus as God's Anointed One chosen to inaugurate God's final rule, would have been familiar with two important religious figures in Jewish thought and literature: the Servant of the Lord and the Righteous One. The Servant, prominent in Isaiah, is God's chosen instrument in the work of salvation. God designates this unnamed figure from birth for a chosen mission, bestowing divine Spirit to aid in his

task. At times the Servant suffers physical and mental abuse, even to the point of death, but through his faithful obedience, God's will is accomplished and the servant is exalted (see Isaiah 52:13—53:12). Later in Israel's history, a similar figure emerges: a righteous, innocent person persecuted for obedient fidelity to God who is ultimately vindicated. In the Book of Wisdom, the Righteous One, also called a "son of God," receives the reward of immortality (Wisdom 2:10—3:12). (Some translations refer to the "Just One" or "Innocent One.")

In various ways, Matthew evokes both of these figures, repeatedly interpreting Jesus as the one in whom their fullest meaning is accomplished. Direct or indirect references to the Suffering Servant and the Righteous One recur in his Passion account, often ironically; unbelievers use them in mockery, but the evangelist unfolds for his hearers their full meaning, embodied in Jesus. He also illumines various facets of meaning in the title "Son of God." The basic narrative of Jesus' Passion and Crucifixion is familiar to most, but Matthew includes particular details in order to present Jesus

Is Jesus angry or, based on what he's just prayed himself, is he understanding the disciples' weakness?

Is Jesus speaking only of the disciples or commenting on his own struggle?

This time, Jesus is a little more confident.

Let Jesus' feeling toward the disciples come through in this narrative line.

Let your voice express this physical and perhaps emotional fatigue.

Take your time here mentioning the third prayer. Color it with the distress mixed with trust of the previous prayers.

The preparation time is over. Now, Jesus is ready. From here on, he is able to accept what unfolds.

Give these words conviction. Jesus seems to speak to both his disciples and himself. "And so it begins . . . "

Don't rush "one of the Twelve." It's significant that Judas is still considered a disciple.

With the appearance of a large, armed crowd, your narration can take on a sinister tone.

What do you think about Judas betraying Jesus with a kiss of friendship? Make a strong choice and let it show both times you refer to the kiss.
Express what you think Jesus is as he calls Judas "Friend"?
Immediately pick up the pace and proclaim these lines with an energy that reflects the violence described.

Pause.

He said to Peter,
  "So you could not keep **watch** with me for one hour?
Watch and **pray** that you may not undergo the **test**.
The **spirit** is **willing**, but the **flesh** is **weak**."
Withdrawing a **second** time, he prayed **again**,
  "My Father, if it is not possible that this cup pass
  without my drinking it, **your** will be done!"
Then he returned once **more** and found them **asleep**,
  for they could not keep their eyes open.
He left them and withdrew again and prayed a **third** time,
  saying the **same** thing **again**.
Then he returned to his disciples and said to them,
  "Are you still **sleeping** and taking your rest?
Behold, the hour is at **hand**
  when the Son of Man is to be handed over to **sinners**.
Get up, let us **go**.
Look, my **betrayer** is at hand."

While he was still speaking,
  Judas, one of the **Twelve**, arrived,
  accompanied by a large crowd, with **swords** and **clubs**,
  who had come from the chief priests and the elders
    of the people.
His betrayer had arranged a **sign** with them, saying,
  "The man I shall **kiss** is the one; arrest him."
Immediately he went over to Jesus and said,
  "**Hail**, Rabbi!" and he **kissed** him.
Jesus answered him,
  "**Friend**, do what you have **come** for."
Then stepping forward they laid **hands** on Jesus and **arrested** him.
And **behold**, one of those who accompanied Jesus
  put his hand to his **sword**, **drew** it,
    and **struck** the high priest's servant, cutting off his **ear**.

as the complete fulfillment of Israel's Scriptures and God's plan of salvation.

Several such details emerge in Matthew's treatment of the betrayer. Only this evangelist specifies the payment that Judas receives for his treachery: thirty pieces of silver. Only Matthew presents a scene of Judas' regret and suicide; when the betrayer attempts to return the payment he received, Jewish leaders object. Blood money cannot be added to the Temple treasury, so it is used to buy a cemetery called "the potter's field." Matthew states that this act fulfills a prophecy of Jeremiah, though the specific text he cites does not appear in the Scriptures. He may have intended to evoke Jeremiah 19, in which the prophet shatters a potter's flask to symbolize the coming destruction of unfaithful Jerusalem. By the time of Matthew's composition, the Romans had again destroyed Jerusalem and the Temple, an event some Christians viewed as divine judgment upon Jews who did not accept Jesus as Messiah. Conversely, some Jews interpreted the disaster as judgment upon those Jews who expressed belief in a crucified Messiah, since Deuteronomy 21:23 pronounced anyone hanged on a tree "a curse of God."

For the most part, Matthew's account of Jesus' supper with the Twelve resembles those of Mark and Luke, but he adds one significant phrase. All three evangelists include core elements already regarded as essential to the Christian celebration of the Lord's Supper, including prayers of thanksgiving (or blessing), bread and cup linked with Christ's body and blood, and reference to covenant relationships. But only Matthew states that Jesus gives his life "for the forgiveness of sins." Some suggest that

Return to a calmer pace with Jesus' response.

Then Jesus said to him,
    "**Put** your sword **back** into its sheath,
    for all who **take** the sword will **perish** by the sword.
Do you think that I cannot call upon my Father
    and he will not provide me at this moment
    with more than twelve **legions** of angels?
But then how would the Scriptures be **fulfilled**
    which say that it **must** come to pass in this **way**?"

Jesus seems amazed at the crowd's actions.

At that hour Jesus said to the crowds,
    "Have you come out as against a **robber**,
    with swords and clubs to **seize** me?
Day after day I sat teaching in the temple area,
    yet you did not arrest me.
But all this has come to **pass**
    that the writings of the prophets may be **fulfilled**."
Then all the disciples left him and **fled**.

The end of the first part of the story. Take a very long pause here and let the assembly breathe for a moment before continuing. Caiaphas = KĪ-uh-fuhs

Those who had arrested Jesus led him away
    to **Caiaphas** the high priest,
    where the **scribes** and the **elders** were assembled.

Drop your voice slightly on this description of Peter's actions.

Peter was following him at a distance
    as far as the high priest's courtyard,
    and going **inside** he sat down with the servants to see
        the outcome.

Sanhedrin = san-HEE-druhn

The chief priests and the entire **Sanhedrin**
    kept trying to obtain false **testimony** against Jesus
    in order to **put** him to **death**,
    but they found **none**,
    though many **false** witnesses came forward.

Don't gloss over "put him to death." This is the first mention of the Sanhedrin's plans.

Finally two came forward who stated,
    "This man said, 'I can **destroy** the temple of God
    and within **three** days rebuild it.'" ➤

this addition indicates that forgiveness was sorely needed in Matthew's community, which struggled with the inclusion of Gentiles into the Christian community. But the evangelist might also intend to evoke the Suffering Servant, whose suffering and self-sacrifice takes away the sins of many (Isaiah 53:12b).

After the supper, Jesus and his disciples depart for the Mount of Olives, and by quoting Scripture, Jesus warns that impending events will shake their faith in him. Describing Jesus' entry into Jerusalem (see Reading at Procession), Matthew has

twice previously called to mind the prophecy of Zechariah. This brief work places great emphasis on God's final act of salvation through a righteous messianic king who replaces those shepherds (kings) who failed to care for the strays, the weak, and the injured (Zechariah 11; 9:9–10; see also Ezekiel 34). Rome will execute Jesus as a pretender to the throne who seeks to undermine the empire's absolute rule. But Matthew suggests his true identity and mission: God's Messiah, the one through whom God will establish a final reign of righteousness and peace. Jesus is king

indeed, but one who rules with the power of self-giving love, not the dominating force exercised by Rome.

Peter and the other disciples all protest that regardless of weakened faith in others, their trust in Jesus will not waver. In one of the most poignant failures of all four Gospel accounts, Peter proclaims that even threat of death would never cause him to deny Jesus. In ensuing scenes, the rock on which the Church is built crumbles, and Peter denies that he even knows Jesus. By the time Matthew composed his account of the Good News, Peter had in fact given his

Contrast the demanding tone of the high priest with the quiet strength of Jesus. The high priest needs his authority on display. Jesus' authority comes from within and his relationship with God.

The high priest is getting desperate, almost frantic, to find something.

Build your energy and intensity from here to the end of this section.

Use force on the words of violence, like "spat," "struck," and "slapped."

Pause to let the scene shift.

Peter has three denials, so raise your intensity gradually. This first one might sound very casual.

The oath indicates he's getting more emphatic (and likely more afraid).

The high priest rose and addressed him,
    "Have you no **answer**?
What are these men **testifying** against you?"
But Jesus was **silent**.
Then the high priest said to him,
    "I **order** you to tell us under **oath** before the living God
    whether you are the **Christ**, the Son of God."
Jesus said to him in reply,
    "**You** have said so.
But I tell you:
    From now on you will see the 'Son of Man
        seated at the right hand of the **Power**'
        and '**coming** on the clouds of heaven.'"
Then the high priest **tore** his robes and said,
    "He has **blasphemed**!
What **further** need have we of witnesses?
You have now **heard** the blasphemy;
    what is your **opinion**?"
They said in reply,
    "He deserves to **die**!"
Then they **spat** in his face and **struck** him,
    while some **slapped** him, saying,
    "**Prophesy** for us, Christ: **who is** it that **struck** you?"

Now **Peter** was sitting outside in the courtyard.
One of the maids came over to him and said,
    "You **too** were with Jesus the Galilean."
But he **denied** it in front of everyone, saying,
    "I do **not** know what you are talking about!"
As he went out to the gate, another girl saw him
    and said to those who were there,
    "**This** man was with Jesus the Nazorean."
Again he denied it with an **oath**,
    "I do not **know** the man!"

life rather than repudiate his faith in Jesus, suggesting that the forgiveness Jesus promised at the supper was surely extended to Peter.

Matthew's scene in Gethsemane follows Mark quite closely, with one brief but notable addition. Perceiving what awaits him, in his anguish Jesus asks God to let this cup pass, if possible; still, he surrenders to whatever must happen in order to accomplish God's will. Finding the disciples asleep, Jesus turns to God a second time; Mark simply states that he prayed "the same thing." Matthew, however, specifically reiterates Jesus' attitude: "Father . . . your will be done." Like the Suffering Servant, if Jesus gives his life for the sins of others, "the LORD's will shall be accomplished through him" (Isaiah 53:10).

By repeating Jesus' explicit surrender to the divine will, the evangelist also emphasizes that the Messiah enters his Passion freely, by choice rather than coercion. It should be noted that in the Bible, understanding the "will of God" emphasized above all the content of God's will or intention for humankind, which is always human salvation: wholeness, well-being, and right relationships with God and with all things. Like Christians today, Jesus must enter into his present experience with trust that whatever happens can and will ultimately lead to salvation.

The betrayer arrives with a crowd sanctioned by some of the Jewish chief priests and elders. Again Matthew's account closely resembles those of Mark and Luke, but he heightens the irony. Only Matthew has Jesus respond to Judas' feigned respectful greeting by addressing him as "Friend." Even in Judas' traitorous act, Jesus offers the forgiveness he promised in the Lord's

The bystanders are getting more insistent as well.

Use the words "curse" and "swear" as if they were curse words.

With real force!

What does Peter feel? Bring that emotion to these lines.

Don't swallow "bitterly." Pause at this scene shift.

A little later the bystanders came over and said to Peter,
    "Surely you **too** are one of them;
    even your speech gives you away."
At that he began to **curse** and to **swear**,
    "I do not **know** the man."
And **immediately** a **cock crowed**.
Then Peter **remembered** the words that Jesus had spoken:
    "Before the cock **crows** you will **deny** me **three** times."
He went out and began to weep **bitterly**.

When it was morning,
    all the chief **priests** and the elders of the people
    took counsel against Jesus to put him to **death**.
They **bound** him, **led** him away,
    and handed him over to **Pilate**, the governor.

Three distinct actions; give each its due.

What does Judas feel as he sees what's happened? Bring that emotion to these lines.

This "deep regret" humanizes Judas for us, and allows us to feel some compassion toward him.

With real regret, and perhaps even fear.

Then **Judas**, his betrayer, seeing that Jesus had
        been condemned,
    deeply **regretted** what he had done.
He returned the thirty pieces of silver
    to the chief priests and elders, saying,
    "I have **sinned** in betraying **innocent** blood."
They said,
    "What is that to **us**?
    Look to it **yourself**."
Flinging the money into the temple,
    he departed and went off and **hanged** himself.
The chief **priests** gathered up the money, but said,
    "It is not **lawful** to deposit this in the **temple** treasury,
    for it is the price of **blood**."

Let your compassion for Judas bring some sadness to this line.

The chief priests are "all business" here, and oblivious to the emotional drama they are involved in.

After consultation, they used it to buy the potter's field
    as a **burial** place for **foreigners**.
That is why that field even today is called the Field of **Blood**. **»**

Supper. Betrayed by one of the Twelve, Jesus will soon be repudiated by another, and like the Servant of the Lord, he suffers deep emotional anguish as well as physical pain. Only Matthew adds Jesus' own statement that these events are unfolding as they must, in order that "the Scriptures be fulfilled."

The following scenes of Jesus' interrogation before Jewish religious authorities and Pilate, the Roman governor, can be read both historically and religiously. Often, the two perspectives overlap. Historically, the empire was on constant guard against the slightest threat to its absolute rule. Those in power were aware that many Jews hoped for a new messianic ruler who would restore their independence as a people and as a nation, freeing them from foreign power. Further, several Roman emperors had claimed divinity, demanding to be revered and honored as "lord" or "son of god." The religious hope and expectation of the Jews awaited a divinely anointed, royal Messiah who enjoyed a filial relationship with God as adopted son. As such, he would govern as God rules, fulfilling the Jewish ideal of kingship by shepherding the covenant people in righteousness and peace (see Psalm 2). Thus in many ways the titles of Messiah, King of the Jews, and Son of God could be interchangeable, equivalent terms; in other ways, they could carry quite different, even contradictory meanings. Further, those familiar with the Old Testament could also associate anyone called a "son of God" with the figure of the suffering and vindicated Righteous One. Finally, by the time of Matthew's composition (about AD 85), Christians recognized Jesus' divinity with the title "Son of God." The multifaceted meanings of these various

Then was **fulfilled** what had been said through **Jeremiah**
        the prophet,
    *And they took the **thirty** pieces of silver,*
    *the value of a man with a **price** on his head,*
    a price set by some of the Israelites,
    *and they paid it out for the **potter's** field*
    just as the Lord *had **commanded** me.*

Pause at this scene shift.

[Now Jesus stood before the governor, and he questioned him,
    "Are you the **king** of the Jews?"
Jesus said, "**You** say so."
And when he was **accused** by the chief priests and elders,
    he made no **answer**.
Then Pilate said to him,
    "Do you not hear how many things they are **testifying**
        against you?"
But he did not answer him one **word**,
    so that the governor was greatly **amazed**.

Pilate is conflicted about what to do with Jesus. What is Pilate's intention? What does he want? Make a strong choice and keep it in mind as you proclaim.

"Don't you want to defend yourself?"

Now on the occasion of the feast
    the governor was accustomed to **release** to the crowd
    one prisoner whom they wished.
And at that time they had a **notorious** prisoner called **Barabbas**.
So when they had assembled, Pilate said to them,
    "**Which** one do you want me to release to you,
    Barabbas, or **Jesus** called **Christ**?"
For he knew that it was out of **envy**
    that they had handed him over.
While he was still seated on the bench,
    his **wife** sent him a message,
    "Have **nothing** to do with that **righteous** man.
I suffered much in a **dream** today because of him."
The chief priests and the elders **persuaded** the crowds
    to **ask** for **Barabbas** but to **destroy Jesus**.
The governor said to them in reply,
    "Which of the two do you want me to **release** to you?"

This message raises the stakes for Pilate. Now he has to be sure to make the right choice about Jesus.

Use a secretive tone to convey the leaders working amidst the crowd.

titles offer Matthew ample opportunity for irony.

In his portrayal of Jesus' interrogation by Jewish and Roman authorities, Matthew suggests numerous ways to interpret the titles of Messiah (Christ), King of Israel, and Son of God. Members of the Sanhedrin, composed of the High Priest and seventy elders, demand to know if Jesus claims to be "the Christ, the Son of God." The Jewish religious leaders have no concern about any threat to Roman power, except as it serves their purposes; they want to know if the Galilean rabbi actually claims to be the

Anointed One chosen to inaugurate God's final rule. Jesus first responds with an indirect affirmation, then quotes the vision of Daniel and Psalm 110 to leave no doubt about his meaning (in Daniel and other Jewish literature, the "Son of Man" appears as a messianic figure; see Daniel 7:13). Once again, Matthew indicates that Jesus fulfills Israel's Scriptures.

For their part, the religious leaders declare him guilty of blasphemy, an offense meriting death. The charge seems vaguely defined in Judaism of the time, but apparently included any affront to God. In the

view of the Sanhedrin, for a man who repeatedly broke the Law, especially the prohibition against work on the Sabbath (a capital offense), to assert that he is God's Messiah surely qualified as blasphemy. Though the Jewish religious court finds Jesus guilty of a transgression meriting death, they cannot carry out the sentence (see John 18:31), and so they hand him over to Pilate, the Roman authority who wields that power.

At first, the governor's interrogation of Jesus closely parallels that of the Sanhedrin. Pilate's wording of questions,

The responses of the crowd should build in volume and intensity.

They answered, "**Barabbas**!"
Pilate said to them,
 "Then what shall I do with **Jesus** called **Christ**?"
They all said,
 "Let him be **crucified**!"
But he said,
 "**Why**? What evil has he done?"
They only shouted the **louder**,
 "Let him be crucified!"
When Pilate saw that he was not succeeding at all,
 but that a **riot** was breaking out instead,
 he took water and **washed** his hands in the sight of the crowd,
 saying, "I am **innocent** of this man's blood.
Look to it **yourselves**."
And the whole people said in reply,
 "His **blood** be upon **us** and upon our **children**."
Then he released Barabbas to them,
 but after he had Jesus **scourged**,
 he handed him over to be **crucified**.

The crowd is so fevered at this point they don't know what they're saying.

Pause slightly.
Proclaim the soldiers' actions with a power that conveys their rough treatment; emphasize especially the words of force.
praetorium = prih-TOHR-ee-uhm

Then the **soldiers** of the governor took Jesus
 inside the **praetorium**
 and gathered the whole cohort around him.
They **stripped** off his clothes
 and threw a scarlet **military** cloak about him.
Weaving a **crown** out of **thorns**, they placed it on his **head**,
 and a **reed** in his right hand.
And **kneeling** before him, they **mocked** him, saying,
 "**Hail**, **King** of the Jews!"
They **spat** upon him and took the reed
 and kept **striking** him on the **head**.
And when they had **mocked** him,
 they **stripped** him of the cloak,
 dressed him in his **own** clothes,
 and led him off to **crucify** him. »

Make sure this sounds like mocking.

The end of the second part of the story.
Pause here for a moment or two before continuing.

however, indicates the empire's major concern: does this Galilean in fact claim to be "king of the Jews?" If so, he is guilty of treason, a capital offense under Roman law. Aside from an indirect acknowledgement, Jesus remains silent. In this way, Matthew calls to mind the Servant of the Lord who, when led like a lamb to slaughter, "did not open his mouth" (Isaiah 53:7). As Jesus remains silent, Pilate's wife informs the governor of a troubling dream and urges him to avoid dealing with "that righteous man." She obliquely declares Jesus to be a Righteous One, a Son of God. Following a

supposed festival custom, Pilate asks the crowds to choose a prisoner for release: Jesus or Barabbas. They demand that Jesus be crucified and call for release of Barabbas, whose name means "son of the father." And so Pilate releases a notorious criminal and delivers up for execution the true Son of God.

The Crucifixion proceeds according to what is known of Roman practice; scourging, stripping and mockery by the soldiers follow common procedure. Often the soldiers' ridicule targeted the charges against a prisoner, so they press a crown of thorns

on this Jew who would be king, shoving a reed into his hand as a scepter to rule over no one. They mimic the bended knee they were required to perform before the emperor, hailing Jesus as "King of the Jews." When Jesus is hoisted up on the cross, the placard proclaiming the charge against him repeats the accusation of treason; this is one who challenged the authority of Rome by claiming to be "King of the Jews."

Such is Rome's understanding of Jesus. For Matthew, Jesus fulfills the Scriptures as true Messiah, the King who gives life itself for God's flock. As Jesus

Cyrenian = sĭ-REE-nee-uhn

As they were going out, they met a Cyrenian named **Simon**;
    this man they pressed into service
    to **carry** his cross.

Golgotha = GAWL-guh-thuh

And when they came to a place called **Golgotha**
    —which means Place of the **Skull**—,
    they gave Jesus **wine** to drink mixed with **gall**.

gall = gawl

Jesus refuses the sedative so as to enter completely into human suffering through his Crucifixion.

But when he had tasted it, he **refused** to drink.
After they had **crucified** him,
    they **divided** his garments by casting **lots**;
    then they sat down and kept **watch** over him there.
And they placed over his head the written charge against him:
    This is **Jesus**, the **King** of the **Jews**.

This is Pilate's insult to the chief priests.

Two **revolutionaries** were crucified with him,
    one on his right and the other on his left.
Those passing by **reviled** him, shaking their heads and saying,
    "You who would **destroy** the temple and **rebuild** it in **three** days,
    save yourself, if you are the Son of God,
    and come **down** from the cross!"

Make sure this sounds like mocking.

Likewise the chief **priests** with the **scribes** and **elders** mocked
    him and said,
    "He saved **others**; he cannot save **himself**.
So he is the **king** of Israel!

No need to draw this out; keep up the pace.

Let him come **down** from the cross now,
    and we will **believe** in him.
He **trusted** in **God**;
    let him **deliver** him now if he wants him.
For he said, 'I am the **Son** of God.'"
The revolutionaries who were crucified with him
    also kept abusing him in the **same** way.

Take this slowly and quietly.

These lines demand emotional depth. Recall a time when you felt completely abandoned and bring that feeling to your proclamation. Raise your volume on the Aramaic; lower it on the translation but keep the emotional intensity.

Eli, Eli, lema sabachthani = ay-LEE, ay-LEE, luh-MAH sah-bahk-TAH-nee

From noon onward, **darkness** came over the whole land
    until **three** in the afternoon.
And about three o'clock Jesus **cried** out in a **loud voice**,
    "*Eli*, *Eli*, *lema sabachthani*?"
    which means, "My **God**, my **God**, **why** have you **forsaken** me?"

hangs on the Cross in final agony, the evangelist again offers multilayered understandings of him as Son of God. Twice he is ridiculed, first by passers-by and then by some of the Jewish religious leaders: if he really is the Son of God, surely he can save himself, or God will save him! In the second taunt, Matthew echoes the Book of Wisdom and Psalm 22; both speak of an innocent person suffering persecution. In both texts, onlookers ridicule a Righteous Son of God who maintains steadfast trust in a God who fails to rescue him. In his last words, Jesus seems to echo the onlookers'

cries. But his words begin Psalm 22, which ends with praise of God for his faithful deliverance. Matthew alludes to the ultimate fate of the persecuted just one: vindication and life forever with God. In three days, these Scriptures will be fulfilled.

Only Matthew refers to Daniel's vision of end-time events that occur at the Death of Jesus: earthquakes, tombs opening, the dead raised (Daniel 12:2). Again the evangelist proclaims that Jesus fulfills Israel's Scriptures and her hope of God's definitive deliverance. However, he places the definitive proclamation of Jesus' true identity

on the lips of Gentiles, the Roman centurion and his men: "Truly, this was the Son of God!"

For Matthew, Jesus' Death fulfills the Scriptures, fully revealing his identity and mission to Jew and Gentile alike: he is the divinely chosen Messiah inaugurating God's Kingdom, ruling like God as a shepherd who gives life itself for his sheep. He is Son of God not only as king but as an obedient Righteous One and Servant of the Lord who suffers rejection and death for his faithfulness to the One who ultimately unites him with the living God forever.

Elijah = ee-LĪ-juh

Some of the bystanders who heard it said,
    "This one is calling for **Elijah**."
Immediately one of them ran to get a **sponge**;
    he soaked it in **wine**, and putting it on a **reed**,
    gave it to him to **drink**.
But the rest said,
    "**Wait**, let us see if Elijah comes to **save** him."
But Jesus **cried** out **again** in a loud voice,
    and **gave** up his **spirit**.

Increase your volume quickly, pause, then immediately drop it.

[Here all kneel and pause for a short time.]

Use the word "behold" to get right back into the story. Quicken your pace considerably on these lines.

And **behold**, the veil of the **sanctuary**
    was torn in **two** from top to bottom.
The earth **quaked**, rocks were **split**, **tombs** were **opened**,
    and the bodies of many saints who had fallen asleep
        were **raised**.
And coming **forth** from their tombs after his **resurrection**,
    they entered the holy city and appeared to **many**.
The **centurion** and the men with him who were keeping watch
        over Jesus
    feared greatly when they saw the earthquake
    and **all** that was happening, and they said,
    "**Truly**, this **was** the Son of **God**!"]

Pause.

centurion = sen-TOOR-ee-uhn

Pause.

Speak of the women with love.

There were many **women** there, looking on from a distance,
    who had followed Jesus from Galilee, **ministering** to him.
Among them were Mary **Magdalene** and **Mary** the mother of
        James and **Joseph**,
    and the **mother** of the sons of Zebedee.

Magdalene = MAG-duh-luhn or MAG-duh-leen

Zebedee = ZEB-uh-dee

When it was evening,
    there came a rich man from **Arimathea** named **Joseph**,
    who was himself a **disciple** of Jesus.
He went to Pilate and asked for the **body** of Jesus;
    then Pilate ordered it to be handed over.
Taking the body, Joseph **wrapped** it in clean **linen**
    and **laid** it in his **new tomb** that he had hewn in the rock. **»**

Arimathea = ayr-ih-muh-THEE-uh

Take these lines slowly and convey Joseph's gentle love and care for the body of Jesus.

hewn = hyoon

After Jesus' Death, he is laid in a tomb provided by Joseph of Arimathea, a wealthy disciple. Two of the faithful women who followed Jesus to the end remain, keeping watch at the tomb. Several days hence, these women, Mary Magdalene and another woman named Mary, will be the first to receive the angelic message that Jesus has been raised up by God; they will be the first Apostles, commissioned to announce this Good News to other disciples. Only Matthew adds that the chief priests and Pharisees ask Pilate for a guard on Jesus' tomb, lest his followers steal the body and claim that he has been raised from the dead. This detail probably reflects an attempt to dismiss Christian claims circulating among unbelieving Jews in the first century. It is one more way that Matthew asserts the firm Christian belief: God's Messiah, true Son of God and Shepherd-king of the final age, has been raised by the God in whom he placed all his trust. M.F.

Pause.

Even after Jesus' Death, their anxiety continues.

A foretaste of exactly what will be said!

Then he rolled a huge **stone** across the entrance to the tomb
  and departed.
But Mary **Magdalene** and the **other** Mary
  remained **sitting** there, **facing** the tomb.

The next day, the one following the day of preparation,
  the chief **priests** and the **Pharisees**
  gathered before **Pilate** and said,
    "Sir, we remember that this **impostor** while still alive said,
    'After **three** days I will be **raised** up.'
Give orders, then, that the grave be **secured** until the **third** day,
  lest his disciples come and **steal** him and say to the people,
  'He has been **raised** from the **dead**.'
This **last** imposture would be worse than the **first**."
Pilate said to them,
  "The guard is **yours**;
  go, **secure** it as best you can."
So they went and **secured** the tomb
  by fixing a **seal** to the stone and setting the **guard**.

[Shorter: Matthew 27:11–54 (see brackets)]

THE 4 STEPS OF *LECTIO DIVINA* OR PRAYERFUL READING

1. *Lectio:* Read a Scripture passage aloud slowly. Notice what phrase captures your attention and be attentive to its meaning. Silent pause.

2. *Meditatio:* Read the passage aloud slowly again, reflecting on the passage, allowing God to speak to you through it. Silent pause.

3. *Oratio:* Read it aloud slowly a third time, allowing it to be your prayer or response to God's gift of insight to you. Silent pause.

4. *Contemplatio:* Read it aloud slowly a fourth time, now resting in God's word.

HOLY THURSDAY: MASS OF THE LORD'S SUPPER

LECTIONARY #39

READING I   Exodus 12:1–8, 11–14

A reading from the Book of Exodus

The LORD said to Moses and Aaron in the land of Egypt,
    "This **month** shall stand at the head of your calendar;
    you shall reckon it the **first** month of the year.
Tell the whole **community** of Israel:
    On the tenth of this month every one of your **families**
    must procure for itself a **lamb**, one apiece for each household.
If a family is too small for a whole lamb,
    it shall **join** the nearest household in procuring one
    and shall **share** in the lamb
    in proportion to the number of persons who partake of it.
The lamb must be a year-old **male** and without **blemish**.
You may take it from either the **sheep** or the **goats**.
You shall keep it until the **fourteenth** day of this month,
    and **then**, with the whole **assembly** of Israel **present**,
    it shall be **slaughtered** during the evening **twilight**.
They shall take some of its **blood**
    and apply it to the two **doorposts** and the **lintel**
    of every **house** in which they partake of the **lamb**.
That same **night** they shall **eat** its roasted flesh
    with **unleavened** bread and bitter **herbs**. »

This narrative is one long set of specific instructions from God. It could sound dry, so don't lose the dramatic story behind the instructions. How would God sound delivering this plan?

Exodus = EK-suh-duhs
Moses = MOH-zis
Aaron = AYR-un

Don't lose "land of Egypt;" it reminds us that the people are enslaved.

The event is so significant the whole year will be reckoned from it.

Keep your pace up.

The celebration is not to be a financial burden on anyone.

Slow down; this is a very strange request.

READING I   This description of the first Passover meal represents centuries of reflection on the meaning of Israel's Exodus and the rituals developed to celebrate it. The account appears within the first five books of the Old Testament, called the Pentateuch, or in Hebrew, the Torah. The final editors, writing with centuries of hindsight, placed the account after the Lord struck Egypt with a tenth and decisive plague; after the death of the first-born humans and animals finally convinces Pharaoh to release God's people from slavery. Long after Israel's passage from Egyptian captivity to a new life of freedom, the Lord's people continued to observe a religious festival in remembrance of this foundational event, as Jews do to this day.

As described in Exodus, the Passover meal appears as a meal-sacrifice, a ritual meant to strengthen bonds of unity between the Hebrew people and God, and among members of the community as well. In Israelite culture, a fellowship meal was a significant way to express and create mutual bonds and mutual commitment. As the ritual developed over centuries, participants told the story of God's deliverance as an act of remembrance. In biblical thought, to "remember" means much more than to simply recall what happened in the past; recounting a previous event makes that ancient reality present, alive, and active here and now. Each time God's people retell the story of their liberation, divine love acts to save them in that moment.

The narrative intersperses description of the impending plague and Israel's escape with elements of the ritual meal. The Passover supper, a family celebration, required an unblemished offering to God; here the lamb's blood marks Hebrew

girt = belted

Another odd set of instructions.

"This is **how** you are to eat it:
   with your loins **girt**, **sandals** on your feet and your **staff**
      in hand,
   you shall **eat** like those who are in **flight**.
It is the **Passover** of the LORD.
For on this **same** night I will go through **Egypt**,
   striking down every **firstborn** of the land, both man and beast,
      and executing **judgment** on all the **gods** of Egypt—**I**, the LORD!
But the **blood** will **mark** the houses where **you** are.
Seeing the blood, I will pass **over** you;
   thus, when I **strike** the land of **Egypt**,
      no destructive blow will come upon **you**.

Don't shy away from these violent actions of
God, but don't overplay them either.

"See how much I care for you!"

No need to play up the phrase "pass over."

"This day shall be a **memorial feast** for you,
   which all your **generations** shall **celebrate**
      with **pilgrimage** to the LORD, as a **perpetual** institution."

Let the joy of the future celebrations come
through in your proclamation.

For meditation and context:

RESPONSORIAL PSALM Psalm 116:12–13, 15–16bc, 17–18
(1 Corinthians 10:16)

R. Our blessing-cup is a communion with the Blood of Christ.

How shall I make a return to the LORD
   for all the good he has done for me?
The cup of salvation I will take up,
   and I will call upon the name of the LORD.

Precious in the eyes of the LORD
   is the death of his faithful ones.
I am your servant, the son of your handmaid;
   you have loosed my bonds.

To you will I offer sacrifice of thanksgiving,
   and I will call upon the name of the LORD.
My vows to the LORD I will pay
   in the presence of all his people.

TO KEEP IN MIND
Use inflection (the high or low pitch
of your voice) to convey attitude
and feeling. High pitch expresses
intensity and excitement; low pitch
expresses sadness, contrition, or
solemnity.

---

homes so that the Lord will "pass over" them but strike the Egyptians with divine judgment. The decisive plague leads to the second and deepest meaning of "Passover": with the Lord leading them, the Chosen People will pass from slavery to freedom. Hence the author stipulates a perpetual celebration of this meal, to "remember" the saving acts of God.

READING II This oldest written account of the Lord's Supper was incorporated into Paul's letter less than thirty years after Jesus' Death and

Resurrection. However, the Apostle's use of technical terms for handing on authentic Christian tradition indicates that it dates from an even earlier time. Paul appeals to the original core of faith and practice to correct the Corinthian community, still struggling to shed ingrained social and cultural divisions. Distinctions according to status, wealth, and even the minister from whom they learned of Christ have plagued the community. Most disturbing to Paul, divisions have appeared among members who gather to celebrate the Lord's Supper,

the meal meant to unite believers to Christ and to one another.

Referring to the earliest faith proclamation, the Apostle links the supper to Jesus' meal with disciples before his Passion. This ancient tradition strove to communicate not simply Jesus' actions but their meaning. The broken bread and outpoured wine recall and make present the very person of the crucified and risen Christ, who gave his entire person and life itself "for you." In New Testament times, "body and blood" signified the whole person as a unity. It is this complete self-sacrifice

The words in this narrative will be very familiar to your assembly. Take time and let them hear it afresh.

Corinthians = kohr-IN-thee-uhnz

Note the progression: From the Lord to Paul to you. Tonight you are another link in that chain.

Be slow and deliberate.

Let the immense love of Jesus come through these words.

Pause.

Again, take your time.

This is not a history lesson. This action will happen shortly right here in your assembly.

READING II   1 Corinthians 11:23–26

A reading from the first Letter of Saint Paul to the Corinthians

Brothers and sisters:
I received from the **Lord** what I also handed on to **you**,
    that the Lord **Jesus**, on the **night** he was handed over,
    took **bread**, and, after he had given **thanks**,
    broke it and said, "This is my **body** that is for **you**.
Do this in **remembrance** of me."
In the same way also the **cup**, after supper, saying,
    "This **cup** is the **new** covenant in my **blood**.
Do this, as often as you **drink** it, in **remembrance** of me."
For as often as you **eat** this bread and **drink** the cup,
    you proclaim the **death** of the Lord until he comes.

A narrative. The intention is clearly stated in the last lines: Be servants to each other. Keep that purpose in mind throughout your proclamation.

Don't stress the word "pass."

A significant statement! Linger over it.

Iscariot = ih-SKAYR-ee-uht

Lower your volume on this aside.

He knows who he is and where his true identity comes from, so he loses nothing by taking the role of a servant.

This is very unexpected. Let the disciples' amazement at this action come through in your proclamation.

GOSPEL   John 13:1–15

A reading from the holy Gospel according to John

Before the feast of **Passover**, Jesus knew that his **hour** had come
    to pass from **this** world to the **Father**.
He **loved** his own in the world and he loved them to the **end**.
The devil had already induced **Judas**, son of Simon the **Iscariot**,
    to hand him **over**.
So, during **supper**,
    fully **aware** that the Father had put **everything** into his power
    and that he had come **from** God and was returning **to** God,
    he **rose** from supper and took **off** his outer garments.
He took a **towel** and tied it around his waist.
Then he poured **water** into a basin
    and began to **wash** the disciples' **feet**
    and dry them with the **towel** around his waist. »

for the good of the other that the community celebrating the Lord's Supper must "remember" (see Reading I). To "proclaim the death of the Lord" means to make present and active here and now his gift of life itself for others, without exception.

GOSPEL Like the other evangelists, John places the Death of Jesus near the time of the Jewish Passover, indicating that his passage through death to new life represents God's new and final act of deliverance. However, the fourth Gospel's account of Jesus' last meal with disciples before his execution differs from the others in significant ways. Lacking an institution account, John instead presents a major aspect of his Eucharistic theology through Jesus' deeply symbolic teaching act at the supper. Like this entire Gospel, today's passage often suggests multiple meanings.

In an earlier chapter, John presented Jesus as the Good Shepherd who would lay down his life for the sheep (John 10.1–18). At the supper, this supreme act of self-sacrificing love approaches, and it is here that disciples are commanded and strengthened to follow his example. The hour has come for Jesus to manifest love for his own "to the end"; in Greek the phrase can mean "to the utmost" or "to the point of death," and surely John intends both. In recounting Jesus laying aside his outer garment, the writer uses the same verb used to describe the Good Shepherd laying down life itself for the sheep. As John signaled at the very beginning of his account, some recognize who Jesus is and what he does, while some reject him. Both, however, share in the supper.

Assuming the role of a slave, Jesus demonstrates the depth of sharing in his

"I can't believe you're going to do this."

Jesus doesn't expect Peter to understand.

Peter is very confused, but if being washed is good, then he wants as much as he can get!

Drop your voice slightly on this aside.
Pause.

Pause; Jesus doesn't expect an answer, but give the disciples a moment to consider before explaining.

Be slow and deliberate; here is the whole point of the story.

He came to Simon **Peter**, who said to him,
　"**Master**, are you going to **wash** my **feet**?"
Jesus answered and said to him,
　"What I am **doing**, you do not **understand now**,
　but you **will** understand **later**."
Peter said to him, "You will **never** wash my feet."
Jesus answered him,
　"**Unless** I wash you, you will have no **inheritance** with me."
Simon Peter said to him,
　"**Master**, then not only my **feet**, but my **hands** and **head**
　　as well."
Jesus said to him,
　"Whoever has **bathed** has no **need** except to have his
　　feet washed, for he is **clean** all over;
　so you are clean, but not **all**."
For he knew who would **betray** him;
　for this **reason**, he said, "Not **all** of you are clean."

So when he had **washed** their feet
　and put his garments back on and reclined at table again,
　he said to them, "Do you **realize** what I have **done** for you?
You call me '**teacher**' and '**master**,' and rightly so, for indeed I **am**.
If **I**, therefore, the master and teacher, have washed **your** feet,
　you ought to wash one **another's** feet.
I have given you a **model** to follow,
　so that as **I** have done for **you**, you should **also** do."

life and mission that partaking in this meal implies, and begins to wash their feet. Resisting this astonishing role reversal, Peter protests and addresses Jesus as *kýrie,* meaning "master" or "lord." Word and act present an astounding juxtaposition, especially in contemporary culture. A lord owned slaves, but most assuredly would never lower himself to behave like one, taking on a most demeaning task. Jesus replies that refusal to participate in this action will mean having no part with Jesus. Typically impetuous, Peter then demands a more complete cleansing. Jesus

responds that those who have bathed need no further washing, though not everyone present is clean. On the surface, John points to the presence of the betrayer, Judas. But the dialogue may also refer to the cleansing of Baptism, since John emphasizes that some accept life offered by Jesus, while others do not. A clear decision is required.

Lest the disciples miss the meaning of his symbolic act, Jesus teaches it again by word: the foot-washing is a model for followers. By the standards of the prevailing culture, one could lower himself no further

in serving another than to do so as a slave, as one owned by the other. By all human standards, one can give nothing more than life itself. Jesus is about to give his whole self, his life itself, for those he loves; a service those who share his supper "should also do." M.F.

GOOD FRIDAY: PASSION OF THE LORD

LECTIONARY #40

READING I   Isaiah 52:13—53:12

A reading from the Book of the Prophet Isaiah

> **See**, my **servant** shall **prosper**,
>   he shall be raised high and greatly **exalted**.
> Even as many were **amazed** at him—
>   so **marred** was his look beyond human semblance
>   and his **appearance** beyond that of the sons of man—
> so shall he **startle** many nations,
>   because of him kings shall stand **speechless**;
> for those who have not been told shall **see**,
>   those who have not heard shall **ponder** it.
>
> Who would **believe** what we have heard?
>   To whom has the arm of the LORD been **revealed**?
> He grew up like a **sapling** before him,
>   like a shoot from the parched **earth**;
> there was in him no **stately** bearing to make us look at him,
>   nor appearance that would **attract** us to him.
> He was **spurned** and avoided by people,
>   a man of **suffering**, accustomed to **infirmity**,
> one of those from whom people **hide** their faces,
>   **spurned**, and we held him in **no** esteem. »

An exhortatory reading, much of it in thought rhyme. Don't let a somber mood overtake this story of good news. Though poignant, it tells of triumph, not defeat. The servant's sufferings contrast with what he accomplishes: he "prospers," is "exalted," placed among "the great."

Isaiah = ī-ZAY-uh

Open strong! Make eye contact with your assembly from the start, and set the tone for the reading. This is good news!

True, he doesn't look like someone you'd expect to be "exalted."

Be amazed, like speechless kings!

Pause.

We know a secret: This story doesn't end with suffering, but with life!

Such things happen in every community. Think of the suffering servants in yours.

Whom do we hide our faces from today? Whom do we spurn?

READING I | Today's First Reading, the fourth "Suffering Servant" song of Isaiah, is one of the most discussed and debated texts in the entire Old Testament. However, the exact identity and occasion of the servant's suffering is far less important than the overall themes rendered here in poetry, which intends to open up various possibilities of meaning rather than report specific factual events.

The "servant songs" appear in the second of three major segments of Isaiah's prophecy; this section most likely dates from the later part of the Babylonian captivity. In this circumstance, the prophet increasingly looks toward God's release and restoration of a defeated and decimated people. In four poems scattered through this part of the Book of Isaiah (chapters 40–55), the prophet describes the Servant of the Lord as a figure chosen by God and anointed with divine spirit to carry out saving activity on behalf of the shattered covenant community.

This last and longest poem often uses the language and imagery of the psalms, especially those that express thanksgiving for God's rescue from debilitating or death-dealing situations. For the original audience of these prophecies, the servant may have represented the covenant people, but the Church's liturgy has followed New Testament interpretations that apply this poem to Jesus. In so doing, these Christian authors made use of Jewish methods of interpreting earlier Scriptures in order to clarify their meaning for the present. Such modes of interpretation often employed creative, poetic approaches to the Old Testament, approaches rooted in the belief that divine guidance aided an ever-deepening understanding of God's Word.

Slow down; you've just learned that those you have dismissed as worthless are actually bearing your own sufferings. How do you feel about this? Let that emotional choice come through in these lines.

How have our communities gone astray? What is our guilt and sorrow?

Pause.

Avoid a tone of pity or sadness as you describe the servant's attitude in these lines; his silence is a sign of his strength and trust in God. Proclaim with that steadfast conviction.

Because God knows what plans are in store for the servant.

Here is the servant's reward for his suffering.

This is good news!

Yet it was **our** infirmities that he bore,
   our **sufferings** that he endured,
while we thought of him as **stricken**,
   as one **smitten** by God and afflicted.
But he was **pierced** for our offenses,
   crushed for our **sins**;
upon **him** was the **chastisement** that makes **us** whole,
   by his **stripes** we were **healed**.
We had **all** gone astray like **sheep**,
   each following his own way;
but the LORD laid upon **him**
   the guilt of us **all**.

Though he was **harshly** treated, he **submitted**
   and opened **not** his **mouth**;
like a **lamb** led to the slaughter
   or a **sheep** before the shearers,
   he was **silent** and opened not his mouth.
Oppressed and **condemned**, he was taken away,
   and who would have thought any **more** of his destiny?
When he was **cut** off from the land of the **living**,
   and **smitten** for the sin of his people,
a **grave** was assigned him among the wicked
   and a burial place with **evildoers**,
though he had done **no** wrong
   nor spoken any **falsehood**.
But the LORD was pleased
   to crush him in **infirmity**.

If he gives his **life** as an **offering** for sin,
   he shall see his **descendants** in a long life,
   and the **will** of the LORD shall be accomplished
      through **him**.

The beginning of the First Reading seems to anticipate its ending by describing such a complete reversal of the servant's fortunes that other nations will fall speechless in amazement. This restoration, of course, must be attributed to the action of God. Though the servant grew up under God's watchful eye, by human standards there was nothing remarkable or noteworthy about him. In fact, as a person accustomed to suffering, he was avoided by others, because Jewish belief assumed that human sorrows resulted from sin.

At this point in the poem, the servant begins to be described as "we," a corporate body that is somehow healed and restored to wholeness through suffering. It appears that ancient Israel did have some level of belief that vicarious suffering of an individual could be redemptive for the whole community. Reference to the people's guilt taken on by the servant may reflect an ancient scapegoat ritual that formed part of atonement rituals. In this symbolic act, the people's offenses were confessed and laid upon a goat that was then driven into the

wilderness, taking away the community's sin and guilt (Leviticus 16:20–22).

Though mistreated, oppressed, and condemned, the servant bears pain, rejection, and abuse in silence. Though he is innocent, the view that suffering implies guilt prevails, and so the servant is designated for burial among the wicked. Again the poem expresses belief that one person's suffering can ultimately bring about renewal for the people as a whole. Through the servant's self-offering, "the will of the LORD shall be accomplished." It is important to be aware that in biblical thought, God's

More good news!

Because of his **affliction**
    he shall see the **light** in fullness of days;
through his suffering, my servant shall **justify** many,
    and their **guilt** he shall bear.

The final triumph!

Therefore I will give him his portion among the **great**,
    and he shall divide the spoils with the **mighty**,
because he surrendered himself to **death**
    and was counted among the **wicked**;

Slow down on this final line, and maintain eye contact with the assembly.

and he shall take away the **sins** of many,
    and win **pardon** for their offenses.

For meditation and context:

RESPONSORIAL PSALM   Psalm 31:2, 6, 12–13, 15–16, 17, 25 (Luke 23:46)

R. Father, into your hands I commend my spirit.

In you, O LORD, I take refuge;
    let me never be put to shame.
In your justice rescue me.
Into your hands I commend my spirit;
    you will redeem me, O LORD,
        O faithful God.

For all my foes I am an object of reproach,
    a laughingstock to my neighbors,
        and a dread to my friends;
    they who see me abroad flee from me.
I am forgotten like the unremembered dead;
    I am like a dish that is broken.

But my trust is in you, O LORD;
    I say, "You are my God.
In your hands is my destiny; rescue me
    from the clutches of my enemies
        and my persecutors."

Let your face shine upon your servant;
    save me in your kindness.
Take courage and be stouthearted,
    all you who hope in the LORD.

> **TO KEEP IN MIND**
> Use inflection (the high or low pitch of your voice) to convey attitude and feeling. High pitch expresses intensity and excitement; low pitch expresses sadness, contrition, or solemnity.

An exhortatory reading. Think of someone you know who is struggling with their faith, especially one who is suffering and in need of encouragement. Proclaim this reading as if you were speaking to that one person.

The challenge of holding onto our faith is easier because we have someone like us who, like a high priest, leads us on the path to God.

our confession = our faith

READING II   Hebrews 4:14–16; 5:7–9

A reading from the Letter to the Hebrews

Brothers and sisters:
Since we have a **great** high priest who has passed through
    the heavens,
    Jesus, the Son of God,
    let us hold fast to our **confession**. »

will always ultimately desires human salvation, healing, and wholeness.

Like a Psalm of thanksgiving, the poem shifts from lament to giving praise and thanks for divine reversal of the sufferer's plight, even before the fact. The prophet describes the most important effect of the servant's sacrificial suffering: the covenant people will be justified: restored to right relationships with God, one another, and all things. The servant who trusted in God's saving might is not disappointed: God purifies, renews, and

justifies the people, and ultimately the servant himself is vindicated.

READING II Because Hebrews is unique among New Testament books in presenting Christ as the perfect high priest, it is important to understand the purpose of the high priest in Jewish religious practice. A major function of the high priest was to offer prayer and sacrifice on the annual Day of Atonement; only he could stand before God in the Temple's Holy of Holies to ask forgiveness for the sins of all the people during the preceding year. The

biblical view of atonement, however, gives precedence to God's saving, renewing action; the people's sacrifice confirms but does cause wholeness and oneness with God.

The Letter to the Hebrews, more a sermon than a letter, is described as a "word of exhortation" (Hebrews 13:22). The author interweaves two major strands: a call to persevere in faith and mutual love in the face of adversity and his interpretation of Christ as both perfect high priest and as actual atonement sacrifice.

Our priest not only goes before us but also stands beside us, and enters into all our suffering.

Don't swallow "sin."

So why wouldn't we ask for mercy and grace from such a person? This is good news! Maintain eye contact with your assembly on this line, and invite them to throw all their cares upon Jesus.

There is nothing wrong with crying out to God in our need like Jesus did.

Suffering, though painful in the moment, can lead to learning and growth.

For we do not have a high priest
   who is unable to **sympathize** with our weaknesses,
   but one who has similarly been **tested** in every **way**,
   yet without sin.
So let us confidently approach the throne of **grace**
   to receive **mercy** and to find **grace** for timely **help**.

In the days when Christ was in the **flesh**,
   he offered **prayers** and **supplications** with loud **cries** and **tears**
   to the one who was able to **save** him from death,
   and he was heard because of his **reverence**.
Son though he was, he learned **obedience** from what he suffered;
   and when he was made perfect,
   he became the source of eternal **salvation** for all who obey him.

John's Passion narrative has Jesus completely in control of all that happens to him. He's not emotionless, but he has a centered intensity, while all those around him are frantic and unbalanced. Keep that contrast evident in your pacing and volume.

Kidron = KID-ruhn

Judas is expecting a fight. Might this tell us something about his intention?

Jesus goes out to them; he is in control.

Nazorean = naz-uh-REE-uhn
Jesus uses the name of God revealed to Moses.

The crowd falls to the ground at the name of God.

GOSPEL   John 18:1—19:42

The Passion of our Lord Jesus Christ according to John

(1) Jesus went out with his disciples across the Kidron valley
   to where there was a **garden**,
   into which he and his disciples entered.
Judas his **betrayer also** knew the place,
   because Jesus had **often** met there with his disciples.
(2) So Judas got a band of **soldiers** and **guards**
   from the chief **priests** and the **Pharisees**
   and went there with **lanterns**, **torches**, and **weapons**.
Jesus, knowing everything that was going to happen to him,
   went out and said to them, "**Whom** are you looking for?"
They answered him, "**Jesus** the **Nazorean**."
He said to them, "**I AM**."
Judas his betrayer was **also** with them.
When he said to them, "**I AM**,"
   they turned away and **fell** to the ground.

The author asserts that as the divine Son of God, Jesus is capable of bringing about atonement. But Christians called to imitate him must also recall that their high priest is fully human, able to understand mortal weakness because he "has similarly been tested in every way." However, regardless of the depth of Jesus' suffering, he never chose to sin. In this he is the supreme example to emulate.

The writer refers to Christ's days "in the flesh," emphasizing his complete identification with humanity. The Greek word here translated "flesh" is *sarkos*, which sig-

nifies the entire human being as susceptible to weakness, suffering, and death. Fully experiencing "the flesh," Jesus called upon divine help in reverent submission to God. His action and attitude provide the model for Christian imitation, for he "learned obedience" through his own suffering.

It is difficult to capture the full original meaning of the phrase translated "when he was made perfect." The Greek term used here can include several meanings: to reach a physical or chronological end, to reach a goal, or to achieve completion. It seems that the author wishes to reassure his readers

that when God's plan reached its completion through the Death and Resurrection of Jesus, he became the source of God's own saving life for all who, like him, learn obedience by trusting and surrendering to God. Christ thus embodies the goal for all his followers: to imitate him in his passage through death to new life in God.

GOSPEL | Any portion of the fourth Gospel must be understood in light of its prologue, in which the author offers a summary-preview of his foundational understanding of Christ: he is

So he **again** asked them,
  "**Whom** are you looking for?"
They said, "**Jesus** the **Nazorean**."
Jesus answered,
  "I **told** you that **I AM**.
So if you are looking for **me**, let these men **go**."
This was to fulfill what he had said,
  "I have not lost **any** of those you gave me."
Then Simon **Peter**, who had a **sword**, **drew** it,
  struck the high priest's slave, and **cut** off his right **ear**.
The slave's name was Malchus.
Jesus said to Peter,
  "Put your **sword** into its **scabbard**.
Shall I not drink the **cup** that the Father gave me?"

So the band of soldiers, the tribune, and the Jewish guards
    seized Jesus,
  bound him, and brought him to **Annas** first.
He was the father-in-law of Caiaphas,
  who was high priest that year.
It was Caiaphas who had counseled the Jews
    that it was better that **one** man should die rather than
      the **people**.

(3) Simon Peter and another disciple **followed** Jesus.
Now the other disciple was **known** to the high priest,
  and he entered the courtyard of the high priest with Jesus.
But **Peter** stood at the gate **outside**.
So the other **disciple**, the acquaintance of the high priest,
    went out and spoke to the **gatekeeper** and brought Peter in.
Then the **maid** who was the gatekeeper said to Peter,
  "**You** are not one of this man's **disciples**, are you?"
He said, "I am **not**." »

Proclaim this moment of sudden violence quickly.

Obviously a threat that, next time, it will be someone's head.

Malchus = MAL-kuhs

Speak with force and authority. There will be no violence from Jesus or on his behalf.

Annas = AN-uhs

Caiaphas = KĪ-uh fuhs

Getting rid of one troublemaker might keep the Romans from punishing the whole city for his actions.

Offhandedly.

God's own self-revealing Word "made flesh" (see Reading II). In Jesus' full humanity, in his words, works, and passage through Death to Resurrection, God proclaims: This is who I am—self-giving love for the re-creation of humankind, my beloved. John's interpretation of Jesus the Christ reflects about seven decades of Christian reflection on his life, Passion, and Resurrection. That reflection portrays, above all, the living, glorified Christ experienced in the present, alive within and among believers in the Spirit. Like any other, this Gospel account must be understood as a faith proclamation in narrative form. Even more than the accounts of Matthew, Mark, or Luke, John's account focuses on the meaning of Jesus in and for the present. The author illuminates his major purpose; he writes not simply to communicate factual details, but to elicit life-giving faith in Jesus as the Messiah and Son of God (John 21:30–31).

Other aspects of John's historical context and literary approach also aid us in understanding his intentions and message. In the New Testament era, mainstream Judaism struggled to identify its most authentic form in a time of varying perspectives and interpretations of the Law of Moses. Some proponents of mainstream Judaism viewed Jewish Christians as members of one among several misguided Jewish sects, and this antagonism surfaces frequently in the Fourth Gospel. The author repeatedly presents Jesus and "the Jews" in debate and opposition, with growing intensity. This name, "the Jews," does not condemn all Jews of all time, but represents strains of Judaism that resisted or fully rejected the Christian movement at the end of the first century.

Now the slaves and the guards were standing around
   a charcoal **fire**
  that they had made, because it was cold,
  and were warming themselves.
Peter was also standing there keeping **warm**.

(4) The high priest questioned Jesus
  about his **disciples** and about his **doctrine**.
Jesus answered him,
  "I have spoken **publicly** to the world.
I have always taught in a **synagogue**
  or in the **temple** area where all the Jews gather,
  and in secret I have said **nothing**. Why ask me?
Ask those who **heard** me what I said to them.
They know what I said."
When he had said this,
  one of the temple guards standing there **struck** Jesus and said,
  "Is **this** the way you answer the high priest?"
Jesus answered him,
  "If I have spoken wrongly, **testify** to the wrong;
  but if I have spoken **rightly**, why do you strike me?"
Then Annas sent him **bound** to **Caiaphas** the high priest.

(5) Now Simon **Peter** was standing there keeping warm.
And they said to him,
  "**You** are not one of his disciples, are you?"
He **denied** it and said,
  "I am **not**."
One of the **slaves** of the high priest,
  a relative of the one whose ear Peter had cut off, said,
  "Didn't I **see** you in the garden with him?"
Again Peter denied it.
And **immediately** the **cock** crowed.

(6, 7) Then they brought Jesus from Caiaphas to the **praetorium**.
It was morning.

Jesus gives a reasoned response, but also implies that the chief priest already knows exactly what Jesus taught. Jesus refuses to play the game the chief priest is setting up.

Speak "struck" sharply to convey the blow.

Keep the guard's anger in his response.

Jesus remains calm and will not return anger with anger. Again, his response is simple and reasoned.

Speak this second denial with more firmness.

Give this description the intensity of Peter's response.

Peter recognizes what he's done.

Pause for a scene shift.

praetorium = prih-TOHR-ee-uhm

John contrasts action inside the praetorium between Pilate and Jesus, and action outside between Pilate and the high priests. The "internal" conversation is about identity and truth. The "external" conversation is about guilt and power and is antagonistic. Change your tone as the scene alternates between inside and outside.

John's interpretation of Christ indicates ways in which Jewish thought, institutions, and observances are replaced by Jesus, God's self-revealing Word made flesh. In the fourth Gospel, Jesus does not speak the Word of God, he *is* that Word. One need not approach the Temple to meet God, one need only encounter Jesus; Jesus does not celebrate God's great saving act of Passover, he himself *is* the new Passover. To convey his message convincingly to those who remain in Judaism, John uses Jewish modes of interpreting the Old Testament, often making creative use of it

to interpret the meaning of Jesus for his time and place (see also Reading I).

The fourth evangelist presents Jesus' Passion and Death as the final and definitive self-revelation of God in Jesus, the divine Word made flesh. For John, Jesus freely chooses to lay down his life for those he loves, so that they may have fullness of life. In his Passion and Death, the word Jesus himself spoke to "the Jews" (John 10:10–18) becomes a Word made flesh, a word enacted. In the fourth Gospel, Jesus appears to be the one in charge of

all proceedings of his Passion, from arrest through his last breath.

Only John names the place of Jesus' arrest as a garden. As the evangelist signaled in the opening words of his prologue ("In the beginning") that a new creation story originates with Jesus, so now he suggests that everything turned awry in the first garden will soon be set right. Unlike the synoptic accounts (Matthew, Mark, and Luke) in which Jesus is seized by religious authorities, in John he steps forward to meet those who will lead him to death, with clear knowledge of what is about to

They stick to the minor details of the Law while doing violence to its intent.

The chief priests must get Pilate to condemn Jesus to death. Their response here is matter-of-fact, but their desperation increases as the scene progresses.

Pilate doesn't want to be bothered.

Keep your voice low throughout the conversations between Pilate and Jesus, as if they were standing very close.

He knows Jesus is no king. What does Pilate want from Jesus? Pilate's power comes solely from his position; perhaps he wants to understand how someone with no position can still hold power.
"Speak for yourself!"

Pilate is puzzled. How could the chief priests be threatened by a nobody like Jesus?

Jesus remains calm in his response: Kingdoms of this world fight; his Kingdom is one of peace.

"My truth comes from within, not from what others think of me."

And they themselves did not enter the praetorium,
   in order not to be **defiled** so that they could eat the **Passover**.
So **Pilate** came out to them and said,
   "What **charge** do you bring against this man?"
They answered and said to him,
   "If he were not a **criminal**,
   we would not have handed him over to you."
At this, Pilate said to them,
   "Take him **yourselves**, and judge him according to your law."
The Jews answered him,
   "We do not have the right to **execute** anyone,"
   in order that the word of Jesus might be **fulfilled**
   that he said indicating the **kind** of death he would die.
So Pilate went back into the praetorium
   and summoned Jesus and said to him,
   "**Are** you the **King** of the **Jews**?"
Jesus answered,
   "Do you say this on your **own**
   or have **others** told you about me?"
Pilate answered,
   "**I** am not a **Jew**, am I?
Your own **nation** and the chief priests handed you over to me.
What have you **done**?"
Jesus answered,
   "My kingdom does not belong to **this** world.
If my kingdom **did** belong to this world,
   my attendants would be **fighting**
   to keep me from being handed over to the Jews.
But as it **is**, my kingdom is not **here**."
So Pilate said to him,
   "Then you **are** a king?"
Jesus answered,
   "**You** say I am a king.
For this I was **born** and for this I came into the world,
   to testify to the **truth**. »

happen. Taking an active role in his own capture, he asks those who confront him who they are looking for. To their reply, "Jesus the Nazorean," he responds three times, with dual meaning, "I AM." In Greek, his answer (*egō eimi*) can simply mean, "It is I" or "I am the one." However, the Greek Old Testament translated the revealed name of God, often rendered "I AM" or "I am who am," with the same words.

John again indicates that the true character of the divine Word made flesh will soon be fully revealed, and it will be manifest in Jesus' chosen act of laying

down life itself for those he loves. Preventing Peter from violence to ward off his arrest, Jesus, in contrast to asking the Father to let the cup of suffering pass, as in the synoptic accounts, instead, freely embraces it. In doing so, he again proclaims his identity as divine Word made flesh.

Most scholars believe that a historical reality underlies the scenes of Jesus brought before Annas, Caiaphas, and Pilate. Ample evidence indicates that historically, some Jews, primarily those in religious leadership, colluded with Roman authorities to eliminate Jesus in order to

protect their own power and position. Throughout his narrative, John has portrayed growing antagonism between "the Jews" and Jesus, and now it reaches a crescendo. Religious leaders in conflict with Jesus would be grateful to Rome for ridding them of this troublesome rabbi who challenges Jewish belief and practice, as well as their supremacy. John intersperses the episodes of Peter's denial of Jesus among the scenes of his confrontation with both Jewish and Roman authorities.

Among the four canonical Gospels, only John indicates a reason for the Jewish

How does Pilate feel about Jesus
at this point? Is he intrigued?
Dismissive? Frightened?

Barabbas = buh-RAB-uhs

scourged = skerjd

This should sound like mocking.

Pilate still doesn't understand why Jesus
would be a threat.

The chief priests and guards are
becoming frenzied.

Everyone who belongs to the truth **listens** to my voice."
Pilate said to him, "What is **truth**?"

When he had said this,
    he **again** went out to the Jews and said to them,
    "I find no **guilt** in him.
(8) But you have a **custom** that I release one prisoner to you
        at Passover.
Do you want me to release to you the **King** of the Jews?"
They cried out **again**,
    "Not this one but **Barabbas**!"
Now Barabbas was a **revolutionary**.

Then Pilate took Jesus and had him **scourged**.
And the soldiers wove a **crown** out of **thorns** and placed it
        on his head,
    and clothed him in a **purple** cloak,
    and they came to him and said,
    "**Hail**, King of the Jews!"
And they **struck** him repeatedly.
(9) Once **more** Pilate went out and said to them,
    "**Look**, I am bringing him **out** to you,
    so that you may **know** that I find no guilt in him."
So Jesus came out,
    wearing the crown of **thorns** and the purple **cloak**.
And he said to them, "**Behold**, the man!"
When the chief priests and the guards saw him they cried out,
    "**Crucify** him, **crucify** him!"
Pilate said to them,
    "Take him **yourselves** and crucify him.
I find no **guilt** in him."
The Jews answered,
    "We have a law, and according to that law he ought to **die**,
    because he **made** himself the **Son** of God."

leadership to accuse Jesus of a capital crime before the Roman governor, Pilate. Though the religious laws of Judaism found Jesus guilty of an offense meriting death (Mark 14:64), execution itself could be carried out only by the ruling empire. The first scene involving Jesus and Pilate involves multilevel meanings, often ironic, which is typical of John. Pilate tests Jesus' response to his inquiry, "Are you the king of the Jews?" Any prisoner answering in the affirmative would be sentenced to death as an insurrectionist, and Jesus initially seems to sidestep the question. He then claims a

kingdom not of this world, echoing John's assertion in the prologue: he is one sent from God as embodiment of divine truth. Pilate can only respond with a question, "What is truth?", for he fails to recognize the truth of God in the prisoner before him. As in the synoptics, Pilate is confronted with repeated calls to release not Jesus, but Barabbas, whose name means "son of the father." And so the Roman governor chooses the revolutionary, Barabbas, instead of the true Son of the Father. In John it is not the crowds who urge the

release of Barabbas, but "the Jews," who cannot accept that Jesus is Son of God.

After having Jesus scourged and mocked, Pilate repeatedly states that he finds no guilt in his prisoner. "The Jews," however, respond that according to their law he must die because he made himself "Son of God." This charge is not made in John's Passion account, but appears earlier in preceding chapters (for example, John 5:18). Pilate threatens Jesus with a claim to hold the power of life and death over him; however, Jesus again speaks as no ordinary prisoner but as one who can claim a

Now when Pilate heard this statement,
he became even **more** afraid,
and went back into the praetorium and said to Jesus,
"Where are you **from**?"
Jesus did not **answer** him.
So Pilate said to him,
"Do you not **speak** to me?
Do you not know that I have power to **release** you
and I have power to **crucify** you?"
Jesus answered him,
"You would have **no** power over me
if it had not been given to you from **above**.
For this reason the **one** who handed me over to you
has the **greater** sin."
Consequently, Pilate tried to release him;
but the **Jews** cried out,
"If you release him, you are not a **Friend** of **Caesar**.
Everyone who makes himself a king opposes Caesar."

When Pilate heard these words he brought Jesus out
and seated him on the **judge's** bench
in the place called **Stone Pavement**, in Hebrew, **Gabbatha**.
It was **preparation** day for **Passover**, and it was about **noon**.
And he said to the Jews,
"**Behold**, your **king**!"
They **cried** out,
"Take him **away**, take him **away**! **Crucify** him!"
Pilate said to them,
"Shall I crucify your **king**?"
The chief priests answered,
"We have **no** king but **Caesar**."
Then he handed him over to them to be **crucified**.

So they took Jesus, and, carrying the cross **himself**,
he went out to what is called the Place of the **Skull**,
in Hebrew, **Golgotha**. »

Pilate is completely unnerved by Jesus.

Pilate is getting desperate. Raise your energy here. Only Jesus remains outside the storm of violence and intrigue swirling about.

Speak "Friend of Caesar" like a title.

Gabbatha = GAB-uh-thuh

The rest of this exchange intensifies very quickly in both pace and energy.

It should sound like a riot is about to break out.

The chief priests have blasphemed (the very charge they brought against Jesus) by claiming Caesar as their king over God. Stop, and let this sink in.

More quietly, then take a significant pause to let the scene subside.

Jesus remains in control; no one helps him and it seems no one needs to.

Golgotha = GAWL-guh-thuh

---

greater authority. When Pilate tries to release Jesus, "the Jews" remind him that such a decision would surely fail to earn him the honorific title "Friend of Caesar."

Finally, battered by continuing insistence of "the Jews," Pilate calls for Jesus' execution. John carefully notes the day and the hour: about noon on preparation day for the Sabbath. His chronology does not match that of the synoptics, but John is far less focused on historical detail than on christological meaning. At this moment, the slaughter of lambs for the Jewish feast of Passover begins. With his chronology, John

instructs his hearers that Jesus is even more than the Suffering Servant of Isaiah, led like a lamb to slaughter (see Reading II); he is, in his person and work, the new Passover for a New Israel of the final age.

Alone among the canonical Gospel accounts, John states that Jesus carries the Cross himself; the Word of God who is one with the Father relies only on divine assistance. The placard indicating the crucified one's crime, part of the usual Roman procedure, mockingly indicates that Jesus dies as an insurrectionist. But John adds another detail to proclaim Jesus' true kingship. When

the chief priests demand that the inscription should not state "King of the Jews" but only that Jesus had made this claim, even the obtuse and unbelieving Pilate decrees, "What I have written, I have written."

Historically, Roman soldiers who carried out a crucifixion were allowed to take portions of the executed person's clothing, but the evangelist John notes deeper meanings as fulfillment of Scripture, quoting Psalm 22. Only John speaks of Jesus providing for mutual care of his mother and the Beloved Disciple ("One of his disciples, the one whom Jesus loved," John 13:23).

Take your time setting this scene.

Perhaps Pilate realized that Jesus had the makings of a king.

There they **crucified** him, and with him two **others**,
    one on either side, with Jesus in the middle.
Pilate also had an inscription written and put on the cross.
It read,
    "**Jesus** the **Nazorean**, the **King** of the **Jews**."
Now many of the Jews read this inscription,
    because the place where Jesus was crucified was near the **city**;
    and it was written in Hebrew, Latin, and Greek.
So the chief priests of the Jews said to **Pilate**,
    "Do not write 'The King of the Jews,'
    but that he **said**, 'I am the King of the Jews.'"
Pilate answered,
    "What I have **written**, I have written."

When the **soldiers** had crucified Jesus,
    they took his clothes and **divided** them into four shares,
    a share for each soldier.
They also took his tunic, but the tunic was **seamless**,
    woven in one piece from the top **down**.
So they said to one another,
    "Let's not tear it, but cast **lots** for it to see whose it will be,"
    in order that the passage of Scripture might be **fulfilled**
        that says:
        They **divided** *my* garments *among them,*
            and for my vesture *they cast* **lots**.
This is what the soldiers did.
Standing by the cross of Jesus were his mother
    and his mother's sister, Mary the wife of Clopas,
    and Mary of Magdala.
When Jesus saw his **mother** and the disciple there whom
        he **loved**
    he said to his mother, "**Woman**, behold, your **son**."
Then he said to the **disciple**,
    "Behold, your **mother**."
And from **that** hour the disciple took her into his **home**.

Pause.

There are four women at the cross. Make sure each is distinct.

Magdala = MAG-duh-luh

A woman without a husband or son would struggle to survive, so Jesus gives her into the disciple's care.

Various interpretations of this act have been given; some believe it points to Jesus' enduring care for those who belong to him, while others perceive an indication that Jesus will soon hand over his work to those who do believe in him.

Jesus approaches the end of his earthly life and of the work the Father has given him, aware that both are reaching completion. John emphasizes this sense of accomplishment, arriving at an intended goal, with words here translated "finished" and "fulfilled." In Greek, the words share a single root which can carry both meanings.

The evangelist portrays Jesus as fully conscious that his total self-gift will end his life in "the flesh" as it brings God's plan to its desired goal. John interprets Jesus' words "I thirst" as fulfilling Scripture; the author may be referring to Psalm 22:16 or 69:22. Both prayers present a faithful sufferer crying out to God in lament, yet expressing hope in ultimate divine deliverance.

Still, John's interpretation of Jesus reaches beyond this Old Testament theme of the vindicated Suffering Righteous One. In response to his cry of thirst, someone offers a sponge soaked with wine, using "a

sprig of hyssop." With this detail, John alludes to the first Passover, when the Lord instructed the Hebrews to mark their door posts with the blood of the lamb sacrificed for the meal before flight from Egypt. They were to sprinkle the lamb's blood with a bunch of hyssop, thus ensuring that God would pass over Hebrew homes on his way to carry out the final plague upon Egypt. With this detail, John suggests again that Jesus himself is the new Passover Lamb of the new and final Passover: a passage through death to fullness of life.

Begin to slow down and speak more quietly.

After this, aware that everything was now **finished**,
in order that the Scripture might be **fulfilled**,
Jesus said, "I **thirst**."
There was a vessel filled with common **wine**.

hyssop = HIS-uhp

So they put a sponge soaked in wine on a sprig of hyssop
and put it up to his mouth.
When Jesus had taken the wine, he said,

There's a tired but satisfied tone here.

"It is **finished**."
And **bowing** his **head**, he handed **over** the **spirit**.

[Here all kneel and pause for a short time.]

Pick up your pace.

Now since it was **preparation** day,
in order that the bodies might not remain
on the cross on the **sabbath**,
for the sabbath day of that week was a **solemn** one,
the Jews asked Pilate that their legs be **broken**
and that they be taken down.
So the soldiers came and **broke** the legs of the **first**
and then of the **other** one who was crucified with Jesus.
But when they came to Jesus and saw that he was already dead,
they did **not** break his legs,
but one soldier thrust his **lance** into his **side**,
and immediately **blood** and **water** flowed out.

An amazing sight!
Lower your voice on this aside.

An **eyewitness** has **testified**, and his testimony is **true**;
he knows that he is speaking the **truth**,
so that you **also** may come to **believe**.
For this happened so that the Scripture passage might be **fulfilled**:
*Not a **bone** of it will be **broken**.*
And again **another** passage says:
*They will **look** upon him whom they have **pierced**.*

Arimathea = ayr-ih-muh-THEE-uh

After **this**, **Joseph** of **Arimathea**,
secretly a disciple of Jesus for **fear** of the Jews,
asked Pilate if he could **remove** the body of Jesus. »

Finally, Jesus himself proclaims what the evangelist has stated: "It is finished." For the third time in three verses, John uses the same word with multilayered meaning. He announces that Jesus has died, and that in so doing, God's plan for human salvation is completed, brought to its intended goal. At this moment, Jesus "handed over the spirit." Yet again, John employs dual meaning. On one hand, the phrase simply states that Jesus has died, returning the life-breath of God to the One who first created his life in the flesh (see

Genesis 2:7). More profoundly, the evangelist proclaims that Jesus, in ending his earthly life, fulfills his promise to send "the Advocate" upon returning to the Father (John 16:1–15). John uses the Greek word *paraklētos*, variously translated but indicating the Holy Spirit; at root, the word designates someone who can be counted upon to stand at the side of another.

In the following passage, Pilate's order to break Jesus' legs may reflect a known Roman practice; if a crucified prisoner did not die within several days, the legs might

be broken to hasten death. For John, however, the scene presents an opportunity for theological commentary. The blood and water flowing from the side of Jesus can be understood to symbolize the Spirit, which John earlier associated with water, and Jesus' life itself, signified by blood, given for those he loves. With a few words drawn from Jewish sacred writings, John announces that Jesus brings to completion three Old Testament motifs: the Paschal Lamb, the Suffering Righteous One, and the

Nicodemus = nik-uh-DEE-muhs (see John 3:1)

myrrh = mer; aloes = AL-ohz (spices to anoint the body)

Truly a burial fit for a king.

You might bring a hint of joy into your mention of the garden, the place of the Resurrection.

> **TO KEEP IN MIND**
> A didactic reading is usually given out of love for the community. Make sure that love is evident in your proclamation.

> **TO KEEP IN MIND**
> Pay attention to the pace of your reading. Varying the pace gives listeners clues to the meaning of the text. The most common problem for proclaimers new to the ministry is going too fast to be understood.

Messiah (Exodus 12:46; Psalm 34:21; Zechariah 12:10).

As in the synoptic Gospel accounts, Joseph of Arimathea asks for and receives for burial the body of Jesus, but the evangelist adds a significant detail. With the burial of Jesus, John returns to the place in which he began his Passion account: a garden. Again he suggests that all that was lacking in the first garden "in the beginning" will now be created anew. The body of Jesus is laid in a new tomb, in which no one has yet been buried; from it will spring the new life of God's new creation. M.F.

And Pilate permitted it.
So he came and **took** his body.
Nicodemus, the one who had first come to him at **night**,
 also came bringing a mixture of **myrrh** and **aloes**
 weighing about one **hundred** pounds.
They took the **body** of Jesus
 and bound it with **burial cloths** along with the **spices**,
 according to the Jewish burial custom.
Now in the place where he had been crucified there was a **garden**,
 and in the garden a **new tomb**, in which no one had yet
 been buried.
So they laid Jesus **there** because of the Jewish preparation day;
 for the tomb was close by.

HOLY SATURDAY: EASTER VIGIL

LECTIONARY #41

READING I   Genesis 1:1—2:2

A reading from the Book of Genesis

[In the **beginning**, when God **created** the heavens and the earth,]
    the earth was a formless **wasteland**, and **darkness** covered
        the **abyss**,
    while a mighty wind **swept** over the waters.

Then God **said**,
    "Let there be **light**," and there **was** light.
God saw how **good** the light was.
God then **separated** the light from the darkness.
God called the light "**day**," and the darkness he called "**night**."
Thus **evening** came, and **morning** followed—the **first** day.

Then God **said**,
    "Let there be a **dome** in the middle of the waters,
    to **separate** one body of water from the other."
And so it **happened**:
    God made the dome,
    and it separated the water **above** the dome from the water
        below it.
God called the dome "the **sky**."
Evening came, and **morning** followed—the **second** day.

Then God **said**,
    "Let the **water** under the sky be gathered into a single **basin**,
    so that the dry **land** may appear." »

A narrative; don't shy away from the rhythm created by the repeated phrasing. It creates the feeling of an unfolding ritual. Let your pacing and intensity increase a bit with each day, like a sunrise.

Use a hushed tone and take your time describing this opening scene.

Let the scene settle a moment.

Keep the volume low, even on God's lines, as if God were almost breathing creation into being.

Speak all these names as if they are brand new.

Raise the volume on God's voice just a bit with each day.

There are options for readings today. Ask your parish staff which ones will be used.

READING I The full range of readings for this greatest of liturgies begins with the story of God's first creation and comes full circle with the beginning of humankind's re-creation through Christ. The First Reading is from the beginning of the Old Testament and the Book of Genesis, the first of two creation narratives. This first creation story most likely came from the hand of a group of priests writing during the Babylonian exile, and the narrative reflects their concern with assuring the captive people that the Lord is their one source of life and future. Thus the writer begins with God bringing life and order out of formless chaos. The Hebrew word *ruach*, here translated "mighty wind," can mean breath, wind, or spirit. The divine power that brings all material creation into being is the same that will bring to life the human creature in the second creation story (Genesis 2:7).

The writer continues to emphasize this divine power at work in a systematic pattern of one day following the next, with specific creatures brought to life in orderly fashion by God's mighty Word. Repeatedly the author notes that what is created is "good"; the original Hebrew word has a vast range of meanings, including "pleasing,

And so it **happened**:
> the water under the sky was **gathered** into its basin,
> and the dry **land** appeared.
God called the dry land "the **earth**,"
> and the basin of the water he called "the **sea**."
God saw how **good** it was.
Then God **said**,
> "Let the earth bring **forth** vegetation:
> every kind of **plant** that bears seed
> and every kind of **fruit** tree on earth
> that bears fruit with its seed in it."
And so it **happened**:
> the earth brought forth every kind of plant that bears **seed**
> and every kind of **fruit** tree on earth
> that bears fruit with its **seed** in it.
God saw how **good** it was.
Evening came, and morning **followed**—the **third** day.

Then God **said**:
> "Let there be **lights** in the dome of the sky,
> to separate **day** from **night**.
Let them mark the fixed **times**, the **days** and the **years**,
> and serve as **luminaries** in the dome of the sky,
> to shed **light** upon the earth."
And so it **happened**:
> God made the **two** great lights,
> the **greater** one to govern the **day**,
> and the **lesser** one to govern the **night**;
> and he made the **stars**.
God **set** them in the dome of the sky,
> to shed **light** upon the earth,
> to **govern** the day and the night,
> and to separate the **light** from the **darkness**.
God saw how **good** it was.
Evening came, and **morning** followed—the **fourth** day.

Now God invites the earth to join with God in bringing life.

Pick up your pacing.

Don't swallow "stars."

valuable, able to fulfill its purpose." God "blessed" living creatures, including human beings, telling them to be fruitful. In ancient Hebrew thought, the notions of blessing and fruitfulness are intimately connected, for a blessing was believed to be permanent and to impart the power to give life. The priestly author-editors, in their precarious situation, continue to reassure God's people that they do have a future—one

envisioned and empowered by God from the beginning of creation.

In this first story, God creates humankind only after providing a sustainable world for this creature. The writer uses the word *adam*, meaning humankind, indicating that God formed the human race as a whole, male and female, in the divine image. This is God's purpose for *adam*; this creature alone can and is meant to reflect the Creator in the world. The author under-

scores the idea that God alone is the source of life for the human creature by using a specific verb meaning "to create"; this Hebrew word (bara') is used only of something formed by God, rather than a human agent. God instructs this unique creature, humankind, to hold "dominion" over the other creatures. To avoid misunderstanding, this statement must be understood in Old Testament context. In the view of ancient Israel, the one true King was the

Let your vocal energy reflect the energy of all the animals. Use the words "teem" and "fly" to emphasize the movement.

Then God **said**,
"Let the water **teem** with an **abundance** of living creatures,
and on the earth let **birds** fly beneath the dome of the sky."
And so it **happened**:
God created the great sea **monsters**
and all kinds of **swimming** creatures with which the
water **teems**,
and all kinds of winged **birds**.
God saw how **good** it was, and God **blessed** them, saying,

God's first blessing is for the animals.

"Be **fertile**, **multiply**, and **fill** the water of the seas;
and let the birds **multiply** on the earth."
Evening came, and **morning** followed—the **fifth** day.

Then God **said**,

The earth is becoming a busy place!

"Let the earth bring **forth** all kinds of living creatures:
cattle, **creeping** things, and wild **animals** of all **kinds**."
And so it **happened**:
God made all **kinds** of wild animals, all kinds of cattle,
and all kinds of creeping things of the earth.
God saw how **good** it was.

Pause here.

Your tone should change to indicate something significant is about to happen. Slow down.

Then [God **said**:
"Let us make **man** in our **image**, after our **likeness**.
Let them have **dominion** over the fish of the sea,
the birds of the air, and the cattle,
and over all the wild animals
and all the creatures that crawl on the ground."
God created **man** in his **image**;
in the image of God he **created** him;

Speak these lines slowly and deliberately. Our creation is good news, so smile with your voice, eyes, and face!

male and **female** he created them.
God **blessed** them, saying:
"Be **fertile** and **multiply**;
fill the earth and **subdue** it.

Pick up your pace again here.

Have **dominion** over the fish of the sea, the birds of the air,
and all the living things that **move** on the earth." »

Lord, and any human king served as his representative. Hence human rulers were expected to rule as God does, ensuring just and peaceful relationships among all people and things.

After ensuring continuing life for the human creature by giving green plants for food, God surveys the whole of creation and once again pronounces it "very good." Closing the orderly pattern of day-by-day creation, the author offers one chief reason

for an important Jewish religious law: avoidance of work on the Sabbath, the seventh day of the week, in order to devote time to praise of God and study of divine teaching. If even God "rested" from work on the Sabbath, how much more ought God's people follow such an example?

The First Reading thus lays the groundwork for the salvation story to unfold in the following readings. The Creator, source, and sustainer of all things,

acts in a purposeful manner, setting all things in right relationship. In the midst of all other creatures, the Lord places the human creature (intended to be the living, acting image of God) in the world. No matter how often and how flagrant the failure to live up to this divine purpose, humankind will be restored and renewed by the God, who first created order out of chaos. The Lord will continue to accomplish the plan of salvation, until the true image of God

Keep your pace up. God cares for all creation, making sure every creature has what it needs to thrive.

God also said:
"**See**, I give you every seed-bearing plant all over the **earth**
and every **tree** that has seed-bearing fruit on it to be your **food**;
and to all the animals of the land, all the birds of the air,
and all the living creatures that crawl on the ground,
I give all the **green** plants for **food**."
And so it **happened**.
God looked at **everything** he had made, and he found it
very good.]

Everything together is very good.

Evening came, and **morning** followed—the **sixth** day.

Thus the heavens and the earth and all their array
were **completed**.
Since on the **seventh** day God was **finished**
with the work he had been doing,
he **rested** on the seventh day from all the **work** he
had undertaken.

[Shorter: Genesis 1:1, 26–31a (see brackets)]

For meditation and context:

RESPONSORIAL PSALM Psalm 104:1–2, 5–6, 10, 12, 13–14, 24, 35 (30)

R. Lord, send out your Spirit, and renew the face of the earth.

Bless the LORD, O my soul!
O LORD, my God, you are great indeed!
You are clothed with majesty and glory,
robed in light as with a cloak.

You fixed the earth upon its foundation,
not to be moved forever;
with the ocean, as with a garment, you
covered it;
above the mountains the waters stood.

You send forth springs into the watercourses
that wind among the mountains.
Beside them the birds of heaven dwell;
from among the branches they send forth
their song.

Or:

You water the mountains from your palace;
the earth is replete with the fruit
of your works.
You raise grass for the cattle,
and vegetation for man's use,
producing bread from the earth.

How manifold are your works, O LORD!
In wisdom you have wrought them all—
the earth is full of your creatures.
Bless the LORD, O my soul!

TO KEEP IN MIND
Parallelism refers to phrases or sentences that have a similar structure or express a similar idea. Use emphasis and rhythm to make sure any parallelism stands out.

appears in the final act of salvation: the mystery of Jesus Christ, crucified and raised up, the beginning of humanity created anew.

READING II Previous to this passage, God promised Abraham that he would be the father of a multitude, but the promise seemed empty as years passed and Abraham and Sarah remained childless. Heavenly messengers assured

them that even in their advanced age, Sarah would conceive a son. This seemingly impossible event came to pass, renewing the promise, only to lead to the shock of today's Second Reading. While this story often arouses revulsion in modern hearers, it has roots in ancient cultures which did in fact practice child sacrifice as an expression of willingness to return everything, even one's most precious object of love, to the god or gods from whom it came. The

writer makes clear from the outset that the story intends to recount a testing of Abraham, a divine inquiry into the degree of Abraham's trusting faith (Genesis 15:1–6).

Several poignant details underscore the cost of following God's terrible command. Abraham is told to take "your son, Isaac, your only one, whom you love" and offer him as a holocaust—an offering burned in its entirety to signify holding back nothing whatsoever from God. On the

For meditation and context:

TO KEEP IN MIND
Be careful not to "swallow" words by mumbling. Articulate carefully so that every word is clearly heard, especially at the end of lines.

RESPONSORIAL PSALM   Psalm 33:4–5, 6–7, 12–13, 20, and 22 (5b)

R. The earth is full of the goodness of the Lord.

Upright is the word of the LORD,
   and all his works are trustworthy.
He loves justice and right;
   of the kindness of the LORD the earth
    is full.

By the word of the LORD the heavens
   were made;
   by the breath of his mouth all their host.
He gathers the waters of the sea as in a flask;
   in cellars he confines the deep.

Blessed the nation whose God is the LORD,
   the people he has chosen for his own
    inheritance.
From heaven the LORD looks down;
   he sees all mankind.

Our soul waits for the LORD,
   who is our help and our shield.
May your kindness, O LORD, be upon us
   who have put our hope in you.

A narrative which we know well, but don't telegraph the end. The scene is full of drama and the stakes are very high—Isaac's life and the promise made to Abraham that he would have many descendants are both in jeopardy.

Abraham has an intimate relationship with God.

Moriah = moh-RĪ-uh

Pause to let this sink in.

We should hear the seriousness of the situation in Abraham's voice.

READING II   Genesis 22:1–18

A reading from the Book of Genesis

[God put **Abraham** to the **test**.
He called to him, "**Abraham!**"
"**Here** I am," he replied.
Then God said:
   "Take your son **Isaac**, your **only** one, whom you **love**,
   and **go** to the land of Moriah.
There you shall **offer** him up as a holocaust
   on a height that I will point out to you."]
Early the next morning Abraham saddled his donkey,
   took with him his son **Isaac** and two of his servants as well,
   and with the **wood** that he had cut for the holocaust,
   set out for the place of which God had told him.

On the third day Abraham got **sight** of the place from afar.
Then he said to his servants:
   "Both of you stay here with the donkey,
   while the **boy** and I go on over **yonder**.
We will **worship** and then come back to you." »

---

way up the mountain, the child himself carries the wood upon which he is to be sacrificed. Addressing Abraham as "Father," Isaac innocently remarks that they have brought wood and fire for a holocaust, but no sheep for sacrifice. His father's initial response already begins to reveal his attitude of trust as he assures the boy that "God himself will provide" for the offering.

After arriving at the place of holocaust and preparing for the sacrifice, Abraham is prevented by a divine messenger from completing the act. Unlike the first call to Abraham, here he is addressed by a repetition of his name. In the Old Testament, calling someone by name twice indicates a closeness of relationship between the speaker and the one addressed. God first speaks to protect Isaac, then assures Abraham that his actions bespeak com-

plete reverence for God. The patriarch's trusting obedience not only would have cost his beloved son but dashed any hope of fulfilling the divine promise of countless offspring. But Abraham had told Isaac that God would provide a sacrificial offering, and his faith proves well-founded; he spies a ram nearby, which ensures a holocaust offering. The naming of the place of offering is a word play easily lost in translation; "the LORD will see" confirms Abraham's

A typical father-son exchange; don't make it sound foreboding.

An honest question.

Convey the sense of dread and horror that Abraham must feel as he does these things.

Pause.

Raise your voice as if you had to stay Abraham's hand.

Quicken your pace; the scene's tension is released.

Yahweh-yireh = YAH-way-YEER-ay

Thereupon Abraham took the wood for the holocaust
    and **laid** it on his son **Isaac's** shoulders,
    while he himself carried the **fire** and the **knife**.
As the two walked on **together**, Isaac spoke to his father
    Abraham:
    "**Father**!" Isaac said.
"**Yes**, son," he replied.
Isaac continued, "Here are the **fire** and the **wood**,
    but **where** is the sheep for the holocaust?"
"**Son**," Abraham answered,
    "God **himself** will provide the sheep for the holocaust."
Then the two continued going forward.

[When they came to the place of which God had told him,
    Abraham built an **altar** there and arranged the **wood** on it.]
Next he **tied** up his son Isaac,
    and **put** him on top of the wood on the altar.
[Then he **reached** out and took the **knife** to **slaughter** his son.
But the LORD's messenger **called** to him from heaven,
    "**Abraham**, **Abraham**!"
"**Here** I am," he answered.
"Do **not** lay your hand on the boy," said the messenger.
"Do not do the **least** thing to him.
I **know** now how **devoted** you are to **God**,
    since you did not withhold from me your **own** beloved son."
As Abraham looked **about**,
    he spied a **ram** caught by its horns in the thicket.
So he went and took the ram
    and offered it up as a **holocaust** in **place** of his son.]
Abraham named the site **Yahweh-yireh**;
    hence people now say, "On the mountain the LORD will **see**."

trust that God would "see to it" that an animal would be available for sacrifice.

Abraham meets his testing with the same unshakeable trust in divine promises that he has shown earlier. In response, God again assures Abraham that the two great promises will be fulfilled: God will give him innumerable descendants, and through the offspring of Abraham, man of obedient faith, all other peoples shall be blessed.

READING III In the Second Reading, God repeated to Abraham the promise of countless descendants. That promise was fulfilled, but according to Old Testament accounts, these descendants eventually found themselves enslaved in Egypt. There, the Lord called Moses to lead the Hebrews out of Egypt to Canaan, a new land of freedom. On the whole, the writer presents the story of the plagues upon Egypt, worked through Moses, as a battle

between the deities of Egypt and the God of Israel. Repeatedly, Egypt's gods prove no match for the Warrior-King of Israel, the Lord,. The Third Reading continues an account of Hebrew flight from slavery, facilitated by God's tenth and final victorious blow upon Egypt.

As the reading begins, the fleeing Hebrews have reached the edge of the sea, only to find themselves seemingly at the mercy of Pharaoh's army. Moses too

The reward is as great as the test was demanding. Keep your pace up to the end.

[**Again** the LORD's messenger **called** to Abraham from heaven
   and said:
"I **swear** by myself, declares the LORD,
that **because** you acted as you did
in not **withholding** from me your **beloved** son,
I will **bless** you **abundantly**
and make your **descendants** as **countless**
as the **stars** of the sky and the **sands** of the seashore;
your descendants shall take **possession**
of the gates of their enemies,
and in **your** descendants **all** the nations of the earth shall
   find **blessing**—
all this because you **obeyed** my command."]

[Shorter: Genesis 22:1–2, 9a, 10–13, 15–18 (see brackets)]

For meditation and context:

TO KEEP IN MIND
Pause in order to break up separate thoughts, set apart significant statements, or indicate major shifts. Never pause in the middle of a single thought. Your primary guide for pauses is punctuation.

RESPONSORIAL PSALM   Psalm 16:5, 8, 9–10, 11 (1)

R. You are my inheritance, O Lord.

O LORD, my allotted portion and my cup,
   you it is who hold fast my lot.
I set the LORD ever before me;
   with him at my right hand I shall not
   be disturbed.

Therefore my heart is glad and my soul
   rejoices,
   my body, too, abides in confidence;
because you will not abandon my soul to the
   netherworld,
   nor will you suffer your faithful one to
   undergo corruption.

You will show me the path to life,
   fullness of joys in your presence,
   the delights at your right hand forever.

appears doubtful that their escape will be complete, but God commands him to raise his staff and split the sea so that the Israelites may continue their journey to freedom. God's mighty power will be even more evident after the Lord himself causes the Egyptians to stubbornly pursue the escaping slaves into the seabed. Their efforts will prove ineffective against the God of Israel, however, who will be glorified by his people's victory. Throughout the

night, God's angel and a column of cloud stand guard for the Israelites. Later in the Exodus journey, this column of cloud will reappear, indicating the Lord's own protective, guiding presence.

Since ancient peoples believed that divine powers directly intervened in all aspects of human life, the writer states that the Lord sends the strong wind to dry up the waters before the Israelites. As the Lord predicted, the pursuing Egyptians fol-

low them, until God, in the form of a cloud of fire, clogs their chariot wheels. At this, Pharaoh's army sounds the retreat, as the author sounds an important theme: the pursuers know they face defeat, because the God of the Hebrews, who has already proved to outrank all the gods of Egypt, fights "for them against the Egyptians." What the Egyptians fear becomes reality as God acts through Moses, and the waters turn back into the sea, bringing total defeat

A well-known narrative, but make the story fresh by proclaiming as if the end were in doubt. Your own excitement will keep the assembly engaged.

Exodus = EK-suh-duhs

We jump into the middle of the story: The Israelites have been complaining against God that they are about to be slaughtered by the Egyptians. God's response is, "Don't you trust me?"

Be deliberate with this line; it would have seemed like a very odd command at first hearing to Moses.

How might God sound as he reveals this plan?

Pause.

Proclaim these amazing events with excitement and energy, as if they were unfolding right before your eyes. Don't read like a dispassionate news reporter, but convey all the intensity, anticipation, danger, and triumph inherent in the story.

What would you feel if you were watching this happen? Bring that emotion to your proclamation.

READING III Exodus 14:15—15:1

A reading from the Book of Exodus

The Lord said to **Moses**, "**Why** are you crying **out** to me?
Tell the Israelites to go **forward**.
And **you**, lift up your **staff** and, with hand **outstretched**
        over the sea,
    split the sea in two,
        that the Israelites may pass through it on **dry** land.
But I will make the Egyptians so **obstinate**
        that they will go in after them.
Then I will receive **glory** through Pharaoh and all his **army**,
        his chariots and charioteers.
The Egyptians shall **know** that **I** am the **Lord**,
        when I receive **glory** through Pharaoh
        and his chariots and charioteers."

The angel of God, who had been **leading** Israel's camp,
        now moved and went around **behind** them.
The column of **cloud** also, leaving the **front**,
        took up its place **behind** them,
        so that it came **between** the camp of the Egyptians
        and that of Israel.
But the cloud now became **dark**, and thus the night passed
        without the rival camps coming any closer together all
            night long.
Then Moses **stretched** out his hand over the **sea**,
        and the Lord **swept** the sea
        with a strong east **wind** throughout the night
        and so **turned** it into **dry** land.
When the water was thus **divided**,
        the Israelites marched into the **midst** of the sea on **dry** land,
        with the water like a **wall** to their right and to their left.

---

and destruction to Pharaoh's army. Awed by this mighty act of power, the Israelites affirm their belief in the Lord and in Moses as God's instrument. The reading ends with the opening line of a great hymn of praise and thanks for God's deliverance. This song is often described as Israel's first creed.

READING IV Earlier readings of this sacred night have described Israel's God as one who always fulfills

promises. That faithfulness was sorely tested by a repeatedly straying people. Many centuries after the Exodus, despite the urgings of numerous prophets, the Chosen People demonstrated their own lack of faithfulness. God allowed the destruction of two Israelite kingdoms, the decimation of the people, and return to their original state as captives in a country far from the Promised Land.

This passage from Isaiah most likely dates from the Babylonian captivity (586–539 BC), probably near its end as God continued to speak words of return and renewal through the prophets. Earlier prophets had likened the relationship between the Lord and the Chosen People to that of faithful and unfaithful spouses. When final destruction befell God's people, the event was imaged as the steadfast husband, the Lord, divorcing his wife, Israel, for

The Egyptians **followed** in pursuit;
    all Pharaoh's horses and chariots and charioteers went
      after them
right into the midst of the sea.
In the night watch just before dawn
    the Lord **cast** through the column of the fiery cloud
    upon the Egyptian force a **glance** that threw it into a **panic**;
    and he so clogged their chariot wheels
    that they could hardly drive.
With **that** the Egyptians sounded the retreat before Israel,
    because the Lord was fighting for them **against** the Egyptians.

Then the Lord told Moses, "**Stretch** out your hand over the sea,
    that the water may flow **back** upon the Egyptians,
    upon their chariots and their charioteers."
So Moses stretched out his hand over the sea,
    and at dawn the sea flowed **back** to its normal depth.
The Egyptians were fleeing head on **toward** the sea,
    when the Lord **hurled** them into its midst.
As the water flowed **back**,
    it **covered** the chariots and the charioteers of Pharaoh's
      whole army
which had followed the Israelites into the **sea**.
Not a **single** one of them escaped.
But the Israelites had marched on **dry** land
    through the **midst** of the sea,
    with the water like a **wall** to their right and to their left.
Thus the Lord **saved** Israel on that day
    from the power of the Egyptians. »

Proclaim this action quickly.

Careful with this awkward construction, and make sure it's clear that "the Lord cast . . . a glance" upon the Egyptians.

Keep the sense of amazement in all these actions.

Here is the victorious conclusion.

Pause.

her repeated infidelities. As prophets like Isaiah turned toward messages of hope for the future, they continued to describe a restored relationship with spousal language and images.

    Isaiah envisions an imminent and astounding reversal of the people's current state. With boundless love and faithfulness, the Lord, Creator and Redeemer of Israel, will restore her as beloved wife. God speaks like a rejected husband who, in a fit of painful loss and anger, cast off the unfaithful partner, but whose love cannot bear the finality of divorce. The Hebrew words with which God speaks of restoring Israel express both the loyalty demanded by covenant relationship ("enduring love") and deeply felt tenderness ("pity"). God reminds the captive people that he has demonstrated fidelity to covenant promises in the past, as in the case of the covenant with Noah. Repeating words of covenant faithfulness and heartfelt love, God promises enduring love; Israel may turn from God, but God will never abandon his beloved Israel.

    Isaiah now turns to address the devastated city, Jerusalem, speaking God's Word to her; she will be rebuilt with even greater glory than before. Most importantly, God will recreate the people and the city that symbolizes their covenant with the Lord in "justice" and "peace." The Hebrew words used here connote wholeness and completeness, a state of being in

When Israel saw the Egyptians lying dead on the seashore
    and beheld the great **power** that the LORD
    had shown against the Egyptians,
    they **feared** the LORD and **believed** in him and in his
        servant **Moses**.

Then Moses and the Israelites **sang** this song to the LORD:
    I will **sing** to the LORD, for he is gloriously **triumphant;**
    horse and **chariot** he has **cast** into the **sea**.

With great joy! Smile with your voice, eyes, and face!

For meditation and context:

RESPONSORIAL PSALM   Exodus 15:1–2, 3–4, 5–6, 17–18 (1b)

R. Let us sing to the Lord; he has covered himself in glory.

I will sing to the LORD, for he is gloriously
    triumphant;
    horse and chariot he has cast into the sea.
My strength and my courage is the LORD,
    and he has been my savior.
He is my God, I praise him;
    the God of my father, I extol him.

The LORD is a warrior,
    LORD is his name!
Pharaoh's chariots and army he hurled into
    the sea;
    the elite of his officers were submerged
        in the Red Sea.

The flood waters covered them,
    they sank into the depths like a stone.
Your right hand, O LORD, magnificent
    in power,
    your right hand, O LORD, has shattered
        the enemy.

You brought in the people you redeemed
    and planted them on the mountain of
        your inheritance—
the place where you made your seat,
    O LORD,
    the sanctuary, LORD, which your hands
        established.
The LORD shall reign forever and ever.

TO KEEP IN MIND
Making eye contact with the assembly connects you with them and connects them to the reading more deeply than using your voice alone. This helps the assembly stay with the story and keeps them engaged.

An exhortatory reading, in which God describes his desire to be in intimate relationship with us.

Isaiah = Ī-ZAY-uh

God wants to be as close to us as a married couple is to each other.

READING IV   Isaiah 54:5–14

A reading from the Book of the Prophet Isaiah

The One who has become your **husband** is your **Maker;**
    his name is the LORD of hosts;
your **redeemer** is the Holy One of **Israel**,
    called God of **all** the earth.

---

which all live in righteous relationship to God and to one another.

READING V Chapters 40–55 of Isaiah are often called the "Book of Consolation," believed to date from near the end of the Babylonian exile (586–539 BC). This part of the lengthy prophecy looks toward God's impending act of liberation from captivity that Israel had deemed a return to the slavery they had known in

Egypt. To designate the hopeful content of this section of Isaiah, the author uses a literary device called an *inclusio*, which forms a set of brackets for a body of material by beginning and ending with similar terms or content. Tonight's reading is the slightly truncated closure of the *inclusio*, and so includes a number of themes from chapter 40: forgiveness, the way, God's renewing action, and the powerful Word of God. In

style, the reading echoes Wisdom literature, priestly exhortation, and prophetic speech.

The Fifth Reading, the beginning of Isaiah 55, opens by addressing the captive people, who are poor and hungry. Like Lady Wisdom, the prophet calls them to a rich and fulfilling banquet. In the centuries following Isaiah, an overflowing banquet came to symbolize God's definitive act of salvation. For Isaiah, it probably carries overtones of renewing unity among partakers of the

Imagine trying to convince a very skeptical person about God's great love. Imagine that this reading is your only chance to do so.

How does God sound reviewing these past actions? How do you sound when you regret the way you treated someone and you try to win them back?

The centerpiece of the reading; proclaim slowly and deliberately.

Pause.

Now raise your intensity and convince your assembly of your sincerity.

carnelians = kahr-NEEL-yuhnz (red semi-precious stones)

carbuncles = KAHR-bung-k*lz (bright red gems)

God takes great joy in securing our peace and our future.

The Lord **calls** you back,
    like a wife **forsaken** and **grieved** in spirit,
    a wife married in youth and then cast **off**,
    says your God.
For a **brief** moment I **abandoned** you,
    but with **great** tenderness I will take you **back**.
In an outburst of **wrath**, for a moment
    I **hid** my face from you;
but with enduring **love** I take **pity** on you,
    says the Lord, your **redeemer**.
This is for me like the days of **Noah**,
    when I **swore** that the **waters** of Noah
    should **never** again **deluge** the earth;
so I have sworn not to be **angry** with you,
    or to **rebuke** you.
Though the mountains **leave** their place
    and the hills be shaken,
my **love** shall **never** leave you
    nor my covenant of **peace** be shaken,
    says the Lord, who has **mercy** on you.
O afflicted one, storm-battered and unconsoled,
    I lay your pavements in **carnelians**,
    and your foundations in **sapphires**;
I will make your battlements of **rubies**,
    your gates of **carbuncles**,
    and all your **walls** of precious **stones**.
All your children shall be **taught** by the Lord,
    and **great** shall be the peace of your children.
In **justice** shall you be established,
    far from the fear of oppression,
    where destruction cannot come near you.

plentiful meal, since Israelite culture understood shared food as a sharing of life and mutual commitment. Through the prophet, God calls the people to listen and so have life. The Hebrew word translated "listen" includes an appeal to listen and respond, to hear and obey. It recalls the Lord's ancient call to a Chosen People expressed in Deuteronomy 6:4–5: "Hear, O Israel! The Lord is our God, the Lord alone . . . you shall love the Lord . . . ." Despite the people's

failure to hear, obey, and love God above all, his forgiveness now offers to renew the ancient covenant, not only with David but with "you," the entire Chosen People. Through the new Exodus of a restored people, all nations will turn toward the God of Israel.

While the phrase "seek the Lord" was often used by priests to invite worshippers to the sanctuary of the Temple, Isaiah broadens its meaning. He seems to ask the

people to find God near at hand. Turning toward God's presence, however, calls for repentance, a complete change of heart and action. The prophet reassures the people that their ever-faithful God will meet them with forgiving mercy. The Hebrew word rendered "mercy" carries overtones of the tender love a woman bears for a child of her womb.

Isaiah begins a kind of conclusion to the entire Book of Consolation by recalling

For meditation and context:

RESPONSORIAL PSALM   Psalm 30:2, 4, 5–6, 11–12, 13 (2a)

R. I will praise you, Lord, for you have rescued me.

I will extol you, O LORD, for you drew
    me clear
    and did not let my enemies rejoice over me.
O LORD, you brought me up from the
    netherworld;
    you preserved me from among those
    going down into the pit.

Sing praise to the LORD, you his faithful ones,
    and give thanks to his holy name.
For his anger lasts but a moment;
    a lifetime, his good will.
At nightfall, weeping enters in,
    but with the dawn, rejoicing.

Hear, O LORD, and have pity on me;
    O LORD, be my helper.
You changed my mourning into dancing;
    O LORD, my God, forever will I give you
    thanks.

An exhortatory reading. Proclaim as if to a specific person you know who is weary and needs a message of hope. This reading is in God's voice and is all good news, so decide how you will maintain that energy throughout.

Make this a strong invitation. Direct your eye contact and vocal energy toward those farthest from you. Take time with this section.

How does God sound conveying this invitation? Make a strong choice. Insist that they come!

How silly!

You will not only be fed, but fed well.

Listening to God brings life!

Pick up your pace here to the end of this section.

READING V   Isaiah 55:1–11

A reading from the Book of the Prophet Isaiah

Thus says the LORD:
All you who are thirsty,
    come to the water!
You who have no **money**,
    come, receive **grain** and **eat**;
come, without **paying** and without **cost**,
    drink **wine** and **milk**!
Why spend your money for what is not **bread**,
    your **wages** for what fails to **satisfy**?
Heed me, and you shall eat **well**,
    you shall **delight** in **rich** fare.
Come to me **heedfully**,
    listen, that you may have **life**.
I will **renew** with you the **everlasting** covenant,
    the benefits assured to **David**.

the core reason for his confidence that return, renewal, and restoration will certainly come to pass. That reason is the power of God's Word. That Word, which carries the very presence of God, comes to earth to give new life and fruitfulness. Because it is God's own word, it bears divine power, and will not fail to accomplish the divine will, which always ultimately desires human healing, wholeness, and deliverance.

READING VI   The Book of Baruch, described as the work of Jeremiah's assistant, actually represents a collection of four different compositions. Set in the early days of the Babylonian exile (586–539 BC), the book is presented as the contents of a scroll read by Baruch to the exiled king and people. Most scholars believe the work was actually written much later, perhaps reaching the stage of final editing within the last two centuries BC. As

a whole, the Book of Baruch follows the theology of Deuteronomy and its author, portraying a cycle of the people's repeated sin, devastation allowed by God as punishment, call to conversion, and the people's repentance. In the first chapter, the people's admission of guilt is expressed in language typical of Deuteronomy and numerous prophets: their primary sin is described as failure to hear and obey God's

As I made him a **witness** to the peoples,
    a leader and commander of **nations**,
so shall you summon a nation you knew **not**,
    and nations that knew you not shall **run** to you,
because of the LORD, your God,
    the Holy One of Israel, who has **glorified** you.

Seek the LORD while he may be **found**,
    call him while he is **near**.
Let the scoundrel **forsake** his way,
    and the **wicked** man his thoughts;
let him **turn** to the LORD for **mercy**;
    to our God, who is **generous** in forgiving.
For **my** thoughts are not **your** thoughts,
    nor are **your** ways **my** ways, says the LORD.
As **high** as the heavens are above the **earth**,
    so high are **my** ways above **your** ways
    and **my** thoughts above **your** thoughts.

For just as from the heavens
    the **rain** and **snow** come down
and do not **return** there
    till they have **watered** the earth,
    making it fertile and fruitful,
giving **seed** to the one who sows
    and **bread** to the one who eats,
so shall my **word** be
    that goes **forth** from my mouth;
my word shall not return to me **void**,
    but shall do my **will**,
    achieving the end for which I **sent** it.

Pause before the next section, a new thought.

Encourage your assembly to sincerely seek out God.

This is not a rebuke, but a declaration of amnesty for all!

"I am more ready to forgive than you are."
How glad we are that God doesn't act as we might!

Pause before the final section.

God uses these metaphors to assure us that the promises made will be fulfilled. Here is your last chance to convince those still skeptical of God's great mercy! These are images of generosity and plenty.

The word you proclaim is a living word, and demands a proclamation worthy of it.

Proclaim with confident assurance: "I will do what I say."

---

voice, spoken through the Mosaic Law and the prophets.

The Sixth Reading comes from a portion of the Book of Baruch patterned after wisdom literature, and virtually equates wisdom with divine teaching given in the Law of Moses. The importance of the message in this section of Baruch is evident in its language; "Hear, O Israel" is the beginning of a prayer that Jews to this day recite daily. The prayer appears in the Torah (Pentateuch) and calls the covenant people to hear and obey the Lord alone, and to love their one and only God above all else (Deuteronomy 6:4–5). The author poses a rhetorical question to the captive people, asking how it came to be that they find themselves in exile; the obvious answer follows: they have forsaken God's teaching, source of all wisdom.

The author calls the people to rediscover wisdom so that they may endure and once again find life and peace. Wisdom, typically personified in the Old Testament as a feminine figure, comes from God, Creator of all things and the sole source of Wisdom, the only One who fully knows her. Still, God has given great wisdom to the covenant people in the form of the Law: "She is the book of the commandments of God." Again echoing Deuteronomy, the author stresses that those who follow her by observing God's teaching will have life,

For meditation and context:

TO KEEP IN MIND
Use inflection (the high or low pitch of your voice) to convey attitude and feeling. High pitch expresses intensity and excitement; low pitch expresses sadness, contrition, or solemnity.

RESPONSORIAL PSALM   Isaiah 12:2–3, 4, 5–6 (3)

R. You will draw water joyfully from the springs of salvation.

God indeed is my savior;
    I am confident and unafraid.
My strength and my courage is the LORD,
    and he has been my savior.
With joy you will draw water
    at the fountain of salvation.

Give thanks to the LORD, acclaim his name;
    among the nations make known his deeds,
    proclaim how exalted is his name.

Sing praise to the LORD for his glorious
        achievement;
    let this be known throughout all the earth.
Shout with exultation, O city of Zion,
    for great in your midst
        is the Holy One of Israel!

An exhortatory reading, encouraging your community to seek wisdom.

Baruch = buh-ROOK

Start strong! Call out to your assembly to pay attention!

"Why do you think you are suffering?"

Here's the answer!
A life of peace is still available to us.

Invite the assembly to grow in their search for wisdom.

The answer to these questions is "God," and by extension, all of us who are in relationship with God.

READING VI   Baruch 3:9–15, 32—4:4

A reading from the Book of the Prophet Baruch

Hear, O Israel, the commandments of **life**:
    listen, and know **prudence**!
How **is** it, Israel,
    that you are in the land of your **foes**,
    grown old in a **foreign** land,
defiled with the dead,
    accounted with those destined for the **netherworld?**
You have forsaken the fountain of **wisdom**!
    Had you walked in the **way** of God,
    you would have dwelt in enduring **peace**.
Learn where **prudence** is,
    where **strength**, where **understanding**;
that you may know **also**
    where are length of days, and **life**,
    where **light** of the eyes, and **peace**.
Who has found the place of **wisdom**,
    who has entered into her **treasuries?**

while those who leave the path of wisdom will surely perish.

The reading closes with an exhortation to repentance, which the prophets often expressed as a call to "turn" or "return." True repentance requires a dual action: turning from the way of evil, and turning toward God and divine wisdom given in the Mosaic Law. God's people have been given a great gift; what pleases God is the way of wisdom, revealed in the Torah.

READING VII Ezekiel, a prophet and priest of the Jerusalem Temple, arrived in Babylon among the first deportees from Judah, and continued to prophesy in the land of exile. The Babylonian conquest of the Kingdom of David and the destruction of both Jerusalem and the Temple represented an unimaginable blow to the Chosen People, a fate they could never have envisioned. Where was all that they had relied upon?

The Promised Land, Davidic kingship, and their very identity as Chosen People of the Lord seemed to have evaporated. To the decimated, captive people, Ezekiel spoke the Word of the Lord, proclaiming both the reasons for their desolation and God's promises of renewal.

Immediately preceding the Seventh Reading, God directed the prophet to address the mountains and hills of ancient Canaan. Ezekiel announced divine assurance

These lines echo tonight's First Reading from Genesis.

The stars are joyous in their response!

Show your excitement in having access to such a God.

God's wisdom isn't just for God; rather, God shares this wisdom with all of us tonight through Jesus Christ.

she = wisdom

Wisdom is available to everyone; this is good news!

Wisdom is the true Law.

Again, invite your assembly to turn to wisdom.

blessed = BLES-uhd

Good news! We know what pleases God! Smile with your voice, eyes, and face.

The One who knows all things knows **her**;
　he has probed her by his **knowledge**—
the One who established the earth for **all** time,
　and **filled** it with four-footed beasts;
he who dismisses the light, and it **departs**,
　calls it, and it **obeys** him trembling;
before whom the **stars** at their posts
　shine and **rejoice**;
when he **calls** them, they answer, "**Here** we are!"
　shining with **joy** for their **Maker**.
Such is our God;
　no **other** is to be compared to him:
he has traced out the whole way of **understanding**,
　and has **given** her to **Jacob**, his servant,
　to Israel, his beloved **son**.

Since then she has **appeared** on earth,
　and **moved** among people.
She is the **book** of the precepts of God,
　the law that endures **forever**;
all who cling to her will **live**,
　but those will **die** who forsake her.
Turn, **O** Jacob, and receive her:
　walk by her light toward **splendor**.
Give not your glory to **another**,
　your privileges to an **alien** race.
Blessed are we, **O** Israel;
　for what pleases God is **known** to us!

that the land itself would be renewed, once again producing fruits of the earth, and in the Promised Land, both cities and people would be rebuilt. The reading begins with another statement of reasons for devastation and loss of the land: its people, the elect people of God, despoiled it themselves by their conduct. They not only shed innocent blood, even blood of their own people, but repeatedly turned to idols instead of the One who chose them. They

were chosen for a purpose: to make their covenant God known to all other nations and peoples by serving the Lord alone. In Hebrew, one word means both to serve and to worship, and their worship of the Lord comprised both communal rituals and an entire way of life. Ezekiel proclaims that their own repeated wandering from the ways of worship have brought divine judgment upon them.

Speaking through the prophet, God confronts the exiles with another reality: their fate has dishonored God's own name. In biblical thought, a name conveys the very essence of what is named, and represents the entire history and reputation of a person named. Nations that witnessed the fall and destruction of the Israelites questioned whether they were in fact the people of God, thus profaning the "name" of the Lord. The promised restoration, therefore,

For meditation and context:

RESPONSORIAL PSALM   Psalm 19:8, 9, 10, 11 (John 6:68c)

R. Lord, you have the words of everlasting life.

The law of the Lord is perfect,
  refreshing the soul;
the decree of the Lord is trustworthy,
  giving wisdom to the simple.

The precepts of the Lord are right,
  rejoicing the heart;
the command of the Lord is clear,
  enlightening the eye.

The fear of the Lord is pure,
  enduring forever;
the ordinances of the Lord are true,
  all of them just.

They are more precious than gold,
  than a heap of purest gold;
sweeter also than syrup
  or honey from the comb.

An exhortatory prophecy of salvation for Ezekiel's audience and for your assembly. Except for the first line, the entire reading is in God's voice. How does God sound as he makes these promises of salvation? Make a strong choice and bring it to your proclamation.

Ezekiel = ee-ZEE-kee-uhl

"Son of man" refers to Ezekiel.

Although these lines speak of God's "fury" and punishment, God is not angry now. Still, he wants faithful behavior.

The people's sins and punishment made God appear weak.

Pause.

Note that our salvation doesn't depend on anything we have done. God gives freely, for his own sake.

READING VII   Ezekiel 36:16–17a, 18–28

A reading from the Book of the Prophet Ezekiel

The **word** of the Lord came to me, saying:
  Son of man, when the house of Israel lived in their **land**,
  they **defiled** it by their conduct and deeds.
Therefore I **poured** out my fury upon them
  because of the **blood** that they poured out on the ground,
  and because they defiled it with **idols**.
I **scattered** them among the nations,
  dispersing them over foreign lands;
  according to their conduct and deeds I **judged** them.
But when they came among the nations wherever they came,
  they served to **profane** my holy name,
  because it was said of them: "These are the people of the Lord,
  yet they had to **leave** their land."
So I have **relented** because of my holy name
  which the house of Israel profaned
  among the nations where they came.
Therefore say to the house of Israel: **Thus** says the Lord God:
  Not for **your** sakes do I act, house of Israel,
  but for the sake of my holy **name**,
  which you profaned among the nations to which you came.

will take place, not for the sake of those whom God has rightly judged, but for the sake of the Lord's own good name as the One who remains forever faithful to Israel.

God then details the renewal that will once again demonstrate that the Lord is a God of covenant faithfulness and enduring love to Israel, despite her numerous infidelities. Not only will the captive people return to a renewed land; God will cleanse them of their sin and the root of their sinful-

ness. The promise of a new heart and new spirit signifies that God will recreate his people at the core of their being. In ancient Israel, the heart represented the core of a human being; a stony heart meant a person closed to God and the divine life within. Genesis 2:7 portrayed divine spirit as the very life-breath of humankind, but the people had shut their hearts to it. With the recreating gift of a new, "natural" heart, God's people will become what they were

intended to be: a community breathing together with God's own life, guided by divine teaching. They will again live as "the people of the Lord," who is always their God of loving fidelity.

EPISTLE   Paul wrote his Letter to the Romans, more a treatise than a letter, near the end of his life, about thirty years after the Death and Resurrection of Jesus. From its earliest

Careful with this awkward construction. The phrase about God's name being profaned is repeated twice; heighten the second instance.

God will take charge.

Now God reveals what is in store! Change your tone; slow down and speak with gentleness, as a loving parent.

God doesn't just cleanse us from our past transgressions, but gives us a new heart to draw us closer to God and help us avoid future transgressions.

It's God's own spirit that God gives us!

Here is our destiny.

Lift your head to maintain eye contact with the assembly; speak this last line slowly and with firm conviction.

For meditation and context:

TO KEEP IN MIND
Proclamation cannot be effective unless it is expressive. As you prepare your proclamation, make choices about emotions. Some choices are already evident in the text.

I will prove the **holiness** of my great name, profaned among
    the nations,
  in whose midst you have profaned it.
Thus the nations shall **know** that I am the LORD, says the
    Lord **GOD**,
  when in their sight I prove my **holiness** through **you**.
For I will take you **away** from among the nations,
    gather you from all the foreign lands,
  and bring you **back** to your **own** land.
I will sprinkle **clean water** upon you
    to **cleanse** you from all your impurities,
  and from all your idols I will **cleanse** you.
I will give you a new **heart** and place a new **spirit** within you,
    taking from your bodies your **stony** hearts
  and giving you **natural** hearts.
I will put **my** spirit within you and make you live by **my** stat-
    utes,
  careful to observe my **decrees**.
You shall **live** in the land I gave your fathers;
    you shall be my **people**, and **I** will be your **God**.

RESPONSORIAL PSALM   Psalm 42:3, 5; 43:3, 4 (2)   **When baptism is celebrated.**

R. **Like a deer that longs for running streams, my soul longs for you, my God.**

Athirst is my soul for God, the living God.
  When shall I go and behold the face
    of God?

I went with the throng
  and led them in procession to the house
    of God,
amid loud cries of joy and thanksgiving,
  with the multitude keeping festival.

Or:

Send forth your light and your fidelity;
  they shall lead me on
and bring me to your holy mountain,
  to your dwelling-place.

Then will I go in to the altar of God,
  the God of my gladness and joy;
then will I give you thanks upon the harp,
  O God, my God!

days, the Church understood Baptism as immersion in Christ, shedding one's former way of life and taking on a way of life patterned according to his passage through death to greater life. The celebration of Christian Initiation at the Easter Vigil thus continues ancient faith and practice. Today's Epistle elaborates both the call and the effects of immersion in Christ's Death and Resurrection.

In the previous chapter, Paul stressed the depth of God's love revealed in Christ, who died for those who were still sinners. In today's Epistle, Paul explains that in Baptism, Christians enter into Christ's manner of dying: death as self-giving love that leads to greater life. The Apostle insists that this death experienced in Baptism is not for its own sake, but is in likeness to, and participation in, Christ. In Baptism the believer is buried "with him" and grows in

oneness with him "through a death like his." It is this likeness to Christ and union with him that brings transformed life, a sharing in his Resurrection.

Paul's view of Baptism calls for nothing less than a complete change of the whole person, a transformation wrought by the interaction of divine power with human choice. For anyone who chooses to die like Christ, the former self or person enslaved to sin dies with him. The "sinful body"

RESPONSORIAL PSALM   Isaiah 12:2–3, 4bcd, 5–6 (3)

When baptism is not celebrated.

R. You will draw water joyfully from the springs of salvation.

God indeed is my savior;
  I am confident and unafraid.
My strength and my courage is the LORD,
  and he has been my savior.
With joy you will draw water
  at the fountain of salvation.

Give thanks to the LORD, acclaim his name;
  among the nations make known his deeds,
  proclaim how exalted is his name.

Sing praise to the LORD for his glorious
  achievement;
  let this be known throughout all the earth.
Shout with exultation, O city of Zion,
  for great in your midst
  is the Holy One of Israel!

Or:

RESPONSORIAL PSALM   Psalm 51:12–13, 14–15, 18–19 (12a)

When baptism is not celebrated.

R. Create a clean heart in me, O God.

A clean heart create for me, O God,
  and a steadfast spirit renew within me.
Cast me not out from your presence,
  and your Holy Spirit take not from me.

Give me back the joy of your salvation,
  and a willing spirit sustain in me.
I will teach transgressors your ways,
  and sinners shall return to you.

For you are not pleased with sacrifices;
  should I offer a holocaust, you would not
  accept it.
My sacrifice, O God, is a contrite spirit;
  a heart contrite and humbled, O God, you
  will not spurn.

> **TO KEEP IN MIND**
> A didactic reading is usually given out of love for the community. Make sure that love is evident in your proclamation.

A didactic reading, but full of good news, so proclaim with intensity. You are speaking to all the baptized in your assembly, but especially those about to be baptized tonight.

Paul sets up a contrast between life and death, but here death is not a bad thing, because death in Christ leads to life in Christ. A challenging teaching! With each repetition, make the progression from death to life very clear.

EPISTLE   Romans 6:3–11

A reading from the Letter of Saint Paul to the Romans

Brothers and sisters:
Are you **unaware** that we who were **baptized** into Christ Jesus
  were baptized into his **death**?
We were indeed **buried** with him through baptism into **death**,
  so that, just as Christ was **raised** from the dead
  by the glory of the **Father**,
  we **too** might live in **newness** of **life**.

(Greek *sóma*) does not signify physical flesh alone, but the human being as a whole, with all its perceptions, attitudes, and behaviors, dominated by sinful influences. One who dies with Christ and like Christ, out of love, is freed from that power and lives in him as a new person, "for God."

GOSPEL   The Gospel according to Matthew appears at the beginning of the Christian Scriptures, a fitting link between the Old and New Testaments. The author, most likely a Jewish convert to belief in Jesus as Messiah,

addresses an audience similar to himself. Matthew's community seems to comprise a primarily Jewish Christian audience, keenly interested in connections between their inherited Scriptures and the person and work of Jesus. The evangelist, very familiar with the sacred writings and hopes of Israel, frequently speaks of Jesus as "fulfilling" or bringing to completion the Old Testament Scriptures. His account of the Good News is laden with direct quotations from, or allusions to, the Old Testament.

Matthew's emphasis on Jesus as fulfillment of the Scriptures also reflects the

time of his writing (the mid-80s), when Judaism was struggling to determine its most authentic form in the midst of differing interpretations of Jewish faith and practice. Apparently some Jews viewed the Christian movement as yet another misguided or heretical Jewish sect.

That circumstance provides the background to the verses immediately before and after today's Gospel reading—verses that are unique to Matthew's narrative. Only this evangelist relates that a group of chief priests and Pharisees asked Pilate to set a guard at Jesus' tomb. These Jewish

Paul makes the point again. Here, emphasize the unity with Christ that Baptism brings.

For if we have grown into **union** with him through a **death**
    like his,
    we shall also be **united** with him in the **resurrection**.
We know that our **old** self was **crucified** with him,
    so that our **sinful** body might be done **away** with,
    that we might no longer be in **slavery** to sin.
For a **dead** person has been **absolved** from sin.
If, then, we have **died** with Christ,
    we believe that we shall also **live** with him.

Paul repeats the point yet again. Slow down.

We know that **Christ**, raised from the dead, dies no **more**;
    death no longer has power over him.
As to his **death**, he died to sin **once** and for **all**;
    as to his **life**, he lives for **God**.

The good news of this night—we no longer need fear death!

Consequently, you **too** must think of yourselves as being **dead**
    to **sin**
    and **living** for **God** in Christ Jesus.

For meditation and context:

RESPONSORIAL PSALM   Psalm 118:1–2, 16–17, 22–23

R. Alleluia, alleluia, alleluia.

Give thanks to the LORD, for he is good,
    for his mercy endures forever.
Let the house of Israel say,
    "His mercy endures forever."

The right hand of the LORD has struck
    with power;
    the right hand of the LORD is exalted.
I shall not die, but live,
    and declare the works of the LORD.

The stone which the builders rejected
    has become the cornerstone.
By the LORD has this been done;
    it is wonderful in our eyes.

> **TO KEEP IN MIND**
> Always pause at the end of the reading, before you proclaim the closing dialogue ("The Word of the Lord" or "The Gospel of the Lord").

> **TO KEEP IN MIND**
> Pray the text, using your favorite method of praying with Scripture.

religious leaders referred to him as an "imposter" who publicly stated that three days after his death, he would be raised up; guarding the tomb would prevent Jesus' followers from removing the crucified body and making the false claim that he had been raised. Immediately after the Resurrection account related in today's Gospel reading, some of the guards reported to Jewish authorities that Jesus' tomb was empty. The guards were quickly instructed to say that while they were asleep, some of his disciples stole the body. It is notable that the chief priests and elders did not deny that the tomb was empty; however, they wanted to promote their own interpretation of that reality.

Matthew's Resurrection narrative recounts that as Mary Magdalene and another woman named Mary arrive at Jesus' tomb, they encounter first an earthquake, and then a resplendent angel. The earthquake resounds with allusions to the Old Testament, signaling both the action of God and the dawning of the final age. In numerous Jewish texts, an earthquake precedes the presence of God, usually acting to save his people (for example, Psalms 77:19 and 68:9). The Book of Daniel and (in Matthew) Jesus himself speaks of earthquakes announcing the end of the old order and the dawn of the final age (Daniel 12:2; Matthew 24:3–14). The evangelist noted in the preceding chapter that the earth quaked at the moment of Jesus' Death, indicating that the old order, under the power of death and sin, was beginning to give way. Now the new age fully dawns, with Jesus' Resurrection confirming the definitive act of God and releasing the power of divine life. The angel's brilliant raiment also symbolizes divine presence and

A narrative which may have lost its power to amaze after centuries of repetition. Your job is to return the sense of wonder, awe, and astonishment to this story.

The amazing events begin.

Paralyzed with fear.

Slowly; this is shocking news.

The women are commissioned to be the first evangelists—the first to share the good news of Jesus' Resurrection. Tonight, you follow in their footsteps.

Quicken your pace.

Let your proclamation include a mix of fear and joy.

Something even more amazing happens!
Slow down.

Knowing their shock, Jesus is gentle and compassionate. Be sure to convey this in your proclamation.

GOSPEL   Matthew 28:1–10

A reading from the holy Gospel according to Matthew

After the **sabbath**, as the first day of the week was **dawning**,
   Mary **Magdalene** and the **other** Mary came to see the **tomb**.
And **behold**, there was a great **earthquake**;
   for an **angel** of the Lord descended from **heaven**,
   approached, rolled back the **stone**, and sat upon it.
His appearance was like **lightning**
   and his clothing was **white** as **snow**.
The guards were **shaken** with fear of him
   and became like **dead** men.
Then the angel said to the **women** in reply,
   "Do not be **afraid**!
I know that you are seeking **Jesus** the **crucified**.
He is not **here**, for he has been **raised** just as he **said**.
Come and **see** the place where he lay.
Then go **quickly** and tell his **disciples**,
   'He has been **raised** from the dead,
   and he is going before you to **Galilee**;
   there you will **see** him.'
Behold, I have **told** you."
Then they went away **quickly** from the tomb,
   fearful yet **overjoyed**,
   and **ran** to announce this to his disciples.
And **behold**, **Jesus** met them on their way and **greeted** them.
They **approached**, embraced his **feet**, and did him **homage**.
Then Jesus said to them, "Do not be **afraid**.
Go tell my brothers to go to **Galilee**,
   and there they will **see** me."

power, which leaves those guarding the tomb immobile with fear.

The angel's words make explicit what the earthquake implied: the presence and power of God has changed not only Jesus but all human existence forever. He who was crucified has been raised, and death gives way to divine life; the old order has passed away, and God rules the new era of salvation.

The impact of the Good News becomes immediately apparent; the women must "announce" it to other disciples. Matthew uses this word frequently employed to describe apostolic activity, thus underscoring that a new age has truly begun. In Jewish society of the time, the testimony of women carried no weight, but now two women are sent to bear witness to the Resurrection. The angel's instruction further directs them to go to Galilee, promising they will "see" Jesus there. Matthew's word choice suggests that in "seeing" Jesus, they will perceive, discern, and understand through experience the meaning of the Risen One. Encountering the resurrected Jesus, the women are sent to proclaim the Good News to others, so that they also may come to "see" Jesus. M.F.

EASTER SUNDAY OF THE RESURRECTION OF THE LORD

LECTIONARY #42

READING I Acts of the Apostles 10:34a, 37–43

A reading from the Acts of the Apostles

Peter proceeded to speak and said:
"You **know** what has happened all over Judea,
beginning in Galilee after the **baptism**
that **John** preached,
how God **anointed** Jesus of **Nazareth**
with the Holy **Spirit** and **power**.
He went about doing **good**
and **healing** all those oppressed by the **devil**,
for God was **with** him.
We are **witnesses** of all that he did
both in the country of the Jews and in Jerusalem.
They put him to **death** by hanging him on a **tree**.
This man God **raised** on the third day and granted
that he be **visible**,
not to all the people, but to **us**,
the witnesses **chosen** by God in advance,
who **ate** and **drank** with him **after** he rose from the dead.
He **commissioned** us to **preach** to the people
and **testify** that **he** is the one appointed by God
as judge of the living and the dead.
To him all the **prophets** bear witness,
that **everyone** who believes in him
will receive **forgiveness** of **sins** through his **name**."

A didactic reading in the form of a narrative. A summary of the life of Christ and what the early Christian community believed about him.

Although Peter is speaking to a crowd, avoid a preachy tone. Instead, imagine yourself speaking to a friend who has just asked, "So who was this Jesus of Nazareth?"

Judea = joo-DEE-uh

How does Peter feel and sound as he recounts the deeds he witnessed?

There might be a tone of sadness in Peter's voice. Pause.

But death was not to be the last word!

You have inherited this commission as a proclaimer of the Word!

Slow down through the end of this line.

Here's the point of Peter's story. Like every reading we proclaim, this is not a history lesson, but a call to all who hear it to act or be differently.

There are options for readings today. Ask your parish staff which ones will be used.

READING I In the Gospel reading for the Easter Vigil, Matthew recounts an angel's announcement to two women that Jesus has been raised. In turn the women, with a mixture of fear and joy, hurry to announce this Good News to other disciples. Mark, Luke, and John also indicate that the first proclamation of Jesus' Resurrection was met with various responses, including fear, doubt, and disbelief. But soon the transforming power of Christ's Resurrection is released in his followers by the power of the Holy Spirit.

The First Reading for Easter Sunday indicates the complete transformation of Peter. The same man, who a short time ago denied even knowing Jesus, quickly comes to such depth of faith and conviction that despite opposition and persecution, he repeatedly proclaims Jesus as Messiah. In preceding chapters, the author, Luke, describes Peter as a fervent Apostle, proclaiming Jesus' Resurrection to fellow Jews first in Jerusalem, then throughout Judea and further Jewish territory.

At the time of today's reading, Peter has begun to open himself to Paul's missionary activity among the Gentiles. By the end of Acts, through the efforts of Peter, Paul, and many coworkers, the Good News of Jesus Christ will spread throughout the Gentile world. Thus unfolds the story of the early Church, in stages outlined by Luke at the beginning of his narrative. Through the resurrected Christ, the divine Spirit comes

For meditation and context:

An exhortatory reading, encouraging your assembly to act like Easter people—a community who has really changed because of the Resurrection. It's brief, so take your time.

Colossians = kuh-LOSH-uhnz

Be concerned with things that bring life.

Death is good news here.

Maintain eye contact with your assembly and smile as you share this good news.

RESPONSORIAL PSALM   Psalm 118:1–2, 16–17, 22–23 (24)

R. This is the day the Lord has made; let us rejoice and be glad.

or

R. Alleluia.

Give thanks to the LORD, for he is good,
    for his mercy endures forever.
Let the house of Israel say,
    "His mercy endures forever."

"The right hand of the LORD has struck
    with power;
    the right hand of the LORD is exalted.
I shall not die, but live,
    and declare the works of the LORD.

The stone which the builders rejected
    has become the cornerstone.
By the LORD has this been done;
    it is wonderful in our eyes.

READING II   Colossians 3:1–4

A reading from the Letter of Saint Paul to the Colossians

Brothers and sisters:
If then you were **raised** with Christ, seek what is **above**,
    where Christ is seated at the right hand of God.
Think of what is **above**, not of what is on **earth**.
For you have **died**, and your life is **hidden** with Christ in **God**.
When Christ your life **appears**,
    then you too will appear **with** him in **glory**.

Or:

---

upon the disciples; in this spirit of power, they will serve as witnesses to Christ "in Jerusalem, throughout Judea and Samaria, and to the ends of the earth" (Acts 1:8).

To what do these disciples bear witness? Peter begins his speech by invoking John the Baptist, the forerunner, and points out that Jesus himself carried out his earthly ministry in the power of the Holy Spirit. His proclamation by word and deed that God was beginning his final reign in Jesus' own person and work is implied in Peter's speech, for though, as his hearers know well, Jesus was crucified, God raised

him to new life. In raising Jesus from death, God demonstrates the truth of the Messiah's message, for only divine power can overcome the rule of sin and death.

Peter emphasizes that those who hear his proclamation are receiving the word of witnesses to the life, Death, and Resurrection of Jesus. They are witnesses in the dual sense of having firsthand experience of what they announce, and of giving public testimony to that experience. As Jesus was brought through death to new life, so these witnesses are transformed

from fearful doubters to fearless witnesses to the Risen Christ.

READING II   **Colossians 3:1–4**. Though Paul did not found the community at Colossae, he was clearly concerned for their faithful understanding and living of the Gospel of Christ as he knew it. The founder of this church, Epaphras, apparently reported to Paul that other teachers had misled some members of the Colossian church into deviant beliefs and practice of faith in Christ. Seeking to correct the teaching of "specious

An exhortatory reading; Paul uses the metaphor of a feast to describe the new life of a resurrected people.

Corinthians = kohr-IN-thee-uhnz

Become completely new! Your old ways, even the smallest detail, can keep you from the fullness of life we celebrate today.

The bread of the feast is unleavened.

Now the feast can begin.

This is the way we live as Christians.

For meditation and context:

TO KEEP IN MIND

You can't proclaim what you don't understand. Read the Scripture passage and its commentary in *Workbook*. Then read it from your Bible, including what comes before and after it so that you understand the context.

READING II   1 Corinthians 5:6b–8

A reading from the first Letter of Saint Paul to the Corinthians

Brothers and sisters:
Do you not **know** that a little yeast leavens **all** the dough?
Clear out the **old** yeast,
   so that you may become a **fresh** batch of dough,
   inasmuch as you are **unleavened**.
For our paschal lamb, Christ, has been **sacrificed**.
Therefore, let us **celebrate** the feast,
   not with the **old** yeast, the yeast of malice and wickedness,
   but with the **unleavened** bread of sincerity and truth.

SEQUENCE   Victimae paschali laudes

Christians, to the Paschal Victim
   Offer your thankful praises!
A Lamb the sheep redeems;
   Christ, who only is sinless,
   Reconciles sinners to the Father.
Death and life have contended in that
      combat stupendous:
   The Prince of life, who died, reigns
   immortal.

Speak, Mary, declaring
   What you saw, wayfaring.
"The tomb of Christ, who is living,
   The glory of Jesus' resurrection;
Bright angels attesting,
   The shroud and napkin resting.
Yes, Christ my hope is arisen;
   to Galilee he goes before you."
Christ indeed from death is risen, our new
      life obtaining.
   Have mercy, victor King, ever reigning!
   Amen. Alleluia.

---

arguments" (Colossians 2:4) imported by these false ministers, Paul in his first chapter clarifies the reality of Christ, then reminds the Colossian church of what the true identity and work of the one Christ implies. In the second chapter he emphasizes the meaning of their Baptism, in which they shared Christ's passage through death to a new kind of life.

Today's Second Reading proceeds from this principle: those who are truly raised to a higher kind of life with Christ will surely seek "what is above," what is in Christ. The minds and hearts of those bap-

tized into Christ must be radically changed. For those who choose to die to a former way of life and share in life "with Christ in God," all is changed; life must be lived differently until Christ appears again in glory.

1 Corinthians 5:6b–8. Paul's motivations for this letter to the Corinthian community apparently arose from reports that reached the Apostle after he had moved on to Ephesus. Distressing news of various divisions and immoral activity within the community reached Paul only a few years after he had established this church. The Apostle addresses one matter, then

another, repeatedly returning to the touchstone of his Gospel: Christ, crucified and raised for all, in fulfillment of the Scriptures. Like Jesus, Paul uses the image of a leavening agent to impress upon the church the dangers of allowing even one member's public immorality to influence the entire community.

Immediately before today's Second Reading, Paul deals with the case of a man openly living with his father's wife. He counsels the church to expel this man for his own sake, but also for the good of the community as a whole. This situation is

A narrative which may have lost its power to amaze after centuries of repetition. Your job is to return the sense of wonder, awe, and astonishment to this story.

Magdala = MAG-duh-luh

This is unexpected.

Quicken your pace to indicate her anxiety.

There should be real fear in your voice.

Out of respect for Peter's position of leadership.

Take time with this line. This is a clue: if the body had been stolen it's unlikely thieves would have taken the time to fold the cloth.

He is the first to believe. Your assembly, too, has seen and believed.

TO KEEP IN MIND

A *narrative* has characters, dialogue, a setting, and action. Help your listeners see the story unfold, keep characters distinct, and be clear about shifts in setting.

GOSPEL   John 20:1–9

A reading from the holy Gospel according to John

On the **first** day of the week,
  Mary of **Magdala** came to the tomb early in the **morning**,
  while it was still **dark**,
  and saw the stone **removed** from the tomb.
So she **ran** and went to Simon **Peter**
  and to the **other** disciple whom Jesus **loved**, and told them,
  "They have **taken** the Lord from the **tomb**,
  and we don't know **where** they **put** him."
So Peter and the other disciple went **out** and came to the tomb.
They both ran, but the other disciple ran **faster** than Peter
  and arrived at the tomb **first**;
  he bent down and saw the **burial** cloths there, but did not go **in**.
When Simon **Peter** arrived after him,
  he went **into** the tomb and saw the **burial** cloths there,
  and the cloth that had covered his **head**,
  not with the burial cloths but rolled up in a **separate** place.
Then the other disciple **also** went in,
  the one who had arrived at the tomb first,
  and he **saw** and **believed**.
For they did not yet **understand** the Scripture
  that he had to **rise** from the **dead**.

---

most likely the "old yeast" that Paul considers a threat to the entire community's life in Christ, and it is Christ who must always provide the life pattern for believers. Paul presents Christ "our Passover lamb" for imitation; Christians must live in his transformed life, dying to the "old yeast" of immorality and leavening the faith community with Resurrection life.

GOSPEL | Though Resurrection accounts differ in details, all four canonical gospels name Mary Magdalene as first or among the first to dis-

cover that Jesus has been raised from death. John opens the scene of this Easter Gospel by noting that Mary comes to the tomb when "it was still dark," invoking the light and darkness symbolism he has used from the beginning of his account. Finding the sealing stone removed, Mary concludes that the body of Jesus has been taken away, and she quickly reports her suspicion to Peter and the Beloved Disciple. They, in turn, hurry to investigate for themselves, but find only burial cloths. The presence of these wrappings, described in some detail, indicates that the body has not simply been

stolen. The face cloth, carefully rolled up and set aside, may intend to evoke Exodus 34:27–35. Moses covered his face to veil its radiance after speaking with the Lord, but now, the full glory of God is revealed in the face of the Risen Christ.

The Beloved Disciple, observing the neatly arranged burial cloths, "saw and believed." For this evangelist, believing is the ultimate goal of any kind of encounter with Jesus. At the end of this chapter, John reiterates the central purpose of his Gospel account, the purpose he proclaimed at its beginning: to elicit faith that Jesus is

AFTERNOON GOSPEL   Luke 24:13–35

A reading from the holy Gospel according to Luke

That **very** day, the **first** day of the week,
    two of Jesus' **disciples** were going
    to a village seven miles from Jerusalem called Emmaus,
    and they were **conversing** about all the things that
        had occurred.
And it happened that while they were conversing and debating,
    Jesus **himself** drew near and walked with them,
    but their eyes were **prevented** from recognizing him.
He asked them,
    "What are you **discussing** as you walk along?"
They stopped, looking **downcast**.
One of them, named **Cleopas**, said to him in reply,
    "Are you the **only** visitor to Jerusalem
    who does not **know** of the things
    that have taken **place** there in these days?"
And he replied to them, "What **sort** of things?"
They said to him,
    "The things that happened to **Jesus** the **Nazarene**,
    who was a prophet **mighty** in deed and word
    before God and all the people,
    how our chief priests and rulers both handed him over
    to a sentence of **death** and **crucified** him.
But we were **hoping** that he would be the one to **redeem** Israel;
    and **besides** all this,
    it is now the **third** day since this took place.
Some **women** from our group, however, have **astounded** us:
    they were at the **tomb** early in the morning
    and did not find his **body**;
    they came back and reported
    that they had indeed seen a **vision** of angels
    who announced that he was **alive**. »

A narrative that suggests how your assembly might meet Jesus today—in the Word, the breaking of the bread, and the stranger. This beloved and powerful story needs careful preparation to make the most of its dialogue, dramatic revelation, and rich insights.

The day of the Resurrection; these disciples have heard the news from the women this morning

The story has much energy and activity. Keep your pace up.

They can't hide their sadness at Jesus' Death and the confusing events since then.

A bit incredulous. Notice how Jesus, who knows the most about what has happened, will pretend ignorance to allow them to share their story and feelings first.
Jesus wants to meet them where they are.

Try alternating these lines between the two speakers. Change tone slightly for each.

The first disciple states the facts.

The second gives an interpretation of the facts.

The first jumps in with even more confusing news.

Let their astonishment come through in this description. They still don't know what to make of it all.

"Can you believe it?"

Messiah and Son of God, and by believing, share fullness of life in him (John 1:12–13, 20:30–31). The unnamed beloved disciple seems to embody the ideal follower: one whom Jesus loves, one who enjoys intimacy with Jesus, one who believes in Jesus. For John, to "believe in" Jesus (the Greek literally means "believe into") implies an intimate relationship, a mutual indwelling of Jesus and the believer. Given his relationship with Jesus, the Beloved Disciple—the ideal disciple—believes even without understanding.

AFTERNOON GOSPEL │ In the Easter Vigil Gospel reading, Matthew recounts the women's discovery of Jesus' empty tomb and the angelic proclamation that "he has been raised." Luke presents a similar narrative, but explicitly adds that other disciples dismissed the women's witness as "nonsense" (Luke 24:9–11). This Easter Gospel reading follows immediately, with Luke describing two disciples who seem to be among those who discounted the women's announcement. This Gospel passage, unique to Luke, reprises some of his major themes, including table fellowship and fulfillment of the Scriptures.

As in several other Resurrection accounts, the dejected pair does not immediately know who has engaged them in conversation; it is the same Jesus they followed, but he has been transformed. Ironically, the discouraged disciples describe Jesus as "a prophet," but they fail to see that his prophetic word concerning his Death and Resurrection (Luke 9:22) has been fulfilled. Jesus himself emphasizes fulfillment of the Scriptures as he chides them for their inability or unwillingness to

The second finishes the story.

"Then some of those with us **went** to the tomb
and found things **just** as the women had described,
but **him** they did not see."

What does Jesus feel as he realizes these disciples still don't understand his messiahship? Disappointment, sadness, compassion?

And he said to them, "Oh, how **foolish** you are!
How **slow** of heart to believe all that the **prophets** spoke!
Was it not **necessary** that the Christ should suffer these things
and enter into his glory?"

Rather than being frustrated and leaving them in their confusion, Jesus is patient and empathetic.

Then beginning with Moses and all the prophets,
he **interpreted** to them what referred to him
in all the Scriptures.
As they approached the village to which they were going,
he gave the impression that he was going on **farther**.

Jesus will not force himself on anyone; he waits to be invited.

But they **urged** him, "**Stay** with us,
for it is nearly evening and the day is almost over."
So he went in to **stay** with them.

Don't rush these four actions; they echo the Last Supper.

And it happened that, while he was with them at **table**,
he took **bread**, said the **blessing**,
broke it, and **gave** it to them.

Now quicken your pace.

With **that** their eyes were **opened** and they **recognized** him,
but he **vanished** from their sight.
Then they said to each other,

Convey their excitement!

"Were not our hearts **burning** within us
while he spoke to us on the way and opened the **Scriptures**
to us?"

Don't swallow "at once." The encounter with Jesus impels them to return to the community immediately.

So they set out at **once** and **returned** to Jerusalem
where they found gathered together
the eleven and those with them who were saying,

Amazing news!

"The Lord has **truly** been **raised** and has appeared to **Simon**!"
Then the **two** recounted

Keep your voice up through the end of the line.

what had taken place on the way
and how he was made **known** to them in the **breaking** of **bread**.

---

perceive their meaning, which he then explains, beginning with Moses.

The two disciples still do not recognize their companion on the journey, but when it seems that he will leave them, they press him to stay. As happens often in Luke, the sharing of a meal with Jesus reveals his true person and mission. In a culture that viewed table fellowship as a profound statement of mutual acceptance and commitment, Jesus frequently dined with sinners and outcasts as a living image of the Kingdom of God that he proclaimed. At the Last Supper, he stated that he would not

share a meal again until the coming of the Kingdom (22:18); now at table with the downcast disciples, Jesus' prophecy is fulfilled, for the Kingdom has begun.

Luke's description of this meal also bears Eucharistic overtones in the use of four key words that reappear in early references to the Lord's Supper: take, bless, break, give. Writing after most if not all of the original disciples have died, Luke reminds his contemporaries and Christians of all time of one very important mode of Jesus' continuing presence. At the close of the episode, the evangelist underscores

the importance of Eucharist as a way of meeting and recognizing Jesus, crucified and raised. Returning to the eleven, who confirm the women's announcement, the two companions relate their own encounter at table with the Risen Christ. M.F.

SECOND SUNDAY OF EASTER (OR SUNDAY OF DIVINE MERCY)

LECTIONARY #43

READING I Acts of the Apostles 2:42–47

A reading from the Acts of the Apostles

They **devoted** themselves
  to the teaching of the apostles and to the communal life,
  to the breaking of bread and to the prayers.
Awe came upon everyone,
  and many **wonders** and **signs** were done through the apostles.
All who believed were **together** and had all things in **common**;
  they would **sell** their property and possessions
  and **divide** them among all according to each one's **need**.
Every **day** they devoted themselves
  to **meeting** together in the temple area
  and to breaking **bread** in their homes.
They ate their meals with **exultation** and **sincerity** of heart,
  praising God and enjoying favor with all the people.
And every day the Lord **added** to their number those who were
    being **saved**.

This narrative describes a fully realized Christian community. Invite your assembly to aspire to this example.

Take time with this reading. Much is described here; make sure it's understood. Distinguish the four things to which they devoted themselves.

Proclaim with the awe of the early community.

This is a community of peace and agreement, free from petty jealousies.

This could be us too, if we put aside our divisions!

Marvel at the blessings God bestows on such a community.

TO KEEP IN MIND
A *narrative* has characters, dialogue, a setting, and action. Help your listeners see the story unfold, keep characters distinct, and be clear about shifts in setting.

READING I The Acts of the Apostles is the second volume of a two-volume composition generally called Luke-Acts. Now separated in our Bibles, the parts were written together, likely near the end of the first century. Luke states at the outset that he draws upon tradition and testimony dating "to the beginning" (Luke 1:2). After recounting the Good News of salvation offered to all people through the life, Death, and Resurrection of Christ in his Gospel account, Luke seeks to show, in Acts of the Apostles, how the faithful witness of the earliest Apostles and disciples

spread the Gospel, first to the people of Israel, and ultimately reached "to the ends of the earth" (Acts 1:8). Today's First Reading summarizes Christian communal life in an idealized portrait of the earliest Church that demonstrates the power of Christ's Resurrection and those who bear faithful witness to it.

In describing the early Christian mission, Luke takes great care to point out continuity between the Gospel and the Scriptures and tradition of Judaism. For this author, the teaching of the first Apostles forms a crucial link connecting Christians of

later ages with Jesus and his saving work. His first summary thus begins by emphasizing the teachings of the Apostles, then stressing the importance of the community's shared life and the Eucharist. Referring to the Eucharist, Luke uses the same phrase he employs in his first volume (his Gospel account). At Emmaus, two bewildered, sorrowing disciples come to recognize the Risen Jesus by sharing with him "the breaking of the bread" (Luke 24:35). Originally the opening of the Jewish ritual meal, this phrase both connects the first Christians to their traditional Jewish worship

For meditation and context:

RESPONSORIAL PSALM   Psalm 118:2–4, 13–15, 22–24 (1)

R. Give thanks to the Lord for he is good, his love is everlasting.
or
R. Alleluia.

Let the house of Israel say,
    "His mercy endures forever."
Let the house of Aaron say,
    "His mercy endures forever."
Let those who fear the LORD say,
    "His mercy endures forever."

I was hard pressed and was falling,
    but the LORD helped me.
My strength and my courage is the LORD,
    and he has been my savior.
The joyful shout of victory
    in the tents of the just.

The stone which the builders rejected
    has become the cornerstone.
By the LORD has this been done;
    it is wonderful in our eyes.
This is the day the LORD has made;
    let us be glad and rejoice in it.

> **TO KEEP IN MIND**
> *Exhortatory* texts make an urgent appeal to listeners. They may encourage, warn, or challenge, and often include a call to action. You must convey the urgency and passion behind the words.

READING II   1 Peter 1:3–9

A reading from the first Letter of Saint Peter

This exhortatory reading is a joyful hymn of praise for faithful Christian life. Through your proclamation, inspire and encourage your assembly to continue to live up to these standards.

Start strong! Blessed = BLES-uhd

Pause only at the commas in this sentence. Note that the first "who" refers to Christ, the second "who" refers to your community.

Blessed be the God and Father of our Lord Jesus Christ,
    who in his great **mercy** gave us a **new** birth to a living **hope**
    through the **resurrection** of Jesus Christ from the dead,
    to an inheritance that is **imperishable**, **undefiled**, and **unfading**,
    kept in heaven for you
    who by the power of God are safeguarded through **faith**,
    to a **salvation** that is ready to be revealed in the final time.

Keep these three qualities distinct.

In this you **rejoice**, although now for a **little** while
    you may have to **suffer** through various trials,
    so that the **genuineness** of your faith,
    more precious than **gold** that is **perishable** even though
        tested by **fire**,
    may prove to be for **praise**, **glory**, and **honor**
    at the revelation of Jesus **Christ**.

Connect "faith" to "may prove" by keeping your pace up or dropping your voice in the aside about gold.

Pause.

Note that Peter says, "You do this already!" Maintain eye contact with the assembly and echo their "indescribable and glorious joy" in your proclamation.

Although you have not **seen** him you **love** him;
    even though you do not see him **now** yet **believe** in him,
    you **rejoice** with an indescribable and **glorious** joy,
    as you attain the **goal** of your faith, the **salvation** of your **souls**.

---

and signals its new meaning: it is now a participation in the self-giving Death and Resurrection of Jesus, the Messiah.

Luke's only use of the word *koinōnia* ("communal life") appears in this passage, emphasizing the mutual responsibility and support that must bind all the baptized. Pooling of resources in order to meet the needs of everyone is one important manifestation of that community bond, and sets them apart from highly stratified surrounding cultures. Luke then describes the fruits of their faithful witness: they give praise to God, receive the people's favor, and enjoy

growth in the community of those saved through proclaiming the Gospel by word and deed.

> **READING II**   Today's Responsorial Psalm of jubilant praise for God's steadfast love ("mercy") provides an excellent transition from the First Reading to the Second. Its joyful tone is especially remarkable in the context of the First Letter of Peter. Though modern scholars debate whether the Apostle or a later follower composed this work, they agree that it speaks to an audience of Christians under-

going unspecified sufferings. Using a traditional greeting formula, the author addresses hearers in several parts of Asia Minor who most likely were Gentile converts to Christian faith. Whether they were enduring formal Roman persecution or the ridicule, exclusion, or economic boycotts often directed at those who refused to conform to the prevailing imperial culture is unknown, but the writer recognizes that his audience is facing various trials and sufferings. Throughout the letter, the author sprinkles numerous references to Baptism and

GOSPEL   John 20:19–31

A reading from the holy Gospel according to John

On the evening of that **first** day of the week,
   when the doors were **locked**, where the disciples were,
   for **fear** of the Jews,
   Jesus came and **stood** in their midst
   and said to them, "**Peace** be with you."
When he had said this, he showed them his **hands** and his **side**.
The disciples **rejoiced** when they saw the Lord.
Jesus said to them again, "**Peace** be with you.
As the **Father** has sent **me**, so **I** send **you**."
And when he had said this, he **breathed** on them and said
      to them,
   "**Receive** the Holy **Spirit**.
Whose **sins** you **forgive** are **forgiven** them,
   and whose sins you **retain** are **retained**."

Thomas, called **Didymus**, one of the **Twelve**,
   was not **with** them when Jesus came.
So the **other** disciples said to him, "We have **seen** the **Lord**."
But he said to them,
   "**Unless** I **see** the mark of the **nails** in his hands
   and put my **finger** into the nailmarks
   and put my **hand** into his **side**, I will not **believe**." »

Marginal notes (left column):

A narrative. For each character—Jesus, Thomas, the disciples—identify an attitude or intention for each and let that help you distinguish them in your proclamation.

This should sound like the surprise that it is!

Immediately, Jesus calms their fears.

Let their joy echo in your proclamation.
We are sent by Jesus as he was sent by the Father.

Pause here to indicate the passage of time.

Didymus = DID-uh-muhs

This is a joyful exclamation!

Careful not to make Thomas sound too obstinate; he longs for direct experience.
Pause again.

---

baptismal liturgies, including what seem to be portions of creeds, hymns, and homilies.

Continuing the usual opening format of a letter, the author gives praise and thanks to God, emphasizing new life and hope given through the Resurrection of Christ Crucified. Christians suffering because of their faith in Jesus are reminded that their unfailing hope must be rooted in this Paschal Mystery. The God who brought Jesus through death to fullness of life continues the same saving, life-giving work in believers who now share in his new life, the "new birth" of Baptism. Like Christ,

Christians might undergo testing and even anguish, but Christians who, like Christ, place unwavering trust in God will know the ultimate joy of salvation. Though now unseen, this Christ is the beloved, sure source and goal of living faith.

Today's Gospel reading can be best understood by reference to its end, which many scholars believe to be also the original conclusion of the Fourth Gospel. John's narrative aims to evoke faith in Jesus as both Messiah and Son of God, leading to fullness of life through him. "Believing" (always a verb in John) and "life" (life in

God) are key words in this Gospel account, completed AD 90–100. Christians of that time, like our own, faced important questions. During Jesus' mortal life, he performed various "signs" that, for those open to perceive, led to insight and, ultimately, to faith in Jesus. For John, such believing deepened into the mutual indwelling of Jesus and the believer: fullness of life, the human sharing in divine life.

But after his Death, Jesus no longer lived as a visible, mortal human being. His disciples then, as now, asked, "How is Jesus present to us now? Through what

There is no chiding in Jesus' words. He knows what Thomas needs and gently offers it.

Now a week **later** his disciples were **again** inside
and Thomas was **with** them.
Jesus came, although the doors were **locked**,
and stood in their **midst** and said, "**Peace** be with you."
Then he said to **Thomas**, "Put your **finger** here and see my **hands**,
and bring your **hand** and put it into my **side**,
and do not be **un**believing, but **believe**."
Thomas answered and said to him, "My **Lord** and my **God**!"
Jesus said to him, "Have you come to **believe** because you have
seen me?

Blessed = BLES-uhd. This line is for your assembly. Pause.

Blessed are those who have **not** seen and **have** believed."

Pick up your pace on this conclusion.

Now, Jesus did many **other** signs in the presence of his **disciples**
that are not written in this book.
But **these** are written that you may come to **believe**

Slow down on the last half of this line.

that **Jesus** is the **Christ**, the Son of **God**,
and that through this belief you may have **life** in his name.

TO KEEP IN MIND
What does the reading ask your assembly to do or to be after hearing your proclamation? Focus on an intention every time you proclaim.

"signs" can he be revealed and encountered, that others may come to believe and participate in divine life?"

At the Last Supper, Jesus promised to send the Advocate (the Spirit) on his return to the God who sent him (John 14:16). In today's Gospel reading, the Risen Jesus fulfills this promise, sending forth the disciples as he was sent; they must now be his revelatory "sign." In the post-Resurrection era, the Church is the presence of the crucified and Risen One in the world, the tangible revelation of God's Word made flesh.

Thomas does not doubt this changed reality—he refuses it: "I will not believe." Thomas desires to experience the concrete, mortal body of Jesus, a sign in the manner he had known before. A week later, Jesus seems to grant his disciple's wish, but Thomas acknowledges a transformed Jesus, recognizing in him the very presence of God. Jesus insists that Thomas also be transformed: blessed are those who have not seen the mortal body of Jesus, but have truly perceived the living sign of his Risen Body on earth, the Church. This body and its Scriptures, the things written "in this

book," are the new mode of encountering Jesus. M.F.

THIRD SUNDAY OF EASTER

LECTIONARY #46

READING I Acts of the Apostles 2:14, 22–33

A reading from the Acts of the Apostles

A didactic reading, in which Peter explains to the crowd who this Jesus really was.

Then **Peter** stood up with the Eleven,
　　raised his voice, and **proclaimed**:
　　"You who are **Jews**, indeed **all** of you staying in Jerusalem.
Let this be **known** to you, and **listen** to my words.
You who are Israelites, **hear** these words.
Jesus the **Nazorean** was a man **commended** to you by God
　　with mighty **deeds**, **wonders**, and **signs**,
　　which God worked **through** him in your midst,
　　　　as you yourselves know.
This man, delivered up by the set plan and **foreknowledge** of God,
　　you **killed**, using **lawless** men to **crucify** him.
But God **raised** him up, **releasing** him from the throes of death,
　　because it was **impossible** for him to be **held** by it.
For **David** says of him:
　　*I saw the Lord ever **before** me,*
　　　　*with him at my right hand I shall not be **disturbed**.*
　　*Therefore my heart has been **glad** and my tongue has **exulted**;*
　　　　*my flesh, too, will dwell in **hope**,*
　　*because you will not abandon my soul to the **netherworld**,*
　　　　*nor will you suffer your holy one to see **corruption**.*
　　*You have made known to me the paths of **life**;*
　　　　*you will fill me with **joy** in your presence.* »

Use eye contact and vocal energy to reach those seated furthest from you.

The message is for Jews and Gentiles.
Pause.

Nazorean = naz-uh-REE-uhn

How might Peter sound describing Jesus' Death?

"But . . . " here's the exciting news!

This quote is exhortatory. Change your tone and keep up your pace.

Slow down on the final line of the quote.
Pause.

READING I In approaching readings from either the Acts of the Apostles or the Gospel According to Luke, it is helpful to know that these two books have one author who clearly composed them as a unified, two-volume work. Luke was not an original eyewitness to the life, Death, and Resurrection of Jesus, but most likely a Gentile convert who wrote his account about fifty-five to sixty years after these events. At the beginning of his work, he indicates major concerns: he reassures hearers that they are receiving authentic teaching passed on from the earliest Apostles and disciples, and he emphasizes that Jesus "fulfills" prophecy. Opening his second volume, Acts, Luke indicates a shift from the Good News of Jesus himself to ways in which the early Church's witness brought the Good News to the Jewish people and, ultimately, to the entire world (see Luke 1:1–4; Acts 1:1–8).

Luke structures Acts according to this geographical spread of Christian faith. As the book opens, the gathered disciples await fulfillment of Jesus' promise of the Spirit. Chapter 2 begins with that fulfillment, as the Holy Spirit descends upon the community of Jesus' followers in Jerusalem. The proclamation of the Good News to fellow Israelites begins immediately with the first of several speeches by Peter. These discourses, arranged by Luke, include key elements of the Christian proclamation, rooted in earliest tradition and the faith experience of foundational Christian communities.

Today's First Reading presents major portions of Peter's first speech. Its opening section, not included in today's liturgy, gives evidence of Luke's concern about fulfilling prophecy. Peter begins by explaining

The teaching continues. Your tone can be, "You know this, right?"

"My brothers, one can **confidently** say to you
    about the patriarch David that he **died** and was **buried**,
    and his **tomb** is in our midst to this day.
But since he was a **prophet** and knew that God had sworn an
      oath to him

Peter is referring back to the quoted psalm.

    that he would set one of his **descendants** upon his throne,
    he **foresaw** and spoke of the **resurrection** of the Christ,
    that neither was he **abandoned** to the netherworld
    nor did his flesh see **corruption**.

Here is the point. Slow down.

God **raised** this Jesus;
    of this we are all **witnesses**.
Exalted at the right hand of God,
    he received the promise of the Holy **Spirit** from the Father
    and **poured** him forth, as you **see** and **hear**."

For meditation and context:

RESPONSORIAL PSALM Psalm 16:1–2, 5, 7–8, 9–10, 11 (11a)

R. Lord, you will show us the path of life.
or
R. Alleluia.

Keep me, O God, for in you I take refuge;
    I say to the LORD, "My Lord are you."
O LORD, my allotted portion and my cup,
    you it is who hold fast my lot.

I bless the LORD who counsels me;
    even in the night my heart exhorts me.
I set the LORD ever before me;
    with him at my right hand I shall not
      be disturbed.

Therefore my heart is glad and my
    soul rejoices,
    my body, too, abides in confidence;
because you will not abandon my soul
    to the netherworld,
    nor will you suffer your faithful one
    to undergo corruption.

You will show me the path to life,
    abounding joy in your presence,
    the delights at your right hand forever.

TO KEEP IN MIND
A *didactic* text makes a point or teaches something. Help your assembly to follow the argument and understand what's being taught.

---

that the Pentecost phenomenon demonstrates "what was spoken through the prophet Joel," who proclaimed that in the final age, God's spirit would be given to all people, without distinctions of age, gender, or social status. Since Jews' expectation about God's final act of salvation included the hope of resurrection, primarily understood as the re-creation of God's people, the rest of Peter's speech strives to illuminate the raising of one individual, Jesus.

Peter reminds his hearers of recent events concerning Jesus and interprets their meaning by repeatedly referring to

Israel's sacred writings. As his audience already knows, Jesus was crucified by Roman power. And yet, proclaims Peter, according to God's mysterious plan of salvation, "God raised him up." The Apostle invokes Psalm 16, attributing it to King David, as were many psalms. The psalmist expresses profound trust in the LORD, who does not abandon a faithful servant to even the power of Sheol, "the pit," which Jews understood as the world of the dead. The Greek terms for this underworld derive from a root word meaning "to be corrupt," and Peter uses a common Jewish approach

to interpretation, wordplay, to proclaim that the psalmist's unbounded trust in the Lord reaches completion in God's saving Jesus from "corruption."

Elaborating his point, Peter refers again to David and another psalm. King David himself died and was buried in a tomb, but God fulfilled the promise that one of his descendants would rule God's people forever. That divine assurance reaches completion in God's act of raising Jesus to the heavenly level "at the right hand of God," sharing divine life. The Lord now

A didactic reading, reminding your community that they have been saved by Christ, and should act accordingly.

We do.

sojourning = SOH-jern-ing

Dismiss these things as worthless.

Pause.

Christ was revealed just for us!
This is good news!

Slow down and speak with assurance.

READING II   1 Peter 1:17–21

A reading from the first Letter of Saint Peter

Beloved:
If you invoke as **Father** him who judges **impartially**
　　according to each one's **works**,
　　conduct yourselves with **reverence** during the time
　　　of your sojourning,
　　realizing that you were **ransomed** from your futile conduct,
　　handed on by your ancestors,
　　not with **perishable** things like silver or gold
　　but with the precious blood of Christ
　　as of a spotless unblemished **lamb**.

He was **known** before the foundation of the world
　　but revealed in the final time for **you**,
　　who through him believe in **God**
　　who **raised** him from the dead and gave him **glory**,
　　so that your **faith** and **hope** are in **God**.

pours forth on all people that divine life, the Holy Spirit, through Jesus, raised by God.

READING II This brief letter attributed to Peter addresses Christians undergoing unspecified sufferings because of their faith in Jesus as Messiah. The author apparently holds the view of most early Christians that Christ would soon return in full glory, bringing to completion the final age of salvation.

Immediately before today's Second Reading, the author urges his hearers to pattern their lives on that of Jesus Christ,

according to the call of God, until he comes again. Christians must bear witness in their actions that they are saved through the self-giving life of Jesus (blood is a Jewish symbol for life). Jesus surrendered his mortal life to God, who raised him to divine life. At his coming in glory, God will also raise up those who put their faith and hope in the One who conquers death and bestows on them the very life of God.

GOSPEL Throughout his account of the Good News, Luke repeatedly refers to Jesus' journey toward

Jerusalem, where he will be crucified and raised. Another key theme for Luke is Jesus' table fellowship, especially with the poor, outcast, and sinners. Today's Gospel Reading continues these themes, now using them to describe the life of Jesus' post-Resurrection followers. Christians continue to journey with Jesus and with one another, together walking the Paschal path through death to greater life; they realize Jesus' continuing, transforming presence among them in one another and in the eucharistic meal.

A narrative that suggests how your assembly might meet Jesus today—in the Word, the breaking of the bread, and the stranger. This beloved and powerful story needs careful preparation to make the most of its dialogue, dramatic revelation, and rich insights.

The day of the Resurrection; these disciples have heard the news from the women this morning.

The story has much energy and activity. Keep your pace up.

They can't hide their sadness at Jesus' Death and the confusing events since then.

A bit incredulous. Notice how Jesus, who knows the most about what has happened, will pretend ignorance to allow them to share their story and feelings first.
Jesus wants to meet them where they are.

Try alternating these lines between the two speakers. Change tone slightly for each.
The first disciple states the facts.

The second gives an interpretation of the facts.

The first jumps in with even more confusing news.

Let their astonishment come through in this description. They still don't know what to make of it all.

"Can you believe it?"

GOSPEL   Luke 24:13–35

A reading from the holy Gospel according to Luke

That **very** day, the **first** day of the week,
   two of Jesus' **disciples** were going
   to a village seven miles from Jerusalem called Emmaus,
   and they were **conversing** about all the things that
     had occurred.
And it happened that while they were conversing and debating,
   Jesus **himself** drew near and walked with them,
   but their eyes were prevented from **recognizing** him.
He asked them,
   "What are you **discussing** as you walk along?"
They stopped, looking **downcast**.
One of them, named **Cleopas**, said to him in reply,
   "Are you the **only** visitor to Jerusalem
   who does not **know** of the things
   that have taken **place** there in these days?"
And he replied to them, "What **sort** of things?"
They said to him,
   "The things that happened to **Jesus** the **Nazarene**,
   who was a prophet **mighty** in deed and word
   before God and all the people,
   how our chief priests and rulers both handed him over
   to a sentence of **death** and **crucified** him.
But we were **hoping** that **he** would be the one to **redeem** Israel;
   and **besides** all this,
   it is now the **third** day since this took place.
Some **women** from our group, however, have **astounded** us:
   they were at the **tomb** early in the morning
   and did not find his **body**;
   they came back and reported
   that they had indeed seen a **vision** of angels
   who announced that he was **alive**.

The Emmaus story follows Luke's account of the faithful women who remained at the Cross and now return to Jesus' tomb in order to anoint his body. There two heavenly messengers announce that no body subject to corruption is to be found, because Jesus "has been raised." The women in turn proclaim this Good News to fellow disciples, who dismiss their testimony. In contrast to the women, who believe based on proclamation, the other disciples as yet refuse to do so. Seeking to verify their witness, Peter runs to the tomb, but sees only empty burial cloths. He is

"amazed," but Luke does not say that he believes; full perception of the Risen One will come only in the familiar yet new table fellowship with Jesus.

By the time Luke wrote his Gospel narrative, most if not all of Jesus' original followers had died. Christians who lacked their experience of Jesus asked, in Luke's day and through the ages, "How can we come to experience and know Jesus today?" In this Sunday's Gospel Reading, Luke offers three major modes: in the faithful testimony of earlier disciples, in the Scriptures, and in the Eucharist.

As the passage begins, two disheartened disciples walk the road from Jerusalem to Emmaus, and soon a third person accompanies them. Jesus continues to journey with his followers, though they do not yet recognize him. Ironically, the two disciples, still dejected, still unseeing, recount the core of Christian belief to their new companion. They tell how the great prophet Jesus worked wonders before God and among the people, but suffered condemnation and crucifixion. They repeat in detail the women's testimony to his

The second finishes the story.

What does Jesus feel as he realizes these disciples still don't understand his messiahship? Disappointment, sadness, compassion?

Rather than being frustrated and leaving them in their confusion, Jesus is patient and empathetic.

Jesus will not force himself on anyone; he waits to be invited.

Don't rush these four actions; they echo the Last Supper.

Now quicken your pace.

Convey their excitement!

Don't swallow "at once." The encounter with Jesus impels them to return to the community immediately.

Amazing news!

Keep your voice up through the end of the line.

Then some of those with us **went** to the tomb
  and found things **just** as the women had described,
    but **him** they did not see."
And he said to them, "Oh, how **foolish** you are!
How **slow** of heart to believe all that the **prophets** spoke!
Was it not **necessary** that the Christ should suffer these things
  and enter into his glory?"
Then beginning with Moses and all the prophets,
  he **interpreted** to them what referred to him
    in all the Scriptures.
As they approached the village to which they were going,
  he gave the impression that he was going on **farther**.
But they **urged** him, "**Stay** with us,
  for it is nearly evening and the day is almost over."
So he went in to **stay** with them.
And it happened that, while he was with them at **table**,
  he took **bread**, said the **blessing**,
  broke it, and **gave** it to them.
With **that** their eyes were **opened** and they **recognized** him,
  but he **vanished** from their sight.
Then they said to each other,
  "Were not our hearts **burning** within us
  while he spoke to us on the way and opened the **Scriptures**
    to us?"
So they set out at **once** and **returned** to Jerusalem
  where they found gathered together
  the eleven and those with them who were saying,
  "The Lord has **truly** been **raised** and has appeared to **Simon**!"
Then the **two** recounted
  what had taken place on the way
  and how he was made **known** to them in the **breaking** of **bread**.

Resurrection, and yet their recitation ends "but him they did not see."

Jesus then confirms the women's announcement by explaining to the travelers how the events they have described fulfill prophecy. Still, they cannot accept either the witness of the faithful women or the testimony of the Scriptures. At their urging, Jesus remains with them as evening draws near. Luke hints at what is to come by reference to the traditional time at which early Christians celebrated the Lord's Supper. With a single deftly written sentence, the evangelist portrays the early

Christian conviction that in this meal, the crucified and Risen One is fully present, teaching, healing, unifying, and transforming his disciples. Using what had quickly become a type of Christian eucharistic formula, Luke includes four key words: take, bless, break, give. In this sacred meal, the pair finally "see" Jesus. Luke's Greek word translated "see" means "to perceive, discern, or know by personal experience." Immediately Jesus vanishes from before their eyes, as Luke emphasizes that truly "seeing" Jesus requires eyes of faith, not merely physical organs.

With new insight, the two disciples reverse the direction of their journey, returning to Jerusalem and other disciples. There they receive the testimony of the Eleven and those gathered with them, sharing their own witness that they, too, have encountered the living Christ "in the breaking of the bread." M.F.

FOURTH SUNDAY OF EASTER

LECTIONARY #49

READING I Acts of the Apostles 2:14a, 36–41

A narrative reading which can encourage your assembly to stay faithful to their commitment to Christ.

A reading from the Acts of the Apostles

Then **Peter** stood up with the Eleven,
    raised his voice, and **proclaimed**:

Be bold in your proclamation!

"Let the whole house of Israel know for **certain**
    that God has made both **Lord** and **Christ**,
    this **Jesus** whom you **crucified**."

Let your voice echo their repentance and regret.

Now when they **heard** this, they were **cut** to the **heart**,
    and they asked Peter and the other apostles,
    "What are we to **do**, my brothers?"
Peter said to them,

Don't scold or demand; rather, invite.

    "**Repent** and be **baptized**, every **one** of you,
    in the name of Jesus **Christ** for the **forgiveness** of your sins;
    and you will **receive** the gift of the Holy **Spirit**.

Here is the good news! Peter is speaking about your assembly.

For the promise is made to **you** and to your **children**
    and to all those **far** off,
    whomever the Lord our God will **call**."

Choose to stand apart, and not go the way of the crowd.

He testified with many other arguments, and was **exhorting** them,
    "**Save** yourselves from this corrupt generation."

More good news!

Those who **accepted** his message were **baptized**,
    and about three **thousand** persons were added that day.

READING I Today's First Reading includes roughly the second half of Peter's speech to fellow Jews in Jerusalem soon after the Pentecost experience of the Holy Spirit (see the commentary for the First Reading of last Sunday for the larger context). Continuing to proclaim the meaning of Jesus as understood in light of Israel's sacred writings and religious hopes, Peter makes an astounding assertion: the man rejected by some Jewish leaders and executed by Rome has been made Lord and Messiah. The power of divine Spirit given through the Risen Christ

clearly empowers Peter, who once, in fear, denied even knowing Jesus. His bold proclamation could easily arouse the wrath, not only of Jewish religious leaders who sought Jesus' Death, but also of imperial Rome, whose emperors enjoyed "Lord" as a title of authority and divinity.

Perhaps the Apostle's obvious transformation serves to "cut to the heart" of his hearers; perhaps they recognize that Peter does proclaim the Word of God, described elsewhere in the New Testament as a piercing sword (Ephesians 6:17; Hebrews 4:12). When fellow Jews ask Peter what

they ought to do in response to his witness, he echoes Jesus' call to "repent," that is, to change the course of their entire lives, and be baptized. Peter's reply indicates core meanings the early Church placed on Baptism: conversion of heart, forgiveness, and imparting of God's Spirit. His call to fellow Israelites to save themselves from "this corrupt generation" may reflect the first century's ongoing antagonism between Jews who accepted Jesus as Messiah and those who considered Christians as an aberrant, even heretical, Jewish sect.

For meditation and context:

RESPONSORIAL PSALM   Psalm 23:1–3a, 3b–4, 5, 6 (1)

R. The Lord is my shepherd; there is nothing I shall want.
or
R. Alleluia.

The LORD is my shepherd; I shall not want.
   In verdant pastures he gives me repose;
beside restful waters he leads me;
   he refreshes my soul.

He guides me in right paths
   for his name's sake.
Even though I walk in the dark valley
   I fear no evil; for you are at my side,
with your rod and your staff
   that give me courage.

You spread the table before me
   in the sight of my foes;
you anoint my head with oil;
   my cup overflows.

Only goodness and kindness follow me
   all the days of my life;
and I shall dwell in the house of the LORD
   for years to come.

A didactic reading. In the second half, Peter quotes Isaiah 52, the Song of the Suffering Servant. You may want to review that for context (see Reading I from Good Friday).

Speak this word of comfort to those who are suffering in your assembly.

Our suffering is compared to Christ's which is compared to the Suffering Servant.

Maintain a gentle tone, consistent with the attitude of the suffering Christ.

Note that the phrase "he handed himself over" refers to his surrendering to God, not to the authorities.

Slow from here to the end.

This is good news!

READING II   1 Peter 2:20b–25

A reading from the first Letter of Saint Peter

Beloved:
If you are **patient** when you suffer for doing what is **good**,
   this is a **grace** before God.
For to this you have been **called**,
   because Christ **also** suffered for **you**,
   leaving you an **example** that you should follow in his **footsteps**.
*He committed no **sin**, and no **deceit** was found in his mouth.*

When he was **insulted**, he returned **no** insult;
   when he **suffered**, he did not **threaten**;
   instead, he **handed** himself over to the one who judges **justly**.
He himself **bore** our sins in his **body** upon the **cross**,
   so that, **free** from sin, we might live for **righteousness**.
By his **wounds** you have been **healed**.
For you had gone **astray** like sheep,
   but you have now **returned** to the **shepherd** and **guardian** of
      your **souls**.

Luke concludes Peter's first address by stating that those who did accept his witness to Jesus were baptized that day, numbering three thousand. This multiplication of "perfect" numbers in Jewish symbolism (three and ten) points to perfection or completion of the age of salvation, which God has inaugurated in Jesus, Lord and Messiah.

READING II The Second Readings for all the Sundays after Easter are taken from a letter attributed to Peter, though this work may have been written by a follower. Like many other New Testament

texts, it often draws upon passages, themes, and characters from the Old Testament. Here the author, addressing Christians undergoing unnamed sufferings, urges his hearers to imitate Christ, who embodies the Suffering Servant described by Isaiah.

In four poems, the prophet described a figure chosen by the Lord for saving work on behalf of God's people. Empowered by divine Spirit, the Servant carries out his mission, though he suffers rejection, physical and mental pain, and even death for his faithfulness. Like the Servant, Jesus brings

healing and oneness with God, the true Shepherd, through his life-giving Death.

GOSPEL Like the two preceding texts, today's Gospel reading employs the Old Testament to interpret the meaning of Jesus. In this passage, Jesus addresses opponents, Jewish leaders who surely understand such allusions. This opening of a lengthy discourse focuses on two things: the identity of Jesus, and the choice presented to those who encounter him, to accept or reject. John portrays Jesus as the Good Shepherd promised to

In this narrative Jesus compares himself to a shepherd and then to the gate of the sheepfold. Jesus uses both metaphors to emphasize that he is the way to abundant life.

This is important! Listen up!

What does Jesus think of these thieves and robbers? Make a choice and make it clear in your proclamation.

Keep your voice gentle, as the shepherd would.

Jesus tries another way to get his message across. Might he be a little frustrated? Raise your energy and be more insistent.

Jesus repeats the metaphor. Be deliberate and emphatic.

Don't swallow "abundantly." It might be the most important word in the reading.

GOSPEL John 10:1–10

A reading from the holy Gospel according to John

Jesus said:
  "Amen, **amen**, I say to you,
    whoever does not enter a sheepfold through the **gate**
    but climbs over **elsewhere** is a **thief** and a **robber**.
But whoever enters through the **gate** is the **shepherd** of the sheep.
The gatekeeper **opens** it for him, and the sheep **hear** his voice,
    as the shepherd **calls** his own sheep by **name** and **leads**
        them out.
When he has driven out all his **own**,
    he walks **ahead** of them, and the sheep **follow** him,
    because they recognize his **voice**.
But they will not follow a **stranger**;
    they will run **away** from him,
    because they do not **recognize** the voice of strangers."
Although Jesus used this figure of **speech**,
    the **Pharisees** did not realize what he was trying to tell them.

So Jesus said **again**, "Amen, **amen**, I say to you,
  I am the **gate** for the sheep.
All who came **before** me are thieves and robbers,
    but the sheep did not **listen** to them.
I am the **gate**.
Whoever enters through **me** will be **saved**,
    and will come **in** and go **out** and find **pasture**.
A thief comes only to **steal** and **slaughter** and **destroy**;
    I came so that they might have **life** and have it
        more **abundantly**."

appear at the culmination of God's plan, thus distinguishing between those Jews who believe in, or oppose, Jesus.

In the Old Testament, God is often portrayed as "Shepherd" of the covenant people. Ezekiel prophesied to the captive Jews in Babylon that their unfaithful kings, also called "shepherds," would be replaced in God's new future with a caring, healing shepherd: none other than the Lord in person (Ezekiel 34:1–16).

After describing himself as "the gate" of the sheepfold, Jesus will identify himself in ensuing verses as "the good shepherd" (John 10:14). In ancient Israel, shepherds sometimes did function as the "gate" to a quickly constructed sheepfold in the wilderness, a rough circle of stones. With the shepherd sleeping in a small opening of the ring, entrance could be gained only through the human "gate." The shepherd's life might well be threatened by a hungry wild animal or human thief. With Jesus as gate or gatekeeper, those who belong to his flock will surely find food and safety.

But who does belong to his flock? Only those who recognize the Shepherd's voice. John again draws his imagery from the real-ities of ancient Palestinian life: sheep are not only defenseless against marauders; left to themselves, they are generally incapable of finding food or water. The sheep's life itself depends upon recognizing and responding to the shepherd's voice. Those who believe in Jesus belong to him, hear and respond to his voice, and so have life. Those who do not recognize the voice of the Lord, true Shepherd, speaking in Jesus, may lose life itself. M.F.

FIFTH SUNDAY OF EASTER

LECTIONARY #52

READING I   Acts of the Apostles 6:1–7

A reading from the Acts of the Apostles

As the number of disciples continued to **grow**,
   the Hellenists **complained** against the Hebrews
   because their **widows**
   were being **neglected** in the daily distribution.
So the Twelve called together the **community** of the disciples
   and said,
   "It is not **right** for us to **neglect** the word of God to **serve**
   at table.
Brothers, select from among you seven **reputable** men,
   filled with the Spirit and wisdom,
   whom we shall **appoint** to this task,
   whereas **we** shall devote ourselves to **prayer**
   and to the ministry of the **word**."
The proposal was **acceptable** to the whole community,
   so they chose **Stephen**, a man **filled** with **faith** and the
      Holy Spirit,
   also **Philip**, **Prochorus**, **Nicanor**, **Timon**, **Parmenas**,
   and **Nicholas** of **Antioch**, a **convert** to Judaism.
They presented these men to the apostles
   who **prayed** and laid **hands** on them. **»**

A narrative, reminding us that even in a model community, conflicts will arise. But when they are handled justly, they become a moment of grace. The emphasis here is not on what decision was made but rather how it was made.

This problem arises because the community is blessed with growth.

Hellenists = Greek-speaking Jewish Christians.

The daily distribution of food to the community from the common store.

Be careful not to make serving at table sound like a menial job. It's simply not the ministry the Twelve are called to.

Note that the community chooses the deacons at the invitation of the Twelve. The Twelve don't act without the assent of the community, nor does the community without the Twelve.

Prochorus = PRAH-kuh-ruhs

Nicanor = nī-KAY-nuhr

Timon = TĪ-muhn

Parmenas = PAHR-muh-nuhs

Antioch = AN-tee-ahk

Pause.

READING I   Previous Easter Time readings from Acts established Luke's purpose: to show the mission of Jesus continuing through the work of the early Church, rapidly spreading among Jews, and finally throughout the Gentile world. As with the Church of today, however, the work of spreading the Gospel did not always proceed smoothly; as the Christian community grew, various needs and even conflicts sometimes called for restructuring of ministries.

Such is the case in today's First Reading. As the Christian community in Jerusalem grew, it incorporated people of differing backgrounds. Not yet distinct from Judaism, Jesus' followers were considered as one of several Jewish sects of the time. In this passage, Hellenists were Jews who spoke only Greek, while Hebrews were Jews who most commonly spoke Aramaic. As today, language differences sometimes led to perceived differences in treatment, and the Greek-speaking Jewish Christians protested that their widows were often ignored in the community's distribution to the needy.

Up to this point, the Twelve had served as leaders of the new Israel of the final age. The Hellenists' complaint seemed to require the aid of leaders who could communicate in Greek and so more easily assist them. The Twelve, who had focused on proclaiming the Good News, did not want to surrender this important work. Reference to table service in this text is ambiguous, but probably refers to distribution of food to members of the community in need. The Twelve therefore call for a new group of leaders among the Hellenists who

More good news!

The word of God continued to **spread**,
    and the **number** of the disciples in Jerusalem
        increased **greatly**;
    even a large group of **priests** were becoming obedient
        to the faith.

This is good and surprising news!

For meditation and context:

RESPONSORIAL PSALM   Psalm 33:1–2, 4–5, 18–19 (22)

R. Lord, let your mercy be on us, as we place our trust in you.
or
R. Alleluia.

Exult, you just, in the LORD;
    praise from the upright is fitting.
Give thanks to the LORD on the harp;
    with the ten-stringed lyre chant his praises.

Upright is the word of the LORD,
    and all his works are trustworthy.
He loves justice and right;
    of the kindness of the LORD the earth is full.

See, the eyes of the LORD are upon those
        who fear him,
    upon those who hope for his kindness,
to deliver them from death
    and preserve them in spite of famine.

TO KEEP IN MIND
Exhortatory texts make an urgent appeal to listeners. They may encourage, warn, or challenge, and often include a call to action. You must convey the urgency and passion behind the words.

An exhortatory reading. Peter emboldens the faithful who are experiencing obstacles in the Christian life. Proclaim with the tone of heartfelt encouragement you would use for someone dear who is dispirited.

Careful with this construction; take your time, and pause only at the commas.

Emphasize the progression: stones become a house become a priesthood.

READING II   1 Peter 2:4–9

A reading from the first Letter of Saint Peter

Beloved:
Come to him, a **living** stone, **rejected** by human beings
    but **chosen** and **precious** in the sight of **God**,
    and, like **living** stones,
    let **yourselves** be built into a **spiritual** house
    to be a holy **priesthood** to offer **spiritual** sacrifices
    acceptable to God through Jesus **Christ**.
For it says in Scripture:
    *Behold, I am laying a **stone** in Zion,*
    *a **cornerstone**, **chosen** and **precious**,*
    *and whoever **believes** in it shall not be put to shame.*

Convey God's care in choosing this special stone.

No matter your struggle, you will not be put to shame.

---

will carry out this ministry, allowing the Twelve to continue preaching the Gospel.

The community finds this an acceptable division of labor, and so chooses seven men who meet the necessary requirements for Christian ministry: faithful disciples "filled with faith and the Holy Spirit." The names of the seven (a "perfect" number symbolizing complete suitability for the task) are all Greek, indicating that they can well serve the Hellenist members of the community. Stephen, named first, will later become a prominent leader and eventually the first Christian martyr. Luke concludes

the episode by focusing again on a favored theme: rapid multiplication of believers in Jesus the Messiah.

READING II   This letter attributed to Peter addresses Christians living in an environment hostile to their way of life. The author repeatedly reminds his hearers of the grace and call of Baptism, urging them to faithfully follow Christ, even in the face of rejection and suffering. The Second Reading reminds those who are baptized into Christ that he is the sure foundation of their lives of faith; he too was

rejected by humans but chosen by God for the work of salvation.

Using a technique common in the New Testament, the writer refers to the Old Testament to clarify the meaning of Christ in the present situation. Isaiah, prophesying to Judah when it too frequently relied on foreign powers rather than on the Lord, reminds the people that God is the cornerstone and sure foundation of Jerusalem, the religious center of Judah and home of God's Temple (Isaiah 28:16). The Old Testament repeatedly looked forward to the age of salvation in which God would

Therefore, its value is for you who have **faith**, but for those
    without faith:
*The stone that the builders **rejected***
*has become the **cornerstone**,*
and
    *a stone that will make people **stumble**,*
    *and a rock that will make them **fall***.
They stumble by **disobeying** the word, as is their **destiny**.

You are "a **chosen** race, a **royal** priesthood,
    a **holy** nation, a people of his **own**,
    so that you may announce the **praises**" of him
    who called you out of **darkness** into his wonderful **light**.

GOSPEL   John 14:1–12

A reading from the holy Gospel according to John

Jesus said to his disciples:
    "Do not let your hearts be **troubled**.
You have faith in **God**; have faith also in **me**.
In my **Father's** house there are many **dwelling** places.
If there were **not**,
    would I have told you that I am going to prepare a **place**
        for you?
And if I **go** and prepare a place for you,
    I will come **back** again and **take** you to myself,
    so that where **I** am you **also** may be.
Where I am going you **know** the way."
Thomas said to him,
    "Master, we do not know where you are **going**;
    how can we know the **way**?"
Jesus said to him, "**I** am the **way** and the **truth** and the **life**.
No one comes to the Father except through **me**.
If you know **me**, then you will also know my **Father**. ≫

It's sometimes hard for others to understand why we make the choice to be faithful to Christ.

Here is the privilege and the responsibility of the Christian. Maintain eye contact and speak directly to the assembly.

A didactic reading in the form of a conversation. Jesus reassures his disciples that he will remain in intimate relationship with them even after he is gone physically. How would you convince a loved one that you will be connected somehow even while separated? Bring that gentle love and concern to your proclamation.

Jesus acknowledges their anxiety.

Our true home is in the house of God; what have we to fear?

Good news!

"You already remain in me."

Thomas (like most of us) wants to know the destination. Jesus asks us to have faith in the journey.

---

create a new Temple, a new house of God that could never be destroyed. The New Testament declares that the Christian community is that new dwelling place where God can be encountered and worshipped, and its cornerstone is Christ (Ephesians 2:19–22). With further allusion to Jewish texts, the author exhorts Christians undergoing trials that they are also the new Israel of the age of salvation, set apart as God's people to offer praise with faithful lives.

GOSPEL   On the Second Sunday of Easter, the Gospel reading

recounted the Risen Christ's bestowal of the Spirit on the disciples. Today the Church recalls Jesus' Last Supper promise to do so—an assurance only dimly grasped at that time. Like his first followers, disciples today may understand more fully with hindsight.

Chapters 14–17 of the fourth Gospel gather much significant material, presented as Jesus' farewell address to the disciples during their supper before his Passion. In biblical writings, a farewell discourse addresses the followers of someone who will soon depart or die, instructing them how to continue the speaker's work and

mission. From the beginning of his Gospel account, John repeatedly presents Jesus as God's Word made flesh; he is sent by the Father to reveal in his own person the character and work of God. Ultimately, for this evangelist, God's person and work are the same: self-giving love that creates oneness and so gives fullness of life, a sharing in divine life.

Today's Gospel reading begins the lengthy Last Supper discourses, presenting several teachings that are repeated throughout. Jesus attempts to prepare the disciples for his departure from his mortal

Reassure your assembly, "You do know him."

Phillip still wants to be sure of the end.

Jesus knows this is difficult for the disciples (and us) to understand, but there might be some frustration in his voice.

"Listen up!" Look directly at your assembly on this final line.

This relationship is so intimate that our works are indistinguishable from the works of Jesus.

From now on you **do** know him and have **seen** him."
Philip said to him,
    "Master, **show** us the Father, and that will be enough for us."
Jesus said to him, "Have I been with you for so long a time
    and you **still** do not know me, Philip?
Whoever has seen **me** has seen the Father.
How can you say, '**Show** us the Father'?
Do you not **believe** that I am in the **Father** and the Father
    is in **me**?
The words that I **speak** to you I do not speak on my **own**.
The Father who **dwells** in me is doing his **works**.
Believe me that **I** am in the **Father** and the **Father** is in **me**,
    or else, believe because of the works themselves.
Amen, **amen**, I say to you,
    whoever **believes** in me will do the works that **I** do,
    and will do **greater** ones than these,
    because I am **going** to the **Father**."

TO KEEP IN MIND
Exhortatory texts make an urgent appeal to listeners. They may encourage, warn, or challenge, and often include a call to action. You must convey the urgency and passion behind the words.

life in this world, but assures them that he will return and take them to himself, promising "where I am you also may be." The disciples do not comprehend Jesus' meaning. Soon he will return to the Father who sent him, raised to the fullness of divine union, so that believers who are one with Jesus can, through him, also share his oneness with God.

The disciples do not yet understand that because of his unique unity with God, Jesus is the living, perceptible image of God, and so to "see" or "know" Jesus is to perceive and experience the Father. In

Hebrew thought, to "know" means perception and understanding derived from intimate experience. For John, "believing in" Jesus also points to personal, affective knowledge born of love, believing as "knowing," or mutual indwelling: "I am in the Father and the Father is in me." In later passages of the discourse, Jesus prays that those who believe in him may enjoy a similar union: that they may be one "as you, Father, are in me and I in you, that they may be one in us" (John 17:21). The principle of such oneness is the Spirit, promised at the Last Supper and breathed into them by the

Risen One (John 20:21–22). John's particular term for the Holy Spirit is "Paraclete"; the Greek root of this word means "one who stands at the side of." In the verse that follows today's Gospel, Jesus promises his disciples that the Paraclete will remain "with you always." M.F.

SIXTH SUNDAY OF EASTER

LECTIONARY #55

READING I   Acts of the Apostles 8:5–8, 14–17

A reading from the Acts of the Apostles

Philip went down to the city of **Samaria**
    and proclaimed the **Christ** to them.
With one **accord**, the crowds paid attention to what was said
      by Philip
    when they heard it and saw the **signs** he was doing.
For unclean **spirits**, crying out in a loud **voice**,
    came out of many **possessed** people,
    and many paralyzed or crippled people were **cured**.
There was great **joy** in that city.

Now when the **apostles** in **Jerusalem**
    heard that Samaria had **accepted** the word of God,
    they sent them **Peter** and **John**,
    who went down and **prayed** for them,
    that they might receive the Holy **Spirit**,
    for it had not yet fallen upon any of them;
    they had only been baptized in the name of the Lord **Jesus**.
Then they laid **hands** on them
    and they **received** the Holy Spirit.

A narrative account of an evangelism success story. How do you feel when recounting a story with a happy ending—a great triumph or success? Bring that same emotion of anticipation and excitement to this proclamation.

Samaria = suh-MAYR-ee-uh

Don't lose "Samaria"; it's significant that the Gospel is being spread beyond the Jews of Judea and Galilee.

Slow down and make Philip's action clear.

This is amazing news!

Show that joy in your voice and face.

Pause.

Two of the leaders are sent, indicating how significant the conversion of the Samaritans was to the Apostles.

There's a sense of satisfied completion in this action.

READING I With Philip's proclamation of Jesus as Messiah, the missionary efforts of the early Church expand from Jerusalem into surrounding areas. In the chapter preceding today's Scripture, Stephen was stoned to death as the first Christian martyr, and persecution of the Church in Jerusalem expanded. In today's First Reading, Philip, a Greek-speaking believer, determines to proclaim the Word to Samaritans. Though some Samaritan beliefs and practices differed from those of Jews, they also held messianic hopes and awaited God's final reign.

Like their Jewish counterparts, Philip's hearers respond to his message of the Messiah when they see signs worked in the name of Jesus, for only the arrival of God's rule could overcome the powers of evil.

The Apostles in Jerusalem rejoice at receiving word that many Samaritans have accepted the Good News of Jesus. They quickly dispatch Peter and John to assist Philip and pray for the Spirit to enliven these new believers. In this case it seems that though the Samaritan converts had received the ritual of Baptism, they had not yet fully experienced the transforming divine presence of God's Spirit. But through those who already live in the power of that Spirit, the new believers also participate in divine life given through Jesus.

READING II The Second Reading for this Sixth Sunday of Easter presents a fifth passage from a brief letter attributed to the Apostle Peter. This work addresses Christians suffering in various unspecified ways because of their allegiance to Jesus, encouraging them to be true to their baptismal calling. Persecution by those who were hostile to Christian faith

For meditation and context:

RESPONSORIAL PSALM   Psalm 66:1–3, 4–5, 6–7, 16, 20 (1)

R. Let all the earth cry out to God with joy.
or
R. Alleluia.

Shout joyfully to God, all the earth,
　　sing praise to the glory of his name;
　　proclaim his glorious praise.
Say to God, "How tremendous are
　　your deeds!"

"Let all on earth worship and sing praise
　　to you,
　　sing praise to your name!"
Come and see the works of God,
　　his tremendous deeds among the children
　　of Adam.

He has changed the sea into dry land;
　　through the river they passed on foot.
Therefore let us rejoice in him.
　　He rules by his might forever.

Hear now, all you who fear God,
　　while I declare
　　what he has done for me.
Blessed be God who refused me not
　　my prayer or his kindness!

An exhortatory reading, cheering the community to keep the faith even when it's a struggle.

Encourage your community to make Christ the center of their lives!

The attitudes of a true evangelist.

If you're always gentle and reverent, no one will believe anything people say against you.

Drop your voice on the aside about God's will.

Our suffering is joined with Christ's.

Slow down on this final line.
Express that this is good news!

READING II   1 Peter 3:15–18

A reading from the first Letter of Saint Peter

Beloved:
Sanctify Christ as Lord in your **hearts**.
Always be ready to give an **explanation**
　　to anyone who asks you for a **reason** for your hope,
　　but do it with **gentleness** and **reverence**,
　　keeping your conscience **clear**,
　　so that, when you are **maligned**,
　　those who **defame** your good conduct in Christ
　　may **themselves** be put to shame.
For it is better to suffer for doing **good**,
　　if that be the will of God, than for doing **evil**.
For Christ **also** suffered for sins once,
　　the **righteous** for the sake of the **unrighteous**,
　　that he might lead you to **God**.
Put to **death** in the **flesh**,
　　he was brought to **life** in the **Spirit**.

---

sometimes took the form of imprisonment and even death, but often it appeared in more subtle forms, such as mockery, shunning, and economic restrictions. Today, some Christians might also experience these modes of discrimination in cultures that consider their faith and practice incompatible with contemporary mores.

The writer instructs believers undergoing trials to claim as Lord the one who passed through Death to Resurrection life. With Christ as model, Christians must always be prepared to explain their ability to face sufferings with hope. Moreover,

they should do so gently, with reverence for even persecutors, because such action both bears testimony to Jesus and reveals the true character of those who cause their travails. If one must suffer, far better to do so for good actions, rather than for evil behavior. In this way, those who find themselves in a "trial by fire" (1 Peter 4:12) both imitate and bear testimony to Christ, remaining faithful to the new life of the baptized. With him, they pass over from death to transformed life.

GOSPEL　Today's Gospel reading continues Jesus' farewell discourse at the supper before his Passion. In John's previous chapter, at this meal Jesus washed the disciples' feet, modelling the humble, selfless love he then commanded them to imitate. He further instructed them that to follow this love command is the most certain sign of true discipleship (John 13). In the lengthy farewell address that follows, Jesus speaks of his coming departure from this world, but assures them of his enduring presence in a different mode. Returning to the One who

A didactic reading, in which Jesus expresses the intimacy of his relationship with us as disciples. Invite your assembly to open themselves to the depth of that relationship.

Let the love and tenderness of Jesus' care for us come through clearly. Don't "teach"; rather, make this an intimate conversation between very close friends.

Proclaim as if you were speaking to one person only.

Jesus has great love and concern for his disciples. He knows how difficult it will be for them, but he is eager to let them know he is not abandoning them. Show this compassion in your proclamation.

Take your time with this line. Make sure the progression is clear, and heighten intensity with each phrase.

The best news of all! Slow down and let your assembly take in this great promise.

TO KEEP IN MIND
Making eye contact with the assembly connects you with them and connects them to the reading more deeply than using your voice alone. This helps the assembly stay with the story and keeps them engaged.

GOSPEL   John 14:15–21

A reading from the holy Gospel according to John

Jesus said to his disciples:
  "If you **love** me, you will keep my **commandments**.
And I will ask the Father,
    and he will give you another **Advocate** to be with you **always**,
    the Spirit of **truth**, whom the world cannot **accept**,
    because it neither **sees** nor **knows** him.
But **you** know him, because he **remains** with you,
    and will be **in** you.
I will not leave you **orphans**; I will **come** to you.
In a little while the world will no longer **see** me,
    but **you** will see me, because I **live** and **you** will live.
On that **day** you will realize that **I** am in my **Father**
    and **you** are in **me** and **I** in **you**.
Whoever has my commandments and **observes** them
    is the one who **loves** me.
And whoever **loves** me will be loved by my **Father**,
    and **I** will love him and **reveal** myself to him."

---

sent him, Jesus will ask the Father to send "another Advocate to be with you always." John uses the word *paraklētos*, a Greek word best understood in its root meaning: "one who stands beside." Jesus' reference to "another" Advocate (Paraclete) suggests that he himself has been the disciples' first Advocate, the one standing beside them to reveal in his humanity the Father's character and will.

After his Death and Resurrection, Jesus will no longer be at his followers' side in tangible, visible flesh, but rather in the Spirit, the Paraclete. By the powerful pres-

ence of the Holy Spirit, those who believe in Jesus will, through him, share in divine life. Once again, John stresses the unique unity of Jesus with God, a oneness now available to believers through Jesus. The evangelist indicates that the power uniting believers, Jesus, and the Father is love.

In light of Jesus' example and command at the supper, this indwelling love must continue to be poured out to and for others, through his followers. Jesus instructs the disciples to love as he does: "to the end" (John 13:1). This phrase carries double meaning: to the end of his life, and

to the utmost. No one can give more than life itself, and soon after the supper, Jesus will freely and wholly offer his life for the good of all. Then and now, he requires no less of believers, but promises divine presence beside and within them, empowering disciples to imitate his total self-gift: the Spirit who remains forever. M.F.

THE ASCENSION OF THE LORD

LECTIONARY #58

READING I   Acts of the Apostles 1:1–11

A reading from the Acts of the Apostles

In the **first** book, Theophilus,
  I dealt with all that Jesus **did** and **taught**
  until the **day** he was taken **up**,
  after giving **instructions** through the Holy **Spirit**
  to the **apostles** whom he had **chosen**.
He presented himself **alive** to them
  by many **proofs** after he had suffered,
  appearing to them during **forty days**
  and speaking about the kingdom of **God**.
While **meeting** with them,
  he enjoined them not to **depart** from Jerusalem,
  but to wait for "the **promise** of the Father
  about which you have heard me **speak**;
  for **John** baptized with **water**,
  but in a few days **you** will be baptized with the Holy **Spirit**."

When they had gathered **together** they asked him,
  "Lord, are you at this time going to **restore** the kingdom
    to Israel?"

A narrative account of an extraordinary event. There's a lot being recounted here. Take your time; use the periods to keep separate thoughts separate.

Theophilus = thee-AWF-uh-luhs

There's a personal and friendly tone to this opening.

Pause slightly after "proofs."

Pause slightly before the quote, and heighten your energy to indicate you are speaking Jesus' words.

Even after all this, the disciples still don't fully understand the nature of Jesus' Messiahship.

READING I   The introduction to Acts of the Apostles, like the introduction to Luke's Gospel account, addresses the reader as Theophilus, a name that means "lover of God." Although Theophilus may have been an actual patron who supported Luke in his writing endeavor, a helpful way for us to hear the account is as a story addressed to each of us personally as lovers of God. We are each Theophilus, knowing that we have an intimate relationship with the God who speaks through the Word. The two closely-connected volumes of Luke and Acts recount the story of God's love manifest in Jesus and in the early Church.

In the final scene of Luke's Gospel, just before Jesus' Ascension, he commissions his gathered disciples, sending them out to all nations (Luke 24:44–53). The scene at the beginning of Acts provides a brief summary of that commissioning, focusing on three essential elements: the disciples are to be Jesus' witnesses; they are to take the Gospel to the ends of the earth; and they do so in the dynamism of the Holy Spirit.

Jesus says that the apostolic task is to be "my witnesses," with "my" embracing a twofold meaning: they will belong to Jesus and they will give testimony about him. As witnesses, they not only give verbal testimony, but they also repeat in their own lives the pattern of Jesus, the one to whom they belong.

We can hear Jesus' words both as a clear command and as an assured promise, since the command he gives his followers will be accomplished by the promised gift of the Holy Spirit. The very breath of God, the Holy Spirit, is the abiding presence of God throughout the entire book of Acts. In fact, the book could appropriately be

Jesus' tone is more "Don't worry about this," than "You aren't allowed to know this."

Jesus commissions his disciples with the phrase, "You will be my witnesses."
Judea = joo-DEE-uh
Samaria = suh-MAYR-ee-uh

Slow down on "ends of the earth."

Don't lose "as they were looking on." It establishes them again as witnesses.
Quicken your pace with this appearance.
Careful not to look toward the sky on this line; rather, look directly at the community.
Pause after the line.

These men want to shake the disciples out of their stunned silence and get them moving again. Proclaim with energy!

Pause a little longer than usual at the end to let the men depart.

For meditation and context:

TO KEEP IN MIND
Be careful not to "swallow" words by mumbling. Articulate carefully so that every word is clearly heard, especially at the end of lines.

He answered them, "It is not for **you** to know the **times**
    or **seasons**
    that the **Father** has established by his own authority.
But you will receive **power** when the Holy **Spirit** comes **upon** you,
    and you will be my **witnesses** in Jerusalem,
    throughout Judea and Samaria,
    and to the **ends** of the **earth**."
When he had **said** this, as they were **looking** on,
    he was **lifted** up, and a **cloud** took him from their sight.
While they were looking intently at the sky as he was going,
    suddenly two men dressed in white garments stood
        beside them.
They said, "Men of **Galilee**,
    why are you standing there looking at the sky?
This **Jesus** who has been taken up from you into heaven
    will **return** in the same way as you have seen him going
        into heaven."

RESPONSORIAL PSALM   Psalm 47:2–3, 6–7, 8–9 (6)

R. God mounts his throne to shouts of joy: a blare of trumpets for the Lord.
or
R. Alleluia.

All you peoples, clap your hands,
    shout to God with cries of gladness,
for the LORD, the Most High, the awesome,
    is the great king over all the earth.

God mounts his throne amid shouts of joy;
    the LORD, amid trumpet blasts.
Sing praise to God, sing praise;
    sing praise to our king, sing praise.

For king of all the earth is God;
    sing hymns of praise.
God reigns over the nations,
    God sits upon his holy throne.

named "Acts of the Holy Spirit," for the Spirit is the one who empowers everyone in the Church to carry out the mission that Jesus gives.

Jesus' Ascension, which Luke describes as his being "lifted up," is the necessary condition for the sending of the Spirit. Only after Jesus is lifted up, exalted into heaven and no longer physically present on earth, can his Spirit be poured out on his disciples. Then, in the power of the Spirit, Jesus' disciples are witnesses—first in Jerusalem—and ultimately they take the Good News to the ends of the earth.

Jesus' Ascension, more than a scene of departure, is one filled with hope, promise, and fulfillment.

READING II Prior to the opening words of this passage, Paul commends the community for their faith, and for the love they have shown. Then he gives thanks to God as he remembers them in prayer. The entire prayer is permeated with an aura of intimacy with the community and thanks to God. Paul asks God that the believers who have already been immersed in the Good News will grow ever more

deeply in wisdom, revelation, and knowledge. Even though each of these terms has an intellectual content, Paul's primary concern is not with understanding apart from relationship with God, but understanding that supports that relationship. The same Spirit that empowers the apostolic mission described in the First Reading is the source of wisdom and revelation, leading Spirit-filled people to knowledge of Christ himself.

While the power of divine beings has often caused people to be in dread of God, Paul prays that enlightened hearts will find hope in God's majesty and supremacy. The

An exhortatory blessing; pray this for your assembly. Take care with the construction, though, and be sure you understand the thoughts being expressed.

Ephesians = ee-FEE-shuhnz

Look directly at your assembly and let them know this is your prayer for them. Smile with your voice, eyes, and face as you pray for an outpouring of gifts from the Spirit.

Keep the structure of this sentence clear. You are blessing your community that they may know three things: hope, riches, and power.

Slightly longer pause at comma, then pick up the thought again with the next phrase. Raise your energy slowly from here to the end.

Pause.

Connect the phrases "gave him" and "to the church" so they form one thought.

Slow down and drop your intensity a bit as you conclude.

READING II   Ephesians 1:17–23

A reading from the Letter of Saint Paul to the Ephesians

Brothers and sisters:
May the God of our Lord Jesus **Christ**, the Father of **glory**,
    give you a Spirit of **wisdom** and **revelation**
    resulting in **knowledge** of him.
May the eyes of your hearts be **enlightened**,
    that you may know what is the **hope** that belongs to his call,
    what are the **riches** of glory
    in his inheritance among the holy ones,
    and what is the surpassing **greatness** of his power
    for us who **believe**,
    in accord with the exercise of his great **might**,
    which he worked in Christ,
    raising him from the **dead**
    and seating him at his **right hand** in the heavens,
    far **above** every principality, authority, power, and dominion,
    and every **name** that is named
    not only in **this** age but also in the one to **come**.
And he put **all** things beneath his feet
    and gave him as **head** over all things to the church,
    which is his **body**,
    the **fullness** of the one who **fills** all things in **every** way.

> **TO KEEP IN MIND**
> Always pause at the end of the reading, before you proclaim the closing dialogue ("The Word of the Lord" or "The Gospel of the Lord").

God of might is not a distant being to be feared, but the one who calls us and gives us an inheritance. God shares the very richness of glory with those who believe. His surpassing greatness of power, and the exercise of his great might find the fullest manifestation in his raising Christ from the dead and seating him at his right hand. By the power of God, Christ too is exalted, and is head of the Church that is his own body. As the body of Christ, the Church has an ongoing sharing in Christ's own exaltation and fullness.

The final words of the reading have a grand expansiveness that connects the believing community with Christ's lordship over all things, filling everything in every way. In the final sentence the repetition of the word "all" (three times) gives the reading both emphasis and richness, and makes it clear that Paul's prayer is for the benefit of all of us who hear it. The Church, the body of Christ, continues his mission, supported by the presence of the risen Christ.

GOSPEL   The final scene in Matthew's Gospel harkens back to earlier chapters in his account and even farther back to the Hebrew tradition. The setting on the mountain reminds us of the mountain of Moses as well as of the many mountain scenes in Matthew's Gospel: the mountains of temptation, of Jesus' great sermon, of prayer, Transfiguration, and feeding. These mountains are places of transcendence, meeting with God, revelation, and teaching. On this final mountain Jesus is a teacher acting with authority that surpasses even that of Moses. He exer-

A brief narrative, with a lot going on. Keep your energy up, but there's no need to rush.

Their doubt shows that the disciples are human. It's a lot for them to take in!

How does Jesus sound as he gives these last instructions?

Take time with this; be very clear with the commission.

Proclaim the Trinitarian formula as if it's being spoken for the very first time. Pause.

Be eager to share Jesus' care for your assembly. Make eye contact and proclaim this line with great compassion and reassurance. Take a longer than usual pause at the end.

GOSPEL   Matthew 28:16–20

A reading from the holy Gospel according to Matthew

The eleven **disciples** went to Galilee,
    to the **mountain** to which Jesus had ordered them.
When they **saw** him, they **worshiped**, but they **doubted**.
Then Jesus **approached** and said to them,
    "All **power** in heaven and on earth has been **given** to me.
Go, therefore, and make disciples of **all** nations,
    baptizing them in the name of the **Father**,
    and of the **Son**, and of the **Holy Spirit**,
    teaching them to **observe** all that I have **commanded** you.
And behold, I am **with** you **always**, until the **end** of the **age**."

THE 4 STEPS OF *LECTIO DIVINA* OR PRAYERFUL READING

1. *Lectio:* Read a Scripture passage aloud slowly. Notice what phrase captures your attention and be attentive to its meaning. Silent pause.

2. *Meditatio:* Read the passage aloud slowly again, reflecting on the passage, allowing God to speak to you through it. Silent pause.

3. *Oratio:* Read it aloud slowly a third time, allowing it to be your prayer or response to God's gift of insight to you. Silent pause.

4. *Contemplatio:* Read it aloud slowly a fourth time, now resting in God's word.

---

cises the exalted power that we heard about in the reading from Ephesians, doing so as his parting gift to his disciples.

The commission that Jesus gives them appears well-nigh impossible, for how can his bewildered followers make disciples of all nations? They have just become disciples themselves, learning from Jesus by traveling with him, hearing his teaching, seeing his deeds of power. Even with Jesus as their teacher, not all were faithful to him, and fear seems to be their constant companion. In this Gospel, we even hear that some doubted. Yet Jesus assures his

followers that after his departure, he will remain with them whenever and wherever they go, never leaving them alone. He will be the one empowering them. He will continue to teach them as they teach others. Baptism and teaching are the means they are to use: making disciples is the purpose of all that they do.

The beginning scenes of Matthew's Gospel as well as this final scene focus our attention on the person of Jesus. The child whose identity was revealed as Emmanuel, God-with-Us, at the beginning of Matthew's Gospel remains Emmanuel to the end of

the ages. When Jesus promises "Behold I am with you always," the single word "behold" alerts all of us who hear the Gospel to pay particular attention to Jesus' words. He will remain as present to us in future ages and in distant places as he was for the earliest disciples gathered on a mountain in Palestine. He is Emmanuel until the end of the age. E.P.

SEVENTH SUNDAY OF EASTER

LECTIONARY #59

READING I   Acts of the Apostles 1:12–14

A reading from the Acts of the Apostles

After Jesus had been taken up to **heaven** the apostles
returned to **Jerusalem**
from the mount called **Olivet**, which is **near** Jerusalem,
a **sabbath** day's journey away.

When they **entered** the city
they went to the **upper room** where they were **staying**,
Peter and **John** and **James** and **Andrew**,
Philip and **Thomas**, **Bartholomew** and **Matthew**,
James son of Alphaeus, Simon the **Zealot**,
and **Judas** son of **James**.
All these devoted themselves with one accord to **prayer**,
together with some **women**,
and **Mary** the mother of **Jesus**, and his **brothers**.

A short narrative relating that after the Ascension, the Apostles return to a life of communal prayer to await the Spirit, who will animate their mission. This reading could motivate your assembly to make prayer and communal life central to their own spirituality.

Insert a brief pause after "heaven."

Olivet = OL-ih-vet

Take your time with the list.

Bartholomew = bahr-THAHL-uh-myoo

Alphaeus = AL-fee-uhs

Zealot = ZEL-uht

This is the point of the story. Slow down and see this group of men and women in your imagination as you describe the scene.

TO KEEP IN MIND

A *narrative* has characters, dialogue, a setting, and action. Help your listeners see the story unfold, keep characters distinct, and be clear about shifts in setting.

READING I   Jesus' commission to his disciples at his Ascension made them truly *Apostles*, that is, "those sent on a mission to act with authority." Once sent, his Apostles do not immediately go to far distant lands. They return instead to the upper room in Jerusalem, a room evocative of the Last Supper, perhaps even the same place. As then, they are again gathered as a community; they are united in prayer as they await the outpouring of the Holy Spirit. While the passage sounds quite serene, the gathered group was probably fearful and anxious, uncertain when or how Jesus' promise would be fulfilled.

Some of the names of the eleven Apostles may be unfamiliar to people today, but each one was most likely well-known and honored by the early Church as men who had faithfully obeyed Jesus' parting mandate. As we hear their individual names, remember that each one was called by Jesus, each one had a unique relationship with him, and each one had an important part to play in fulfilling the mission that Jesus gave them.

The eleven are not alone in the upper room. Among the one hundred twenty, some women are gathered, just as women had followed Jesus during his ministry. The only one named beyond the eleven is Mary, the mother of Jesus. As she prepared for the birth of her son at the opening of Luke's Gospel, now she prayerfully prepares for the outpouring of the Holy Spirit, which we celebrate as the birth of the Church.

READING II   The opening of the exhortation from the Letter of Peter juxtaposes two words that seem to

For meditation and context:

An exhortatory reading. The Christian life is hard, whether we suffer persecution or just try to live our authentic call from God. Proclaim this reading to encourage your assembly to persevere.

We suffer for something worthwhile: life in Christ.

Emphasize the contrast between the insult and the blessing. Blessed = BLES-uhd

This kind of suffering has no place in Christian life.

Don't let the challenges of following Christ make you second-guess your commitment.

Play up "the name."

RESPONSORIAL PSALM   Psalm 27:1, 4, 7–8 (13)

R. I believe that I shall see the good things of the Lord in the land of the living.
or
R. Alleluia.

The LORD is my light and my salvation;
　whom should I fear?
The LORD is my life's refuge;
　of whom should I be afraid?

One thing I ask of the LORD;
　this I seek:
to dwell in the house of the LORD
　all the days of my life,
that I may gaze on the loveliness
　　of the LORD
　and contemplate his temple.

Hear, O LORD, the sound of my call;
　have pity on me, and answer me.
Of you my heart speaks; you my glance seeks.

READING II   1 Peter 4:13–16

A reading from the first Letter of Saint Peter

Beloved:
Rejoice to the extent that you share in the **sufferings** of Christ,
　so that when his **glory** is revealed
　you may also rejoice **exultantly**.
If you are **insulted** for the name of Christ, **blessed** are you,
　for the Spirit of **glory** and of **God** rests upon you.
But let **no** one among you be made to suffer
　as a **murderer**, a **thief**, an **evildoer**, or as an **intriguer**.
But whoever is made to suffer as a **Christian** should not
　　be **ashamed**
　but **glorify** God because of the **name**.

be opposites: rejoicing and suffering. This seemingly unreasonable combination continues in the next sentence with the pairing of insult and blessing. Such paradoxical statements are part of Jesus' own words, including one of his best-known teachings in the beatitudes. In fact, Peter uses the same word for "blessed" (*makarioi*) that we find in the beatitudes. To be blessed is to be the recipient of God's freely-given kindness, even in the midst of suffering, insults, mourning or persecution.

Neither the beatitudes nor Peter's exhortation are promoting self-imposed

suffering. Rather, suffering with Christ is a deep participation, a true communion with the person of Christ who suffered for us. For Christ, as well as for Christians, the other side of suffering is glory. Thus we share not only in the suffering of Christ, but we also share in God's glory: the radiance, splendor, magnificence, and weighty majesty of God. This is a glory that we already experience, and which will be revealed fully in the future. It is a cause for present hope and rejoicing.

Before a final teaching about Christian suffering, Peter inserts sources of suffering

that should not be a part of the lives of any among us. Most who hear this part of the exhortation can readily say, "I am neither a murderer nor a thief." Yet the final two terms are much broader, and can be reminders of the more insidious ways by which we may suffer and bring suffering to others. An "evildoer" is someone who does harm or injury to self, to someone else, or even to our world. An "intriguer" could be a spy or informer, but more commonly simply one who meddles in other people's business. In contrast to these forms of malignant suffering, those whose suffering is in

An exhortatory prayer of Jesus, showing his intimacy with God and his deep love for us.

Don't raise your eyes; maintain eye contact with the assembly.
"I have accomplished what I was sent to do."

Grace comes from God to Jesus to us. This progression occurs a few times in this reading, and shows the intimacy between God and Jesus, between Jesus and us, hence between God and us.

Don't make Jesus sound like a braggart, extolling his own accomplishments. He maintains his humility by simply telling the truth.

Note again the progression from God to Jesus to us.

Look directly at your assembly: you are affirming them for what they believe.

Don't gloss over this short line. Proclaim deliberately and with tenderness.

Slow down. This is the whole reason for Jesus' prayer—he will no longer be physically present in the world, yet he will continue to pray for us.

GOSPEL   John 17:1–11a

A reading from the holy Gospel according to John

Jesus raised his eyes to **heaven** and said,
    "**Father**, the hour has **come**.
Give **glory** to your son, so that your son may glorify **you**,
    just as you gave him **authority** over all people,
    so that your son may give eternal **life** to all you gave him.
Now **this** is eternal life,
    that they should **know** you, the only **true** God,
    and the one whom you **sent**, Jesus **Christ**.
I glorified you on **earth**
    by accomplishing the **work** that you gave me to do.
Now glorify **me**, Father, with **you**,
    with the glory that I had with you before the world **began**.

"I revealed your **name** to those whom you gave me out
        of the world.
They **belonged** to you, and you **gave** them to me,
    and they have **kept** your word.
Now they know that everything you gave me is from **you**,
    because the words you gave to **me** I have given to **them**,
    and they **accepted** them and truly understood that I **came**
        from you,
    and they have **believed** that you sent me.
I **pray** for them.
I do not pray for the **world** but for the ones you have **given** me,
    because they are **yours**, and everything of **mine** is yours
    and everything of yours is **mine**,
    and I have been **glorified** in them.
And now I will no **longer** be in the world,
    but **they** are in the world, while **I** am coming to **you**."

Christ have no cause to be ashamed and magnify the very glory of God.

GOSPEL | When Jesus performed his first sign at Cana in Galilee, he told his mother, "My hour has not yet come" (John 2:4). At that stage in the narrative, the significance of the hour remained mysterious, moving us to expect deeper revelation. Now, as Jesus is gathered with his disciples at a final meal, he prays aloud, "Father, the hour has come." By listening in on this intimate conversation with his Father, we, along with Jesus' disciples at the Last Supper, learn that Jesus' hour is a departure out of this world to return to the Father who had sent him.

Jesus' relationship with his Father gives shape to this prayer, just as it gave shape to the entirety of Jesus' life. By accomplishing the work the Father gave him, Jesus glorified his Father, and now asks that the Father will give glory to him. Jesus ever acted with divine authority so that all would know the Father as the only true God, would believe in him, and would know the Father's name. Those who belong to Jesus have first belonged to his Father, and Jesus gave to them, and to us, the words from the Father.

The profound intimacy of Jesus with his Father radiates out to embrace all those the Father has given to him, including ourselves. His gift to us is eternal life, already begun here and now. This prayer is usually referred to as Jesus' high priestly prayer, perhaps best understood as his priestly intercession before the Father for all of us. E.P.

PENTECOST SUNDAY: VIGIL

LECTIONARY #62

READING I   Genesis 11:1–9

A reading from the Book of Genesis

The whole world spoke the same **language**, using the same **words**.
While the people were **migrating** in the east,
    they came upon a valley in the land of **Shinar** and **settled** there.
They said to one another,
    "**Come**, let us mold **bricks** and harden them with **fire**."
They used bricks for **stone**, and **bitumen** for **mortar**.
Then they said, "Come, let us build ourselves a **city**
    and a **tower** with its top in the **sky**,
    and so make a **name** for ourselves;
    otherwise we shall be **scattered** all over the earth."

The LORD came down to **see** the city and the tower
    that the people had built.
Then the LORD said: "If **now**, while they are **one** people,
    all speaking the same **language**,
    they have started to do this,
    nothing will later **stop** them from doing whatever they **presume** to do.
Let us then go down there and **confuse** their language,
    so that one will not **understand** what another says."
Thus the LORD **scattered** them from there all over the earth,
    and they stopped **building** the city. »

A narrative originally intended to explain the diversity of languages, but in the context of Genesis, part of the continuing saga of sin and alienation that began in the garden.

God has commanded that the people populate the whole world, but they decide instead to stay together in one place.
Shinar = SHĪ-nahr

Speak as though you're the person with this idea; be excited about hatching this plan!

bitumen = bih-TYOO-m*n

It's folly to try to make a name for ourselves; our real identity is found in God.

But the people believe they can ensure their own future.

Usurping God's role results in chaos and confusion.

There are options for readings today. Ask your parish staff which ones will be used.

Pentecost is a solemnity both of reversal and renewal. Through the action of the Holy Spirit, God reverses the long-standing division of peoples and tongues, and brings about a multifaceted renewal: new community, new prophetic word, and new life. Each reading for Vigil and Day contributes to these interwoven dimensions of faith.

READING I — **Genesis 11:1–9.** The account of the tower at Babel is a dramatic tale of division brought about by people's pride-filled actions. The story appears in the Book of Genesis as part of the continuing saga of sin and alienation that began in the garden. At Babel, the attempt to build a city and tower to the sky further separates people from God and one another. The name *Babel* itself, based on the Hebrew verb *balal*, "to confuse," points to the consequences of their foolish efforts. Their attempt to take over God's realm leads to confusion and chaos in their own realm.

As we hear this reading at the Vigil of Pentecost, we can understand well the need for God's action of reversing the situation. A precise reversal would be a return to a time when "the whole world spoke the same language." In response to the ongoing reality of misunderstanding and division, the reversal accomplished by the Spirit will do something even greater. It will bring about understanding and unity among peoples from different places and different tongues, creating unity in their diversity. No longer will there be confusion but comprehension.

That is why it was called **Babel**,
     because there the LORD **confused** the speech of all the world.
It was from that place that he **scattered** them all over the **earth**.

Or:

READING I   Exodus 19:3–8a, 16–20b

A reading from the Book of Exodus

Moses went up the mountain to **God**.
Then the LORD **called** to him and said,
     "**Thus** shall you say to the house of **Jacob**;
     tell the **Israelites**:
     You have **seen** for yourselves how I treated the **Egyptians**
     and how I **bore** you up on **eagle** wings
     and brought you here to **myself**.
Therefore, if you **hearken** to my voice and keep my **covenant**,
     you shall be my special **possession**,
     dearer to me than all **other** people,
     though **all** the earth is mine.
You shall be to me a kingdom of **priests**, a **holy** nation.
That is what you must tell the Israelites."
So Moses went and summoned the **elders** of the people.
When he set before them
     all that the LORD had **ordered** him to tell them,
     the people all answered together,
     "**Everything** the LORD has said, we will **do**."

On the morning of the **third** day
     there were peals of **thunder** and **lightning**,
     and a heavy **cloud** over the mountain,
     and a very loud **trumpet** blast,
     so that all the people in the camp **trembled**.

Margin notes (left column):

Babel = BAB-*l

The unhappy consequence of Babel is a scattering of people and confusion of languages, but on Pentecost, God brings understanding and unity amidst the diversity.

A narrative relating how God made the Covenant with Moses for the Israelites. There's a lot happening here; take your time.

Exodus = EK-suh-duhs

Moses = MOH-zis

Make this an intimate conversation with Moses, contrasting with the more spectacular, public conversation later.

God's love is the basis of the covenant. Let that love come through in your voice.

How does God sound as he says these things?

Pause after this line.

Proclaim "we will do" slowly and with great self-assurance.

Pause.

God now appears to the people in this awesome display. Let it sound awesome!

Raise your intensity on each of these three effects.

Contrast the people's fear with Moses' confident leadership.

Exodus 19:3–8a, 16–20b. If the account of the Tower of Babel demonstrated the need for God's action of reversing the divisions among peoples, the account of the covenant on the mountain generates hope that God would again renew this ancient covenant. The story is particularly appropriate at Pentecost. Originally a harvest festival, Pentecost later became associated with the giving of the Law at Sinai and with its renewal.

The description of the event at Sinai uses powerful audio-visual imagery: thunder and lightning, trumpet blast, smoke, and fire. Such imagery throughout the biblical tradition is used to convey some of the mystery and power of God's presence. Reflecting on this scene in the first century, the Jewish writer Philo commented that the voice of God on Mount Sinai was so mighty that it became truly visible. Another Jewish tradition held that the voice of God divided into different voices or languages so that all could understand it. These interpretations, which share terminology with the New Testament account of Pentecost, envision Moses' encounter with God as a display of the vigor of the divine Word, and the far-reaching destination of God's Covenant, intended for all nations.

By New Testament times, the celebration of Pentecost included a recommitment to the covenant made on Mount Sinai. It was a time to remember God's saving actions in the past, and to again live as a kingdom of priests and a holy nation. The reading from Exodus prepares the way for God to renew the covenant, thereby fulfilling the feast of Pentecost.

Ezekiel 37:1–14. A plain filled with lifeless dry bones! What could be more in need of reversal and renewal? Ezekiel's

Drop your voice to a whisper to express the mystery here.

Now raise it again while describing the fire and smoke.

A conversation between trumpets and thunder!

Pause.

Now God invites Moses again into an intimate conversation. Pause a bit longer than usual at the end.

But Moses led the people **out** of the camp to meet **God**,
 and they stationed themselves at the **foot** of the mountain.
Mount Sinai was all wrapped in **smoke**,
 for the LORD came down upon it in **fire**.
The smoke **rose** from it as though from a **furnace**,
 and the whole mountain trembled **violently**.
The **trumpet** blast grew louder and louder, while Moses
   was speaking,
 and God **answering** him with **thunder**.

When the LORD came **down** to the top of Mount Sinai,
 he summoned **Moses** to the **top** of the mountain.

Or:

READING I   Ezekiel 37:1–14

A reading from the Book of the Prophet Ezekiel

A narrative which includes exhortatory passages, relating the infinite depth of God's desire to bring life to all.

Ezekiel = ee-ZEE-kee-uhl

The hand of the LORD came upon me,
 and he led me out in the **spirit** of the LORD
 and set me in the center of the **plain**,
 which was now filled with **bones**.
He made me **walk** among the bones in every direction
 so that I saw how **many** they were on the surface of the plain.

Convey the quiet sadness in this scene of desolation.

There's absolutely no life in them!

How **dry** they were!
He asked me:
 Son of **man**, can these bones come to **life**?
I answered, "Lord GOD, you **alone** know that."
Then he said to me:
 Prophesy over these bones, and **say** to them:
 Dry bones, **hear** the word of the LORD!

Raise intensity for this first exhortatory passage.

Proclaim as if to someone desperate for God to bring life.

This is good news! Smile with your voice, eyes, and face!

Thus says the Lord GOD to these bones:
 See! I will bring **spirit** into you, that you may come to **life**. **»**

---

vision begins when the spirit of the Lord leads him out to see the bone-filled valley. We can almost see through Ezekiel's eyes and feel his shock as he views dry bones in every direction; we can hear the rattling when bone is rejoined to bone. Sinews, flesh, and skin are not enough to bring the bones to life. Only God's spirit can raise them up.

Ezekiel had this vision when he, along with others from Jerusalem, were in exile in Babylon. The exile was an experience of such lifelessness, away from land and Temple, that the whole community seemed comparable to the field filled with dry bones. For them, there was no life in exile. Yet the vision reveals that the deadness of exile is not the end of the story. Ezekiel proclaims that God will send the life-giving Spirit to his people even outside their own land, bringing life in faraway Babylon. For Ezekiel, the vision brought about a change in his prophetic message. He was no longer announcing punishment for the sins of the people, but proclaiming the possibility of new life for them.

Throughout this reading, the prophet employs a clever play on the Hebrew word *ruah*, which means both "spirit" and "breath." No spirit means no breath, no life. God's own spirit-breath will restore the dry bones. Spirit-generated restoration is more than physical reenfleshment, but means a full and rich life, leading people to know that God is the Lord. In keeping with the common biblical perspective, knowing is not a simple intellectual comprehension, but expresses an intimate relationship. The restored life of the whole field of dry bones is for the sake of an intimate, fruitful, and faithful covenant relationship.

sinews = sin-YOOZ

prophesied = PROF-uh-sīd
How does Ezekiel feel as he watches this?
Frightened, amazed, maybe a little of both?
Bring those emotions to your proclamation.

Let God's excitement come through in the
encouragement of Ezekiel.

Demand that the spirit come!

Let the weariness of those in dryness come
through in your voice.

A final exhortatory prophecy expressing
God's love and longing for us.

This shouldn't sound like, "Then you'll be
sorry!" Rather, "Then you'll know how much
I love you!"
At this phrase, look directly at the assembly
and fill your voice with love.

These lines restate the same ideas as above;
slow down to let them sink in more deeply.
How does God sound?

Pause.

Take significant pauses at each comma; slow
down on "I will do it," and proclaim with
steadfast assurance.

I will put **sinews** upon you, make **flesh** grow over you,
　　cover you with **skin**, and put **spirit** in you
　　so that you may come to **life** and know that I am the LORD.
I, Ezekiel, prophesied as I had been told,
　　and even as I was prophesying I heard a **noise**;
　　it was a **rattling** as the bones came **together**, **bone** joining **bone**.
I saw the **sinews** and the **flesh** come upon them,
　　and the **skin** cover them, but there was no **spirit** in them.
Then the LORD said to me:
　　Prophesy to the spirit, **prophesy**, son of man,
　　and **say** to the spirit: **Thus** says the Lord GOD:
　　From the four winds **come**, O spirit,
　　and **breathe** into these slain that they may come to **life**.
I **prophesied** as he told me, and the spirit **came** into them;
　　they came **alive** and stood **upright**, a vast **army**.
Then he said to me:
　　Son of man, these bones are the whole house of **Israel**.
They have been saying,
　　"Our bones are **dried** up,
　　our hope is **lost**, and we are **cut** off."
Therefore, prophesy and **say** to them: Thus says the Lord **GOD**:
　　O my people, I will **open** your **graves**
　　and have you **rise** from them,
　　and bring you **back** to the land of **Israel**.
Then you shall **know** that I am the LORD,
　　when I **open** your graves and have you **rise** from them,
　　O my people!
I will put my **spirit** in you that you may **live**,
　　and I will **settle** you upon your land;
　　thus you shall know that I am the LORD.
I have **promised**, and I will **do** it, says the LORD.

Or:

Joel 3:1–5. "Thus says the LORD." Joel begins his prophecy by announcing that we will hear not his own words, but an authentic and certain declaration from God. The time and manner in which the prophecy will be fulfilled remain in an unknown future, perhaps only accomplished at the end of days, on the "day of the Lord. Though we do not know the time, fulfillment of each of God's promises is guaranteed, for the Word comes directly from God.

First, God will pour out the divine spirit on all flesh, so that young and old, as well as men and women servants will all become prophets. Through the power of the spirit, the ancient gift of prophecy will be renewed, not for a designated few, but for the entire spirit-filled community. Along with Joel, these spirit-filled prophets can prepare the people for the second promise, God's dramatic portents on heaven and earth. Wonders, blood, and fire are evocative of the plagues in Egypt; columns of smoke remind us of God's presence to the people in the desert. These dramatic signs at the time of the exodus as well as in Joel's prophecy are a means of directing people away from sin and toward God.

The third promise follows logically: those who call on the name of the Lord will be rescued, just as the faithful Hebrews were rescued at the time of the exodus. The promises of God's action are strongly connected with human response. Calling on the name of the Lord entails more than a verbal crying out to God. Those who call out to God live in trust and fidelity. They are renewed by God's own Spirit.

An exhortatory prophecy, describing an exciting vision of what God's spirit can accomplish.

Joel = JOH-*l

Linger over the word "pour," a lavish image.

prophesy = PROF-uh-sī

God's generosity knows no bounds of class or gender.

The world will know the power of God through these signs.

Raise your intensity as you describe these "wonders."

Express the tenderness of God in rescuing all who call on the name of the Lord.

READING I   Joel 3:1–5

A reading from the Book of the Prophet Joel

Thus says the LORD:
I will pour out my **spirit** upon all **flesh**.
Your **sons** and **daughters** shall **prophesy**,
   your **old** men shall dream **dreams**,
   your **young** men shall see **visions**;
even upon the **servants** and the **handmaids**,
   in those days, I will **pour** out my spirit.
And I will work **wonders** in the heavens and on the earth,
   blood, **fire**, and columns of **smoke**;
the **sun** will be turned to **darkness**,
   and the **moon** to **blood**,
at the **coming** of the day of the LORD,
   the **great** and **terrible** day.
Then everyone shall be **rescued**
   who calls on the **name** of the LORD;
for on Mount Zion there shall be a **remnant**,
   as the LORD has said,
and in Jerusalem **survivors**
   whom the LORD shall **call**.

READING II   **Romans 8:22–27**. The reading from Romans is part of Paul's longer reflection on present suffering and future glory: "I consider the sufferings of this present time are as nothing compared with the glory to be revealed for us" (Romans 8:18). In this context, Paul uses the image of labor pains and groaning to illustrate in a well-understood physical way the necessity of suffering now for the sake of new life to come. As he writes about the movement from suffering to glory, Paul simultaneously develops the themes of reversal and renewal. The Spirit, of whom we have already received the "firstfruits," is the source of transformation and new life.

Throughout this text, Paul repeatedly uses the word "we," making it clear that he cosuffers with all creation and with the Roman community. With Paul, all of us share in suffering, in the firstfruits of the Spirit, in waiting, in endurance, and in hope. The presence of God's own Spirit does not mean escape from suffering, for Jesus himself endured suffering before his glorification. Paul emphasizes this just a few verses before today's reading (verse 17) when he writes that we cosuffer with Christ so that we may be coglorified. Suffering is the necessary means of shaping believers into the image of Christ.

It is in the very experience of suffering that hope arises. As one who suffers along with the community, Paul knows personally the need for faith-filled and patient hope. Five times he uses that word "hope," an emphatic reminder of how we are to bear present suffering. Hope leads us to rely on the Spirit in our weakness, whatever form that weakness may take, from every kind of suffering to the debility that arises from sin. One form of weakness in an inability even

For meditation and context:

An exhortatory reading about enduring in hope, waiting for the fulfillment of God's reign.

Don't lose "all creation." Paul asserts that the whole universe awaits its redemption, not just human beings.

Paul encourages us not to lose hope. Although we are saved, we shouldn't expect our lives to be perfect and easy. Our full redemption is still to come.

We only hope in something we don't yet see.

Again, we wait for something more, something yet to come.

The Spirit knows our longings even when we can't express them.

RESPONSORIAL PSALM   Psalm 104:1–2a, 24, 35c, 27–28, 29bc–30 (30)

R. Lord, send out your Spirit, and renew the face of the earth.
or
R. Alleluia.

Bless the LORD, O my soul!
  O LORD, my God, you are great indeed!
You are clothed with majesty and glory,
  robed in light as with a cloak.

How manifold are your works, O LORD!
  In wisdom you have wrought them all—
the earth is full of your creatures;
  bless the LORD, O my soul! Alleluia.

Creatures all look to you
  to give them food in due time.
When you give it to them, they gather it;
  when you open your hand, they are filled
    with good things.

If you take away their breath, they perish
  and return to their dust.
When you send forth your spirit,
  they are created,
    and you renew the face of the earth.

READING II   Romans 8:22–27

A reading from the Letter of Saint Paul to the Romans

Brothers and sisters:
We know that all **creation** is groaning in **labor** pains even
    until **now**;
  and not **only** that, but we **ourselves**,
  who have the **firstfruits** of the Spirit,
  we also **groan** within ourselves
  as we wait for **adoption**, the **redemption** of our bodies.
For in hope we were **saved**.
Now hope that **sees** is not **hope**.
For who **hopes** for what one **sees**?
But if we hope for what we do **not** see, we wait with **endurance**.

In the **same** way, the Spirit **too** comes to the aid of our **weakness**;
  for we do not know **how** to pray as we ought,
  but the Spirit himself **intercedes** with inexpressible **groanings**.
And the one who **searches hearts**
  knows what is the **intention** of the Spirit,
  because he **intercedes** for the holy ones
  according to God's **will**.

---

to know how to pray, but the Spirit will intercede for us. The Spirit will be the source of transformation, giving newness of life, accomplished according to God's will.

GOSPEL   From the first of Jesus' signs at Cana in which he changed water to wine, to the water from his pierced side, to the appearance of the risen Jesus on the beach of the Sea, water flows throughout John's Gospel. In this scene at the feast of Tabernacles, John brings together the abundant Jewish symbolism of water with Jesus' new interpreta-

tion. During the week-long celebration of Tabernacles, a procession of throngs of people, led by priests and Levites, went each day to the Pool of Siloam to draw water that was poured into vessels on the altar. The Siloam waters had multiple symbolic links with other life-giving waters, such as water from the rock in the desert, God's gift of rain, the thirst-quenching gift of Torah, and prophecies of living water flowing out from Jerusalem (Zechariah 14:7, 8).

On the last day of the feast, Jesus stretches the water symbolism to apply life-giving waters to himself. Much more

than the amount of water poured onto the altar, whole rivers of living water will flow, in an overwhelming abundance. But does the living water flow from Jesus, or from the one who believes in him? Ultimately, the verse affirms that the manifold benefits of water celebrated in the feast and recorded in the biblical tradition are all fulfilled In Jesus and shared with his disciples.

A series of active verbs draws our attention to people's response to Jesus' gift of living water: thirst; come; drink; believe. The first three verbs are common actions that all people experience. Typical of John's

A brief didactic reading with an exhortatory passage. Don't rush it.

GOSPEL   John 7:37–39

A reading from the holy Gospel according to John

On the **last** and **greatest** day of the feast,
　　Jesus stood up and **exclaimed**,
　　"Let anyone who **thirsts** come to me and **drink**.
As Scripture says:
　　*Rivers of **living** water will flow from within him* who
　　　　believes in me."

The setting gives this teaching great importance.

Raise your energy and encourage your assembly to respond to this invitation.

He said this in reference to the **Spirit**
　　that those who came to believe in him were to **receive**.
There was, of course, no Spirit **yet**,
　　because Jesus had not yet been **glorified**.

This is us! We have received this spirit!

Drop your voice slightly on this concluding comment.

Gospel, ordinary human realities have a deeper (and higher) meaning. To *thirst* it to yearn for life, refreshment, and restoration; most profoundly it is to long for God. To *come* is to take the initial steps, however halting and unsure, in responding to Jesus' invitation to follow him. To *drink* is to partake openly and gratefully in all that he gives to us, specifically to the gift of living water. The final verb, *believe*, moves beyond the ordinary, to the language of relationship with Jesus. To *believe* in him is to live in trust, fidelity and commitment of life. Although the phrase reads "believe in me," the literal translation is "believe *into* me," connoting a dynamic immersion into the very life of Christ.

　　At the feast of Tabernacles, no one had yet received the Spirit. The final verb, *were to receive*, points to the future when those who believe would welcome the Spirit as God's gift of life-sustaining breath. This short Gospel reading promises an abundance of life for the audience in Jesus' day and in our own. The Spirit is again the source of renewal. E.P.

PENTECOST SUNDAY: DAY

A narrative with exciting emotional intensity.

Build your intensity slowly through this line.

Articulate this complex line carefully.

Be amazed at this!

Pause.

Take your time with this line.

Let their astounded amazement come through in your proclamation.

Don't let this list of place names throw you. Practice the pronunciations, but then proclaim as if they were all places you were very familiar with. If you make a mistake, just keep moving.

Parthians = PAHR-thee-uhnz; Medes = meedz; Elamites = ee-luh-mīts

Mesopotamia = mes-uh-poh-TAY-mee-uh; Judea = joo-dee-uh; Cappadocia = cap-uh-DOH-shee-uh

Pontus = PON-tuhs; Phrygia = FRIJ-ee-uh; Pamphylia = PAM-fil-ee-uh

Libya = LIB-ee-uh; Cyrene = sī-REE-nee

LECTIONARY #63

READING I   Acts of the Apostles 2:1–11

A reading from the Acts of the Apostles

When the time for **Pentecost** was **fulfilled**,
　　they were all in one place **together**.
And **suddenly** there came from the **sky**
　　a noise like a **strong** driving **wind**,
　　and it **filled** the entire **house** in which they were.
Then there appeared to them **tongues** as of **fire**,
　　which **parted** and came to **rest** on each **one** of them.
And they were all **filled** with the **Holy Spirit**
　　and began to speak in different **tongues**,
　　as the Spirit **enabled** them to **proclaim**.

Now there were **devout** Jews from every **nation** under heaven
　　staying in Jerusalem.
At this **sound**, they gathered in a large **crowd**,
　　but they were **confused**
　　because **each** one heard them **speaking** in his own **language**.
They were **astounded**, and in **amazement** they asked,
　　"Are not all these people who are speaking **Galileans**?
Then how does **each** of us hear them in his **native** language?
We are **Parthians**, **Medes**, and **Elamites**,
　　inhabitants of **Mesopotamia**, **Judea** and **Cappadocia**,
　　Pontus and **Asia**, **Phrygia** and **Pamphylia**,
　　Egypt and the districts of **Libya** near **Cyrene**,
　　as well as travelers from **Rome**,

READING I　The opening verses of the Pentecost account introduce an important motif of the solemnity: fullness. Pentecost is fulfilled; a noise filled the entire house; all were filled with the Holy Spirit. Such repetition and variation of the vocabulary of fullness emphasizes the expansiveness and power of the Spirit. Luke, the supposed author of Acts of the Apostles, describes this fullness at Pentecost with graphic imagery, depicting the event both as an audible and visible phenomenon: noise like a strong driving wind; visible tongues as if of fire. The imagery is strongly reminiscent of God's manifestation at Sinai, where God descended on the mountain in fire (Exodus 19:18), and with a great noise (Exodus 19:16). Use of imagery associated with the Sinai theophany creates the impression of a similarity, even continuity, between the events on Mount Sinai and at Pentecost, indicating that the Covenant between God and his people is now being renewed.

After describing the event itself, Luke shifts focus to the participants and witnesses, again emphasizing fullness or totality; the disciples were all together, and every nation under heaven is gathered in Jerusalem. It isn't surprising that such a multitude would be present, since Pentecost was one of the major pilgrim festivals, drawing devout Jews from far away to celebrate in Jerusalem. This multitude is confused, literally "poured together." We can imagine a whole crowd poured together in massive bewilderment. Their confusion, however, is not like that at Babel, where people *cannot* understand the many languages. At Pentecost, they are confused precisely because they *can* understand, each in their own tongue.

Cretans = KREE-tuhnz

Slight pause after "yet."

Pause a little longer than usual at the end.

both **Jews** and **converts** to Judaism, **Cretans** and **Arabs**,
yet we hear them **speaking** in our own **tongues**
of the mighty **acts** of **God**."

For meditation and context:

RESPONSORIAL PSALM   Psalm 104:1, 24, 29–30, 31, 34 (30)

R. Lord, send out your Spirit, and renew the face of the earth.
or
R. Alleluia.

Bless the LORD, O my soul!
  O LORD, my God, you are great indeed!
How manifold are your works, O LORD!
  the earth is full of your creatures.

If you take away their breath, they perish
  and return to their dust.
When you send forth your spirit,
   they are created,
  and you renew the face of the earth.

May the glory of the LORD endure forever;
  may the LORD be glad in his works!
Pleasing to him be my theme;
  I will be glad in the LORD.

> **TO KEEP IN MIND**
> A *narrative* has characters, dialogue, a setting, and action. Help your listeners see the story unfold, keep characters distinct, and be clear about shifts in setting.

A familiar and powerful didactic reading: regardless of differences in talents, ministries, ethnicity, or class all are one in the Body of Christ.

Corinthians = kohr-IN-thee-uhnz

This is the key; all who believe in Jesus are one in the Spirit.

Put a slight pause before the word "but" in each of these phrases.

Keep these two lines together.

Pause.

Contrast "one" and "many" in this line.

Slow and deliberate.

"So why do you divide yourselves over differences that don't matter?"

READING II   1 Corinthians 12:3b–7, 12–13

A reading from the first Letter of Saint Paul to the Corinthians

Brothers and sisters:
No one can say, "**Jesus** is **Lord**," except by the Holy **Spirit**.

There are different **kinds** of spiritual **gifts** but the same **Spirit**;
  there are different forms of **service** but the same **Lord**;
  there are different **workings** but the same **God**
   who produces **all** of them in **everyone**.
To **each** individual the **manifestation** of the Spirit
  is given for some **benefit**.

As a body is **one** though it has many **parts**,
  and **all** the parts of the body, though **many**, are **one** body,
  so also **Christ**.
For in **one** Spirit we were all **baptized** into **one body**,
  whether **Jews** or **Greeks**, **slaves** or **free** persons,
  and we were all given to **drink** of one **Spirit**.

Their questions express astonished wonderment. The disciples who received visible fiery tongues (*glossa*) now speak audibly in other tongues (*glossa*) as the Spirit gave them to speak. Whatever the words they spoke, the crowd understands that they are proclaiming the mighty acts of God. The outpouring of the Spirit is the mighty work of God that creates unity, understanding, and covenant renewal.

 READING II Different, different, different, same, same, same. As Paul repeats these words in the context of

ministry in the Corinthian church, he develops further the unity-in-diversity theme we saw in the First Reading. He is addressing a community beset with factions, incorrect belief, and immoral behavior. In the face of these problems, Paul teaches them about unity, faith, and right living.

  He begins by affirming Jesus' Lordship—a belief one can assert only through the power of the Spirit. That same Spirit is the unifying force at work in the different kinds of spiritual gifts. The same Lord is the source of different forms of service. The same God brings about different

workings. Although Paul doesn't have a developed theology of the Holy Trinity, the designations Spirit, Lord (Jesus), and God (the Father) present a foundation for later understanding of God as three-in-one. Drawing on this theological insight, we can see that the three distinct persons united in one God present an image of unity beneficial for our own reflection.

  While the concept of the Trinity would have been foreign to Paul's Corinthian community, the analogy of the body would be readily understandable. It was a metaphor commonly used in the ancient world to

For meditation and context:

SEQUENCE Veni, Sancte Spiritus

Come, Holy Spirit, come!
And from your celestial home
    Shed a ray of light divine!
Come, Father of the poor!
Come, source of all our store!
    Come, within our bosoms shine.
You, of comforters the best;
You, the soul's most welcome guest;
    Sweet refreshment here below;
In our labor, rest most sweet;
Grateful coolness in the heat;
    Solace in the midst of woe.
O most blessed Light divine,
Shine within these hearts of yours,
    And our inmost being fill!

Where you are not, we have naught,
Nothing good in deed or thought,
    Nothing free from taint of ill.
Heal our wounds, our strength renew;
On our dryness pour your dew;
    Wash the stains of guilt away:
Bend the stubborn heart and will;
Melt the frozen, warm the chill;
    Guide the steps that go astray.
On the faithful, who adore
And confess you, evermore
    In your sevenfold gift descend;
Give them virtue's sure reward;
Give them your salvation, Lord;
    Give them joys that never end. Amen.
    Alleluia.

GOSPEL   John 20:19–23

A reading from the holy Gospel according to John

On the evening of that **first** day of the week,
    when the doors were **locked**, where the **disciples** were,
    for fear of the **Jews**,
    Jesus came and **stood** in their midst
    and said to them, "**Peace** be with you."
When he had **said** this, he showed them his **hands** and his **side**.
The disciples **rejoiced** when they saw the Lord.
Jesus said to them **again**, "**Peace** be with you.
As the **Father** has sent **me**, so **I** send **you**."
And when he had said this, he **breathed** on them and said to them,
    "**Receive** the Holy **Spirit**.
Whose sins you **forgive** are **forgiven** them,
    and whose sins you **retain** are **retained**."

A brief narrative; take your time. All the emotions—fear, surprise, joy, peace, love—are heightened and need to be fully expressed.

This should sound like the surprise that it is!

Immediately, Jesus calms their fears.

Let their joy echo in your proclamation.

As Jesus is sent by the Father, we are sent by Jesus.

Linger over the word "breathed." It implies that Jesus is in very close proximity to those present.

illustrate the diversity and interdependence in a community. Beyond the conventional use of this image, Paul relates the body image specifically to Christ. In the power of the Spirit the divisions within Christ's body, the Church, are reversed, and the body is renewed.

GOSPEL The Risen Jesus and the Spirit of God are not limited by the ordinary categories of time and space. Thus the locked doors do not prevent Jesus from joining the gathering of his fearful disciples. Standing in their midst, he

gives them the gifts that they will need to fulfill the mission he passes on to them.

The first gift is that of peace. Much more than the absence of war or conflict, peace is a blessing of health, wholeness, harmony, and everything good. Along with peace, Jesus gives them the gift of the Holy Spirit, the very power and presence of God that Jesus breathes into them. His gifts of peace and the Holy Spirit transform the disciples' fear into rejoicing—a transformation they need to fulfill the mission Jesus gives them. He is sending them out, as the Father

had sent him, so that they can continue Jesus' own mission.

Throughout his lifetime, Jesus repeatedly offered the gift of forgiveness. Now his followers, empowered by the Holy Spirit, are to be instruments of Jesus' own forgiveness. Peace, the Holy Spirit, and forgiveness are the abiding gifts from the risen Jesus to all. E.P.

THE MOST HOLY TRINITY

A narrative relating a stunning event: God reveals his name and essence to Moses. The story conveys a core truth of our faith: we believe in a God of mercy and forgiveness.

Exodus = EK-suh-duhs
Moses = MOH-zis
Sinai = SĪ-nī

The scene following is full of drama. Use your best storytelling skills.

God agrees to Moses' request to see his glory (Exodus 33:12–23).

Note that it is God who proclaims the name, "Lord."

God speaks here in the third person, saying, "This is who I am!" How might this sound? Try out different possibilities.

Imagine your own response as you describe Moses.

Moses begs God not just for forgiveness, but for God's very presence to remain with the people.

LECTIONARY #164

READING I Exodus 34:4b–6, 8–9

A reading from the Book of Exodus

Early in the morning **Moses** went up Mount **Sinai**
 as the Lord had **commanded** him,
 taking along the two stone **tablets**.

Having come down in a **cloud**, the Lord **stood** with Moses there
 and proclaimed his **name**, "Lord."
Thus the Lord **passed** before him and **cried** out,
 "The Lord, the Lord, a **merciful** and **gracious** God,
 slow to **anger** and rich in **kindness** and **fidelity**."
Moses at once bowed down to the **ground** in **worship**.
Then he said, "If I find **favor** with you, O Lord,
 do come along in our **company**.
This is indeed a **stiff**-necked people; yet **pardon** our wickedness
 and sins,
 and **receive** us as your **own**."

READING I The heart of Moses' experience on Mount Sinai is the revelation of God's identity. At this point in the story of the Israelites in the desert, the Israelites need a deeper understanding of God's name and nature to restore their damaged relationship with God. They had repeatedly rejected Moses and God by their idolatry, most shockingly by their worship of a golden calf. As a result of this grave sin, Moses had broken the stone tablets, in effect annulling the covenant between God and Israel (Exodus 32–33). Now with a new set of tablets, Moses meets God to restore the broken covenant.

The encounter with God is mysterious, enshrouded in a cloud, typical of theophanies, or manifestations of God. When God somehow "appears," there is still something hidden and concealed. Then, from the cloud, God proclaims the divine name: Lord, in Hebrew, *YHWH*, the revealed personal name of Israel's God. In the description that follows, God reveals more about what that name means. The Lord is merciful and gracious, two qualities that are almost synonymous. The first one has a stronger familial meaning; it is related to the Hebrew word for "womb," suggesting a love that a mother has for her child. That God is slow to anger would be a reassuring affirmation to the people who have so often provoked the anger of both Moses and God. The final two qualities, kindness and fidelity, are further assurances that the Lord will remain faithful and steadfast, even though the people are stiff-necked and wicked.

When Moses asks God to receive the people again in covenant relationship, we are right to expect God to do so, given that

For meditation and context:

RESPONSORIAL PSALM   Daniel 3:52, 53, 54, 55 (52b)

R. Glory and praise for ever!

Blessed are you, O Lord, the God
 of our fathers,
  praiseworthy and exalted above all forever;
and blessed is your holy and glorious name,
  praiseworthy and exalted above all for
   all ages.

Blessed are you in the temple of your
  holy glory,
  praiseworthy and glorious above
   all forever.

Blessed are you on the throne
  of your kingdom,
  praiseworthy and exalted above all forever.

Blessed are you who look into the depths
  from your throne upon the cherubim, ·
  praiseworthy and exalted above all forever.

A beautiful exhortatory reading about Christian community life. Practice so you can make eye contact with the community at significant points in the reading.

Corinthians = kohr-IN-thee-uhnz

Express with your voice, eyes, and face that this is good news

Pause a little longer at each comma in this list. Be encouraging as the reading suggests!

Take this final blessing slowly, and really pray over your assembly. There are three phrases; make them distinct.

READING II   2 Corinthians 13:11–13

A reading from second Letter of Saint Paul to the Corinthians

Brothers and sisters, **rejoice**.
Mend your ways,
    encourage one another,
   agree with one another, live in **peace**,
   and the **God** of love and peace will **be** with you.
Greet one another with a **holy** kiss.
All the **holy** ones greet you.

The **grace** of the Lord Jesus Christ
   and the **love** of God
   and the **fellowship** of the Holy Spirit be with **all** of you.

God's very identity, almost equivalent to the divine name, is mercy and compassion.

 The final words of a letter can leave the reader with a parting message or summary. These three verses of Paul's Second Letter to the Corinthians are his concluding words to a community that needed more than one letter to address their multiple wrong beliefs and immoral behaviors. After writing at length about so many problems in the church, Paul signs off with words of exhortation and blessing. First, he urges the

Corinthians to rejoice, putting the rest of his imperatives in a positive setting, for the community will indeed experience joy when they live in accordance with Paul's counsel. The four imperatives that follow are indicative of the ongoing problems in the community, particularly the lack of unity and peaceful relationships. If people take these exhortations to heart, they can expect God's own peace to reign among them.

Paul's parting words also include a blessing asking for God's gracious favor, love, and fellowship (in Greek, *koinonia*, best understood as "communion") to be

with the community. As he does elsewhere, Paul uses divine designations that are foundational for our understanding of God as Trinity: Jesus Christ, God, Holy Spirit. It is fitting on the Solemnity of the Most Holy Trinity to hear of the grace, love, and communion from God to be poured out on the community of Corinth as well as on all of us. God was, is, and will be the source of the peace and unity that Paul envisions.

GOSPEL   In the reading from John's Gospel account, we hear part of Jesus' conversation with Nicodemus,

A well-known exhortatory passage, full of good news. Proclaim with joy, and as if you were reading it for the very first time.

Imagine you've just been asked, "How much does God love us?" Convince your inquirers of the immensity of God's love.

This is good news! Smile with your voice, eyes, and face!

You're explaining a principle of the spiritual life—the consequence of a choice.

TO KEEP IN MIND

Use inflection (the high or low pitch of your voice) to convey attitude and feeling. High pitch expresses intensity and excitement; low pitch expresses sadness, contrition, or solemnity.

GOSPEL   John 3:16–18

A reading from the holy Gospel according to John

God so **loved** the world that he gave his only **Son**,
    so that everyone who **believes** in him might not **perish**
    but might have eternal **life**.
For God did not send his Son into the world to **condemn**
        the world,
    but that the world might be **saved** through him.
Whoever **believes** in him will **not** be condemned,
    but whoever does **not** believe has **already** been condemned,
    because he has not believed in the name of the only **Son**
        of **God**.

---

a Pharisee who came to Jesus by night. The setting in a time of darkness may be symbolic of the dim understanding that Nicodemus had of Jesus and his mission. Jesus' teaching to him is intended to bring light, both to Nicodemus and to all who hear his words. In fact, just a few verses before today's reading, Jesus addresses his words to "you" in the plural, indicating a widening of the audience he is speaking to, along with Nicodemus the inquirer.

That audience, most broadly, is "the world," everyone to whom God offers the gift of his own Son. God does this for only one reason: an immense love that did not spare even his only Son. Each person in the world has the opportunity to accept God's gift. Although God's purpose in sending Jesus is not condemnation, but eternal life, some people choose not to accept Jesus, and by their decision bring condemnation on themselves.

Yet God's plan in sending his Son is that the whole world may believe in him, living in a loving and faithful relationship with him. Such belief will result in eternal life, beginning here and now and extending beyond death into eternity; it is God's own life shared with believers. God sent his Son so that the world "might be saved through him"—another way of speaking about the same reality. The biblical writers use many terms to proclaim this magnificent gift: eternal life, salvation, deliverance, redemption, justification, each one highlighting an aspect of God's overwhelming generosity. E.P.

THE MOST HOLY BODY AND BLOOD OF CHRIST (CORPUS CHRISTI)

LECTIONARY #167

READING I   Deuteronomy 8:2–3, 14b–16a

A reading from the Book of Deuteronomy

Moses said to the people:
    "**Remember** how for **forty** years now the **Lord**, your God,
    has directed **all** your journeying in the **desert**,
    so as to **test** you by affliction
    and find out whether or not it was your **intention**
    to **keep** his commandments.
He therefore let you be **afflicted** with hunger,
    and then **fed** you with **manna**,
    a food **unknown** to you and your fathers,
    in order to show you that not by bread **alone** does one live,
    but by every **word** that comes forth from the mouth
        of the LORD.

"Do not **forget** the LORD, your God,
    who brought you **out** of the land of Egypt,
    that place of **slavery**;
    who **guided** you through the vast and terrible **desert**
    with its saraph **serpents** and **scorpions**,
    its parched and **waterless** ground;
    who brought forth **water** for you from the flinty **rock**
    and **fed** you in the desert with **manna**,
    a food **unknown** to your fathers."

A narrative, in which Moses tells the people not to forget all that God has done for them while in the wilderness. Your proclamation can help your assembly recall and be grateful for all God has done for us as well.

Deuteronomy = doo-ter-AH-nuh-mee
Moses = MOH-zis
Keep your pace up through this section.

Slow down. Here is the point of the miracle of the manna.

This section repeats the same theme as above. Raise your intensity.
Note the three phrases here, each beginning with "who." Don't run them together.

saraph = SAYR-uhf (fiery)

READING I Moses is gathered with the Israelites on the plains of Moab, where they are poised to enter the Promised Land. This reading from Deuteronomy is comprised almost entirely of the words of Moses as he gives his final instructions and exhortations. Because the first word of the book in Hebrew is *devarim*, "words," the book is called *Devarim* in the Jewish tradition, a well-chosen title, considering Moses' lengthy speeches, the many words he speaks to Israel in the desert.

This passage is from his second discourse that also includes the Ten Commandments and lengthy legal instructions. Before he presents that Law, Moses tells the people: "Not with our ancestors did the Lord make this covenant but with us, all of us who are alive here this day" (5:3). When he tells the people in today's reading "Remember . . . do not exalt yourself, forgetting the Lord," he continues this view. Moses is talking to a later generation as if they had been present for God's saving action at the exodus from Egypt, the making of the covenant, and the Lord's wondrous acts of kindness in the desert. Remembrance of the God who accom-

plished all these saving events of the past is a means of reassuring the people that God will continue to save them in the present and in the future. Remembrance also functions to call the people of every generation, including our own, to obedience and fidelity.

Central to Israel's memory are the abundant blessings God manifest in bringing the people out of Egypt and guiding them in the desert. In the midst of the affliction, the hunger, and the terrors in the wilderness the Lord provided food unknown to their ancestors, and brought out water from the rock. As essential as

For meditation and context:

TO KEEP IN MIND

Pay attention to the pace of your reading. Varying the pace gives listeners clues to the meaning of the text. The most common problem for proclaimers new to the ministry is going too fast to be understood.

RESPONSORIAL PSALM   Psalm 147:12–13, 14–15, 19–20 (12)

R. Praise the Lord, Jerusalem.
or
R. Alleluia.

Glorify the LORD, O Jerusalem;
   praise your God, O Zion.
For he has strengthened the bars
    of your gates;
   he has blessed your children within you.

He has granted peace in your borders;
   with the best of wheat he fills you.
He sends forth his command to the earth;
   swiftly runs his word!

He has proclaimed his word to Jacob,
   his statutes and his ordinances to Israel.
He has not done thus for any other nation;
   his ordinances he has not made known
    to them.
Alleluia.

An exhortatory reading about our communion with Christ and each other. It may look like a simple, brief teaching, but it is a deep mystery.

Corinthians = kohr-IN-thee-uhnz

Start strong; be deliberate and upbeat.

More slowly, so your listeners can ponder the meaning.

Your delivery on this question should echo that of the question about the blood.

For this final, important point, take care with the structure.

READING II   1 Corinthians 10:16–17

A reading from the first Letter of Saint Paul to the Corinthians

Brothers and sisters:
The cup of **blessing** that we **bless**,
   is it not a participation in the **blood** of Christ?
The **bread** that we **break**,
   is it not a participation in the **body** of Christ?
Because the loaf of bread is **one**,
   we, though **many**, are one **body**,
   for we all partake of the **one loaf**.

TO KEEP IN MIND

Repetition of the same word or phrase over the course of a reading emphasizes a point. Make each instance distinct, and build your intensity with each repetition.

food and drink were, and continue to be, Moses asserts that the manna should show them that such bread alone is not enough for life. They, we, all generations, are fed by every word that comes from the mouth of God. Ongoing remembrance of the *devarim* unites us with the God who continues to sustain us with life-giving words.

 READING II   In the opening chapter of his First Letter to the Corinthians, Paul tells the community "God is faithful, and by him you were called to fellowship (in Greek *koinonia*) with his Son,

Jesus Christ our Lord" (1:9). What is the meaning of fellowship for the community? How is it attained? How is it sustained? Today's reading gives at least a partial answer to these questions.

Paul begins with his own twofold question: Isn't partaking together in the cup of blessing and in the broken bread a participation, a *koinonia,* in the Body and Blood of Christ? When he asks these questions, he seems to expect the community to know the answers, and to respond affirmatively. Perhaps if their theology is correct, right behaviors will follow. Underlying

his questions, Paul is saying in effect that since God has first called the community into *koinonia*, he has also provided the means by which they can experience it. The Eucharistic celebration will transform the bread and the wine into the Body and Blood of Christ. By sharing in this food and drink, they will have a true communion/*koinonia* with and in Christ.

Paul's main purpose in writing about participation in the Body and Blood of Christ becomes clearer in the last sentence of today's reading. Addressing a community beset with factions that surface even

For meditation and context:

TO KEEP IN MIND
Making eye contact with the
assembly connects you with them
and connects them to the reading
more deeply than using your voice
alone. This helps the assembly stay
with the story and keeps them
engaged.

SEQUENCE   Lauda, Sion, Salvatorem

Laud, O Zion, your salvation,
Laud with hymns of exultation,
   Christ, your king and shepherd true:

Bring him all the praise you know,
He is more than you bestow.
   Never can you reach his due.

Special theme for glad thanksgiving
Is the quick'ning and the living
   Bread today before you set:

From his hands of old partaken,
As we know, by faith unshaken,
   Where the Twelve at supper met.

Full and clear ring out your chanting,
Joy nor sweetest grace be wanting,
   From your heart let praises burst:

For today the feast is holden,
When the institution olden
   Of that supper was rehearsed.

Here the new law's new oblation,
By the new king's revelation,
   Ends the form of ancient rite:

Now the new the old effaces,
Truth away the shadow chases,
   Light dispels the gloom of night.

What he did at supper seated,
Christ ordained to be repeated,
   His memorial ne'er to cease:

And his rule for guidance taking,
Bread and wine we hallow, making
   Thus our sacrifice of peace.

This the truth each Christian learns,
Bread into his flesh he turns,
   To his precious blood the wine:

Sight has fail'd, nor thought conceives,
But a dauntless faith believes,
   Resting on a pow'r divine.

Here beneath these signs are hidden
Priceless things to sense forbidden;
   Signs, not things are all we see:

Blood is poured and flesh is broken,
Yet in either wondrous token
   Christ entire we know to be.

Whoso of this food partakes,
Does not rend the Lord nor breaks;
   Christ is whole to all that taste:

Thousands are, as one, receivers,
One, as thousands of believers,
   Eats of him who cannot waste.

Bad and good the feast are sharing,
Of what divers dooms preparing,
   Endless death, or endless life.

Life to these, to those damnation,
See how like participation
   Is with unlike issues rife.

When the sacrament is broken,
Doubt not, but believe 'tis spoken,
   That each sever'd outward token
      doth the very whole contain.

Nought the precious gift divides,
Breaking but the sign betides
   Jesus still the same abides,
      still unbroken does remain.

[Shorter form begins here.]
Lo! the angel's food is given
To the pilgrim who has striven;
   See the children's bread from heaven,
      which on dogs may not be spent.

Truth the ancient types fulfilling,
Isaac bound, a victim willing,
   Paschal lamb, its lifeblood spilling,
      manna to the fathers sent.

Very bread, good shepherd, tend us,
Jesu, of your love befriend us,
   You refresh us, you defend us,
   Your eternal goodness send us
In the land of life to see.

You who all things can and know,
Who on earth such food bestow,
   Grant us with your saints, though lowest,
   Where the heav'nly feast you show,
Fellow heirs and guests to be. Amen. Alleluia.

when they gather for the Lord's Supper, Paul teaches them that sharing in the one loaf of bread, the very Body of Christ, makes the community itself into one body as well. Paul's theology is for the sake of conversion within the fractured church at Corinth. In the milieu of the time, sharing in any meal was regarded as establishing a bond among the participants, and much more so in the case of sharing at the Lord's table. The cup of blessing and the broken bread are both sign and source that can heal their divisions, and transform the community into the very Body of Christ in which they have shared. Their *koinonia,* and ours as well, is attained and sustained by loving recognition of and respect for the body of Christ present in the transformed bread and wine as well as in the transformed community.

GOSPEL   Jesus' words to the crowds in the Gospel reading are a continuation of his long discourse that follows the multiplication of the loaves and fish. He had already told the crowds that he is the Bread of Life, an announcement that met with murmuring and hostile questioning. Now Jesus expands on his earlier teaching: the bread that he will give is his own flesh for the life of the world. Not surprisingly, there is further quarreling and questioning. Now he teaches with shocking boldness, four times repeating that his flesh is food and his blood is drink.

The words "flesh and blood" are often used together and have a richness of meaning that can be understood on several levels. To be "flesh and blood" can mean simply that one is a real human being. For Jesus, being flesh and blood can be seen as an allusion to the Incarnation, in which he

An exhortatory teaching. It's difficult to read this without thinking of the theology of the Eucharist, but Jesus' hearers had no such context. To them, it was shocking news indeed. Try to proclaim as if these words were being spoken for the very first time.

Slow down and let this sink it.

Don't gloss over the word "flesh." It's precisely the words "flesh" and "blood" in all their rawness that cause dissension among Jesus' listeners.

Listen up!

Jesus always teaches out of love, even when the teaching is hard to accept. Let the assembly hear and see that love in you as you proclaim.

This is the ultimate outcome of our communion with Christ.

We have the same intimacy with Jesus that he has with the Father.

The phrase "bread from heaven" recalls the manna in the wilderness, but as Jesus points out, he is the real bread that gives eternal life.

GOSPEL   John 6:51–58

A reading from the holy Gospel according to John

Jesus said to the Jewish crowds:
    "**I** am the **living** bread that came down from **heaven**;
    whoever **eats** this bread will live **forever**;
    and the **bread** that **I** will give
    is my **flesh** for the **life** of the world."

The Jews **quarreled** among themselves, saying,
    "How can this man give us his **flesh** to eat?"
Jesus said to them,
    "Amen, **amen**, I say to you,
    unless you **eat** the **flesh** of the Son of Man and **drink** his **blood**,
    you do not have **life** within you.
Whoever **eats** my flesh and **drinks** my blood
    has **eternal** life,
    and I will **raise** him on the last day.
For my flesh is **true food**,
    and my blood is **true drink**.
Whoever **eats** my flesh and **drinks** my blood
    remains in **me** and I in **him**.
Just as the living Father sent **me**
    and I have **life** because of the Father,
    so also the one who **feeds** on me
    will have life **because** of me.
This is the bread that came down from **heaven**.
Unlike your ancestors who ate and still **died**,
    whoever eats **this** bread will live **forever**."

took on our humanity. The terms can also be seen as looking ahead to his Death on the Cross when he poured out his blood in sacrifice. Those two meanings are surely included when he speaks of his flesh and blood. But Jesus is saying something further, for he says that we are to *eat* his flesh and *drink* his blood. Here "flesh and blood" is referring to sharing in a ritual meal in which we are nourished by his very person. We share, through eating and drinking, in the totality of who he is, in his "flesh and blood."

The result of this eating and drinking is immediate as well as far-reaching. Two of

John the Evangelist's most important theological words highlight the effects of eating Jesus' flesh and drinking his blood. First, we are given life (*zoe*). This life that Jesus gives is both a present reality, given to us now when we share in this meal, and is also a promise of future eternal life, when *zoe* will be given in fullness. *Zoe* is life that doesn't end, and is a participation in God's own life. A second gift to those who share in this meal is that they *remain* in Jesus, and Jesus *remains* in them. Among the evangelist's most frequently used words, "remain," (*meno*) entails more than a physi-

cal presence, but indicates a personal, abiding relationship. As Jesus explains at the Last Supper, we remain in him as vines on a branch, abiding always in his love. E.P.

TWELFTH SUNDAY IN ORDINARY TIME

An exhortatory prayer. Jeremiah is pouring his heart out to God; be sure his anguish is heard.

Jeremiah = jer-uh-MĪ-uh

There is real fear in Jeremiah's voice.

Start low and raise your volume through the end of this line.

How does Jeremiah sound describing faithless friends? How does he feel about God allowing his torment?

Give this line a conspiratorial tone so your assembly knows this is a quote.

Pause slightly, then change your emotion as Jeremiah turns to praise God, affirming what he knows to be true.

It's very human to want to see your enemies punished.

This is the point of the prayer. Take it slowly.

End the prayer with this joyous expression of confidence!

LECTIONARY #94

READING I Jeremiah 20:10–13

A reading from the Book of the Prophet Jeremiah

Jeremiah said:
    "I hear the **whisperings** of many:
    '**Terror** on every side!
    Denounce! let us **denounce** him!'
All those who were my **friends**
    are on the watch for any **misstep** of mine.
'Perhaps he will be **trapped**; then we can **prevail**,
    and take our **vengeance** on him.'
But the LORD is **with** me, like a mighty **champion**:
    my persecutors will **stumble**, they will **not** triumph.
In their **failure** they will be put to utter **shame**,
    to lasting, unforgettable **confusion**.
O LORD of hosts, you who **test** the just,
    who probe **mind** and **heart**,
let me witness the **vengeance** you take on them,
    for to **you** I have **entrusted** my cause.
Sing to the LORD,
    praise the LORD,
for he has **rescued** the life of the **poor**
    from the **power** of the **wicked**!"

READING I Imprisoned, flogged, plotted against, mocked, abandoned! Jeremiah's prophetic mission has resulted in intense suffering and persecution. Who is to blame for Jeremiah's trials? Jeremiah shouts his answer: "You seduced me, LORD, and I let myself be seduced; you were too strong for me, and you prevailed" (20:7). The Word of the Lord that should have been a source of strength for Jeremiah has instead brought "reproach and derision all day long" (20:8). Today's First Reading continues that lament. Jeremiah can hear people whispering

"Terror on every side!" Shortly before, he had used the name "Terror on Every Side" for the priest Pashhur after he put Jeremiah in stocks. Now he hears people repeating the name as a way to humiliate him and deride his prophecy. Even those who were Jeremiah's supposed friends join in watching for his downfall.

Jeremiah's tormented prayer is his sixth lament to God for his suffering. Taken cumulatively, these prayers seem to depict Jeremiah on the edge of despair. He will even curse the day he was born, and ask why he came forth form the womb (20:14,

18). In the context of such extreme lamentation, Jeremiah's declaration that "the Lord is with me" and his jubilant "sing to the Lord, for he has rescued the life of the poor" express an extraordinary mood shift. Such an abrupt shift is surprising, but common in the psalms of lament. Even cries of pain are an expression of belief that God does hear those who grieve. Praise of God before the rescue occurs is surely a hope-filled prayer of confidence, even in the midst of suffering.

For meditation and context:

TO KEEP IN MIND

You can't proclaim what you don't understand. Read the Scripture passage and its commentary in *Workbook*. Then read it from your Bible, including what comes before and after it so that you understand the context.

RESPONSORIAL PSALM   Psalm 69:8–10, 14, 17, 33–35 (14c)

R. Lord, in your great love, answer me.

For your sake I bear insult,
    and shame covers my face.
I have become an outcast to my brothers,
    a stranger to my children,
because zeal for your house consumes me,
    and the insults of those who blaspheme
        you fall upon me.

I pray to you, O LORD,
    for the time of your favor, O God!
In your great kindness answer me
    with your constant help.
Answer me, O LORD, for bounteous is
        your kindness;
    in your great mercy turn toward me.

"See, you lowly ones, and be glad;
    you who seek God, may your hearts
        revive!
For the LORD hears the poor,
    and his own who are in bonds he
        spurns not.
Let the heavens and the earth praise him,
    the seas and whatever moves in them!"

A didactic reading which at first seems complex, but its structure is simple. Paul contrasts two persons (Adam and Christ), their actions (sin and redemption), and the results of those actions (death and life).

Paul starts by explaining how Adam's sin brought death to all.

Sin was in the world even before Moses received the Law that defined sin.

Adam is the "type" of Christ; that is, Adam is human just as Christ is fully human.

Pause briefly, raise your energy, and smile as you proclaim the good news that Christ's gift is much greater than Adam's transgression.

READING II   Romans 5:12–15

A reading from the Letter of Saint Paul to the Romans

Brothers and sisters:
Through one man **sin** entered the world,
    and through sin, **death**,
    and thus death came to **all** men, inasmuch as **all** sinned —
    for up to the time of the **law**, **sin** was in the world,
    though sin is not **accounted** when there is no **law**.
But **death** reigned from Adam to Moses,
    even over those who did **not** sin
    after the **pattern** of the trespass of Adam,
    who is the **type** of the one who was to **come**.

But the **gift** is not like the **transgression**.
For if by the **transgression** of the one the many **died**,
    how much **more** did the **grace** of God
    and the **gracious** gift of the one man Jesus **Christ**
    overflow for the **many**.

READING II   To illustrate the extraordinary scope of God's grace, freely given to us, Paul sets up a contrast between Adam and Christ, and between sin and grace. As he develops his argument, Paul uses complicated sentences and logic. He presents Adam as a "type" of Christ, doing so in an unusual way. A "type" in the Old Testament is most often seen as a positive foreshadowing that is brought to fullness or perfection in the New Testament, particularly in Christ. In this passage, however, Adam is a negative foreshadowing.

Adam's sin contrasts sharply with Christ's gift of grace.

Beginning with Adam, sin and death spread throughout the world. Like a virus, sin infected the whole human race: all "men." (Paul uses the word *anthropos* in Greek, "human person.") But the grace of God is far more powerful than sin. Yes, Paul says, sin and death entered into the world through the one *anthropos* Adam. But from another *anthropos*, Christ, we receive something so much greater. Paul's language is expansive as he writes about God's gracious gift that is not like the trans-

gression. The grace of Christ overflows, offering gifts that are fuller and more comprehensive than the effects of Adam's sin: the greatest gift is, in fact, Jesus Christ himself, the freely given gift from the Father.

GOSPEL   Jesus is continuing his instruction to his closest disciples, the Twelve, to prepare them for their mission. He has already told them that he is sending them out as sheep among wolves, that they will endure extreme persecution, and that even families will be divided. As he speaks with the Twelve, all

A didactic reading, celebrating and teaching about God's providence. Jesus is quite clear—there is nothing to be afraid of within God's loving care. What tone feels most in tune with that message?

Take this line slowly and deliberately, then return to a normal pace.

There are no secrets that can do you harm.

Strongly encourage your assembly to be bold!

Gehenna = geh-HEN-nah

Pause.

They are worth little in the marketplace.

Amazing!

Emphasize "do not be afraid;" it's the second time Jesus says this.

GOSPEL   Matthew 10:26–33

A reading from the holy Gospel according to Matthew

Jesus said to the Twelve:
  "Fear **no** one.
Nothing is concealed that will not be **revealed**,
  nor **secret** that will not be **known**.
What I **say** to you in the **darkness**, **speak** in the **light**;
  what you **hear whispered**, **proclaim** on the **housetops**.
And do not be **afraid** of those who kill the **body**
    but cannot kill the **soul**;
  rather, be afraid of the one who can destroy
  both soul and body in **Gehenna**.
Are not two **sparrows** sold for a small **coin**?
Yet not **one** of them falls to the ground
    without your Father's **knowledge**.
Even all the **hairs** of your head are **counted**.
So do **not** be afraid; you are worth **more** than **many** sparrows.
Everyone who **acknowledges** me before **others**
  I will **acknowledge** before my heavenly **Father**.
But whoever **denies** me before others,
  I will **deny** before my heavenly Father."

TO KEEP IN MIND
Pause in order to break up separate thoughts, set apart significant statements, or indicate major shifts. Never pause in the middle of a single thought. Your primary guide for pauses is punctuation.

---

disciples throughout the centuries can hear him instructing them as well as they share in the mission of the first followers. Jesus opens up his teaching for all generations when he proclaims that things concealed and secret will be revealed and made known. Disciples themselves (ourselves) are to speak in the light what Jesus spoke in darkness, and to proclaim from the housetops what was a mere whisper.

Jesus calls his disciples to a stunning boldness even in the face of persecution. Three times in this part of his instruction, he tells them not to be afraid. The first

time, he exhorts them not to be afraid of those who will persecute them. They should expect persecution, for they, as disciples, are not above their teacher (10:24). What Jesus endured, they too must endure. In the second instance, Jesus tells them not to be afraid of those who can kill the body, but cannot kill the soul. The grammatical form of this second "Do not be afraid" is different from the first one, and implies that the disciples are already afraid. It might be translated, "Stop being afraid." Similarly, in the third counsel, his disciples should stop being afraid, reassured of the

value that God places on them. Jesus' instruction to stop being afraid reveals his intimate knowledge of his disciples. If even tiny sparrows and each hair on the head are counted, they should lay aside their fear for they can surely count on the Father's constant care for them. E.P.

THIRTEENTH SUNDAY IN ORDINARY TIME

LECTIONARY #97

A narrative about hospitality. Consider how to make these characters sound distinctive and true to their role in the story.

Elisha = ee-LĪ-shuh

Shunem = SHOO-nuhm

The woman, not her husband, takes the initiative.

Let her evident friendliness and warmth come through here.

Her attention to these small, hospitable details gives us a clue about her character and the way she would sound.

Lower your voice as if the woman were near.

Gehazi = geh-HAY-zī: Gehazi understands Elisha's intention and is excited to share his idea.

Elisha is not just predicting the future; he's bestowing a gift. How might that sound?

READING I   2 Kings 4:8–11, 14–16a

A reading from the second Book of Kings

One day **Elisha** came to Shunem,
    where there was a **woman** of influence, who **urged** him to
        dine with her.
Afterward, **whenever** he passed by, he used to stop there to **dine**.
So she said to her husband, "I **know** that Elisha is a **holy** man of
        God.
Since he visits us **often**, let us arrange a little **room** on the roof
    and **furnish** it for him with a bed, table, chair, and lamp,
        so that when he comes to us he can **stay** there."
Sometime later Elisha **arrived** and stayed in the room overnight.

Later Elisha asked, "Can something be **done** for her?"
His servant **Gehazi** answered, "**Yes!**
    She has no **son**, and her husband is getting **on** in years."
Elisha said, "**Call** her."
When the woman had been called and **stood** at the door,
    Elisha **promised**, "**This** time next year
    you will be fondling a baby **son**."

READING I   The First Reading opens and closes with reference to Elisha, the prophetic successor to Elijah. Like Moses, Samuel, David, and Elijah himself, Elisha is given the designation "man of God," an honorific title bestowed on men who are both worthy and extraordinary. A man of God is one through whom God works. Aware that Elisha is a holy man of God, a woman of Shunem is motivated to have a room built where he can stay when he passes through their town. The Shunemite woman is first described as wealthy, and her generous hospitality visi-

bly displays that wealth. Offering a meal when he stops in Shunem, the woman and her husband then build him his own well-furnished room. Contrary to the norms of a patriarchal society, it is the woman and not her husband who speaks to Elisha, prevails upon him to stay for a meal, and has the plan for Elisha's upper chamber. And it is to her, not her husband, that Elisha makes the promise of a son to be born. While her recognition of Elisha as a holy man of God may be a seminal statement of faith, Elisha rewards her not for her faith, but for her generous hospitality.

Typically in biblical annunciations of an extraordinary birth, it is the child to be born who is the focus of attention. Here, in contrast, the woman and the prophet Elisha are at the center. The episode is part of the saga in which Elisha is depicted as a prophet powerful in word and deed, a worthy heir to Elijah. The Shunemite woman illustrates how one is to receive both prophet and the prophetic word: with openness and eager welcome.

READING II   Paul is addressing members of a community in Rome

For meditation and context:

RESPONSORIAL PSALM Psalm 89:2–3, 16–17, 18–19 (2a)

R. Forever I will sing the goodness of the Lord.

The promises of the LORD I will sing
    forever,
  through all generations my mouth shall
    proclaim your faithfulness.
For you have said, "My kindness is
    established forever";
  in heaven you have confirmed your
    faithfulness.

Blessed the people who know the joyful
    shout;
  in the light of your countenance,
    O LORD, they walk.
At your name they rejoice all the day,
  and through your justice they are exalted.

You are the splendor of their strength,
  and by your favor our horn is exalted.
For to the LORD belongs our shield,
  and to the Holy One of Israel, our king.

A didactic reading that reflects on a central mystery: we are baptized into Christ's death to rise with him to new life. This might be challenging for your audience to understand, so make the progression from death to life very clear.

Are you unaware = Don't you know

Emphasize we were buried through Baptism.

Follow the punctuation carefully throughout this reading: brief pauses at commas, longer pauses at semicolons and longest at periods.

Slow down.

Good news indeed—we no longer need fear death!

Encourage your assembly to recognize that sin and death hold no power over them any longer. We live for God!

READING II Romans 6:3–4, 8–11

A reading from the Letter of Saint Paul to the Romans

Brothers and sisters:
Are you **unaware** that we who were **baptized** into Christ Jesus
    were **baptized** into his **death**?
We were indeed **buried** with him through **baptism** into death,
    so that, just as **Christ** was **raised** from the dead
    by the **glory** of the Father,
    we **too** might live in **newness** of life.

If, then, we have **died** with Christ,
    we **believe** that we shall also **live** with him.
We **know** that Christ, **raised** from the dead, dies no **more**;
    death no longer has **power** over him.
As to his **death**, he died to sin **once** and for **all**;
    as to his **life**, he lives for **God**.
Consequently, you too must think of yourselves as **dead** to sin
    and **living** for God in Christ Jesus.

---

who have already been baptized. As he explains the meaning of Baptism, he includes himself, using "us" and "we" repeatedly, making it clear that he is one with them in all that Baptism implies. Here he is using theology to provide a foundation so that they will "walk" in accordance with the new life they received through Baptism.

Paul frequently uses this pattern in his letters. He begins with an explanation of what the community believes, and follows with the implications for life that flow from that belief. Here Paul begins here with the understanding that those baptized into

Christ have been baptized into this Death. As he does elsewhere when writing about Baptism (as in Galatians 3:27), he uses the preposition "into" (*eis*), indicating a dynamic immersion *into* the very person of Christ, and *into* his Death. Such immersion into Christ means that the baptized will share in his pattern of Death and Resurrection; they are conformed to Christ in the totality of his Passion, Death, and Resurrection. Just as Christ's Death means that he will die no more, so too those who are baptized, having once died to sin are to be ever dead to sin. They are to walk in the

newness of life that comes from being plunged into Christ, and will remain alive to God in him. As Paul continues to exhort the community in the verses that follow today's reading, he provides specifics on how they are to live, having been brought from death to new life through the grace of Baptism.

GOSPEL   In Matthew's Gospel, Jesus gives five lengthy speeches. Today's Gospel is the conclusion of the second of these discourses. Throughout this instruction Jesus teaches the Twelve the meaning of discipleship before sending

Two didactic teachings connected by the idea that disciples become as their master is.

The first teaching: As disciples, we must give of ourselves as completely as Jesus did. These are hard sayings, but remember, a didactic proclamation is given out of love. Let that love come through here. Take your time.

"For my sake" breaks the parallelism and is the key idea here.

Pause.

The second teaching: As Jesus bears the Father who sent him, disciples bear Jesus. To receive Jesus through his disciples (among whom are prophets and the righteous) brings reward.

Emphasize the smallness of this gesture, which is rewarded nonetheless. Don't pause until the dash.

TO KEEP IN MIND
Pray the text, using your favorite method of praying with Scripture.

GOSPEL   Matthew 10:37–42

A reading from the holy Gospel according to Matthew

Jesus said to his apostles:
  "Whoever loves father or mother **more** than me is not **worthy**
    of me,
  and whoever loves son or daughter **more** than me is not **worthy** of me;
  and whoever does not take up his **cross**
  and follow **after** me is not **worthy** of me.
Whoever **finds** his life will **lose** it,
  and whoever **loses** his life for **my** sake will **find** it.

"Whoever receives **you** receives **me**,
  and whoever receives **me** receives the one who **sent** me.
Whoever receives a **prophet because** he is a prophet
  will receive a prophet's **reward**,
  and whoever receives a **righteous** man
  because he is a **righteous** man
  will receive a **righteous** man's reward.
And whoever gives only a **cup** of cold water
  to one of these **little** ones to drink
  because the little one is **a disciple**—
  amen, I say to you, he will **surely** not **lose** his reward."

---

them out on their mission. The section consists of two parts. In the first, Jesus tells the Twelve about the challenging demands of discipleship; then he announces rewards, not the rewards given to the disciples themselves, but rewards that will be given to those who welcome them.

In explaining the demands of discipleship, three times Jesus uses the phrase "is not worthy of me." If one is not worthy of Jesus, he or she cannot belong to him. In the first two examples, Jesus speaks of well-known relationships of father or mother, and son or daughter, family bonds

in which people do belong to one another. As desirable as are these ties, Jesus is teaching that, in order to be worthy, the new family formed in him must take priority. In the third example, Jesus gives a succinct description of a disciple: one who takes up the cross and follows him. Paradoxically those who take up the cross will find life, even as they lose it for his sake.

Because disciples belong to Jesus, those who welcome them in fact welcome Jesus himself. All who welcome prophets and righteous persons will receive the reward of a prophet and righteous one. We

can easily think of the Shunemite woman who welcomed the righteous prophet Elisha and received a reward for her actions. Jesus' disciples, like Jesus himself, are numbered among the prophets and righteous persons. In addition, disciples are also included among the little ones. Those who welcome them will be rewarded. E.P.

FOURTEENTH SUNDAY IN ORDINARY TIME

An exhortatory proclamation of how the world will be when the Reign of God is fulfilled. Give it energy and excitement. Maintain as much eye contact as you can, and take your time, relishing these images of peace and joy.

Zechariah = zek-uh-RĪ-uh

Express this enthusiasm and joy in your face as well as well as your voice. Don't lose "heartily"—it creates a dynamic image.

Pour your excitement into the word "See."

Ephraim = EE-fray-im; EF-r*m

These implements of war will be gone! Keep your energy up.

Slow down especially on this line.

He reigns over the whole earth. Be expansive in your proclamation.

LECTIONARY #100

READING I   Zechariah 9:9–10

A reading from the Book of the Prophet Zechariah

> **Thus** says the LORD:
> Rejoice **heartily**, **O** daughter Zion,
>   shout for **joy**, **O** daughter Jerusalem!
> **See**, your **king** shall come to you;
>   a just **savior** is he,
> **meek**, and riding on an **ass**,
>   on a **colt**, the **foal** of an ass.
> He shall **banish** the **chariot** from Ephraim,
>   and the **horse** from Jerusalem;
> the warrior's bow shall be **banished**,
>   and he shall proclaim **peace** to the nations.
> His dominion shall be from **sea** to **sea**,
>   and from the River to the **ends** of the earth.

TO KEEP IN MIND

Making eye contact with the assembly connects you with them and connects them to the reading more deeply than using your voice alone. This helps the assembly stay with the story and keeps them engaged.

READING I   Zechariah is one of the last of the Hebrew prophets, writing in the year 520 BC, the time of restoration after the Babylonian exile. The second part of the book, chapters 9–14, was probably written at a later date when the earlier hopes of rebuilding the Temple and renewing the land were still not realized. It announces an ideal though distant future brought about by the power of God.

Today's reading is one of the clearest visions of such a hopeful future. The prophet depicts God speaking directly to Jerusalem, twice described as "daughter;" presenting an intimate, familial relationship with the city and its inhabitants. At last they can rejoice shouting out their joy, for the king coming to them will embody all of the great expectations awaited since the return from Babylon. He is a just (*saddiq*) king who pursues right relationships with God, all people, and the land itself. He is their savior who will lead them out of any darkness, whether it be imprisonment, exile, slavery, or any other situation of human need, individual or collective. Though king and savior, he will come to them in humility. Riding the foal of an ass is a sign that he comes in peace, not as a military commander. Banishing the means of war from both Ephraim in the north and Jerusalem in the south, he will extend his reign to the nations, including the Gentiles. He will rule even to the ends of the earth, always with peace, bringing integrity and harmony to land and people.

Both Rabbinic Judaism and Christianity have seen in these verses a reference to the Messiah, with the Gospel writers depicting them as fulfilled in Jesus' entry into Jerusalem at the beginning of his Passion. His kingly rule, like that depicted

For meditation and context:

RESPONSORIAL PSALM   Psalm 145:1–2, 8–9, 10–11, 13–14 (1)

R. I will praise your name for ever, my king and my God.
or
R. Alleluia.

I will extol you, O my God and King,
   and I will bless your name for ever
   and ever.
Every day will I bless you,
   and I will praise your name for ever
   and ever.

The LORD is gracious and merciful,
   slow to anger and of great kindness.
The LORD is good to all
   and compassionate toward all his works.

Let all your works give you thanks, O LORD,
   and let your faithful ones bless you.
Let them discourse of the glory of your
   kingdom
   and speak of your might.

The LORD is faithful in all his words
   and holy in all his works.
The LORD lifts up all who are falling
   and raises up all who are bowed down.

In this didactic reading Paul contrasts living in the flesh (death), with living in the spirit (life). Your assembly is meant to live in the spirit; this reading reminds them to live that way.

READING II   Romans 8:9, 11–13

A reading from the Letter of Saint Paul to the Romans

Brothers and sisters:
You are **not** in the flesh;
   on the **contrary**, you are in the **spirit**,
   if **only** the Spirit of God **dwells** in you.
Whoever does not have the **Spirit** of Christ does not **belong**
      to him.
If the **Spirit** of the one who raised Jesus from the dead **dwells**
      in you,
   the **one** who raised Christ from the dead
   will give **life** to your mortal bodies **also**,
   through his Spirit that **dwells** in you.
Consequently, brothers and sisters,
   we are not **debtors** to the flesh,
   to live **according** to the flesh.
For if you live according to the **flesh**, you will **die**,
   but if by the **Spirit** you put to **death** the deeds of the body,
   you will live.

Remind your assembly that they are not in the flesh.

Keep the pace up in this line, pausing briefly at commas, so as not to lose the train of thought.

The same Spirit brings the same Resurrection.

The body is not evil; it will be raised to new life.
Pause.
We need not live according to the flesh, as if the Spirit of God didn't dwell within us. Rather, we can choose to live out our true identity in God.

Death is the natural consequence of life outside our home in God.

With deliberate emphasis.

---

by Zechariah, reaches all peoples, encircling them in peace.

   "Home" implies a place of welcome, intimacy, and belonging. All of these features are implied when Paul writes, "the Spirit of God dwells in you." God's own Spirit makes a home within us, and because of that in-dwelling we belong to God, living in intimate union with Father, Son, and Spirit.

READING II   Paul uses "spirit" in two ways in this reading. In the first sense, spirit refers to a person living in right relationship and communion with God. Living in the spirit contrasts with living in the flesh, a life alienated from God, earthbound, rather than oriented to the things of heaven. Neither spirit nor flesh refers to separate aspects of a person, but to a person either open and turned toward God, or one hostile and turned away from God.

   The second way Paul uses "Spirit" is to refer to God's own Spirit. Paul writes about this Spirit in a variety of ways: Spirit of God, Spirit of Christ, Spirit of the one who raised Jesus from the dead. The Spirit is, in a mysterious way, God's own presence that breathes within us. The word "spirit" (*pneuma*) in fact means "breath," that which gives life. The same life-giving Spirit who raised Christ from the dead will give life to us as well. God's life-imparting gift, the Spirit empowers us to shun life according to the flesh, which brings death. As we make a home for the Spirit, the Spirit gives us a share, a down-payment, in eternal life even now.

An exhortatory reading in two parts, both spoken by Jesus: a prayer of praise to God and a call to his followers to rest on him.

"Exclaimed" gives us a clue to Jesus' emotion here: great joy and excitement. Give this exhortation that same energy.

Is Jesus' gratitude expressed exuberantly or quietly and thoughtfully? You choose.

And the Son has revealed the Father to all of us.

Pause.

Change your tone to one of comfort and encouragement, but keep your energy up. How would you speak to someone weary and troubled? Look directly at the assembly and invite them to come and rest!

You can take a more intimate, quiet tone here, and slow down through to the end.

TO KEEP IN MIND
What does the reading ask your assembly to do or to be after hearing your proclamation? Focus on an intention every time you proclaim.

GOSPEL   Matthew 11:25–30

A reading from the holy Gospel according to Matthew

At that time Jesus **exclaimed**:
  "I give **praise** to you, Father, Lord of heaven and earth,
  for although you have **hidden** these things
  from the **wise** and the **learned**
  you have **revealed** them to **little** ones.
Yes, Father, such has been your **gracious** will.
All things have been handed over to **me** by my **Father**.
No one knows the **Son except** the **Father**,
  and **no** one knows the **Father** except the **Son**
  and **anyone** to whom the Son wishes to **reveal** him.

"**Come** to me, **all** you who labor and are **burdened**,
  and I will give you **rest**.
Take my **yoke** upon you and **learn** from me,
  for I am **meek** and **humble** of heart;
  and you will find **rest** for yourselves.
For my yoke is **easy**, and my burden **light**."

GOSPEL Jesus gives thanks to his Father for the revelation given to little ones, those who are receptive as opposed to those who are closed because they believe they are wise. Jesus then addresses two groups who could be considered to be among these little ones: his own disciples (those "to whom the Son wishes/chooses to reveal him," and those who are burdened. The disciples, both those in Jesus' own day and those in the centuries since, could be included among the burdened. For all, Jesus' comforting words promise rest.

When we pray for those who have died, we ask that God will give them eternal rest. This concept of rest is of an eternal Sabbath spent in God's loving embrace. Jesus assures those who labor and are burdened that he will give them rest when they come to him, indicating that rest is not only for them after death, but a gift in the present time. It is a taste of eternal life, Sabbath peace, even now. The rest that Jesus promises is a joyful refreshment in the midst of the burdens of life, and is a secure communion with God, God's people, and creation.

Jesus, meek and humble of heart, does not add encumbrances to those who are already burdened. Using an image that would be familiar to his first-century audience, Jesus says that his yoke is easy, unlike the heavy burdens placed on people's shoulders by the Pharisees, who according to Matthew's Gospel, did nothing to ease the weighty burden (23:4). Jesus' yoke is well fitted and matched to each person. E.P.

FIFTEENTH SUNDAY IN ORDINARY TIME

In this exhortatory reading, God speaks, assuring us that all his promises will be fulfilled. Show your assembly God's bold confidence and care; stand up straight, and proclaim directly to your listeners.

Isaiah = ī-ZAY-uh

This is one long sentence with three thoughts. Keep your pace up through the first thought ("Just as . . . who eats"), pausing briefly at the commas. This sets up the metaphor.

These are images of generosity and plenty.

Pause before beginning the second thought ("so shall . . . ")

Remember, the Word you proclaim is a living Word, and demands a proclamation worthy of it!

A longer pause before the final thought ("my word . . . "). This thought reiterates the theme of the reading; slow down, and proclaim with confident assurance.

LECTIONARY #103

READING I   Isaiah 55:10–11

A reading from the Book of the Prophet Isaiah

Thus says the LORD:
Just as from the **heavens**
    the **rain** and **snow** come down
and do not **return** there
    till they have **watered** the earth,
    making it **fertile** and **fruitful**,
giving **seed** to the one who **sows**
    and **bread** to the one who **eats**,
so shall my **word** be
    that goes **forth** from my mouth;
my word shall not return to me **void**,
    but shall do my **will**,
    achieving the end for which I **sent** it.

READING I "Thus says the Lord" immediately announces to us that everything that follows will be words from God. While "Thus says the Lord" is a common introduction to prophetic pronouncements, it is particularly important here since the message focuses on the power and purpose of God's Word. Before any mention of that divine communication, Isaiah presents a vivid, well-developed image. In theological terms, Isaiah has a sacramental worldview, seeing in the elements of the natural world signs that point to God. Isaiah has observed the world, and

finds an analogy for what he cannot see. He builds a picture for us: the waters sent from God return to the heavens from whence they came, having accomplished their purpose. Without use of scientific language, Isaiah presents the cycle of nature that he has observed, and sees there a way of explaining the Word of God.

Of all the things that Isaiah could have said about the effects of rain and snow, he chose those that lead to food production: earth that is fertile and fruitful, seed spread by the sower that sprouts forth, and is used for bread for all who eat. As the heaven-

sent waters are essential for the nourishment of land and people, the Word that goes forth from the mouth of God is essential for feeding our minds and hearts. And as the rain does not return to the heavens without providing food, neither does the Word of God. It will accomplish its purpose of giving a banquet to God's people.

The reason the Word is effective is that it is God's own speech. Isaiah emphasizes the personal quality of God's Word by use of the first person pronoun: *my* word, *my* mouth, *my* will; it will not return to *me* void. And the final phrase gives a strong

For meditation and context:

TO KEEP IN MIND
The Word you have the privilege of proclaiming desperately needs to be heard. Recognize how important it is for you to work to help the Word of God come alive for the assembly.

A didactic reading. Paul makes four points: (1) We await a future of glory. (2) Creation, too, will be redeemed. (3) Creation "groans" as that redemption is born in it. (4) We, too, "groan" in anticipation and hope.

The first point. Be dismissive of these "sufferings of this present time."

The second point. Don't lose the word "creation." Express the eagerness you describe in your voice.

A long phrase ("for creation . . . children of God"); keep it together, pausing briefly for a quick breath at each comma.

Paul asserts that the whole universe awaits its redemption, not just human beings.

Pause.

The third point.

The fourth point.

We who already can taste the future still await the fullness of that redemption to be born.

Though we must wait and perhaps even suffer, encourage your assembly not to lose hope.

RESPONSORIAL PSALM   Psalm 65:10, 11, 12–13, 14 (Luke 8:8)

R. The seed that falls on good ground will yield a fruitful harvest.

You have visited the land and watered it;
    greatly have you enriched it.
God's watercourses are filled;
    you have prepared the grain.

Thus have you prepared the land: drenching
        its furrows,
    breaking up its clods,
softening it with showers,
    blessing its yield.

You have crowned the year with your bounty,
    and your paths overflow with a rich
        harvest;
the untilled meadows overflow with it,
    and rejoicing clothes the hills.

The fields are garmented with flocks
    and the valleys blanketed with grain.
    They shout and sing for joy.

READING II   Romans 8:18–23

A reading from the Letter of Saint Paul to the Romans

Brothers and sisters:
I consider that the **sufferings** of this present time are as **nothing**
    compared with the **glory** to be revealed for us.
For **creation** awaits with **eager** expectation
    the **revelation** of the children of God;
    for creation was made subject to **futility**,
    not of its **own** accord but because of the one who **subjected** it,
    in hope that creation **itself**
    would be set **free** from **slavery** to corruption
    and **share** in the glorious **freedom** of the children of God.
We know that **all** creation is **groaning** in labor pains even
        until **now**;
    and not only **that**, but we **ourselves**,
    who have the **firstfruits** of the Spirit,
    we **also** groan within ourselves
    as we wait for **adoption**, the **redemption** of our bodies.

assurance that the Word will achieve the end for which *I* sent it. The God who controls the rain and snow may seem distant, the Lord of heaven and earth. But the God who speaks is an intimate presence who is speaking to all of us.

Today's Responsorial Psalm continues the imagery of water and the fruitfulness of the land that God provides. Although it doesn't mention the Word of God, all that it says about God enriching the earth and crowning the year with bounty applies equally well to the fruitfulness and bounty of God's Word. The joy and singing of the

psalm are apt responses to the Word of God proclaimed in our hearing.

READING II | Paul's reflection in today's Second Reading is filled with hope and confidence in the midst of suffering, something that each person experiences in a unique, individual way. As he writes about suffering, Paul addresses all of us, nudging us to reflect on our own understanding, since human responses to suffering are as individual as the sufferings themselves. In his Second Letter to the Corinthians, Paul describes his own

response: "We are afflicted in every way, but not constrained, perplexed, but not driven to despair; persecuted, but not abandoned; struck down, but not destroyed" (2 Corinthians 4:8–9). Clearly, Paul has endured intense suffering, but it did not lead to despair.

According to Paul, creation itself shares in suffering, and has done so from the very beginning. Creation is in travail, is in "slavery to corruption," and is "groaning in labor pains." Like Paul and all of us, creation also has a response to its suffering: it waits with eager expectation to be set free

A narrative (a parable) within another narrative about Jesus' ministry. Matthew points out how large the crowds are that gather to hear Jesus, no doubt because he was such a good storyteller. Let the story be your focus as you proclaim.

These lines set the scene; don't linger over them. Keep your pace up.

Jesus describes four outcomes of this sowing; keep each one distinct.

The first outcome happens quickly; match your pace accordingly.

Pause.

Pause.

Raise your energy and smile at this good news.
"Pay attention!"

A longer pause to indicate the passage of time.

We have to respond to the Word of God for it to bear fruit in us. Those who respond will bear much fruit; those who do not will bear nothing.

GOSPEL   Matthew 13:1–23

A reading from the holy Gospel according to Matthew

[On that day, **Jesus** went out of the house and sat down by the **sea**.
Such **large** crowds gathered around him
    that he got into a **boat** and sat down,
    and the whole crowd stood along the **shore**.
And he spoke to them at length in **parables**, saying:
    "A **sower** went out to **sow**.
And as he sowed, some seed fell on the **path**,
    and **birds** came and **ate** it up.
Some fell on **rocky** ground, where it had **little** soil.
It sprang up at **once** because the soil was not **deep**,
    and when the **sun** rose it was **scorched**, and it **withered** for
        lack of **roots**.
Some seed fell among **thorns**, and the thorns grew up and
    choked it.
But **some** seed fell on **rich** soil, and produced **fruit**,
    a **hundred** or **sixty** or **thirtyfold**.
Whoever has **ears** ought to **hear**."]

The disciples approached him and said,
    "**Why** do you speak to them in **parables**?"
He said to them in reply,
    "Because **knowledge** of the mysteries of the kingdom of
        heaven
    has been granted to **you**, but to **them** it has **not** been granted.
To anyone who **has**, **more** will be given and he will grow **rich**;
    from anyone who has **not**, even what he **has** will be
    taken away. »

---

from the present slavery and pain. We can envision the earth itself striving even now to participate in God's glory.

For creation and for us in particular, Paul considers present sufferings, no matter how serious or difficult they may be, as miniscule in comparison with future glory. Because of what lies ahead, we wait with eager longing, and hope for the glorious freedom of the children of God, for adoption, and the redemption of our bodies.

Eager expectation; hope; waiting. Each of these responses is a way of looking to the future as better than the present,

regarding it as a time when the distress of this moment will be no more. The image of labor pains expresses this well. The groaning associated with the pain of giving birth will be transformed to wondrous joy when the child is born.

For Paul, present suffering that will be changed to future joy is only part of the truth to be revealed. He says that even now we already have the first fruits of the Spirit; we already have a taste or a down payment of the glory that will be ours fully in the future. That means that we not only await glory, but we experience it even now, even

in the midst of our hardships. Paul is announcing here the Good News of God's glory that encompasses past, present, and future. No wonder he has such lively hope!

| GOSPEL | As the Gospel begins, we see Jesus seated on the |

shore of the Sea of Galilee. Shortly before this seaside scene, he had been involved in controversies with the Pharisees who were seeking to destroy him (12:14) and had accused him of being in league with Beelzebul (12:24). The Pharisees, however, do not seem to be among the throng

They take no action, make no choices, upon hearing the Word proclaimed.

How does Jesus feel about the people's hardness of heart? How do you feel when someone you love is making poor choices, and you're seemingly powerless to prevent it?

There is still hope for the people, if they allow Jesus to be in relationship with them and heal them.

Blessed = BLES-uhd. Speak these lines directly to your assembly. How does Jesus feel as he acknowledges the faithfulness of his disciples (your assembly)? Pleased, joyful, excited? Let that emotion come through in your proclamation.

Pause.

Again, keep each of the four outcomes distinct as you explain them. How does Jesus feel about each of these hearers of the word? Make a distinct emotional choice for each, and let it come through especially as you proclaim the outcome of each kind of sowing.

This is **why** I speak to them in parables, because
   they **look** but do not **see**, and **hear** but do not **listen**
      or **understand**.
Isaiah's prophecy is **fulfilled** in them, which says:
   *You shall indeed **hear** but not **understand**,*
      *you shall indeed **look** but never **see**.*
   ***Gross** is the heart of this people,*
      *they will hardly **hear** with their ears,*
      *they have **closed** their eyes,*
      *lest they **see** with their eyes*
      *and **hear** with their ears*
   *and **understand** with their hearts and be **converted**,*
      *and I **heal** them.*

"But **blessed** are your eyes, because they **see**,
   and your **ears**, because they **hear**.
Amen, I say to you, many **prophets** and **righteous** people
   longed to see what you see but did **not** see it,
   and to **hear** what you hear but did **not** hear it.

"**Hear** then the parable of the sower.
The seed sown on the **path** is the one
   who **hears** the word of the kingdom without **understanding** it,
   and the **evil** one comes and **steals** away
   what was sown in his **heart**.
The seed sown on **rocky** ground
   is the one who hears the word and receives it at **once** with **joy**.
But he has no **root** and lasts only for a **time**.

gathered around Jesus beside the sea. So great is the crowd that Jesus gets into a boat, not to escape them, but to teach them. Since sound travels easily over water, Jesus' words spoken even at a distance from the shore would clearly reach his audience.

Teaching them from the boat, Jesus would be looking at the people and the land on which they were standing. He begins, "A sower went out to sow." As Jesus tells about the places on which the seed fell, he may have been able to see birds pecking along a path, have observed rocky ground, weeds and thorns, and some

plants growing vigorously. The people listening could look around them and see exactly what Jesus was talking about. Parabolic teaching draws on what is familiar and observable to illustrate what is unfamiliar and unseen.

Parables should get listeners engaged in active thought that also moves them to new ways of thinking, behaving, and relating. The description of the seed falling on different kinds of soil readily brings to mind different people to whom the images apply. Given that Jesus had so recently been in controversy with the Pharisees, it is easy to

see seed falling on rocky soil, and seed withered and failing to thrive, applied to them. Yet parables are intended to get individuals to apply the message to themselves. That is why Jesus concluded his parable with the admonition, "Whoever has ears ought to hear." Rather than pointing fingers at others, the parable should prod us to ask what kind of soil we provide for the seed. Are our ears ready to listen? How is the parable calling us to conversion?

Jesus' disciples, among those who heard his parable, ask him, "Why do you speak to them in parables?" Jesus' answer

Be expansive as you proclaim the bountiful harvest the seed yields!

When some **tribulation** or **persecution** comes because of the word,
  he **immediately** falls away.
The seed sown among **thorns** is the one who hears the word,
  but then worldly **anxiety** and the **lure** of riches **choke** the word
  and it bears **no** fruit.
But the seed sown on **rich** soil
  is the one who **hears** the word and **understands** it,
  who indeed **bears** fruit and yields a **hundred** or **sixty**
    or **thirtyfold**."

[Shorter: Matthew 13:1–9 (see brackets)]

recalls his concluding words about the necessity of hearing. Those who are attentive and open with both eyes and ears will understand and be converted. Those who have closed their eyes and ears will not understand, and will be confused. Thus the *purpose* of teaching in parables is not to confuse, but the *result* of this teaching is confusion to those who do not heed Jesus' advice to listen. Because his disciples have seen and heard, Jesus pronounces them blessed; the blessing, or beatitude, is "knowledge of the mysteries of the kingdom."

In the final scene, Jesus provides an allegorical interpretation of the parable. Rather than considering the soil, he looks at the seed that is sown; it represents various ways in which people hear the Word. Though many seeds do not bear lasting fruit, some will produce in great abundance. This final image, given to his disciples, is one of hope and growth, brought about by the power of God's Word in those who have heard and understood. E.P.

SIXTEENTH SUNDAY IN ORDINARY TIME

LECTIONARY #106

READING I Wisdom 12:13, 16–19

A reading from the Book of Wisdom

There is no god besides **you** who have the **care** of all,
    that you need **show** you have not **unjustly** condemned.
For your **might** is the source of **justice**;
    your **mastery** over all things makes you **lenient** to all.
For you show your **might** when the perfection of your power
      is **disbelieved**;
    and in those who **know** you, you rebuke **temerity**.
But though you are **master** of might, you judge with **clemency**,
    and with much **lenience** you govern us;
    for **power**, whenever you **will**, **attends** you.
And you **taught** your people, by these deeds,
    that those who are **just** must be **kind**;
and you gave your children good ground for **hope**
    that you would permit **repentance** for their **sins**.

An exhortatory hymn praising God for being all-powerful and just as well as merciful and lenient. This should sound like a hymn of praise! Keep your energy up and smile where you feel it's fitting.

An awkward construction. The core thought is "There is no one to whom you need to prove yourself." Drop your voice on the parenthetical phrase, "who have the care of all."

In these lines, contrast power and might with clemency and leniency.

temerity = tuh-MER-uh-tee (insolence)

Speak directly to your assembly. We are to do as God does—tempering power and authority with kindness and mercy.

READING I An ancient Latin saying "*lex orandi, lex credendi*" (the law of prayer is the law of belief) means that the way we pray expresses what we believe about God, about ourselves, and about the world. Today's reading from Wisdom is a notable example of a prayer addressed to the Lord that conveys what the Jewish people believed about God and how they were called to live in accordance with that belief. The prayer, like wisdom literature in general, combines ways of thinking, believing, and living, teaching those who hear how to be faithful to the God in whom they believe.

The prayer begins with a restatement of the fundamental belief that there is only one God who cares for all people. The One who cares for everyone is the same God who judges them justly. Thus God's concern for all is coupled with an attribute that could be considered its opposite. The God who is compassionate is also the God who can condemn. As the prayer develops, the description of God continues to combine traits that manifest differing, often apparently contradictory, perspectives: God's sovereignty is linked with leniency; God shows divine power when people doubt or do not believe in that power.

Only God, who is all-powerful and all-loving, can exercise that power and love in a way that is totally free, not controlled by what people think or expect or even deserve. This prayer implies that what limits humanity's exercise of justice and power does not limit God's. Yet, though only God can manifest all of these characteristics fully, perfectly, and with absolute freedom, people are called to act in a similar way. God's actions in creation and his-

For meditation and context:

> **TO KEEP IN MIND**
> Pay attention to the pace of your reading. Varying the pace gives listeners clues to the meaning of the text. The most common problem for proclaimers new to the ministry is going too fast to be understood.

A very brief didactic reading. Don't rush it. This is important news—the Spirit knows what we need and intercedes for us, even when we can't. That's very good news.

As always, before you begin, make sure you have the full attention of your assembly.

This line sets up the main idea; set it apart.

God is the "one who searches hearts."

We are the holy ones.

> **TO KEEP IN MIND**
> Use inflection (the high or low pitch of your voice) to convey attitude and feeling. High pitch expresses intensity and excitement; low pitch expresses sadness, contrition, or solemnity.

RESPONSORIAL PSALM   Psalm 86:5–6, 9–10, 15–16 (5a)

R. Lord, you are good and forgiving.

You, O LORD, are good and forgiving,
  abounding in kindness to all who call
    upon you.
Hearken, O LORD, to my prayer
  and attend to the sound of my pleading.

All the nations you have made shall come
  and worship you, O LORD,
  and glorify your name.
For you are great, and you do wondrous
    deeds;
  you alone are God.

You, O LORD, are a God merciful and
    gracious,
  slow to anger, abounding in kindness
    and fidelity.
Turn toward me, and have pity on me;
  give your strength to your servant.

READING II   Romans 8:26–27

A reading from the Letter of Saint Paul to the Romans

Brothers and sisters:
The **Spirit** comes to the **aid** of our **weakness**;
  for we do not know how to **pray** as we **ought**,
  but the Spirit **himself** intercedes with inexpressible **groanings**.
And the **one** who searches **hearts**
  knows what is the intention of the Spirit,
  because he **intercedes** for the **holy** ones
  according to God's **will**.

---

tory have taught people how they are to pattern their own lives. Like God, people who are just must also be kind, and the human exercise of power must be tempered with leniency. This wisdom prayer expresses well that the way of praying, the *lex orandi*, becomes not only *lex credendi*, the way of believing, but also the *lex vivendi*, the way that people are to live based on their prayer and their faith.

 It is not always easy to pray or to speak to God with the self-assurance of the wise that we heard in the First Reading. Though Paul's letters are filled with beautiful prayers, he also knew that we need the help of God's own Spirit as we attempt to pray—and Paul includes himself in that need: "*we* do not know how to pray as *we* ought."

Weakness limits us. We might contrast this weakness with the sovereign power of God described in the reading from Wisdom. Fundamentally a human condition, the weakness that we experience in prayer, and in all of life, is in part physical, in part intellectual, as well as spiritual and emotional. Paul recognizes that we need help!

The word that he uses for "help" is found in only one other passage in the New Testament when Martha asks that her sister Mary come to her aid (Luke 10:40). The verb means to share the responsibility of the task, to take part in the action *with* the other, not to take it over, but to join in it. As Martha wanted Mary's help, we likewise want the assistance of God's Spirit, the Spirit working within us, when we pray.

Twice Paul describes the Spirit's help as *interceding* for us, noting that this intercession is according to God's will. We can also understand the Spirit as pleading for

A narrative (parable) within a larger narrative.

Focus here on telling a good story, not on its meaning. Identify an intention (purpose) and emotion for each character—the householder, his enemy, and his servant.

Lower your voice to convey the secrecy of the enemy's action.

A legitimate question that should sound like a question.

The owner is confident that he can deal with the problem.

Pause.

Emphasize the contrast between the small and large.

Be expansive with your voice and face to convey the bounty that comes from this seed.

Pause.

Again, use your voice to convey the expansive effect of a small amount of yeast.

A longer pause.

GOSPEL   Matthew 13:24–43

A reading from the holy Gospel according to Matthew

[**Jesus** proposed another **parable** to the crowds, saying:
"The kingdom of **heaven** may be likened to a man
   who sowed **good** seed in his field.
While everyone was **asleep** his **enemy** came
   and sowed **weeds** all through the **wheat**, and then went off.
When the crop **grew** and bore **fruit**, the weeds appeared as **well**.
The slaves of the householder came to him and said,
   '**Master**, did you not sow **good** seed in your field?
Where have the **weeds** come from?'
He answered, 'An **enemy** has done this.'
His slaves said to him,
   'Do you want us to go and **pull** them up?'
He replied, '**No**, if you pull up the **weeds**
   you might uproot the **wheat** along with them.
Let them grow **together** until harvest;
   then at harvest time I will say to the harvesters,
   "First collect the **weeds** and tie them in bundles for **burning**;
   but gather the **wheat** into my **barn**."'"]

He proposed **another** parable to them.
"The kingdom of heaven is like a **mustard** seed
   that a person took and **sowed** in a field.
It is the **smallest** of all the seeds,
   yet when full-**grown** it is the **largest** of plants.
It becomes a **large** bush,
   and the '**birds** of the sky come and **dwell** in its branches.'"

He spoke to them **another** parable.
"The kingdom of heaven is like **yeast**
   that a woman took and **mixed** with three measures
     of wheat flour
   until the **whole** batch was **leavened**."

---

us before God, expressing what we ourselves are unable to articulate. In addition, Paul describes the Spirit's intercession as groaning, comparable to the groaning of the whole creation and of ourselves as we eagerly await God's gifts of redemption (Romans 8:22–23).

Weak though we are, we have already received the firstfruits, the very presence of God's Spirit who breathes within us as we come before God in prayer. Paul's assertion here that the Spirit will help us in our weakness reinforces his boasting elsewhere of his own weakness; the Lord

informed him, "My grace is sufficient for you, for my power is made perfect in weakness" (2 Corinthians 12:9). The good news for us is that weakness, even in prayer, is the very place God's grace is brought to perfection.

GOSPEL What is the Kingdom of Heaven? How can we understand something that we cannot readily see or measure or touch? The Kingdom of Heaven is a mystery so multifaceted, that there is always more to understand. With so much to grasp while

leaving so much still to comprehend, Jesus chose the language of poetry and parable to offer sketches of God's Kingdom. Whether lengthy stories or simple metaphors, Jesus' parables have the power to ignite the imagination and to open up possibilities of meaning, even as they raise intriguing questions for further reflection.

As he invites his audience to consider the meaning of the Kingdom of Heaven, Jesus presents three parables, each one drawing on what is familiar to illustrate dimensions of the Kingdom. In each of the three parables, Jesus says that the

This is a more intimate setting. Lower your volume and intensity to indicate the closeness of the space.

They're confused.

Gently, with patience.

Pause.

The focus of this action is clearing the world of all evil.

In his compassion, no doubt Jesus feels some of this pain himself as he describes the fate of the evildoers.

Use the word "then" to change your tone as you describe the joyous fate of the righteous.

All these things Jesus spoke to the crowds in **parables**.
He spoke to them **only** in parables,
    to **fulfill** what had been said through the prophet:
        *I will open my mouth in **parables**,*
            *I will **announce** what has lain **hidden** from*
            *the **foundation** of the world.*

Then, **dismissing** the crowds, he went into the house.
His **disciples** approached him and said,
    "**Explain** to us the parable of the weeds in the field."
He said in **reply**, "He who sows **good** seed is the Son of **Man**,
    the field is the **world**, the good seed the **children**
        of the kingdom.
The **weeds** are the children of the **evil** one,
    and the **enemy** who sows them is the **devil**.
The **harvest** is the end of the age, and the harvesters are **angels**.
Just as **weeds** are collected and burned up with **fire**,
    so will it be at the **end** of the age.
The Son of Man will send his **angels**,
    and they will collect out of his kingdom
    all who cause **others** to sin and all **evildoers**.
They will **throw** them into the **fiery** furnace,
    where there will be **wailing** and **grinding** of teeth.
Then the righteous will **shine** like the sun
    in the kingdom of their Father.
Whoever has ears ought to **hear**."

[Shorter: Matthew 13:24–30 (see brackets)]

Kingdom of Heaven "may be compared," or "is like." He doesn't give a definition, but presents pictures that are windows into the mystery of the Kingdom. The first parable, the most developed of the three, begins with one person who sowed seed and another who sowed weeds. This is the only parable for which Jesus gives an interpretation to his disciples. Viewed as an allegory, the sower is Jesus himself, the Son of Man; the enemy who sows weeds is the Devil. Though wheat and weeds are allowed to grow together, at the final judgment the evil and the righteous will be separated, one to a fiery punishment and the other to "shine like the sun." In this interpretation, the children of the Kingdom within the *Church* are contrasted with the children of the evil one in the *world*.

Since parables are open-ended, offering more than one way to understand them, we can also see the admixture of wheat and weeds within the Church itself where we experience both healthy, vigorous wheat, and unhealthy, destructive weeds growing and struggling and striving. Further, we can see in ourselves both good and evil, wheat and weeds present in our hearts, our thoughts, and our actions. Whichever way we look at the parable, we see that God who sows the good seed remains present, patient, and attentive. And ultimately, whether it is the world, the Church, or ourselves, the final judgment is left to God, not to us. E.P.

SEVENTEENTH SUNDAY IN ORDINARY TIME

LECTIONARY #109

A narrative that calls your assembly to live or act differently.

Solomon = SOL-uh-muhn

Emphasize "dream" rather than "night."
Solomon feels overwhelmed by the responsibility he's been given. Let his anxiety and self-doubt come through in his prayer.

"Not knowing at all how to act" is a refreshingly honest statement.

Here the vastness of Israel is a reason for Solomon's concern. Recall a time you you felt overwhelmed and project that feeling here.

Let God's pleasure show in your voice and eyes and face.

Try to imagine wisdom and understanding of this great depth.

READING I   1 Kings 3:5, 7–12

A reading from the first Book of Kings

The LORD appeared to **Solomon** in a **dream** at night.
God said, "**Ask** something of me and I will **give** it to you."
Solomon answered:
  "O LORD, my **God**, you have made me, your servant, **king**
      to succeed my father **David**;
    but I am a mere **youth**, not knowing at **all** how to act.
I serve you in the midst of the people whom you have **chosen**,
      a people so **vast** that it cannot be **numbered** or **counted**.
Give your servant, therefore, an **understanding** heart
      to **judge** your people and to distinguish **right** from **wrong**.
For **who** is able to govern this **vast** people of yours?"

The LORD was **pleased** that Solomon made this request.
So God said to him:
    "Because you have asked for **this**—
    not for a **long** life for yourself,
    nor for **riches**,
    nor for the life of your **enemies**,
    but for **understanding** so that you may know what is **right**—
    I **do** as you requested.
I give you a heart **so** wise and understanding
      that there has never been **anyone** like you up to now,
      and **after** you there will come no one to **equal** you."

READING I At the shrine of Gibeon where he had offered sacrifice, King Solomon has a dream in which the Lord appears to him. As in other dreams in the biblical tradition, it is a divine communication in which God takes the initiative, offering Solomon whatever he wants. Before making his request, Solomon recalls God's steadfast love to his father David. He describes himself as God's servant, adding, "I am a mere youth"—meaning that he lacks the leadership experience necessary for a king. Solomon also speaks of the great number of people he must gov-

ern. For these reasons, taking into consideration both his own limitations and the vast number of people, Solomon asks God for an understanding heart so he will be able to govern justly, discerning between right and wrong.

The one word that best describes what Solomon requests is "wisdom." That Solomon asks to be able to rule with understanding and right judgment, rather than a long life, riches, or defeat of enemies, is one sign that he already has a certain amount of wisdom. His humble stance before God is another. God—generous both

in taking the initiative and in the gift—imparts even more than Solomon asks for. God grants Solomon a heart so wise that neither before nor after him will anyone be equal in wisdom. His wisdom will be a benefit not only for Solomon but also for his kingdom.

READING II Today's reading is the culmination of Paul's discourse in which he ponders suffering, weakness, and the presence of God's Spirit in the midst of any travail we may experience. Thus when he says "*all* things work

For meditation and context:

TO KEEP IN MIND

A *didactic* text makes a point or teaches something. Help your assembly to follow the argument and understand what's being taught.

RESPONSORIAL PSALM   Psalm 119:57, 72, 76–77, 127–128, 129–130 (97a)

R. Lord, I love your commands.

I have said, O LORD, that my part
   is to keep your words.
The law of your mouth is to me more precious
   than thousands of gold and silver pieces.

Let your kindness comfort me
   according to your promise to your
     servants.
Let your compassion come to me that
   I may live,
     for your law is my delight.

For I love your commands
   more than gold, however fine.
For in all your precepts I go forward;
   every false way I hate.

Wonderful are your decrees;
   therefore I observe them.
The revelation of your words sheds light,
   giving understanding to the simple.

A short but significant didactic reading about the generosity and justice in God's great plan.

READING II   Romans 8:28–30

A reading from the Letter of Saint Paul to the Romans

Be very deliberate with this statement. It's the key to the whole reading. Keep the two phrases together, with a very short pause at the comma.

This is why all things work for good—because we have been made into the image of Jesus.

Each of these statements is better news than the previous one. Heighten them by starting with a natural pace, then slowing on the second, and slowing even more on the final phrase and the word "glorified."

Brothers and sisters:
We know that **all** things work for **good** for those who **love** God,
   who are **called** according to his **purpose**.
For those he **foreknew** he also **predestined**
   to be **conformed** to the **image** of his Son,
   so that he might be the **firstborn**
   among **many** brothers and sisters.
And those he **predestined** he also **called**;
   and those he **called** he also **justified**;
   and those he **justified** he also **glorified**.

---

for good" he is affirming that there is good even in the midst of the many ways humans suffer. He also means that God is clearly the one whose actions accomplish that good. This does not mean that pain and suffering will be eliminated, but that God will bring good even out of that suffering.

As Paul continues his reflection, he presents a rich array of God's actions: God calls, foreknows, predestines, conforms, justifies, and glorifies. The one divine action that has probably caused the most confusion is that of predestining. The notion of predestination that says God decides from

all eternity that some will be saved and others will be doomed forever is not what Paul means here. Rather, all the verbs, including predestining, indicate that God has a plan and the power to bring it to fulfillment. In the divine plan God knows all things, calls slave and free, women and men, Jews and Gentiles (Galatians 3:28); God conforms them all to Jesus, justifies and glorifies them. Paul's focus is not on individuals, but on the "grand scheme," a predetermined plan to bring all things and all people together in Christ (see Ephesians 1:10). God's purpose is positive, inclusive, power-

ful, and generous. We joyfully proclaim God's eternal, salvific plan in this reading.

GOSPEL   Jesus' parables in today's Gospel present inanimate objects as images of the Kingdom of Heaven: a treasure, fine pearls, and a net cast into the sea. Each highlights a different dimension of the mysterious Kingdom of Heaven. In the first two parables, the hidden treasure and a fine pearl are objects of great value. In both cases, someone finds the precious item, and then sells all they have to buy it. With these common elements, we

A string of narrative parables. Why does Jesus share so many different images of the Kingdom with his disciples? He really wants them, and us, to understand. Bring this same sense of urgency to your proclamation.

Proclaim with the joy of the treasure hunter.

Proclaim with the excitement of the merchant.

Keep the sense of Jesus' urgency.

Pause.

This is a real question. Look directly at your assembly and ask them.

"Ok, then, if you understand, you must act as if you do!"

GOSPEL   Matthew 13:44–52

A reading from the holy Gospel according to Matthew

[Jesus said to his disciples:
   "The kingdom of **heaven** is like a **treasure** buried in a **field**,
   which a person **finds** and **hides** again,
   and out of **joy** goes and sells **all** that he has and **buys** that field.
Again, the kingdom of heaven is like a **merchant**
   searching for fine **pearls**.
When he finds a pearl of great **price**,
   he goes and **sells** all that he has and **buys** it.]
Again, the kingdom of heaven is like a **net thrown** into the sea,
   which collects fish of **every** kind.
When it is **full** they haul it **ashore**
   and sit down to put what is **good** into buckets.
What is **bad** they throw **away**.
Thus it will be at the **end** of the age.
The **angels** will go out and separate the **wicked**
     from the **righteous**
   and throw them into the fiery **furnace**,
   where there will be **wailing** and **grinding** of teeth.

"Do you **understand** all these things?"
They answered, "**Yes**."
And he replied,
   "Then every **scribe** who has been **instructed** in the kingdom
     of heaven
   is like the **head** of a household
   who brings from his storeroom both the **new** and the **old**."

[Shorter: Matthew 13:44–46 (see brackets)]

---

can easily see that the Kingdom is of immense worth. The differences in the two parables bring to light less obvious insights. The person who found the treasure wasn't looking for it, but found an unexpected windfall, whereas the merchant was actually out looking for fine pearls. The Kingdom breaks into the world whether people are oblivious of God's hidden grace or are actively seeking it.

Like the parable of the pearl, that of the net cast into the sea involves people who are expecting to find something of worth. An added aspect is the separation of the good and the bad fish, symbolic of the division of the righteous and the evil at the end of the age. Like the seeds and the weeds in last week's Gospel, they remain together in the present age.

The treasure, pearl, and net are not the only pictures of the Kingdom of Heaven. So too are the people involved. Their actions indicate how people are engaged in Kingdom pursuit. Hope of possessing a great treasure or fine pearls or a good catch of fish directs their actions even before they acquire anything. Seeking a way to obtain the desired object and working diligently toward obtaining it are hope-filled actions. Similarly, hope for the Kingdom of Heaven directs the actions of all of us who would be Jesus' disciples. E.P.

THE TRANSFIGURATION OF THE LORD

LECTIONARY #614

READING I   Daniel 7:9–10, 13–14

A reading from the book of the Prophet Daniel.

As I **watched**:
　　Thrones were set up
　　　and the **Ancient One** took his throne.
His clothing was **bright** as **snow**,
　　and the hair on his head as **white** as **wool**;
His **throne** was **flames** of fire,
　　with **wheels** of burning **fire**.
A surging **stream** of **fire**
　　flowed out from where he **sat**;
Thousands upon **thousands** were ministering to him,
　　and **myriads** upon **myriads** attended him.
The **court** was **convened** and the **books** were **opened**.

As the **visions** during the night **continued**, I saw:
　　One like a **Son of man** coming,
　　　on the clouds of **heaven**;
when he reached the **Ancient One**
　　and was **presented** before him,
the one like a **Son of man** received **dominion**, **glory**,
　　and **kingship**;
　　all **peoples**, **nations**, and **languages serve** him. **»**

A dramatic narrative describing a vision. Vivid details help set the scene and heighten the impact of the concluding insight about the mysterious figure Christians interpret as Christ.

Because the passage is so powerful and full of detail, take a brief pause after each sentence.

These numbers are signs of universality.

This Old Testament figure is seen in the Christian tradition as an allusion to Christ.

myriads = MEER-ee-uhdz

Take a longer pause at the end of this line.

We seldom hear the readings for the Transfiguration because it is not an obligatory feast. When it falls on a Sunday in Ordinary Time, however, it takes precedence. That is why we are honored with its readings today rather than those for the Eighteenth Sunday in Ordinary Time.

READING I The Book of Daniel is named for the hero of the stories in its first six chapters. Daniel, who has a special gift of wisdom, has been chosen along with three other young Jewish exiles in Babylon, to be educated and to serve in the court of the Babylonian king. There they face many trials, such as the famous fiery furnace and the lion's den. In each case, their steadfast faith in the Hebrew God wins the day. Beginning in chapter 7, from which today's reading comes, the book presents a series of Daniel's visions. These visions belong to the "apocalyptic" genre—a type of vivid, dramatic narrative written during times of persecution. Daniel's visions were composed in the second century BC when Jews were being forced to adopt Greek culture and religious practices. They were intended to comfort the persecuted Jews, strengthen them in their faith, and assure them that justice will triumph in the end.

In this powerful vision, an enthroned figure, the Ancient One, with dazzling white clothing and hair is worshipped by "thousands upon thousands." Verses omitted from today's reading describe this as a court of judgment in which terrible beasts who have exercised power over the world are condemned and removed from power. Our reading picks up when a new figure enters the scene: "one like a Son of man," who arrives coming "on the clouds of

His **dominion** is an **everlasting** dominion
　　that shall not be taken away,
　his **kingship** shall not be **destroyed**.
The word of the Lord.

The final verse reveals what God bestows on Christ, and it is a reign of cosmic proportions. Proclaim it boldly.

For meditation and context:

RESPONSORIAL　Psalm 97:1–2, 5–6, 9–12 (1a, 9a)

R. **The Lord is king, the Most High over all the earth.**

The Lord is king; let the earth rejoice;
　let the many islands be glad.
Clouds and darkness are round about him,
　justice and judgment are the foundation
　　of his throne.

R. **The Lord is king, the Most High over all the earth.**

The mountains melt like wax before the Lord,
　before the Lord of all the earth.
The heavens proclaim his justice,
　all peoples see his glory.

R. **The Lord is king, the Most High over all the earth.**

Because you, O Lord, are the Most High
　　over all the earth,
　exalted far above all gods.

R. **The Lord is king, the Most High over all the earth.**

TO KEEP IN MIND
Use inflection (the high or low pitch of your voice) to convey attitude and feeling. High pitch expresses intensity and excitement; low pitch expresses sadness, contrition, or solemnity.

This didactic reading serves as Peter's eyewitness testimony to the events described in today's Gospel.

Reading II　2 Peter 1:16–19

A reading from the second Letter of Saint Peter

Beloved:
We did not follow cleverly devised **myths**
　　when we made **known** to you
　　the **power** and **coming** of our Lord Jesus Christ,
　　but we had been **eyewitnesses** of his **majesty**.
For he received **honor** and **glory** from **God** the **Father**
　　when that unique **declaration** came to him from the
　　　majestic glory,

The first- and second-person plural pronouns—"we," "our," "ourselves," "you," and "your"—can be adopted by you and proclaimed anew to the Church before you.

---

heaven." He is presented to the enthroned figure and given "dominion, glory, and kingship." Through this vision, Jews drew strength from the Lord and the Messiah dispatching the evil forces. Christians in later centuries were also comforted by this scene of heavenly justice, but saw a prophecy of God the Father entrusting the world to the care of his Son, Jesus Christ. That interpretation makes this reading a particularly appropriate choice for the Feast of the Transfiguration of the Lord.

READING II　Today all three readings point to Christ as the one empowered and sent to us by the Father. This passage from the Second Letter of Peter, written in the persona of the Apostle Peter (but most likely authored by later followers) takes up this theme with the same purpose as the author of the Book of Daniel: to encourage his audience to hold fast to their faith, in this case, faith in Jesus Christ. The author first reminds us of the Father's voice from heaven at Jesus' baptism: "This is my Son, my beloved, with whom I am well pleased." Then, as an eye-

witness to the events reported in today's Gospel, ("We ourselves heard . . . ") he refers to the voice of God again commending Jesus Christ to us. What stronger confirmation of the "prophetic message" about Christ's identity could we desire? He urges us to "be attentive" to it as if it were "a lamp shining in a dark place."

GOSPEL　We heard this Gospel reading on the Second Sunday of Lent, but today we hear it in a different context—Ordinary Time, when the Scriptures have been chosen to help us under-

Pause slightly before you deliver this line so that the assembly is poised to recognize the link with the narrative of Jesus' own baptism.

These final images of light—"lamp shining," "day dawns," and "star rises"—are wonderful. Visualize them as you proclaim them forthrightly and clearly.

"**This** is my **Son**, my beloved, with whom I am **well pleased**."
We **ourselves** heard this voice come from heaven
    while we were **with** him on the holy **mountain**.
Moreover, we possess the prophetic **message** that is
    altogether **reliable**.
You will do **well** to be **attentive** to it,
    as to a **lamp shining** in a dark place,
    until day **dawns** and the morning star **rises** in your **hearts**.

A dramatic narrative with compelling characters and supernatural effects. Give it your best storytelling skills.

Pronounce each name carefully.

Set the scene clearly so that your listeners can visualize it.

Let your voice convey that a vision is unfolding.

This is truly amazing!

Moses = MOH-zis; Elijah = ee-LĪ-juh

Pause slightly before "Then Peter."

Peter is overcome with the excitement of the moment. Quicken your pace for his words.

Slow down and build suspense for the most dramatic moment that is coming: the voice.

Emphasize the words from the cloud; they echo the words from above heard at Jesus' baptism.

Gospel   Matthew 17:1–9

Jesus took **Peter**, **James**, and his brother, **John**,
    and led them up a high **mountain** by **themselves**.
And he was **transfigured** before them;
    his face **shone** like the **sun**
    and his **clothes** became **white** as **light**.
And **behold**, **Moses** and **Elijah appeared** to them,
    conversing with him.
Then **Peter** said to Jesus in reply,
    "**Lord**, it is **good** that we are here.
If you wish, I will make **three tents** here,
    one for **you**, one for **Moses**, and one for **Elijah**."
While he was still speaking, behold,
    a **bright** cloud cast a **shadow** over them,
    then from the **cloud** came a **voice** that said,
    "**This** is my beloved **Son**, with whom I am **well pleased**;
    listen to him."
When the **disciples** heard this, they fell prostrate
    and were very much **afraid**.
But **Jesus** came and **touched** them, saying,
    "**Rise**, and do not be **afraid**." »

stand the demands of discipleship. Just as the passages from Daniel and 2 Peter were written to strengthen the faith of their audiences, so the experience of Peter, James, and John on the mountain can revitalize our faith as disciples.

    Previous to today's Gospel reading, Jesus had presented major points of his teaching on a mountain, a setting that recalls God's gift of the Torah to Moses on Mount Sinai. Matthew thus portrays Jesus as true interpreter of the Law of Moses. In today's account of Jesus' Transfiguration, Matthew depicts Jesus as the one who ful-

fills the Law and the Prophets, symbolized by the figures of Moses, the Lawgiver, and Elijah, prominent among the great prophets of Israel. These figures appear with Jesus, but fade into the background after the revelation of divine presence in Jesus.

    The "bright cloud" reminds us of the guiding presence of God as a pillar of cloud in Israel's desert journey. The voice from the cloud describes Jesus as "beloved Son," recalling the divine voice heard at Jesus' baptism. On the mountain, God's voice adds the command to "listen to him." In the Old Testament, to hear and obey God's

Word was the identifying mark of a genuine response to God. In the Transfiguration story, God calls all disciples to listen to his Son's teaching, in the words he speaks and in the self-giving death he will embrace. M.F./M.C./ed.

And when the disciples raised their eyes,
    they saw **no one** else but **Jesus alone**.

As they were coming down from the **mountain**,
    Jesus **charged** them,
    "Do not tell the **vision** to **anyone**
    until the Son of Man has been **raised** from the **dead**."

Slow your pace for this last statement.

TO KEEP IN MIND
You can't proclaim what you don't understand. Read the Scripture passage and its commentary in *Workbook*. Then read it from your Bible, including what comes before and after it so that you understand the context.

NINETEENTH SUNDAY IN ORDINARY TIME

LECTIONARY #115

READING I   1 Kings 19:9a, 11–13a

A reading from the first Book of Kings

At the mountain of God, **Horeb**,
    Elijah came to a **cave** where he took shelter.
Then the LORD said to him,
    "Go **outside** and **stand** on the mountain before the LORD;
    the **Lord** will be passing by."
A strong and heavy **wind** was **rending** the mountains
    and **crushing** rocks before the LORD—
    but the LORD was **not** in the wind.
After the wind there was an **earthquake**—
    but the LORD was **not** in the **earthquake**.
After the earthquake there was **fire**—
    but the LORD was **not** in the **fire**.
After the fire there was a tiny **whispering** sound.
When he **heard** this,
    Elijah **hid** his face in his cloak
    and went and **stood** at the entrance of the cave.

A powerful narrative, proclaiming that our God appears not only in great displays of power, but in the most intimate—and unexpected—places.

Horeb = HOHR-eb

Elijah = ee-LI-īuh

Pause.

Raise your intensity and convey the power of a wind strong enough to split rocks! Use the words "rending" and "crushing" to describe this power.

Again, raise your energy—it's an earthquake!

Raise your intensity one final time to describe the fire, as if it were a raging blaze covering the mountain.

Slow down and speak softly; lean in a little closer to the microphone (if there is one) so you can still be heard.

Keep a quiet tone, and proclaim these lines with awe and reverence, as if Elijah were narrating his own actions.

READING I   At Mount Horeb the prophet Elijah has an astounding, multisensory experience. As the First Book of Kings relates, Elijah had been fleeing the wrath of Jezebel, and then, following the instructions of an angel, traveled for forty days to the mountain of God. There, Elijah complains to God about the idolatry of the people who have killed other prophets and plan to take his life as well. God's responds by commanding Elijah to come out of his sheltering cave to see the Lord pass by. At the mouth of the cave, Elijah hears a mountain-splitting and rock-crushing wind, and then feels earthquake and fire. Such natural marvels are typical of theophanies, displays of God's power and presence. But God was not in any of these. After that prelude of dramatic wonders, Elijah hears only a single small whisper. He wraps his cloak around his face, a sign of reverence, as he recognizes God's mysterious presence, not in awesome phenomena, but in something apparently insignificant.

On Mount Horeb, also called Mount Sinai, Moses spent forty days and forty nights with God (Exodus 24:18). Like Elijah, Moses experienced a grand theophany of clouds and fire on the mountain, and the cave of Elijah reminds us of the cleft in the rock where the Lord passed before Moses—a divine self-revelation as mysterious as the whisper heard by Elijah (Exodus 33:18–23). The clear similarities between Moses and Elijah have led people to see Elijah as the fulfillment of God's promise to Moses, "I will raise up a prophet like you" (Deuteronomy 18:18). Elijah foreshadows an even greater prophet like Moses, Jesus, both prophet and manifestation of God's presence.

For meditation and context:

In this exhortatory reading, the emotions are plainly stated: "great sorrow and constant anguish." Recall a situation in your own life when you have experienced a similar rejection by those closest to you. Proclaim with the emotions that arise.

You're about to share a painful truth, known to yourself and to the Spirit, and now your assembly.

Be careful not to sound angry. Like a loving parent, you're willing to take on any punishment if it means life for your children.

You might show a hint of joy as you relate the gifts showered on these people. It's because they are so loved by God that Paul experiences such sorrow at their rejection of the Christian community.

RESPONSORIAL PSALM   Psalm 85:9, 10, 11–12, 13–14 (8)

R. Lord, let us see your kindness, and grant us your salvation.

I will hear what God proclaims;
    the LORD—for he proclaims peace.
Near indeed is his salvation to those who
    fear him,
    glory dwelling in our land.

Kindness and truth shall meet;
    justice and peace shall kiss.
Truth shall spring out of the earth,
    and justice shall look down from heaven.

The LORD himself will give his benefits;
    our land shall yield its increase.
Justice shall walk before him,
    and prepare the way of his steps.

READING II   Romans 9:1–5

A reading from the Letter of Saint Paul to the Romans

Brothers and sisters:
I speak the **truth** in Christ, I do not **lie**;
    my conscience joins with the Holy Spirit in bearing
        me **witness**
    that I have great **sorrow** and constant **anguish** in my heart.
For I could wish that I myself were **accursed** and cut **off**
        from Christ
    for the **sake** of my own people,
    my **kindred** according to the flesh.
They are **Israelites**;
    theirs the **adoption**, the **glory**, the **covenants**,
    the giving of the **law**, the **worship**, and the **promises**;
    theirs the **patriarchs**, and from **them**,
    according to the flesh, is the **Christ**,
    who is **over** all, God **blessed forever**. Amen.

READING II Paul's anguish in this passage is the setting for his explanation of how the Jews fit into God's plan of salvation. His grief over his fellow Jews' rejection of Christ is so great that he would even consider being "accursed and cut off from Christ" for the sake of his "kindred." From the time of his conversion, having failed to evangelize other Jews, Paul has been a missionary to the Gentiles. But he always retained a deep love for his own people.

After emphasizing his personal involvement, Paul lists privileges that God has already given to his people. These are ancient favors, but Paul makes it clear that God has not withdrawn them. First, they are Israelites, the people with whom God made the covenant. Because of the covenant, Israel is adopted by God, making them into God's own sons and daughters. Next, God's gift of glory is a tangible manifestation of divine presence to Israel throughout their history. Israel's covenants express their oft-renewed pact with God, first made with Abraham, solemnized with Moses, and extending to King David. The Law, worship, and promises, beginning with the patriarchs, are further assurance of the continuing relationship with God. Most importantly, Christ himself, the promised anointed one, has come from this people. By concluding his list of benefits with "God blessed forever, Amen," Paul moves from anguish to praise.

GOSPEL As Matthew often does, in today's Gospel he combines a portrait of Jesus with a portrait of his disciples. In this episode, Jesus again goes away by himself while he sends his disciples into a boat. This is the second

An exciting narrative. It shouldn't sound like you're relating an everyday occurrence or the evening news. Let all the emotions and drama come through.

This is the setup. Don't linger, but keep your energy and pace up to engage your assembly in the story.

Just before dawn; it is difficult to see clearly.

Don't rush "walking on the sea." It should sound as strange and startling as it is!

Of course they would be!

Quickly, and with anxiety.

Jesus speaks quickly but calmly. His is not a rebuke but words of comfort.

Invite gently.

Take this slowly; it's just as amazing as Jesus' appearance. Stand up straight and proclaim with the confidence of Peter.

Immediately pick up your pace and raise your energy through to Peter's cry.

Don't swallow "sink."

Keep your pace up.

How does Jesus sound? Fill the line, and especially the word "O," with that emotion.

Pause.

Slowly, with reverence and awe, and perhaps even some fear.

GOSPEL   Matthew 14:22–33

A reading from the holy Gospel according to Matthew

After he had **fed** the people, Jesus made the disciples get
    into a **boat**
  and **precede** him to the other side,
  while he **dismissed** the crowds.
After doing so, he went up on the mountain by **himself** to pray.
When it was **evening** he was there **alone**.
Meanwhile the **boat**, already a few miles **offshore**,
  was being **tossed** about by the waves, for the **wind** was
    against it.
During the **fourth** watch of the night,
  he came **toward** them **walking** on the **sea**.
When the disciples **saw** him walking on the sea they
  were **terrified**.
"It is a **ghost**, " they said, and they cried out in **fear**.
At **once** Jesus spoke to them, "Take **courage**, it is **I**; do **not**
  be **afraid**."
Peter said to him in reply,
  "**Lord**, if it **is** you, command me to **come** to you on the water."
He said, "**Come**."
Peter got **out** of the boat and began to **walk** on the **water**
  toward Jesus.
But when he saw how **strong** the wind was he became
  frightened;
  and, beginning to **sink**, he **cried** out, "Lord, **save** me!"
Immediately Jesus stretched out his **hand** and **caught** Peter,
  and said to him, "**O** you of **little** faith, why did you **doubt**?"
After they got into the boat, the wind **died** down.
Those who were in the boat did him **homage**, saying,
  "**Truly**, you are the Son of **God**."

disciples-in-a-boat scene in Matthew's Gospel, and each has been interpreted both realistically and figuratively. A long tradition sees the boat as a symbol of the Church; "being tossed about," literally "being tortured," gives a vivid picture of what the Church experiences. In such tossing, Jesus seems to be absent until his disciples see him walking on the water, an action only God can do (Isaiah 43:16). The disciples are understandably terrified, but Jesus commands them to stop being afraid. He then says simply, "It is I," the same way that God had identified himself to Moses at the burning bush (Exodus 3:13–15). Jesus' portrait is majestic, mysterious, and redolent of the God known to the Jewish people.

Peter represents both a Church leader and a typical disciple. That he urges Jesus to command him to come to him on the water, and addresses him as "Lord" both indicate a certain amount of faith. Yet when Peter becomes more focused on the wind than on Jesus, he falters. Though Peter does have some faith, Jesus recognizes its littleness, addressing Peter as if his name were "Man of Little Faith." Peter's only hope is to call out to Jesus to save him. His plea is the plea of the whole Church, asking that the Lord protect her against the torturing storms of life. When Jesus, along with Peter, gets into the boat, everyone there worships him and acknowledges him as Son of God, present in the Church as her Savior. E.P.

THE ASSUMPTION OF THE BLESSED VIRGIN MARY: VIGIL

LECTIONARY #621

READING I 1 Chronicles 15:3–4, 15–16; 16:1–2

A narrative. See the story unfold before you as you proclaim. Let your face and voice reflect your emotions as you watch.

Chronicles = KRAH-nih-k*ls

This is a big deal! Everyone is there.

Aaron = AYR-uhn
Levites = LEE-vīts

This is a solemn event, but also one of great joy!

Let the excitement of the day come through as you describe the music.

lyres = līrz
cymbals = SIM-buhlz

You can lower your energy a bit to indicate the mystery unfolding here.

Don't lose the word "blessed." Convey this blessing to your community as well.

A reading from the first Book of Chronicles

David assembled **all** Israel in **Jerusalem** to bring the **ark** of the LORD
    to the place that he had **prepared** for it.
David also called together the sons of **Aaron** and the **Levites**.

The Levites **bore** the ark of God on their **shoulders** with **poles**,
    as Moses had ordained according to the word of the LORD.

David **commanded** the chiefs of the Levites
    to appoint their kinsmen as **chanters**,
    to play on musical instruments, **harps**, **lyres**, and **cymbals**,
    to make a **loud** sound of **rejoicing**.

They brought in the **ark** of God and **set** it within the tent
    which David had **pitched** for it.
Then they offered up **burnt** offerings and **peace** offerings to God.
When David had **finished** offering up the burnt offerings and
    peace offerings,
    he **blessed** the people in the **name** of the LORD.

READING I | King David had a deep and intense desire to bring the ark of the covenant to Jerusalem, settling it in a place of honor that he had prepared for it. His first attempt to transfer the ark failed, apparently because of David's impetuous actions that ignored cultic obligations. David admits, "The wrath of the LORD our God burst upon us, for we did not seek him aright" (1 Chronicles 15:13). In this account, describing the second attempt to transfer the ark, David observes all the cultic requirements of the Torah; only the Levites were to carry the ark, as ordained by Moses. Because of the holiness of the ark, those who handled it—the priests and Levites—were required to carefully sanctify themselves. The chanting and musical instruments add both solemnity and joy as the holy object, sign of God's glory and presence among the people, is brought to Jerusalem. When the ark is safely set within the tent, the offering of sacrifice and the blessing of the people give honor to God and express the unity of those who celebrate.

All of the rituals recounted in this reading emphasize the holiness of the ark; it is God's own dwelling place, welcomed with joyful music. This ancient ark of the covenant has long been understood by Christians as a type or foreshadowing of Mary. She is a new ark of God, the place where God has made a home. In her, God's holiness dwells; she too is cause for joy. The honor given to her, like the honor given to the ark in the Hebrew tradition, is fundamentally honor given to God, and expresses the unity of mind and heart of all who celebrate her feast.

For meditation and context:

TO KEEP IN MIND

Exhortatory texts make an urgent appeal to listeners. They may encourage, warn, or challenge, and often include a call to action. You must convey the urgency and passion behind the words.

An exhortatory reading which also teaches the central tenet of our faith: life has conquered death through Jesus Christ.

Corinthians = kohr-IN-thee-uhnz

Proclaim with expectant hope!

Paul quotes this poem or hymn. Let it be heard as a quotation, resounding with equal energy and joy.

Slight pause after "But." Take this slowly and look directly into the community.

RESPONSORIAL PSALM   Psalm 132:6–7, 9–10, 13–14 (8)

R. Lord, go up to the place of your rest, you and the ark of your holiness.

Behold, we heard of it in Ephrathah;
   we found it in the fields of Jaar.
Let us enter into his dwelling,
   let us worship at his footstool.

May your priests be clothed with justice;
   let your faithful ones shout merrily for joy.
For the sake of David your servant,
   reject not the plea of your anointed.

For the LORD has chosen Zion;
   he prefers her for his dwelling.
"Zion is my resting place forever;
   in her will I dwell, for I prefer her."

READING II   1 Corinthians 15:54b–57

A reading from the first Letter of Saint Paul to the Corinthians

Brothers and sisters:
When that which is **mortal** clothes itself with **immortality**,
   then the word that is **written** shall come about:

> **Death** is swallowed up in **victory**.
> **Where**, O death, is your **victory**?
> **Where**, O death, is your **sting**?

The **sting** of death is **sin**,
   and the **power** of sin is the **law**.
But **thanks** be to **God** who gives us the **victory**
   through our **Lord** Jesus **Christ**.

READING II The Resurrection of Jesus is a mystery so rich and multifaceted that there is always more for reflection. In chapter 15 of his First Letter to the Corinthians, Paul writes extensively about the Resurrection, reacting to the Corinthians' lack of belief, which is shocking and distressing to Paul. "How can some among you say there is no resurrection of the dead?" (15:12), he asks, using the question as a springboard for his teaching. Presenting two other questions, "How are the dead raised? With what kind of body will they come back?" (15:35), he explores the implications of Jesus' Resurrection for mortals who have "fallen asleep," or who are still there "at the last trumpet." Having begun his explanation of this mystery, Paul brings it to a conclusion in the portion we hear in today's reading.

Though we now wear mortal clothing, we will change our temporary garments to be clothed with immortality. Paul's imagery evokes the transfigured Jesus, whose clothing was radiant and dazzling white. Just as death was not victorious over Jesus, neither is it for those who die in him. No victory! No sting! Paul's confident proclamation combines prophecies from Isaiah and Hosea, both of which announce God's power over death. Even greater than the message from these Hebrew prophets, Christ's victory over death is also his victory over sin. Paul maintains here (and elsewhere in his letters) that death is the result of sin. But sin and death alike are conquered by Christ, victoriously risen. The Resurrection of Jesus is the powerful and mysterious source for our own victory over sin and death, moving Paul to conclude his exposition with a short but profound thanksgiving to God.

A short narrative with two exhortations. Don't rush it.

Raise your voice and energy. The woman is overcome with excitement and can't help but cry out these words of praise.
Blessed = BLES-uhd

Pause; don't drop your energy but lower your volume. Blessed = BLES-uhd

Careful not to make Jesus' reply sound like a rebuke. He doesn't negate the woman's blessing of his mother, but offers an even better blessing, available to everyone.

GOSPEL   Luke 11:27–28

A reading from the holy Gospel according to Luke

While Jesus was **speaking**,
a **woman** from the crowd **called out** and said to him,
"**Blessed** is the **womb** that **carried** you
and the **breasts** at which you **nursed**."
He replied,
"**Rather**, **blessed** are those
who **hear** the word of God and **observe** it."

THE 4 STEPS OF *LECTIO DIVINA* OR PRAYERFUL READING

1. *Lectio:* Read a Scripture passage aloud slowly. Notice what phrase captures your attention and be attentive to its meaning. Silent pause.

2. *Meditatio:* Read the passage aloud slowly again, reflecting on the passage, allowing God to speak to you through it. Silent pause.

3. *Oratio:* Read it aloud slowly a third time, allowing it to be your prayer or response to God's gift of insight to you. Silent pause.

4. *Contemplatio:* Read it aloud slowly a fourth time, now resting in God's word.

GOSPEL The beatitudes that are most familiar to us are those in Jesus' Sermon on the Mount: "Blessed are the poor in spirit, for theirs is the kingdom of heaven" (Matthew 5:3), followed by other proclamations of God's generous blessing. The beatitudes in Jesus' sermon, like the others in the Old and New Testaments, are exclamations acknowledging God's abiding, grace-filled relationship with the one who is blessed. In today's Gospel, we hear two beatitudes, the first one from a woman in the crowd, and the second from Jesus himself.

The beatitude shouted out by the anonymous woman simultaneously honors both mother and son, with the mother praised precisely because of her son. Similarly, the remembrance of Sarah, Hannah, and other women both named and unnamed in the Old Testament is closely connected with the memorable stories of their noteworthy sons. Thus the beatitude proclaimed by the woman in today's Gospel is grounded in the Jewish tradition that reveres mothers because of their sons. Jesus' beatitude provides another, much broader, reason for God's blessing. All those who hear the Word of God and keep it are recipients of God's loving kindness. His own mother is a living example in Luke's Gospel of one who heard and obeyed God's Word. Beginning with the Annunciation and continuing throughout Luke's opening chapters, Mary listens and responds with an absolute "yes." That is the reason she, and all those who likewise hear and keep God's Word, are blessed by God. E.P.

THE ASSUMPTION OF THE BLESSED VIRGIN MARY: DAY

LECTIONARY #622

READING I   Revelation 11:19a; 12:1–6a, 10ab

A reading from the Book of Revelation

God's **temple** in heaven was **opened**,
    and the **ark** of his covenant could be **seen** in the temple.

A great **sign** appeared in the sky, a **woman** clothed with the **sun**,
    with the **moon** under her **feet**,
    and on her **head** a **crown** of twelve **stars**.
She was with **child** and **wailed** aloud in pain as she **labored** to
      give birth.
Then **another** sign appeared in the sky;
    it was a huge red **dragon**, with seven **heads** and ten **horns**,
    and on its heads were seven **diadems**.
Its tail **swept** away a third of the **stars** in the sky
    and **hurled** them down to the **earth**.
Then the dragon **stood** before the woman about to give birth,
    to **devour** her child when she gave birth.
She gave **birth** to a son, a **male** child,
    destined to rule **all** the nations with an iron **rod**.
Her child was **caught up** to God and his **throne**.
The woman herself **fled** into the **desert**
    where she had a place prepared by **God**. »

A narrative filled with fantastical images. It demands great energy and passion in its telling.

Start with heightened intensity.

Each part of this image is more amazing than the last!

Your voice might have a sinister tone, but keep your energy up to convey the ferocity of this creature.

Slow down on "huge red dragon," then return to a normal pace.

Use the words "swept" and "hurled" to show the beast's power.

Pause.
Slow down and lower your intensity a little. This is moment of joy.

Pick up your pace again; "caught up" and "fled" indicate quick action.

A sense of relief; all will be well. Pause.

READING I Taken from the Book of Revelation, this reading is an example of "apocalyptic" literature—characterized by visions, secret revelations, and language that is highly symbolic and imaginative. Frequent features of this literary genre include conflict between good and evil that extends beyond earth to shake the entire cosmos; divine judgment in which wickedness is finally destroyed; and veiled, mysterious images that are open to multiple interpretations.

The reading opens with a vision in heaven where we see familiar earthly objects: the Temple and the ark of the covenant. Whereas the holiest place in the earthly Temple is accessible only to the high priest and only once a year, the heavenly temple is open to all. As the vision continues, a great sign appears in the sky: a woman surrounded by heavenly bodies of sun, moon, and stars. This celestial woman, first described in images far removed from human and earthly experience, is then described in terms well known and graphic. She is with child, wailing in pain as she labors to give birth.

After the brief introduction to the woman, another sign appears, a beastly dragon that sweeps away a full third of the stars in the sky, and stands ready to devour the woman's child. The expected apocalyptic conflict has begun. Without explaining how the woman and her child escape the dreaded dragon, we hear that the son to whom she gives birth is destined to rule all nations and that he was caught up to God, while the woman fled safely to the desert.

Given apocalyptic multifaceted symbolism, the woman has been understood as representing Israel, the Church, or the

Then I heard a **loud** voice in heaven say:
  "**Now** have **salvation** and **power** come,
    and the **Kingdom** of our **God**
    and the **authority** of his **Anointed** One."

For meditation and context:

TO KEEP IN MIND
A didactic reading is usually given out of love for the community. Make sure that love is evident in your proclamation.

A didactic reading about the implications of Resurrection; there is great joy in this teaching.
Corinthians = kohr-IN-thee-uhnz

Paul repeats the same point: that Christ's Resurrection prefigures our own in different ways.

This should sound self-evident.

What follows is a list of three events.

This is good news. The world will be freed from every oppression and evil. Don't make it sound like a terrible Armageddon.

Slight pause after "for" so the final phrase sounds like a quote.

RESPONSORIAL PSALM Psalm 45:10, 11, 12, 16 (10bc)

R. **The queen stands at your right hand, arrayed in gold.**

The queen takes her place at your right hand in gold of Ophir.

Hear, O daughter, and see; turn your ear, forget your people and your father's house.

So shall the king desire your beauty; for he is your lord.

They are borne in with gladness and joy; they enter the palace of the king.

READING II 1 Corinthians 15:20–27

A reading from the first Letter of Saint Paul to the Corinthians

Brothers and sisters:
Christ has been **raised** from the dead,
  the **firstfruits** of those who have fallen **asleep**.
For since **death** came through **man**,
  the **resurrection** of the dead came **also** through man.
For just as in **Adam** all **die**,
  so too in **Christ** shall **all** be brought to **life**,
  but each one in proper **order**:
  Christ the **firstfruits**;
  then, at his **coming**, those who **belong** to Christ;
  then comes the **end**,
  when he **hands** over the **Kingdom** to his **God** and Father,
  when he has **destroyed** every **sovereignty**
  and every **authority** and **power**.
For he must **reign** until he has put **all** his enemies under his feet.
The **last** enemy to be destroyed is **death**,
  for "he subjected **everything** under his feet."

mother of Jesus. Whichever meaning is ascribed to her, she is in conflict with evil, the seven-headed dragon that is unable to destroy her child. She and the child are ultimately victorious, finding refuge by God's power. While the woman can easily be interpreted in different ways, the child, whether born of Israel, the Church, or Mary, is clearly Jesus. After these mysterious and polyvalent signs, the end of the reading is a loud proclamation, unmistakable in its meaning: Jesus is the Anointed One, the Christ, in whom salvation, power, authority, and the Kingdom of God have

come. This apocalyptic vision has portrayed conflict ending with victory.

READING II The opening sentence of this reading presents Paul's foundational, deeply held belief: Jesus has been raised from the dead. Paul's transformation from persecutor of Christians to ardent Apostle of Jesus Christ, his extensive missionary activity, his endurance through persecution, his teaching, and letter-writing, all flow from his conviction that Christ has been raised from the dead. As the firstfruits of those who have died, the

risen Christ is the promise, the source, and the pattern of Resurrection for those who belong to him. Just as the firstfruits of a crop display what is expected for the rest of the harvest, so too does Christ's Resurrection reveal the destiny of all who are in communion with him.

In order to explain this mystery for the Corinthian community, Paul draws on the Jewish tradition, in which he is well versed. As death came to all humanity through one person, Adam, so too will life come through one person, Christ. Employing imagery from the Psalms (8:7 and 110:1), Paul says

A narrative which includes an exhortation.

Keep up your pace to indicate Mary's haste.

Judah = JOO-duh

Zechariah = zek-uh-RĪ-uh

Immediately smile as you convey Elizabeth's joy.

Let your voice "leap" as well.

There's great excitement in Elizabeth's voice.
Blessed = BLES-uhd

She can't contain her excitement.

GOSPEL   Luke 1:39–56

A reading from the holy Gospel according to Luke

Mary set out
    and traveled to the hill country in **haste**
    to a town of **Judah,**
    where she entered the house of **Zechariah**
    and greeted **Elizabeth.**
When Elizabeth **heard** Mary's greeting,
    the infant **leaped** in her womb,
    and Elizabeth, **filled** with the Holy **Spirit,**
    cried out in a **loud** voice and said,
    "**Blessed** are you among women,
    and **blessed** is the **fruit** of your **womb.**
And how does this happen to **me,**
    that the mother of my **Lord** should come to **me?**
For at the **moment** the sound of your greeting reached my **ears,**
    the **infant** in my womb **leaped** for **joy.**
Blessed are you who believed
    that what was **spoken** to you by the **Lord**
    would be **fulfilled.**"

that the reigning risen Christ will subject everything, putting all enemies under his feet—even death itself, that came to all through Adam.

The "proper order" in which this happens, as Paul describes it, begins with Christ's Resurrection; then, at his coming again, known as the Parousia, those who belong to him will also be raised. After this, the end will come, when Christ hands over everything to his Father, and every enemy will be vanquished. Paul's proclamation about Christ's Resurrection, his Parousia, and the final conquering of all enemies is a

promise of hope for believers. On this solemnity celebrating the Assumption of Mary, we look to her as the first of those who have received this glorious promise.

GOSPEL   The title usually given to this Gospel account is "The Visitation," a title we can understand from a variety of perspectives. It is, on the narrative level, the visit of Mary, having traveled in haste from Galilee to Judah, to be with her cousin Elizabeth. Though separated by age and distance, the two women have each been visited by a miraculous divine

action that brings about their pregnancies. Though the account does not describe details of their meeting, it is easy to imagine the shared wonder, questions, and joy as they tell their stories.

We can also see the meeting of the two women as the visitation of God with the people. Mary has carried in her womb the very person of the Lord, joyfully acknowledged by Elizabeth. Filled with the Holy Spirit, Elizabeth pronounces blessing on both the mother and the child in her womb. Along with her blessing, she questions how "the mother of my Lord" could

This song pours from Mary's heart, as if Elizabeth's greeting has banished all fear and anxiety from her, and her pent-up joy overflows into praise. Keep your energy and pace up.

Proclaim as if Mary is speaking directly to Elizabeth—someone with whom she can share her most intimate thoughts; blessed = BLESD

These images portray God as the help of the poor and lowly, vanquisher of the rich and powerful.

Pause, as if to allow Mary to catch her breath.

Drop your energy slightly and take your time on this last line.

> **TO KEEP IN MIND**
> In a narrative, find an emotion or point of view for each character, keeping in mind that these might change during the reading.

And **Mary** said:

"My soul proclaims the **greatness** of the Lord;
   my spirit **rejoices** in God my Savior
      for he has with **favor** on his lowly servant.
From this day **all** generations will call me **blessed**:
   the Almighty has done **great** things for me
      and **holy** is his Name.
He has **mercy** on those who fear him
   in **every** generation.
He has shown the **strength** of his arm,
   and has scattered the **proud** in their conceit.
He has cast down the **mighty** from their **thrones**,
   and has **lifted** up the **lowly**.
He has **filled** the hungry with **good** things,
   and the **rich** he has sent away **empty**.
He has come to the **help** of his servant Israel
   for he has remembered his promise of **mercy**,
      the promise he made to our **fathers**,
      to Abraham and his children for **ever**."

Mary remained with her about three months
   and then **returned** to her home.

come to her. Elizabeth's question resonates with King David's wonder at the visit of the ark of the covenant to him (2 Samuel 6:9). Both the ark of the covenant and the Virgin Mary are tangible signs of God's presence among the people, and cause for great joy. King David was even moved to dance before the ark. When Elizabeth's unborn child leaps for joy in her womb at the sound of Mary's greeting, we are reminded of David's spontaneous dance before the Lord's presence in the ark.

In the second part of the scene, Mary proclaims her prayer of praise. As she reflects on all that God has done in the past, she echoes the poetry and praise of other Hebrew women: Miriam, Hannah, and Judith. We can hear her joyful wonder at the many ways God visited the people throughout their history. Her prayer is an expansive review of God's saving actions for Israel in every generation, rightly called the Magnificat, since she enlarges the portrait of God for all of us to see. Mary praises God, not only for mercy in the past, but also in her own life, and offers a foretaste of what God will accomplish in the Son she carries in her womb. E.P.

TWENTIETH SUNDAY IN ORDINARY TIME

LECTIONARY #118

An exhortatory passage, in the voice of God, proclaiming God's openness and availability to all. Give your proclamation a welcoming tone.

Isaiah = ī-ZAY-uh

Slight pauses after "right" and "just."

Take care with the structure of this sentence. Keep the two subject phrases ("The foreigners who join . . ." and "all who keep the sabbath . . .") connected to the action: "them I will bring to my holy mountain."

Pause after "servants—"

profanation = prah-fuh-NAY-shuhn

Pause after "covenant."

Human divisions means nothing; God welcomes all who love him. This is good news; let that be seen in your voice, eyes, and face.

Slow down on this last phrase.

READING I   Isaiah 56:1, 6–7

A reading from the Book of the Prophet Isaiah

Thus says the Lord:
Observe what is **right**, do what is **just**;
  for my **salvation** is about to **come**,
  my **justice**, about to be **revealed**.

The foreigners who **join** themselves to the Lord,
  ministering to him,
loving the name of the Lord,
  and becoming his **servants**—
all who keep the sabbath **free** from profanation
  and **hold** to my covenant,
them I will bring to my holy mountain
  and make **joyful** in my house of prayer;
their burnt **offerings** and **sacrifices**
  will be **acceptable** on my altar,
for my **house** shall be called
  a house of **prayer** for **all** peoples.

READING I   As the reading begins, Isaiah is reminding the Judean community of their covenantal obligations: doing what is right and just is essential to their identity as God's covenant partners. The reminder is timely, because God's own justice is about to be revealed. Justice, for humans and for God means living in right relationship. The people had long understood their duty to live in right relationship with God by loving the Lord's name, being his servants, observing the Sabbath, and holding to the covenant.

Then Isaiah announces that foreigners who join themselves to the Lord in the same way as Jews will also be brought into saving relationship with God. During the time of exile in Babylon and the return to Zion, many foreigners had had close contact with the Judeans, and became attracted to their religion and way of life. God is making it clear that when they act on this attraction by observing his Law, he will bring them to the holy mountain, Zion. Prayer, burnt offering and sacrifices, so important for worship among the Jews, will be equally acceptable when offered by for-

eigners. Although the Torah states that such offerings would be allowed in the Temple (as in Numbers 15:14–16; Leviticus 22:18–25), Isaiah's prophecy goes further. He tells the Jews that foreigners who observe covenant obligations can be like members of their own community. In effect, through Isaiah God is telling the Chosen People that God has also chosen all men and women who join themselves to him. The final verse expresses beautifully this universality of God's invitation: God's own house, the Temple, will be a house of prayer for all.

For meditation and context:

An exhortatory reading, with a complex, bittersweet tone. Let your assembly hear both Paul's joy in his ministry to the Gentiles, and his pain that his own people, the Jews, have not yet accepted the Gospel.

Their rejection can only lead to something even better when they accept. Set this key thought apart.

irrevocable = ih-REV-uh-kuh-b*l

Make the comparison clear. Emphasizing the bolded words and pausing only at commas will help.

Drop your voice slightly on this parenthetical phrase.

God's plan will win out in the end!

RESPONSORIAL PSALM   Psalm 67:2–3, 5, 6, 8 (4)

R. O God, let all the nations praise you!

May God have pity on us and bless us;
   may he let his face shine upon us.
So may your way be known upon earth;
   among all nations, your salvation.

May the nations be glad and exult
   because you rule the peoples in equity;
   the nations on the earth you guide.

May the peoples praise you, O God;
   may all the peoples praise you!
May God bless us,
   and may all the ends of the earth fear him!

READING II   Romans 11:13–15, 29–32

A reading from the Letter of Saint Paul to the Romans

Brothers and sisters:
I am speaking to you **Gentiles**.
Inasmuch as I am the **apostle** to the Gentiles,
   I **glory** in my ministry in order to make my race **jealous**
   and thus **save** some of them.
For if their **rejection** is the **reconciliation** of the world,
   what will their **acceptance** be but **life** from the dead?

For the **gifts** and the **call** of God are **irrevocable**.
Just as **you** once **disobeyed** God
   but have **now** received **mercy** because of **their** disobedience,
   so **they** have now **disobeyed** in order that,
   by virtue of the mercy shown to **you**,
   they **too** may now receive mercy.
For God delivered **all** to disobedience,
   that he might have **mercy** upon all.

READING II   In the reading from Isaiah, the prophet spoke to the Jews about including foreigners, or Gentiles, in God's saving plan. In the reading from Romans, we hear an opposite perspective. Here Paul speaks to Gentiles about how Jews are included in God's plan of salvation. Though the Jewish people had long understood themselves as God's chosen people, Paul is in anguish that most of his own kindred have not accepted the Messiah, apparently making Gentile believers now God's chosen ones. This personally heartrending situation motivates Paul's reflection.

Paul uses his own ministry to explain what he sees as the historical change-of-situation. Raised in Judaism, proud of his heritage, and intense in his fidelity to the Law, Paul was nevertheless, quite surprisingly, called by God to bring the Good News of the Messiah to the Gentiles. By converting Gentiles, Paul maintains, he will make his own people jealous, leading some of them to salvation.

Next, Paul reminds his Gentile audience that just as they once were disobedient, but have received God's mercy, so too will God show mercy to the presently disobedient Jews. In fact, Jewish refusal to accept Jesus as the Messiah was the very reason that Paul brought the Good News to the Gentiles. Jewish rejection of Jesus as the Messiah thus had a positive divine purpose: to bring God's mercy to the Gentiles. In the final step of Paul's logic, he concludes that God delivered everyone to disobedience so that God might have mercy on all.

A unique narrative in which a foreign woman persuades Jesus to change his mind. Don't suggest the end from the beginning, as if Jesus is only testing the woman. The drama of the encounter comes from seeing Jesus change his mind.

Tyre= tīr

Sidon = SĪ-duhn

Canaanite = KAY-nuh-nīt

What does the woman want? Healing for her daughter, yes, but also acknowledgment of her dignity.
Jesus has no intention of helping her.

The disciples ask Jesus to give her what she wants because they're bothered by her, not because they think she deserves dignity.
Give the woman a quiet intensity; she insists on being acknowledged while still respecting Jesus.
A harsh rebuke; don't try to soften it.

Pause. This is surprising; she's up to the task of arguing with Jesus!

How does Jesus sound? Amazed, impressed, compassionate?

> **TO KEEP IN MIND**
> A *narrative* has characters, dialogue, a setting, and action. Help your listeners see the story unfold, keep characters distinct, and be clear about shifts in setting.

GOSPEL   Matthew 15:21–28

A reading from the holy Gospel according to Matthew

At that time, **Jesus** withdrew to the region of Tyre and Sidon.
And **behold**, a **Canaanite woman** of that district came
    and **called** out,
  "Have **pity** on me, Lord, Son of **David**!
My daughter is **tormented** by a **demon**."
But Jesus did not say a **word** in answer to her.
Jesus' **disciples** came and asked him,
  "Send her **away**, for she keeps **calling** out after us."
He said in reply,
  "I was sent **only** to the lost sheep of the house of **Israel**."
But the woman came and did Jesus **homage**, saying,
    "Lord, **help** me."
He said in reply,
  "It is not **right** to take the food of the **children**
  and throw it to the **dogs**."
She said, "**Please**, Lord, for **even** the **dogs** eat the scraps
  that fall from the table of their masters."
Then Jesus said to her in reply,
  "**O** woman, **great** is your faith!
Let it be **done** for you as you **wish**."
And the woman's daughter was **healed** from that hour.

GOSPEL | After arguing with the Pharisees on what makes a person clean or unclean, Jesus withdraws into the pagan territory of Tyre and Sidon, an area considered unclean by Jesus' opponents. It is not surprising that Jesus would encounter Gentiles in that region; it is surprising, however, that a Canaanite woman there would approach Jesus so directly to heal her daughter, and even more that she would address him with a title rich in meaning for Jews: Lord, Son of David. Jesus' disciples urge him to send the woman away because she has behaved improperly in approaching Jesus, and because as a Canaanite, she belongs to an ancient enemy of the Jews. Jesus even tells her that food for the children ought not be thrown to the dogs, using a derogative term, "dog," that was often applied to Gentiles by Jews of the time.

Perhaps because Jesus has already crossed a boundary by entering into pagan territory, the woman boldly asks him to cross another one. She appears neither insulted nor deterred in pushing for the cure of her daughter, and in fact uses a humorous play on Jesus' reference to dogs. Surely, she insists, the pet dogs under the table can have some scraps that fall from the master's table.

Both her words and her actions show a greatness of faith that stands in sharp contrast with the littleness of faith that Jesus' own disciples have shown (see Matthew 8:26; 14–31). What started out as a rejection culminates in the healing of her daughter. Jesus' insistence that he came for the lost sheep of Israel does not mean that Gentiles who come in faith will be excluded. Jesus' love and compassion has no boundaries. E.P.

TWENTY-FIRST SUNDAY IN ORDINARY TIME

LECTIONARY #121

An exhortatory reading, in God's voice.

Isaiah = Ī-ZAY-uh

Shebna = SHEB-nah

God is clearly angry at Shebna (who is more concerned with fortifications and political alliances than with trusting God; see Isaiah 22:10–19). Let this sound like anger.

Eliakim = ee-LĪ-uh-kim

Hilkiah = hil-KĪ-uh

Emphasize how different Eliakim will be. Let your feelings show about your choice.

Today's Gospel refers to this passage; slow a little.

Take pleasure in the good work that Eliakim will do.

READING I Isaiah 22:19–23

A reading from the Book of the Prophet Isaiah

Thus says the LORD to **Shebna**, master of the **palace**:
"I will **thrust** you from your office
  and **pull** you down from your station.
On **that** day I will summon my **servant**
  Eliakim, son of Hilkiah;
I will **clothe** him with your **robe**,
  and **gird** him with your **sash**,
  and give **over** to him your **authority**.
He shall be a **father** to the inhabitants of Jerusalem,
  and to the house of Judah.
I will place the **key** of the House of David on **Eliakim's**
  shoulder;
  when he **opens**, no one shall **shut**,
  when he **shuts**, no one shall **open**.
I will **fix** him like a **peg** in a **sure** spot,
  to be a place of **honor** for his family."

[handwritten annotations:]
Contrary to what God said, then Isaiah — Shebna pushed King Hezekiah to go to war.
① Has governing power
② He can allow or prohibit access to palace + to King.
③ Like tent peg He will keep people secure.

READING I The brief condemnation of Shebna, a steward in charge of the royal palace of King Hezekiah, is actually the conclusion of a longer indictment against him. Shebna's "crimes" are not specified, but they are significant enough that he is deposed, with the transfer of power shifted to Eliakim, son of the high priest Hilkiah. The rest of the reading focuses on Eliakim's authority and the role that he will assume, all in God's own words. The Lord will clothe him with robe and sash, symbols of his divinely given authority, explained further by three images. First, calling him "father" indicates a relationship with the people that goes far beyond that of palace steward; as a father to the inhabitants of Jerusalem and Judah, he will participate in the governing power of the Davidic dynasty for the whole southern kingdom. Second, as keeper of the key of the House of David, Eliakim will have the power to allow or prohibit entrance into the palace; he thus has authority to decide who will have access to the king. The third image is that of a peg that securely fastens the tent. This image presents Eliakim as the one who will see to the safekeeping of those in his care.

According to the Second Book of Kings (22:8), Eliakim's father Hilkiah had brought honor to his family by finding a copy of the book of the Law that was the impetus for reforms instituted by King Josiah. Now Eliakim has the opportunity to bring further honor by acting as a wise father, a careful guardian, and a living symbol of stability.

READING II Faced with the reality that most of his Jewish kindred have not accepted Jesus, Paul utilized his

For meditation and context:

RESPONSORIAL PSALM   Psalm 138:1–2, 2–3, 6, 8 (8bc)

R. Lord, your love is eternal; do not forsake the work of your hands.

I will give thanks to you, O Lord, with all
   my heart,
  for you have heard the words of my mouth;
in the presence of the angels I will sing
   your praise;
  I will worship at your holy temple.

I will give thanks to your name,
   because of your kindness and your truth:
when I called, you answered me;
  you built up strength within me.

The Lord is exalted, yet the lowly he sees,
  and the proud he knows from afar.
Your kindness, O Lord, endures forever;
  forsake not the work of your hands.

> **TO KEEP IN MIND**
> Use inflection (the high or low pitch of your voice) to convey attitude and feeling. High pitch expresses intensity and excitement; low pitch expresses sadness, contrition, or solemnity.

An exhortatory exclamation in praise of God's wisdom. Keep your energy up throughout.

Fill the word "Oh" with Paul's joy, wonder, and excitement.
inscrutable = in-SKROO-tuh-b*l (unknowable)

No one!

Pause.

Pause at the period after "forever."

READING II   Romans 11:33–36

A reading from the Letter of Saint Paul to the Romans

Oh, the depth of the riches and **wisdom** and **knowledge** of God!
How **inscrutable** are his judgments and how **unsearchable**
   his ways!
   For **who** *has* **known** *the mind of the Lord*
     or **who** *has been his* **counselor***?*
   Or who has given the Lord **anything**
     that he may be repaid?
For **from** him and **through** him and **for** him are **all** things.
To him be glory **forever**. **Amen**.

---

own experience and education in creating a solution to this painful situation. Drawing on the heritage of the Old Testament, as well as Hellenistic forms of rhetoric, Paul concluded that God's salvation would extend to everyone. Yet, even after all his complicated explanation, Paul seemed to realize that his arguments couldn't answer all his questions; the mystery of God's saving plan is beyond human comprehension. God's judgments, Paul says, are inscrutable; God's ways are unsearchable.

Just as he had found language and images in the Old Testament to conclude

that God will have mercy on all (Romans 11:32), Paul also found biblical passages that pointed to the difficulty of comprehending God's ways. Not surprisingly, he relied on Isaiah, the prophet most frequently cited by New Testament writers. Paul quotes Isaiah 40:13–14, part of a longer passage where the prophet asks questions about creation, God, and humanity's relationship with God. Both Isaiah and Paul pose questions in order to push their audiences to reflect more and more deeply on the grandeur, the immensity, and "the depth of the riches and wisdom and knowl-

edge of God!" Having exhausted his capacity to provide a cogent explanation about God's plan of salvation, Paul shifts to give praise and glory to God. Ultimately, it is not logical explanation of the great mysteries, but lived participation in them, enhanced by prayer, that is most important for Paul and for all who believe in Jesus.

GOSPEL Who is Jesus? Answers to this question are woven throughout the Gospel accounts, inspiring all who hear the story to answer the question for themselves. Today, Jesus asks his

A narrative which is mostly dialogue. Identify an intention and emotion for each character—Jesus, Peter, and the disciples.

Caesarea Philippi = sez-uh-REE-uh fih-LIP-ī

Jesus really wants to know what people think.

Proclaim as if these three answers are given by three different disciples.

Clearly the crowds don't fully understand him, so Jesus asks his closest friends.

Jesus is excited, even relieved, that Peter understands!

Jesus trusts Peter to continue his ministry after he is gone. How does Jesus sound as he entrusts Peter with this ministry?

Drop your voice slightly to convey the intimacy and trust in this relationship.

> **TO KEEP IN MIND**
> Pray the text, using your favorite method of praying with Scripture.

GOSPEL   Matthew 16:13–20

A reading from the holy Gospel according to Matthew

Jesus went into the region of Caesarea Philippi and
    he asked his disciples,
   "**Who** do people say that the Son of Man **is**?"
They replied, "**Some** say John the **Baptist**, others **Elijah**,
    still others **Jeremiah** or one of the **prophets**."
He said to them, "But who do **you** say that I am?"
Simon **Peter** said in reply,
   "You are the **Christ**, the **Son** of the living **God**."
Jesus said to him in reply,
   "**Blessed** are you, **Simon** son of **Jonah**.
For **flesh** and **blood** has not revealed this to you, but my
     heavenly **Father**.
And so I **say** to you, **you** are **Peter**,
   and upon this **rock** I will build my **church**,
   and the gates of the **netherworld** shall **not** prevail against it.
I will give you the **keys** to the kingdom of **heaven**.
Whatever you **bind** on earth shall be **bound** in heaven;
   and whatever you **loose** on earth shall be **loosed** in heaven."
Then he **strictly** ordered his disciples
   to tell **no** one that he was the **Christ**.

---

disciples what other people are saying about him. Suggestions that Jesus is John the Baptist, Elijah, Jeremiah, or one of the prophets have a common insight: Jesus acts like the great prophets of Judaism, each of whom anticipates the inauguration of God's reign. When Jesus asks his disciples how *they* would answer the question, Simon Peter speaks for the group. Jesus is the Christ, the long-awaited Messiah. The hopes for what this Messiah would be varied widely, but people commonly expected him to be a powerful advocate for the Jewish people. Added to the messianic title,

Peter declares Jesus to be Son of the living God, an exalted title expressing the unique filial relationship of Jesus with his Father.

Although Peter's later words will indicate that he didn't understand the full meaning of his testimony, Jesus praises him, calling him blessed and the recipient of God's revelation. Making a word play on the nickname "Peter" (*Petros*), Jesus declares him to be the rock (*petra*) on which he will build his Church. The keys that Jesus gives him recall those given to Eliakim. Like Eliakim, Peter will act with

authority; what he declares on earth will be affirmed in heaven.

Jesus' final words to the disciples order them to tell no one he is the Christ. All who encounter Jesus will understand his messiahship only when he completes his journey. His Passion, Death, and Resurrection will reveal the mysterious answer to the question, "Who is Jesus?" E.P.

TWENTY-SECOND SUNDAY IN ORDINARY TIME

LECTIONARY #124

An exhortatory lament directed to God. Let all of Jeremiah's frustration, pain, and anger come through in your proclamation.

Jeremiah = jayr-uh-MĪ-uh

Note that Jeremiah puts the responsibility for his situation on both God and himself.

How do you feel when others mock and laugh at you?

Use the words "cry out," "violence" and "outrage" to convey the intensity of the prophet's feelings.

This is defiance; makes sure it sounds like it!

Pause.
Feel the fire burning in your body. Start the lines slowly and build intensity through to the end.
Pause at the end before speaking the closing dialogue calmly.

READING I Jeremiah 20:7–9

A reading from the Book of the Prophet Jeremiah

You **duped** me, **O** Lord, and I **let** myself be duped;
    you were too **strong** for me, and you **triumphed**.
All the day I am an object of **laughter**;
    everyone mocks me.

Whenever I **speak**, I must **cry** out,
    violence and **outrage** is my message;
the word of the Lord has brought me
    derision and **reproach** all the day.

I say to myself, I will not **mention** him,
    I will speak in his name no **more**.
But then it becomes like fire **burning** in my heart,
    imprisoned in my bones;
I grow **weary** holding it in, I cannot **endure** it.

READING I Jeremiah's vocation, received when he was first called by God, involves both destruction and rebuilding (Jeremiah 1:10). He is an unwilling prophet to unwilling audiences, and here we find him experiencing disillusionment, anger, and self-pity. He sees himself as persecuted by people who plot against him, and persecuted even more harshly by the God who called him. As he shouts his lament before God, Jeremiah sees his own life as a living example of the destruction he was called to preach.

Jeremiah cries out that God is responsible for all of his suffering. God enticed Jeremiah, and Jeremiah allowed himself to be tricked. Although the purpose of his preaching was to bring people to repentance, it results instead in making Jeremiah an object of scorn. As much as he tries to resist continuing his prophecy of judgment against people, priests, and kings, Jeremiah cannot stop! When he says that he *must* cry out, he refers simultaneously to the abiding impact of his God-given vocation, the strength of God's Word, and the urgency of the message. The power of God's Word overwhelms him; it is like fire burning within him, imprisoned in his very bones.

Today's reading is only a brief portion of one of the six laments among Jeremiah's prophecies. Vehement and accusing as he is, it is significant that he continues to address all his pain to God. God alone is the one who can understand the depths of Jeremiah's grief, and the only one who can rebuild prophet and people.

For meditation and context:

RESPONSORIAL PSALM   Psalm 63:2, 3–4, 5–6, 8–9 (2b)

R. My soul is thirsting for you, O Lord my God.

O God, you are my God whom I seek;
    for you my flesh pines and my soul thirsts
    like the earth, parched, lifeless and
        without water.

Thus have I gazed toward you in the
    sanctuary
    to see your power and your glory,
for your kindness is a greater good than life;
    my lips shall glorify you.

Thus will I bless you while I live;
    lifting up my hands, I will call upon
        your name.
As with the riches of a banquet shall my soul
        be satisfied,
    and with exultant lips my mouth shall
        praise you.

You are my help,
    and in the shadow of your wings I shout
        for joy.
My soul clings fast to you;
    your right hand upholds me.

An exhortation encouraging your community to conform themselves completely to Christ. It's brief, so take your time.

READING II   Romans 12:1–2

A reading from the Letter of Saint Paul to the Romans

Don't make this sound like a rebuke. Rather, you might even smile as you give your community some excellent advice which will bring them life!

Of course not!

Take your time and make each of these three fruits distinct.

I **urge** you, brothers and sisters, by the **mercies** of God,
    to offer your bodies as a **living** sacrifice,
    holy and **pleasing** to God, your spiritual worship.
Do not **conform** yourselves to this age
    but be **transformed** by the **renewal** of your **mind**,
    that you may **discern** what is the will of God,
    what is **good** and **pleasing** and **perfect**.

READING II   Today's brief passage from Romans, addressed to both Jewish and Gentile Christians, provides the foundation for the pattern of life to be embraced by all believers. It follows Paul's exposition in Romans 9–11 where he presents God's merciful plan of salvation. Although Paul is writing to the entire community, his appeal is also made to each individual member of the body of Christ. The word "therefore" in the original Greek text (but not carried over in the Lectionary reading we hear) connects this passage with the section that precedes it, the

description of God's merciful plan for salvation: ("I urge you, *therefore*"). Paul is thus signaling that their way of life is a response to God's mercy. The behavior that he is urging on them will guide them in living in accordance with the mercy that God has showered on them.

Paul first explains that the believers' own bodies are to become living sacrifices. The Hebrew prophets had taught that sacrifices are meaningless unless accompanied by repentance and living in accordance to the covenant. Paul, expanding on this insight, is teaching that believers' entire

way of life is sacrificial; their whole existence is offered to God. Whereas the offering of sacrifices in the Jewish Temple is a fleeting act, the living sacrifice of believers embraces every moment and every dimension of their lives. Paul says that their minds must be transformed so that they no longer conform to the limited, temporary, and earthbound way of thinking of this age. Their transformation in Christ, through the mercy of God, will empower them to discern God's will. More than simply a new understanding, the renewal of the minds of believers is a participation in the newness

A narrative focusing on Peter and Jesus. Make sure you know what each of them wants (their intentions) and feels (their emotions). It might be more complex than it first appears. Could Jesus be tempted by Peter's suggestion? Is he conflicted?

Speak these lines with Jesus' emotion. How does he feel about these sufferings?

Don't gloss over this announcement. It would have been shocking to the disciples.

Note that Peter has taken Jesus aside for a one-on-one conversation. Proclaim with intensity rather than volume.

Raise your volume on this rebuke.

In these lines, Jesus is speaking about his followers, but he's also speaking about himself and his own free choice to give up his life. How does he feel about this choice?

Nothing!

GOSPEL   Matthew 16:21–27

A reading from the holy Gospel according to Matthew

Jesus began to **show** his disciples
    that he must go to **Jerusalem** and **suffer** greatly
    from the elders, the chief priests, and the scribes,
    and be **killed** and on the **third** day be **raised**.
Then **Peter** took Jesus aside and began to **rebuke** him,
    "God **forbid**, Lord! No such thing shall **ever** happen to you."
He turned and said to Peter,
    "Get **behind** me, Satan! You are an **obstacle** to me.
You are thinking not as **God** does, but as human **beings** do."

Then Jesus said to his disciples,
    "Whoever wishes to come **after** me must **deny** himself,
    take up his cross, and **follow** me.
For whoever wishes to **save** his life will **lose** it,
    but whoever **loses** his life for **my** sake will **find** it.
What **profit** would there be for one to gain the whole **world**
    and forfeit his **life**?
Or **what** can one give in **exchange** for his life?
For the Son of Man will come with his **angels** in his
        Father's **glory**,
    and then he will **repay** all according to his **conduct**."

TO KEEP IN MIND
Use inflection (the high or low pitch of your voice) to convey attitude and feeling. High pitch expresses intensity and excitement; low pitch expresses sadness, contrition, or solemnity.

---

of all creation accomplished through the Paschal Mystery of Christ.

GOSPEL   After Simon Peter had identified Jesus as the Messiah, Son of the living God, Jesus began to teach his disciples what kind of Messiah he is. Like most of their contemporaries, Jesus' disciples expected the Messiah to be powerful and to give them a privileged place. How shocking and distressing Jesus' teaching about suffering and death must have been! And his words about rising on the third day would not have calmed their angst. With many Jews of the era, they would have believed in resurrection on the last day, but would have been mystified at the notion of Jesus' rising before the final conquering of all evil.

Peter, the one who had spoken for the group in answering the question "But who do *you* say that I am?" now expresses the concern in all of their minds. He rebukes Jesus for even suggesting something so unthinkable. Peter is the tempter, Satan, urging Jesus to change the path that must pass through suffering and death. Now Jesus gives another epithet to Peter.

Instead of being a foundational rock, he is an obstacle, literally a *skandalon*, a stumbling stone, put in someone's path that causes them to trip. Jesus tells Peter to "get behind" him; that is, he must follow Jesus, taking up a cross as Jesus did. What Jesus says about his own dying and rising, his own loss and finding of life, teaches his disciples of every age about their own death and resurrection, about losing their lives to find them again eternally. E.P.

TWENTY-THIRD SUNDAY IN ORDINARY TIME

LECTIONARY #127

READING I   Ezekiel 33:7–9

A reading from the Book of the Prophet Ezekiel

Thus says the LORD:
> **You**, son of man, I have appointed **watchman** for the house
>   of Israel;
> when you **hear** me say anything, you shall **warn** them for me.
If I tell the wicked, "**O** wicked one, you shall **surely** die,"
>   and you do not **speak** out to dissuade the wicked from his way,
>   the wicked shall **die** for his guilt,
>   but I will hold **you** responsible for his death.
But if you **warn** the wicked,
>   trying to **turn** him from his way,
>   and he **refuses** to turn from his way,
>   **he** shall die for his guilt,
>   but **you** shall **save** yourself.

A narrative that unfolds entirely in God's voice, in which he sets high expectations for Ezekiel's ministry.

Ezekiel = ee-ZEE-kee-uhl

God addresses Ezekiel. How might this sound?

Implicit in this statement is " . . . if you don't change your ways."

Keep your pace up. These are simple and clear instructions; there's no need to linger.

READING I   God speaks directly to the prophet Ezekiel, "You, son of man," giving him a frequently repeated designation rich in meaning. As a son of man, the prophet is a weak human being who shares in human suffering, often in the depths of humiliation. Along with fellow Jews, Ezekiel had been exiled to Babylon, far from land and Temple, sharing in the suffering of all the exiles. From his own place of humiliation, Ezekiel preaches his dramatic, often disturbing message in words and symbolic actions. He also serves as a mediator between God and the peo-ple, and is in some way a representative of the whole nation.

In this passage, God reaffirms Ezekiel's initial prophetic call and assigns to him the role of watchman. A sentinel looks out over the city and must warn the people of impending danger, whether from inside or outside the city walls. In this case, Ezekiel must pass on the warning that comes directly from God. Ezekiel's responsibility is a heavy one; if he fails to warn the wicked according to God's words, Ezekiel himself will be responsible for their death. However, he will not be responsible if they refuse to heed his message. As a divinely appointed prophet, Ezekiel's task is to deliver God's words; the task of the people is to listen and repent. Through the prophet, God's warnings offer the people a chance for new life, even in exile, if only they will take heed. Listen, repent, and receive God's blessings: this is a prophetic message reiterated by all of Israel's proph-ets, including the greatest prophet, Jesus.

READING II   In last Sunday's reading from Romans, Paul tells the community members to offer their entire

For meditation and context:

TO KEEP IN MIND
Proclamation cannot be effective unless it is expressive. As you prepare your proclamation, make choices about emotions. Some choices are already evident in the text.

RESPONSORIAL PSALM   Psalm 95:1–2, 6–7, 8–9 (8)

R. If today you hear his voice, harden not your hearts.

Come, let us sing joyfully to the LORD;
    let us acclaim the rock of our salvation.
Let us come into his presence with
        thanksgiving;
    let us joyfully sing psalms to him.

Come, let us bow down in worship;
    let us kneel before the LORD who made us.
For he is our God,
    and we are the people he shepherds,
        the flock he guides.

Oh, that today you would hear his voice:
    "Harden not your hearts as at Meribah,
        as in the day of Massah in the desert,
    where your fathers tempted me;
        they tested me though they had seen
            my works."

A didactic reading, but it demands a passionate proclamation.

READING II   Romans 13:8–10

A reading from the Letter of Saint Paul to the Romans

Brothers and sisters:
Owe **nothing** to anyone, except to **love** one another;
    for the one who **loves** another has **fulfilled** the law.
The commandments, "You shall not commit **adultery**;
    you shall not **kill**; you shall not **steal**; you shall not **covet**,"
    and whatever **other** commandment there may be,
    are summed up in this saying, **namely**,
    "You shall **love** your **neighbor** as **yourself**."
Love does no **evil** to the neighbor;
    hence, **love** is the **fulfillment** of the law.

Move through these quickly; they're not what Paul is emphasizing.

Slight pause after "saying."

Slow down; set this line apart.

The word "hence" gives us a clue that this is the key to the reading. Take this final phrase slowly and deliberately.

lives in sacrifice. He continues his exhortation by giving specific examples of behavior and attitudes that flow from a sacrificial life. In today's reading, Paul summarizes the way of life of believers with one word: love. Not only does love summarize the life of Christians, it is also a fulfillment of the Law of the Jewish tradition. In these three verses, Paul uses forms of the word "love" (*agape*) five times. Prior to this summary, Paul had written about diverse details of Christian obligations, from the practice of hospitality, to blessing those who persecute us, to associating with the lowly, to

the paying of taxes. All such actions are included under the rubric of love.

After telling the Roman community about the obligation of paying taxes, Paul continues, saying they should owe nothing, except to love. Paying taxes or any other monetary debt does not discharge the lifelong debt of loving one another. The commandments of the Law are examples of how we pay this debt of love. Rather than being restrictive, they offer a pathway for loving relationships with God and neighbor.

Both Jesus and Paul cite Leviticus 19:18 regarding loving our neighbor as our-

selves, thereby fulfilling the Law (Matthew 5:43; Romans 13:9). The great Rabbi Hillel (around 70–10 BC) had a similar insight: "What is hateful to you, do not do to your neighbor: that is the whole Torah, while the rest is commentary on it. Go and learn." Love is the essence and the summit of the Law, and of life in Christ.

GOSPEL   In today's Gospel, taken from Jesus' discourse on the Church, he explains to his disciples a means of reconciling when one member of the community has sinned against another.

A didactic reading with insightful advice on how to deal with disagreement. This shouldn't sound like a law school lecture; rather, be eager to help your community resolve their conflicts.

Smile at this outcome.

Jesus is not suggesting "ganging up" on your offender; rather, you need to find others who agree with you that you were wronged. Offenders have a chance to make their case as well—and you might have to admit some fault yourself.
The whole community is responsible for and to each other.
"Then" . . . and only then.
Listen up!

How you treat others is how God will treat you; this teaching is echoed in the Our Father.

Jesus is present in every manifestation of true community.

GOSPEL   Matthew 18:15–20

A reading from the holy Gospel according to Matthew

Jesus said to his disciples:
   "If your brother **sins** against you,
     go and **tell** him his fault between you and him **alone**.
If he **listens** to you, you have **won** over your brother.
If he does **not** listen,
     take one or two **others** along **with** you,
     so that 'every fact may be established
     on the testimony of two or three **witnesses**.'
If he **refuses** to listen to **them**, tell the **church**.
If he refuses to listen **even** to the church,
     then treat him as you would a **Gentile** or a **tax** collector.
Amen, I say to you,
     whatever you **bind** on earth shall be **bound** in heaven,
     and whatever you **loose** on earth shall be **loosed** in heaven.
Again, amen, I say to you,
     if two of you **agree** on earth
     about **anything** for which they are to **pray**,
     it shall be **granted** to them by my heavenly Father.
For where **two** or **three** are gathered together in my **name**,
     there am I in the **midst** of them."

THE 4 STEPS OF *LECTIO DIVINA* **OR PRAYERFUL READING**

1. *Lectio:* Read a Scripture passage aloud slowly. Notice what phrase captures your attention and be attentive to its meaning. Silent pause.

2. *Meditatio:* Read the passage aloud slowly again, reflecting on the passage, allowing God to speak to you through it. Silent pause.

3. *Oratio:* Read it aloud slowly a third time, allowing it to be your prayer or response to God's gift of insight to you. Silent pause.

4. *Contemplatio:* Read it aloud slowly a fourth time, now resting in God's word.

Throughout his life, Jesus taught the importance of forgiveness, offering it even to those who had crucified him. Important as universal forgiveness is, Jesus' instruction here explains a process of reconciliation *within* the church, bringing a sinful member back into communion.

The three-step process that Jesus describes has roots in Judaism. In the Torah (Leviticus 19:17–18), reproving a fellow Israelite is a sign of love and keeps resentment from growing between them. If such correction is unsuccessful, bringing in one or two witnesses is the next step, keeping the division as private as possible. This shows respect for the erring brother or sister, and keeps the disagreement from spreading throughout the community. Only if these efforts fail is the whole group brought in. Jesus had earlier conferred the power to bind and loose on Peter (Matthew 16:19); now he extends that power to the wider Church. The Church will treat recalcitrant members as outsiders, such as Gentiles and tax collectors. Remember: even Gentiles and tax collectors are welcomed into the community if they believe in Jesus and show the fruits of repentance in their lives. So too will anyone who finally repents be welcomed home.

Throughout the process of healing divisions, Jesus remains present in the community. Even with as few as two or three witnesses, he is present in their efforts at reconciliation. E.P.

TWENTY-FOURTH SUNDAY IN ORDINARY TIME

LECTIONARY #130

READING I   Sirach 27:30—28:7

A reading from the Book of Sirach

Wrath and anger are **hateful** things,
   yet the sinner **hugs** them tight.
The vengeful will suffer the Lord's vengeance,
   for he **remembers** their **sins** in detail.
Forgive your neighbor's injustice;
   then when you pray, your **own** sins will be **forgiven**.
Could anyone nourish **anger** against another
   and expect **healing** from the Lord?
Could anyone refuse **mercy** to another like himself,
   can he seek **pardon** for his **own** sins?
If one who is but **flesh** cherishes **wrath**,
   who will forgive **his** sins?
Remember your last days, set **enmity** aside;
   remember death and decay, and **cease** from **sin**!
Think of the commandments, **hate not** your neighbor;
   remember the Most High's covenant, and **overlook faults**.

A didactic reading, proclaimed out of love for your community.

Sirach = SEER-ak or SĪ-ruhk

A compelling image!

God will treat the vengeful the same way they treat others.

Change your tone: "Don't be like that! Rather . . . "

Ridiculous!

These lines are complex; articulate them carefully.

Pause.

Really encourage your community! "Do it!"

Emphasize the phrases "hate not your neighbor" and "overlook faults."

READING I The book of Sirach, part of Israel's Wisdom literature, observes ordinary circumstances of life, and addresses the question: "How do I live wisely?" To answer, Sirach reflects on our shared humanity and on the covenant relationship with God. In this passage, he considers anger, vengeance, and forgiveness, and God's response to them.

When unchecked, anger can lead to vengeance, exacting "an eye for an eye," or even more severe reprisals. Sirach may have seen this personally, or be thinking of the biblical teaching against vengeance:

"Take no revenge and cherish no grudge against your own people" (Leviticus 19:18). Through Moses, God declared that only he can effect retribution: "Vengeance is mine" (Deuteronomy 32:35).

Sirach's insights on vengeance and forgiveness have a twofold application. First, he exhorts people to let go of anger and any desire for retaliation, to always be ready to reconcile. Second, he emphasizes each person's need for forgiveness. Certainly we hope for human forgiveness, but Sirach focuses on divine forgiveness. The Lord will heal those who forgive their

neighbors. At the end of life, we don't want to take anger with us to the grave. Rather, we set enmity aside and rely on the mercy of our God who will overlook our faults, as we have overlooked those of others.

The Book of Sirach came late in the biblical tradition, and Jesus' teaching, actions, and prayers of forgiveness soon amplified Sirach's instruction: "Forgive us our debts, as we forgive our debtors" (Matthew 6:12) and from the Cross: "Father, forgive them. . . . " (Luke 23:34). Jesus' whole life answers the question, "How do I live wisely?"

For meditation and context:

RESPONSORIAL PSALM   Psalm 103:1–2, 3–4, 9–10, 11–12 (8)

R. The Lord is kind and merciful, slow to anger, and rich in compassion.

Bless the LORD, O my soul;
    and all my being, bless his holy name.
Bless the LORD, O my soul,
    and forget not all his benefits.

He pardons all your iniquities,
    heals all your ills.
He redeems your life from destruction,
    he crowns you with kindness and
        compassion.

He will not always chide,
    nor does he keep his wrath forever.
Not according to our sins does he deal
        with us,
    nor does he requite us according
        to our crimes.

For as the heavens are high above the earth,
    so surpassing is his kindness toward
        those who fear him.
As far as the east is from the west,
    so far has he put our transgressions
        from us.

TO KEEP IN MIND
Be careful not to "swallow" words by mumbling. Articulate carefully so that every word is clearly heard, especially at the end of lines.

A didactic reading. Paul emphasizes the community's unity in Christ.

It's a short reading, so take your time, and use the commas to make sure you're understood.

Differences and disagreements shouldn't be the cause of division—we're all fundamentally the same in Christ.

This is indeed good news! Smile with your voice, eyes, and face!

READING II   Romans 14:7–9

A reading from the Letter of Saint Paul to the Romans

Brothers and sisters:
None of us **lives** for **oneself**, and no one **dies** for **oneself**.
For if we **live**, we live for the **Lord**,
    and if we **die**, we die for the **Lord**;
        so then, whether we **live** or **die**, we are the **Lord's**.
For **this** is why Christ **died** and came to **life**,
    that he might be **Lord** of both the **dead** and the **living**.

A didactic passage followed by a narrative. Jesus is an excellent storyteller. Be sure you proclaim this story with all the drama and emotion he puts into it.

Peter is eager to show he's willing to go beyond what would be expected.

GOSPEL   Matthew 18:21–35

A reading from the holy Gospel according to Matthew

Peter approached Jesus and asked him,
    "Lord, if my brother **sins** against me,
        how **often** must I **forgive**?
As many as **seven** times?"

READING II   Paul's poetic parallelism throughout this short reading suggests he may be quoting from an early Christian hymn: "Lives for oneself . . . dies for oneself . . . live for the Lord . . . die for the Lord." Perhaps this was a hymn sung in celebration of Christ's Death and Resurrection. Through this central mystery, Jesus manifests his lordship. The earliest believers, coming from the Jewish tradition, understood in a new way that God's covenant relationship with them transcends the border between life and death. Thus the risen Lord reigns over both the living and the dead.

This lovely poem also has a baptismal ring, a reminder that in Baptism each believer dies and rises to new life in Christ. Once baptized, we no longer belong to ourselves, but to Christ, and are members of his body. Belonging to Christ means that our lives are lived in communion with him. Our attitudes, way of thinking, our relationships, and behaviors are patterned on Christ's own. Belonging to him must also mean belonging to one another. Since we do not live for ourselves, we live for one another.

Paul's final acclamation celebrates our abiding union with Christ. We remain united to him, whether we live or die, for Christ's lordship embraces both the living and the dead. We live joyfully, confident that we will always belong to him.

GOSPEL   Jesus' teaching to Peter in today's Gospel continues his long discourse on Church life. Peter's initiating question flows naturally from Jesus' instruction on the process of forgiveness that we heard in last Sunday's Gospel. Now Peter is asking just how far forgive-

The answer is not about the specific number, but indicates that a change of heart is what is really required. Pause.

Don't swallow "debtor."

Emphasize "huge." You can comment on this action with sadness and compassion for the debtor.

Let the desperation of the debtor come through in his plea.

Slowly.

Don't gloss over this. This outcome would be very surprising to Jesus' listeners.

Pick up your energy and intensity to convey the violence.

"Can you believe it?"

Pause.

The master's act of mercy came with the unspoken expectation that his servants follow his example. Let his anger show.

Pause.

Take your time with this final line, the point of the parable.

Jesus answered, "I say to you, not **seven** times
    but **seventy-seven** times.
That is **why** the kingdom of heaven may be likened to a **king**
    who decided to settle **accounts** with his **servants**.
When he began the accounting,
    a **debtor** was brought before him who owed him
        a **huge** amount.
Since he had **no way** of paying it back,
    his master ordered him to be **sold**,
    along with his **wife**, his **children**, and all his **property**,
    in **payment** of the debt.
At **that**, the servant fell **down**, did him **homage**, and said,
    'Be **patient** with me, and I **will** pay you back in **full**.'
Moved with **compassion** the **master** of that servant
    let him **go** and **forgave** him the loan.
When that servant had left, he found one of his **fellow** servants
    who owed him a much **smaller** amount.
He **seized** him and started to **choke** him, demanding,
    '**Pay back** what you owe.'
Falling to his knees, his fellow servant **begged** him,
    'Be **patient** with me, and I **will** pay you back.'
But he **refused**.
Instead, he had the fellow servant put in **prison**
    until he **paid** back the debt.
Now when his **fellow** servants **saw** what had happened,
    they were **deeply** disturbed, and went to their **master**
    and **reported** the whole affair.
His master **summoned** him and said to him, 'You **wicked** servant!
I forgave **you** your **entire** debt because you **begged** me to.
Should **you** not have had **pity** on your **fellow** servant,
    as **I** had pity on **you**?'
Then in **anger** his master handed him over to the **torturers**
    until he should **pay** back the **whole** debt.
So will my heavenly Father do to **you**,
    unless **each** of you **forgives** your brother from your **heart**."

ness should extend. What limits can he put on forgiving a member of the Church who has sinned against him? When Peter suggests forgiving as many as seven times, he apparently thinks he is being magnanimous. After all, Peter and his fellow Jews knew well that God punished foreign nations after only three transgressions (see Amos 1:3–13). Some Jewish teachers at the time of Jesus interpreted this to mean that forgiving three times was sufficient. Forgiving seven times goes far beyond the "rule of three" forgiveness. Forgiving seven

times also draws on the Jewish symbolism of seven, signifying completeness.

Picking up on the symbolism, Jesus must have shocked Peter and the disciples by expanding to an almost impossible offer of forgiveness: seventy-seven times, or even seventy times seven. Forgiveness, according to Jesus, has no bounds. He illustrates such overwhelming forgiveness through a parable in three scenes. in the first, the king forgives an excessive amount to a slave who begs forgiveness. Scene two presents a huge contrast when the same slave refuses to forgive a much smaller

debt. The parable concludes with the king calling back the unforgiving servant and punishing him for his lack of mercy. The twofold teaching of the parable, coupled with Jesus' initial response to Peter, emphasizes God's extravagant mercy, and the necessity of exercising the same mercy in our own lives, even to seventy times seven. E.P.

TWENTY-FIFTH SUNDAY IN ORDINARY TIME

LECTIONARY #133

An exhortatory reading in God's voice. This is all good news, so maintain that energy throughout.

Isaiah = ī-ZAY-uh

Make this appeal to your listeners urgent and heartfelt.

This is not a rebuke, but a declaration of amnesty for all!

"I am more ready to forgive than you are."

How glad we are that God doesn't act as we might!

God is so much more merciful than we are, we can hardly imagine it!

TO KEEP IN MIND

Exhortatory texts make an urgent appeal to listeners. They may encourage, warn, or challenge, and often include a call to action. You must convey the urgency and passion behind the words.

READING I   Isaiah 55:6–9

A reading from the Book of the Prophet Isaiah

> **Seek** the LORD while he may be **found**,
>   **call** him while he is **near**.
> Let the scoundrel **forsake** his way,
>   and the **wicked** his thoughts;
> let him **turn** to the LORD for **mercy**;
>   to our **God**, who is **generous** in forgiving.
> For **my** thoughts are not **your** thoughts,
>   nor are **your ways my** ways, says the LORD.
> As **high** as the heavens are above the **earth**,
>   so high are **my** ways above **your** ways
>   and **my** thoughts above **your** thoughts.

READING I In one of the most familiar prophecies of Isaiah, he addresses "all you who are thirsty" (Isaiah 55:1), instructing them with rich and varied imagery and with actions that draw them into relationship with God: come, eat, listen. Today's reading continues this prophecy. *Seeking* the Lord and *calling* on God are fundamental ways of quenching the perennial thirst of the human heart. Both verbs are a summons to turn towards God in worship and in daily life; both verbs are also ways in which God acts toward humanity. Isaiah thus intimates that seek-ing and calling out to God are responses to God's initiative in seeking and calling us.

As the exhortation continues, the prophet appeals to the scoundrels and the wicked, beckoning them to repent and to rely on God's mercy and generosity in forgiving. Here Isaiah is not talking about a different group of people, but is referring to sinful behavior *within* the community. He is, in effect, advising everyone to walk in the way of the Lord, and not in the way of sinners. His prophecy echoes that of the psalmist: "Blessed the man who follows not / the counsel of the wicked" (Psalm 1:1).

Isaiah is well aware how easy it is to seek after other gods, to forsake the ways of God and follow easier paths. In comparing the distance between God's thoughts and ours to the distance between heaven and earth, he isn't suggesting that following God's ways is impossible. Rather, he is directing our thoughts and actions toward God. Seek God, call upon God's name, turn toward God in repentance and ask for mercy.

Isaiah addresses this audience in broad terms that can include people in varied historical circumstances, including the

For meditation and context:

RESPONSORIAL PSALM   Psalm 145:2–3, 8–9, 17–18 (18a)

R. The Lord is near to all who call upon him.

Every day will I bless you,
   and I will praise your name forever
      and ever.
Great is the LORD and highly to be praised;
   his greatness is unsearchable.

The LORD is gracious and merciful,
   slow to anger and of great kindness.
The LORD is good to all
   and compassionate toward all his works.

The LORD is just in all his ways
   and holy in all his works.
The LORD is near to all who call upon him,
   to all who call upon him in truth.

TO KEEP IN MIND

Words in bold are significant words about which you must make a choice to help their meaning stand out. You may (or may not) choose to stress them.

An exhortation expressing Paul's faith and joy in Christ, his devotion to spreading the Gospel, and his concern for the community at Philippi. Proclaim this with Paul's ardent devotion to his ministry.

Philippians = fih-LIP-ee-uhnz

Life and death are equally desirable to Paul.

How do you feel when you must choose between two equally good options? It can be more difficult than choosing good over evil!

Pause.

Paul has decided to remain and is pressing his listeners here: "If I'm going to remain in the flesh for your benefit, you'd better make it worth my time!"

READING II   Philippians 1:20c–24, 27a

A reading from the Letter of Saint Paul to the Philippians

Brothers and sisters:
Christ will be **magnified** in my body, whether by **life** or by **death**.
For to me **life** is Christ, and **death** is gain.
If I go on living in the **flesh**,
   that means **fruitful** labor for me.
And I do not know **which** I shall choose.
I am **caught** between the two.
I long to **depart** this life and be with **Christ**,
   for that is far **better**.
Yet that I **remain** in the flesh
   is more necessary for **your** benefit.

Only, conduct yourselves in a way **worthy** of the **gospel** of Christ.

---

widely diverse conditions of this century. In our own day, Pope Francis' exhortation has a message similar to Isaiah's "Whenever we take a step toward Jesus, we come to realize that he is already there, waiting for us with open arms. . . . How good it feels to come back to him whenever we are lost!" (*Evangelii Gaudium*, 3).

READING II   Paul writes his Letter to the Philippians while imprisoned, not knowing what the outcome will be. His fundamental conviction is that no matter what befalls him, Christ will be mag-

nified in his body. Paul uses the word "body" (*soma*) to refer to his whole being, embracing the entirety of who he is; his *soma* is where Paul first met the risen Jesus, and where Jesus continues to dwell. At death, Paul's body, like that of Christ himself, will be transformed, yet will still remain his body. By declaring that Christ will be "magnified," in his body, Paul says that Christ will be increased and glorified in all that Paul experiences. Since Christ will be magnified in either case, Paul can see reasons to choose either life or death. He is "caught between the two"; the verb he

chooses to describe his situation means to be pushed from both sides, to feel a physical, intense pressure. (The same verb describes the crowds pressing upon Jesus at Luke 8:45.)

As Paul reflects on his present condition, he does so with a view to the ministry to which he was called. In particular he considers the impact his continued life or his death would have on the Philippian Christians. If he endures in the flesh, in his present mortal state, he can continue his fruitful labor for the churches he loves. It would be for the benefit of others, not for

A narrative which reminds us that God's ideas of justice and mercy are far different from our own. (See Reading I.)

This is the setup. Don't linger over these details.

Keep your pace up. By now we know what's going to happen.

Pause at the end of this line.

Slow down on "usual daily wage," so it's clear what is happening.

A reasonable assumption, one we would all likely make.

GOSPEL　Matthew 20:1–16a

A reading from the holy Gospel according to Matthew

Jesus told his disciples this **parable**:
　"The kingdom of **heaven** is like a **landowner**
　　who went out at dawn to hire **laborers** for his vineyard.
After **agreeing** with them for the **usual** daily wage,
　he sent them into his **vineyard**.
Going out about **nine** o'clock,
　the landowner saw **others** standing **idle** in the marketplace,
　and he said to them, 'You **too** go into my vineyard,
　and I will give you what is **just**.'
So they **went** off.
And he went out again around **noon**,
　and around **three** o'clock, and did **likewise**.
Going out about **five** o'clock,
　the landowner found **others** standing around, and said to them,
　'Why do you stand here **idle** all day?'
They answered, 'Because no one has **hired** us.'
He said to them, 'You **too** go into my vineyard.'
When it was **evening** the owner of the vineyard said
　　to his foreman,
　'**Summon** the laborers and give them their **pay**,
　beginning with the **last** and ending with the **first**.'
When those who had started about **five** o'clock came,
　each received the **usual** daily wage.
So when the **first** came, they thought that they would
　　receive **more**,
　but each of them **also** got the usual wage.

his own benefit, that Paul would choose to remain in this life.

Yet, in the fullest sense, "life" for Paul is his existence in Christ. Death is therefore gain, resulting in the fullest and most advantageous state. If he were to depart this life, he would be with Christ forever, no longer experiencing the limits of time, space, and flesh. The last line of the reading comes from a later verse after Paul has decided to remain and serve the community for the sake of their advancement and joy in the faith. And like Paul himself, they are to conduct themselves as worthy ser-

vants of the Gospel. When Paul ultimately departs this life, the Good News will continue to be proclaimed by the communities he served.

GOSPEL　Jesus addresses his parables to different groups, ranging from opponents plotting against him to the assembly of his closest followers. In today's parable, Jesus is teaching his disciples, having just told them, "many who are first will be last, and the last will be first." The parable he tells them provides an illustration of the reversal of last and first,

and he reiterates this saying about reversals as the parable's conclusion.

The characters, hiring process, and other details of the story reflect the real life situation of Jesus' day. The custom of workers gathering at the marketplace, waiting to be hired, was common practice, and continues in many places today. At dawn, the first workers are hired, with an agreed-upon wage for the day. Each time the landowner goes back to the marketplace, he chooses laborers who are still waiting to be hired. We can presume that even those who are hired at the end of the day would

A complaint we've all no doubt heard frequently. Don't make the workers sound too whiny or the assembly won't be able to see themselves in this story.

Be gentle and understanding in your response. The landowner isn't angry.

Take your time with this line, then pause.

> TO KEEP IN MIND
> What does the reading ask your assembly to do or to be after hearing your proclamation? Focus on an intention every time you proclaim.

And on receiving it they **grumbled** against the landowner, saying,
  'These last ones worked only **one** hour,
  and you have made them **equal** to us,
  who bore the day's **burden** and the **heat**.'
He said to one of them in reply,
  'My **friend**, I am not **cheating** you.
Did you not **agree** with me for the usual daily wage?
Take what is yours and **go**.
What if I wish to give this last one the same as **you**?
Or am I not **free** to do as I **wish** with my own money?
Are you **envious** because I am **generous**?'
Thus, the **last** will be **first**, and the **first** will be **last**."

have happily gone to the vineyard earlier had the landowner given them the chance.

Most of Jesus' parables have a surprising element, and this parable is no exception. Not only are we as hearers of the story surprised by the landowner's action, but the characters in the story are even more astounded. If those who came last are given the wages for a full day's work, surely those who have labored for hours under the hot Palestinian sun will be paid a greater wage. No! They are paid what the landowner had originally agreed with them.

The landowner, a vivid image of God, acts with generosity. God's gift of salvation is an act of overwhelming liberality, as well as one of divine justice. God gives much more than anyone can earn by a lifetime of good works and acts of devotion. God freely offers salvation to those who appear to be last and least in the eyes of the world, as well as to those who welcome God's generosity at the last moment of their lives. Jesus' own disciples needed to hear this parable. Rather than being resentful of people who did not labor long years as they

did, Jesus teaches them that they should delight in God's generosity. As should all of us. E.P.

TWENTY-SIXTH SUNDAY IN ORDINARY TIME

LECTIONARY #136

An exhortatory reading which continues the theme from previous Sundays on the wideness of God's mercy. Review Reading I and the Gospel from the past couple of weeks.

Ezekiel = ee-ZEE-kee-uhl

This should sound as childish as it appears.

Pause briefly at the commas.

Ignore the comma after "iniquity."

A reasonable outcome.

Good news!

Slowly.

READING I   Ezekiel 18:25–28

A reading from the Book of the Prophet Ezekiel

Thus says the LORD:
You say, "The LORD's way is not **fair**!"
Hear now, house of Israel:
    Is it **my** way that is unfair, or **rather**, are not **your** ways unfair?
When someone virtuous turns **away** from virtue to commit
        iniquity, and **dies**,
    it is because of the **iniquity** he committed that he must die.
But if he **turns** from the wickedness he has committed,
    and does what is **right** and **just**,
    he shall **preserve** his life;
    since he has turned **away** from all the sins that he
        has committed,
    he shall surely **live**, he shall **not** die.

For meditation and context:

RESPONSORIAL PSALM   Psalm 25:4–5, 6–7, 8–9 (6a)

R. Remember your mercies, O Lord.

Your ways, O LORD, make known to me;
    teach me your paths,
guide me in your truth and teach me,
    for you are God my savior.

Remember that your compassion, O LORD,
    and your love are from of old.
The sins of my youth and my frailties
        remember not;
    in your kindness remember me,
    because of your goodness, O LORD.

Good and upright is the LORD;
    thus he shows sinners the way.
He guides the humble to justice,
    and teaches the humble his way.

TO KEEP IN MIND

Pause in order to break up separate thoughts, set apart significant statements, or indicate major shifts. Never pause in the middle of a single thought. Your primary guide for pauses is punctuation.

READING I   Ezekiel preached to the people of Judah when they were in exile in Babylon, and he shared in their humiliation and loss. It was a time of questioning, "How could this happen to us? Is it the guilt of our ancestors that brought us to a foreign land, where they taunt and shame us?" Ezekiel's task was difficult, since he, too, was suffering; he was to teach those far away from their own land new truths about God and about themselves.

In the midst of their suffering, it isn't surprising that people cried out "The Lord's way is not fair!" Ezekiel had to break through their self-pity and defensiveness, likely shouting above their shouting. He told them that God wasn't punishing them on account of the actions of their parents, as was a common way of thinking. Ezekiel corrects this notion, telling them, "Only the one who sins shall die!" (Ezekiel 18:20). Everyone must take individual responsibility for their actions, and accept that they brought their misery upon themselves.

When Ezekiel says that people must die on account of their iniquity, he may not be referring to physical death. The exile itself was a symbol of death. Yet even in Babylon there is the possibility for restored life if they repent, and live in justice and right. When the prophet tells them that God shall preserve life for those who turn away from wickedness, he offers hope. Transformed lives will result in a new possibility of life, even in exile.

READING II   On Palm Sunday and on the Feast of the Exaltation of the Holy Cross we hear the magnificent hymn to Christ that we hear again today. The hymn proclaims Christ's emptying of himself. It is often referred to as "The

An exhortatory reading, ending with the great Christological hymn. In Paul's voice, encourage the assembly to conform themselves completely to Christ, bringing all your energy and skill to the task.

Philippians = fih-LIP-ee-uhnz
Pause briefly at each comma and raise your intensity on each phrase through "mercy."

solace = SOL-uhs (comfort)
Pause.

Longer pause at the period.
vainglory = VAYN-glohr-ee (excessive pride)

Christ is the model for the behavior to which you call them.

The hymn begins with strength, diminishes to a quiet middle, then rises again to the great proclamation at the end. Pacing and volume will indicate the changes in intensity.

Now begin to diminish your energy slightly.

Arrive at this line with a quiet intensity. Drop your volume and pace, but don't lose contact with the assembly.

pause after "on a cross."

Now, gradually pick up your pace and energy from here to the end. It's one long sentence; pause only at the commas.

Keep building your energy.

READING II   Philippians 2:1–11

A reading from the Letter of Saint Paul to the Philippians

[Brothers and sisters:
If there is any **encouragement** in Christ,
    any **solace** in love,
    any **participation** in the **Spirit**,
    any **compassion** and **mercy**,
    complete my joy by being of the same **mind**, with the
        same **love**,
    united in heart, thinking **one** thing.
Do **nothing** out of **selfishness** or out of **vainglory**;
    rather, humbly regard **others** as more **important**
        than yourselves,
    each looking out not for his **own** interests,
    but also for those of **others**.

Have in you the **same** attitude
    that is also in Christ **Jesus**,]
Who, though he was in the **form** of God,
    did not regard **equality** with God
    something to be **grasped**.
    Rather, he **emptied** himself,
    taking the form of a **slave**,
    coming in **human** likeness;
    and found **human** in appearance,
    he **humbled** himself,
    becoming **obedient** to the point of **death**,
    even death on a **cross**.
Because of this, God greatly **exalted** him
    and **bestowed** on him the **name**
    which is above **every** name,
    that at the name of **Jesus**
    every **knee** should bend,
    of those in **heaven** and on **earth** and **under** the earth, »

Kenosis Hymn" since the Greek word *kenosis*, "emptying," is a key theme of the hymn. Christ empties himself by not clinging to his equality with God, by taking the form of a slave, and by obediently emptying himself to death on a cross. The hymn was likely already known to Paul's Philippian community, probably sung when they gathered for the Eucharist, where they remembered and celebrated Christ's *kenosis*, his humility, and obedience.

In his Letter to the Philippians, Paul takes this familiar christological hymn and adds an ecclesiological meaning. That is, he uses the story of Christ to present a pattern for the Philippian church, showing them that they too, as a community, are to live in humility, obedience, and self-emptying. All in the church are to "humbly regard others as more important," repeating the example of Christ who humbly did not regard equality with God something to be grasped. Paul tells the community to "do nothing out of selfishness or out of vainglory"; the word "vainglory" is literally "empty, (*keno*) glory," an attitude focusing on glory or honor given to oneself, in sharp contrast with Christ's *kenosis* of himself, leading to the glory of God the Father.

In every moment of his life, Jesus' actions were for the sake of others. We can listen, pray, and sing this hymn both to honor Christ, and as an inspiration for our own humble and obedient self-emptying.

GOSPEL   Today's Gospel parable is directed to the chief priests and elders, among the most powerful of Jesus' opponents. At this point in Matthew's Gospel, their enmity against Jesus has escalated; they are indignant

Keep your energy up; slow down just a bit and proclaim this final line deliberately and with great joy.

and every **tongue** confess that
Jesus **Christ** is **Lord**,
　to the **glory** of **God** the Father.

[Shorter: Philippians 2:1–5 (see brackets)]

GOSPEL　Matthew 21:28–32

A reading from the holy Gospel according to Matthew

Simple narrative; important message: God does not judge by appearances but by actions and the attitude of the heart. These cautionary tales about being authentic and leading with integrity apply to all of us, and even more so to those of us in ministry.

Ask this question directly to your assembly. They will be eager to pay attention!
Relate the story; let the community make the judgement.
Don't make this a command, but a request. Then the son's refusal sounds even more shocking.
Be defiant!

Be eager in your response!

"Of course!"

"Well, then . . ."
Slowly; make sure they get the message.
This is the truth. State it simply.

You can see Jesus shaking his head in disbelief. Let your voice ring with incredulity.

Jesus said to the chief **priests** and **elders** of the people:
　"What is your **opinion**?
A man had two **sons**.
He came to the **first** and said,
　'**Son**, go out and work in the **vineyard** today.'
He said in reply, 'I will **not**,'
　but **afterwards** changed his **mind** and **went**.
The man came to the **other** son and gave the **same** order.
He said in reply, '**Yes**, sir,' but did **not** go.
Which of the two did his father's **will**?"
They answered, "The **first**."
Jesus said to them, "**Amen**, I say to you,
　tax collectors and **prostitutes**
　　are entering the kingdom of God before **you**.
When **John** came to you in the way of **righteousness**,
　you did not **believe** him;
　　but tax collectors and prostitutes **did**.
Yet **even** when you saw **that**,
　you did not later **change** your minds and **believe** him."

---

when he enters Jerusalem to the cries of "Hosanna!" and challenge Jesus' authority. Just before today's account, Jesus had asked them whether the baptism of John was from heaven or from humankind. Arguing among themselves about the effects of either answer, they admit that they do not know. Following this episode, Jesus tells them the parable, which prods them to answer another question.

　　The story features a father and two sons, a familiar motif both in narratives of the ancestors and in Jesus' own parables: Cain and Abel; Jacob and Esau; the prodigal son and his jealous brother. In all of these tales, the brothers represent contrasting words and actions. In this parable, the first son sounds disobedient, but in fact does as his father asks. The second reverses the scenario, sounding obedient, but not following through. Although Jesus' audience of priests and elders did not answer his question about John the Baptist, they seem to be caught off guard when they answer that the first son did the father's will. By their answer, they unwittingly show their own prejudice. They considered tax collectors and prostitutes to be outsiders, but

Jesus sees the outsiders entering the Kingdom of God even before those who looked down on them. Unlike the seemingly righteous priests and elders, the so-called sinners believed and repented; they are the truly righteous ones. E.P.

TWENTY-SEVENTH SUNDAY IN ORDINARY TIME

LECTIONARY #139

READING I   Isaiah 5:1–7

An exhortatory prophecy in the form of a song. Prepare to be expressive; these are tender, loving—and challenging—images of God.

Isaiah = ī-ZAY-uh

The story starts in the third person (about my "friend"), then switches to first person, but proclaim the whole story as if it were in first person, as if you were the owner of the vineyard.

Let your great love and care for the vineyard come through in these lines.

spaded = SPAY-d*d

With excitement and anticipation.

Wild grapes would be sour, unfit for winemaking. Pause.

Address these questions directly to your assembly.

There's more hurt than irritation here.

Pause.

Heighten your energy and let your feelings come through—anger, frustration, sadness.

A reading from the Book of the Prophet Isaiah

Let me now **sing** of my **friend**,
   my friend's **song** concerning his **vineyard**.
My friend had a vineyard
   on a **fertile** hillside;
he **spaded** it, cleared it of **stones**,
   and planted the **choicest** vines;
within it he built a **watchtower**,
   and hewed out a **wine** press.
Then he looked for the crop of **grapes**,
   but what it yielded was **wild** grapes.

Now, inhabitants of **Jerusalem** and people of **Judah**,
   judge between me and my vineyard:
What **more** was there to do for my vineyard
   that I had not **done**?
Why, when I looked for the crop of grapes,
   did it bring forth **wild** grapes?
Now, I will let you know
   what I mean to **do** with my vineyard:
take away its **hedge**, give it to **grazing**,
   break through its wall, let it be **trampled**! »

Today's reading, a song of a vineyard, is a parable whose meaning is not revealed until the end.

   The song is sung by Isaiah himself, telling of the vineyard carefully tended by his friend. It is actually the friend's own song, recounting all the labors through each stage of growth, beginning with spading, and culminating with the expectation of rich harvest. There is no hint of backbreaking fatigue, just loving attention. With all of that care, how could the friend's vineyard produce only wild grapes?

READING I At this point, when Isaiah's audience may be wondering at such an unnatural harvest, the speaker changes. Now it is the owner of the vineyard who addresses them. Clearly the owner has not stinted in any way, and asks the question that has such pathos and emotion in it: "What more was there to do for my vineyard that I had not done?" Sadly, having spent so much effort on the vineyard, he will now let it fall into ruin. Even more, the owner says he will command that no rain fall on it. With such a forceful word of authority, we now see the identity

of the vineyard's owner. It is God speaking, God who had so lovingly tended the vineyard, who judges it, and announces the coming punishment. The very ones listening to the song are themselves the vineyard, God's cherished plant, and are subject to God's judgment for their failure to produce a good harvest.

   With the skill of an accomplished poet, Isaiah concludes with a play on words that evokes the contrast between a good crop of grapes and a worthless harvest. God looked for judgment (*mishpat*), but instead got bloodshed (*mispah*); God

A long pause; let the image settle before you announce the meaning of the parable.

Deliberately; make sure the community understands who is who.

Take your time with these lines. Drop your inflection on "judgment" and "justice"; raise it quickly on "bloodshed" and "outcry."

Yes, I will make it a **ruin**:
　　it shall not be **pruned** or **hoed**,
　　but overgrown with **thorns** and **briers**;
I will command the clouds
　　not to send rain upon it.
The **vineyard** of the LORD of hosts is the house of **Israel**,
　　and the people of **Judah** are his cherished **plant**;
he looked for **judgment**, but see, **bloodshed**!
　　for **justice**, but hark, the **outcry**!

For meditation and context:

RESPONSORIAL PSALM　Psalm 80:9, 12, 13–14, 15–16, 19–20 (Isaiah 5:7a)

R. The vineyard of the Lord is the house of Israel.

A vine from Egypt you transplanted;
　　you drove away the nations and planted it.
It put forth its foliage to the Sea,
　　its shoots as far as the River.

Why have you broken down its walls,
　　so that every passer-by plucks its fruit,
the boar from the forest lays it waste,
　　and the beasts of the field feed upon it?

Once again, O LORD of hosts,
　　look down from heaven, and see;
take care of this vine,
　　and protect what your right hand
　　　　has planted,
　　the son of man whom you yourself
　　　　made strong.

Then we will no more withdraw from you;
　　give us new life, and we will call upon
　　　　your name.
O LORD, God of hosts, restore us;
　　if your face shine upon us, then we shall
　　　　be saved.

---

wanted justice (*sedeq*), but heard instead an outcry (*se'aqah*). Having listened to Isaiah's prophecy, perhaps the people will be moved to repentance.

READING II　Paul is writing to his beloved Philippian Christians while he is imprisoned and the community itself is facing persecution. Just before these verses, he had told the church in Philippi to rejoice, for "The Lord is near" (Philippians 4:5). Paul's conviction that the risen Lord is present among them, and that he will come again in glory, is fundamental

to everything he says. We can almost hear Paul repeating his belief in the Lord's nearness after each piece of advice. Whether one is imprisoned or enslaved or free, in poverty or in riches, persecuted or honored, have no anxiety: "The Lord is near." They should offer prayer in all forms, with thanksgiving, confident that God will hear: "The Lord is near." The peace that God will give surpasses understanding. By using the verb "surpassing" (*hyperexousa*), Paul assures his audience that God's peace is "superior to" human intelligence. By human standards or understanding, both Paul and

the Philippian church have ample reason to experience anxiety, rather than peace. Yet, like a guardian of a fortress, God's peace will protect the entirety of every person. "The Lord is near."

Next, Paul enjoins on the church specific behaviors or virtues that will bring about peace. Listing virtues and vices was a common practice in Paul's Hellenistic milieu, including in the New Testament (see 2 Corinthians 6:6–8 and Galatians 5: 22–23). Jews, Gentiles, Christians, and Greek philosophers all used these catalogues as a technique to promote right living. Paul not

An exhortatory reading. Take your time; there's a lot of good news here; you don't want to rush through any of it!

Philippians = fih-LIP-ee-uhnz

Speak this vital message directly to the assembly. You are commissioned to bring it and must make your community understand.

Imagine what this peace would feel like! Let that show in your voice, eyes, and face.

Here is the conclusion and advice. Continue slowly and deliberately.

Raise your intensity very slightly with each phrase.

"You're already doing it; keep it up!"

Pause.

READING II   Philippians 4:6–9

A reading from the Letter of Saint Paul to the Philippians

Brothers and sisters:
Have **no** anxiety at all, but in **everything**,
    by **prayer** and **petition**, with **thanksgiving**,
    make your requests **known** to God.
Then the **peace** of God that surpasses **all** understanding
    will **guard** your hearts and minds in Christ **Jesus**.

Finally, brothers and sisters,
    whatever is **true**, whatever is **honorable**,
    whatever is **just**, whatever is **pure**,
    whatever is **lovely**, whatever is **gracious**,
    if there is any **excellence**
    and if there is anything **worthy** of praise,
    think about **these** things.
Keep on **doing** what you have **learned** and **received**
    and **heard** and **seen** in me.
Then the God of **peace** will be **with** you.

A narrative. Review the notes for today's Reading I; Jesus intentionally echoes Isaiah's parable in this one.

Note who the parable is directed to: not the crowd but the leaders.

Speak of this work with the same enthusiasm as the "friend" in Reading I.

Continue to show enthusiasm and confidence; don't telegraph what's about to happen.

GOSPEL   Matthew 21:33–43

A reading from the holy Gospel according to Matthew

Jesus said to the chief **priests** and the **elders** of the people:
    "Hear another **parable**. *(God)*
There was a **landowner** who planted a **vineyard**, *Israel*
    put a **hedge** around it, dug a **wine** press in it, and built
        a **tower**.   *Jewish Leadership*
Then he leased it to **tenants** and went on a **journey**.
When **vintage** time drew near,
    he sent his **servants** to the tenants to obtain his **produce**. »
        prophets

only exhorts the community to manifest whatever is true, honorable, just, and ultimately, worthy of praise; he also tells them that they are to *think* about these qualities. Paul seems to suggest a meditative stance in support of virtuous living: *think* about what you are doing. They are also to observe Paul's own behavior, for his life was patterned on Christ's. Bringing his advice to a close, Paul again promises God's peace. And we can again say with him: "The Lord is near."

GOSPEL   Jesus continues his teaching in parables directed to the chief priests and elders. These leaders, as well as Matthew's first-century audience, would be well steeped in Judaism, know its traditions, imagery, and prophecies. They would know Isaiah's Song of the Vineyard that we heard in the First Reading, as well as Psalm 80, today's Responsorial Psalm. They would readily see the vineyard as an image for the Jewish people, and the landowner as representing God. With that initial allegorical interpretation, they could see the rest of the parable telling the story

of Israel's relationship with God. The owner gives responsibility for care of the vineyard to tenants, understood as the leaders of Israel; the servants sent by the owner are the prophets, harshly treated and even killed. The prophecy of Jeremiah can be heard in the background: "I kept on sending all my servants the prophets to you. Yet they have not listened to me . . . they have stiffened their necks and done worse than their ancestors" (Jeremiah 7:25–26).

The landowner still does not give up, but sends his son. Now the interpretation moves from the past to the present. The

Now you can take on a sinister tone. Don't rush through the descriptions of what happened to each of the three servants.

The landowner's trust in his tenants remains, despite this violence.

With strength and conviction.

Lower your voice as if whispering in conspiracy.

Use the power in the verbs "seized," "threw," and "killed" to convey the violence.

Pause before asking the question.

There's an arrogance to their answer. "Of course we're right!" They're clueless that Jesus is speaking about them.

"You don't get it, do you?"

Treat this as a statement, not a question.

Slowly, so the message sinks in.

We are the people to whom the vineyard has been given. We must work to ensure that we produce fruit!

TO KEEP IN MIND
Making eye contact with the assembly connects you with them and connects them to the reading more deeply than using your voice alone. This helps the assembly stay with the story and keeps them engaged.

But the tenants **seized** the servants and one they **beat**,
   another they **killed**, and a third they **stoned**.
Again he sent **other** servants, more **numerous** than the first ones,
   but they treated them in the **same** way.
Finally, he sent his **son** [Jesus] to them, thinking,
   'They will **respect** my son.'
But when the tenants saw the son, they said to one another,
   'This is the **heir**.
Come, let us **kill** him and acquire his **inheritance**.'
They **seized** him, **threw** him out of the vineyard, and **killed** him.
What will the **owner** of the vineyard **do** to those tenants when
      he comes?"
They answered him,
   "He will put those **wretched** men to a wretched **death**
   and lease his vineyard to **other** tenants [Gentiles]
   who will **give** him the produce at the proper **times**."
Jesus said to them, "Did you **never** read in the Scriptures:
   *The **stone** that the builders **rejected**
      has become the **cornerstone**;*
   *by the **Lord** has this been done,*
      *and it is **wonderful** in our eyes?*
Therefore, I say to you,
   the kingdom of God will be taken away from **you**
   and given to a **people** that will **produce** its fruit."

Son, of course, is Jesus himself. The treatment of the son seems desperate and illogical. What could the tenants hope to gain? With such a shocking conclusion to the parable, Jesus puts the question that demands an answer: "What will the owner do?" The answer from the priests and elders points to their own guilt and the consequences in rejecting the son.

   In a way that would jolt his audience, Jesus abruptly asks them another question, intimating that they have not read the Scriptures. In citing Psalm 118, Jesus connects the rejected stone and the murdered son. However, rejecting the stone and killing the son, is not the end of the story, for the son will become a cornerstone. Because of their actions, leadership will be taken away from those who rejected Jesus and given to others. Immediately following Jesus' words, Matthew states that the chief priests and Pharisees knew he was speaking about them. They tried to arrest him but feared the crowds, who regarded Jesus as a prophet. E.P.

TWENTY-EIGHTH SUNDAY IN ORDINARY TIME

LECTIONARY #142

READING I   Isaiah 25:6–10a

A reading from the Book of the Prophet Isaiah

On this **mountain** the LORD of hosts
    will provide for **all** peoples
a feast of **rich** food and **choice** wines,
    juicy, rich food and **pure**, choice wines.
On this mountain he will destroy
    the **veil** that veils all peoples,
the **web** that is woven over all nations;
    he will destroy death **forever**.
The Lord GOD will wipe **away**
    the tears from **every** face;
the reproach of his people he will **remove**
    from the **whole** earth; for the LORD has **spoken**.
    On **that** day it will be said:
"**Behold** our God, to whom we looked to **save** us!
    This is the LORD for whom we looked;
    let us **rejoice** and be **glad** that he has **saved** us!"
For the hand of the LORD will rest on **this** mountain.

An exhortatory prophecy of God's abundant care for us. Keep your energy up throughout. This is all good news, so smile with your voice, eyes, and face.

Isaiah = ī-ZAY-uh

Savor the words describing this mouth-watering feast. Make the community hungry for it.

Slowly, with deliberate emphasis.
With gentleness and love.

Any cause for punishment or disapproval will be forgotten!
Pause.

Raise your energy and let the community hear your excitement as you praise God.

Pause.
Lower your volume a bit and proclaim slowly and with confidence.

READING I   In his poem, the prophet Isaiah depicts the Lord of hosts as a lavish provider, as well as a mighty warrior who is victorious over every evil and source of sorrow, including death itself. The Lord of hosts is a biblical image of a warrior God who commands the heavenly armies in battle, is always triumphant, and holds sway over every element of creation. Isaiah emphasizes God's universal power throughout the poem: all peoples, all nations, every face, and the whole earth will experience God's might.

The poem opens with a scene of glad feasting on the mountain, most likely referring to the holy city Jerusalem, the symbolic locale of God's abiding presence. The rich food and drink that God will provide there manifests divine control over nature itself, as God sets a plentiful table for all peoples. Following the image of God offering a banquet is one that depicts God's ability to destroy. The power that the Lord of hosts manifests, however, does not bring rampant ruin, for God destroys only that which inhibits life and wholeness. First, God will destroy the veil that veils all peo-

ples, the web over all nations. This veil or web has several possible meanings. We may imagine it as ignorance of God, or as illusions that confuse and divide people. More concretely, we may see it as the shroud that covers all who die; all nations appear to be wrapped in the mourning veil as a sign of universal grief. God will conquer both grief and death that causes such sadness. When we hear that the Lord God wipes away tears from every face, we can add another piece in the portrait of God: the one who acts with motherly tenderness.

For meditation and context:

TO KEEP IN MIND
Words in bold are significant words about which you must make a choice to help their meaning stand out. You may (or may not) choose to stress them.

A narrative that gives us a glimpse into Paul's personal strength. Make sure you proclaim with Paul's deep trust in God. What difference would it make in your life to have Paul's confidence?

Philippians = fih-LIP-ee-uhnz

Don't make too much of the difference between being in need and having abundance. The point is that no change in external circumstances can shake your confidence in God.

Set this statement apart; here is your secret!

Paul is genuinely grateful for the concern of the community. Smile as you recall someone who has stood by you in your times of distress. Pause.

Speak confidently to your community assuring them of God's abundant care.

Proclaim this closing exhortation with energy and excitement. Raise your inflection slightly on "Amen." You're saying "Yes, indeed!"

RESPONSORIAL PSALM   Psalm 23:1–3a, 3b–4, 5, 6 (6cd)

R. I shall live in the house of the Lord all the days of my life.

The LORD is my shepherd; I shall not want.
  In verdant pastures he gives me repose;
beside restful waters he leads me;
  he refreshes my soul.

He guides me in right paths
  for his name's sake.
Even though I walk in the dark valley
  I fear no evil; for you are at my side
with your rod and your staff
  that give me courage.

You spread the table before me
  in the sight of my foes;
you anoint my head with oil;
  my cup overflows.

Only goodness and kindness follow me
  all the days of my life;
and I shall dwell in the house of the LORD
  for years to come.

READING II   Philippians 4:12–14, 19–20

A reading from the Letter of Saint Paul to the Philippians

Brothers and sisters:
I **know** how to live in **humble** circumstances;
  I know also how to live with **abundance**.
In **every** circumstance and in **all** things
  I have learned the **secret** of being well fed and of going hungry,
  of living in **abundance** and of being in **need**.
I can do **all** things in **him** who **strengthens** me.
Still, it was **kind** of you to **share** in my distress.

My God will **fully** supply **whatever** you need,
  in accord with his **glorious** riches in Christ **Jesus**.
To our **God** and **Father**, glory **forever** and **ever**. **Amen**.

Those who look to God in hope will not be disappointed, for all God's actions are for the sake of salvation. Most importantly, God's saving actions are for *us*! The concluding verses are personal acclamations of faith and hope, because this universally powerful Lord of hosts has saved us. The response of Isaiah's original audience is the same as ours today: "Let us rejoice and be glad!"

 READING II   In the final portion of Paul's Letter to the Philippians, he gives a theological reflection on his own

circumstances and those of his beloved Philippian church. When he tells the community that he "knows" how to live both in humble situations and in abundance, he is not speaking theoretically or from a merely intellectual perspective. Paul's knowledge comes from his personal experience, for his ministry has often brought him into situations of persecution and distress, as well as abundance that flows from living in union with Christ.

In referring to his humble circumstances, Paul uses the same root word that describes Jesus in the *kenosis* hymn: "he

humbled himself" (Philippians 2:8). Paul had also urged the Philippians to have the same mind as in Christ Jesus, and "humbly regard others as more important than yourselves" (2:3). This attitude was not common in the Hellenistic world; humility was considered the status of a slave, indicative of subservience typical of the lower class. Yet both Paul and the Church find in Christ the pattern for their own acceptance of lowliness.

In contrast with his living in humility, Paul says he has also lived in abundance. Earlier in the letter Paul had used the same verb when he prayed that the love of the

GOSPEL Matthew 22:1–14

A reading from the holy Gospel according to Matthew

[Jesus **again** in reply spoke to the chief **priests** and **elders**
of the people
in **parables**, saying,
"The kingdom of **heaven** may be likened to a **king**
who gave a **wedding** feast for his son.
He dispatched his servants
to **summon** the invited guests to the feast,
but they **refused** to come.
A **second** time he sent **other** servants, saying,
'Tell those invited: "**Behold**, I have **prepared** my banquet,
my calves and fattened cattle are **killed**,
and **everything** is ready; **come** to the feast."'
Some **ignored** the invitation and went **away**,
one to his **farm**, another to his **business**.
The rest laid **hold** of his servants,
mistreated them, and **killed** them.
The king was **enraged** and sent his **troops**,
destroyed those murderers, and **burned** their city.
Then he said to his servants, 'The feast is **ready**,
but those who were invited were not **worthy** to come.
Go **out**, therefore, into the main roads
and invite to the feast **whomever** you find.' ❯❯

Another narrative exchange between Jesus and the leaders of the community. See the notes from the last two weeks' Gospels.

Remember, Jesus draws large crowds in part because he's an excellent storyteller. Give this proclamation all the passion and emotion he would have.

Express the surprise (and confusion) of the servants on receiving such a response. Pause.

Apparently, a little marketing is required to interest these guests! Really sweeten the deal and make this sound like an amazing, not-to-be-missed happening!

"Please, come!"

Be dismissive, uninterested.

Quickly; the violence is sudden and unexpected.

Keep your pace and intensity up; violence begets violence.

There might still be a tinge of anger in his voice.

Philippian church would abound (1:9), indicative of their full life in Christ. The abundance that is most important both for Paul and the community is richness that overflows from their mutual union with Christ who remains present and gives strength whatever their situation.

Both Paul and the Philippians shared in distress (*thlipsis*). When Paul uses this term, he means more than the trials of hunger or poverty or physical ailments. *Thlipsis* refers to the suffering associated with the end-time tribulation and affliction. Certain as suffering and trials are at the end-time,

even more assured is God's triumph over evil. The God who has strengthened Paul during his lifetime will continue to strengthen the faithful at the end of the ages. Confident in Christ's abiding and strong presence, Paul concludes his reflection with a prayer of praise, rejoicing in the glorious riches in Christ Jesus.

GOSPEL The parable of the wedding feast is the final of three parables Jesus addressed to the Jewish leaders. He likens the Kingdom of Heaven to a king giving a lavish banquet, a motif

often associated with heavenly fulfillment. As with the other parables, allegorical interpretation may highlight the significance of the symbols for Jesus' audience, as well as Matthew's.

The king of the parable is God, who has planned a celebration for his Son, Jesus. The servants sent by God are the prophets of Israel. Two times God sends out the invitation, clearly expecting people to come to the feast. The first time, people simply refused. At the second invitation, we hear more specifics about their declining: too distracted; too occupied. Refusing

Note that the "bad" are invited as well as the "good."

Smile; the feast has begun! Pause.

"Friend" indicates the king is not (yet) angry; he gives the man a chance to explain.

It's his lack of response—like that of the invited guests—that seems to anger the king.

The invitation to the Kingdom of Heaven is open and generous, but once invited, we must do our part to bring the Kingdom to fullness.

TO KEEP IN MIND

A *narrative* has characters, dialogue, a setting, and action. Help your listeners see the story unfold, keep characters distinct, and be clear about shifts in setting.

The servants went out into the streets
and gathered **all** they found, bad and good **alike**,
and the hall was **filled** with guests.]
But when the king came in to **meet** the guests,
he saw a man there **not** dressed in a wedding garment.
The king said to him, 'My **friend**, how is it
that you came in here **without** a wedding garment?'
But he was reduced to **silence**.
Then the king said to his attendants, '**Bind** his hands and feet,
and **cast** him into the **darkness outside**,
where there will be **wailing** and grinding of **teeth**.'

Many are **invited**, but **few** are **chosen**."

[Shorter: Matthew 22:1–10 (see brackets)]

---

the king for such paltry reasons is bad enough, but the worst is killing the messengers, the prophets sent by God. Enraged, the king punishes those whose actions are tantamount to rebellion. Matthew's audience may see this as a reference to the destruction of Jerusalem.

Still, the feast must go on, so the king invites everyone who can be found—the bad and good alike. The seeming illogic of a man punished for not having a wedding garment when he was just recently pulled off the street reminds us of the allegorical character of the parable: exaggeration, inconsistency, and shocking details nudge us to look for possible symbolism. The wedding garment may indicate righteousness or faith or good works. "Being clothed in Christ" is an early way of describing Baptism. Having no wedding garment suggests someone who initially responded to God's invitation, but did not continue life in Christ. Matthew's audience could well ask themselves if they are living with or without a proper wedding garment.

The final verse summarizes the meaning of the parable for Jesus' audience, for Matthew's, and for us. Many (in the biblical idiom, "many" signifies "all") are called by God's widespread invitation. Few, however, choose to accept the invitation, or accept it only partially and temporarily. E.P.

TWENTY-NINTH SUNDAY IN ORDINARY TIME

LECTIONARY #145

READING I   Isaiah 45:1, 4–6

A reading from the Book of the Prophet Isaiah

An exhortatory reading in God's voice, describing the powerful yet hidden ways God acts for his people. This is not a history lesson, but a reminder that God is always present, even in the darkest situations.

Isaiah = ī-ZAY-uh

Cyrus = Sī-ruhs

Let your energy convey the drive and determination with which God acts, knocking down every barrier that stands in the way of freedom for Israel.
Pause.

Thus says the LORD to his **anointed**, **Cyrus**,
    whose right hand I **grasp**,
subduing **nations** before him,
    and making kings **run** in his service,
opening **doors** before him
    and leaving the gates **unbarred**:
For the sake of **Jacob**, my servant,
    of **Israel**, my **chosen** one,
I have **called** you by your **name**,
    giving you a **title**, though you knew me **not**.

God can use any person or circumstance to bring good.

An expression of God's power over all events.

I am the **Lord** and there is no **other**,
    there is **no** God besides me.
It is **I** who arm you, though you know me **not**,
    so that toward the **rising** and the **setting** of the sun
    people may **know** that there is **none** besides me.

"I do it so everyone may know that I have the power to carry out my plan for my people."

The second time this phrase appears; slowly and with great deliberateness.

I am the **Lord**, there **is** no **other**.

"There is no God besides me." When the Lord, the God of Israel, spoke to Cyrus, the king of Persia, telling him that there is no other God, Cyrus must have been shocked. According to a sixth century BC artifact called the Cyrus cylinder, Cyrus had been chosen by Marduk, the chief god of the Babylonians, to bring peace and order. Cyrus said that Marduk had bestowed great destiny upon him and pronounced blessing over him. But now another God, one who declares "There is no God besides me," addresses Cyrus. By grasping Cyrus by the right hand, the Lord God, not Marduk, is conferring royal authority upon him. The Lord is the only God, and has called Cyrus by name for the sake of God's Chosen People.

READING I God's choice of Cyrus must have been a shock to Israel as well, particularly since God referred to Cyrus as "anointed," a title expected for Davidic kings, and not for a foreign ruler. Cyrus did not even know the Lord, yet was chosen as the instrument to free the people from their exile in Babylon. When Cyrus allows the exiles to return to their own land, other nations will recognize the power and fidelity of the God of Israel. Thus, the royal title and authority that God gives to Cyrus is not for his own sake, but for that of others. The revelation to Cyrus is that Israel's God has a universal dominion. All peoples, from the rising of the sun to its setting, all people from east to west, are to know that only the Lord is God.

READING II The greetings in Paul's letters are more than formal salutations, for they contain rich insights into the life and faith of the early Church.

For meditation and context:

TO KEEP IN MIND
Repetition of the same word or phrase over the course of a reading emphasizes a point. Make each instance distinct, and build your intensity with each repetition.

RESPONSORIAL PSALM　Psalm 96:1, 3, 4–5, 7–8, 9–10 (7b)

R. Give the Lord glory and honor.

Sing to the LORD a new song;
　sing to the LORD, all you lands.
Tell his glory among the nations;
　among all peoples, his wondrous deeds.

For great is the LORD and highly
　　to be praised;
　awesome is he, beyond all gods.
For all the gods of the nations are things
　　of nought,
　but the LORD made the heavens.

Give to the LORD, you families of nations,
　give to the LORD glory and praise;
　give to the LORD the glory due his name!
Bring gifts, and enter his courts.

Worship the LORD, in holy attire;
　tremble before him, all the earth;
say among the nations: The LORD is king,
　he governs the peoples with equity.

An exhortatory greeting and blessing from Paul and his companions to the community at Thessalonica, but which you proclaim to your community.

Thessalonians = thes-uh-LOH-nee-uhnz

Silvanus = sil-VAY-nuhs

Pause.

Don't rush this short line.

A long sentence; pause at the commas except where noted. Keep your energy up.

Pause and take a breath here so you can keep the next phrases together (through "Father").

No pause here.

Pause at the end of the line.

Drop your voice slightly on the parenthetical phrase.

Pause at the end of the line.

Keep your energy up to the end.

Short pauses after "power" and "Spirit."

READING II　1 Thessalonians 1:1–5b

A reading from the first Letter of Saint Paul to the Thessalonians

Paul, **Silvanus**, and **Timothy** to the church of the **Thessalonians**
　in God the **Father** and the Lord Jesus **Christ**:
　grace to you and **peace**.
We give **thanks** to God **always** for all of you,
　remembering you in our **prayers**,
　　unceasingly calling to mind your work of **faith** and labor
　　　of **love**
　and endurance in **hope** of our Lord Jesus **Christ**,
　before our God and Father,
　knowing, brothers and sisters loved by God,
　how you were chosen.
For our gospel did not come to you in word **alone**,
　but also in **power** and in the Holy **Spirit** and with
　　much conviction.

The first words of the letter tell us that Paul is not engaged in the missionary enterprise in isolation; he is joined by his companions, Silvanus and Timothy. They greet the community in Thessalonica warmly, affirming that the believers live "in God the Father and the Lord Jesus Christ." At the end of the greeting, Paul also writes of the power of the Holy Spirit. Taken together, we see here one of the earliest foundations of belief in God as Father, Son, and Holy Spirit. Through Baptism the Thessalonians have been immersed into this Trinitarian life.

Paul and companions send, as they typically do, their wish of grace and peace, followed by a prayer of thanksgiving. As they recall the reasons for gratitude, we hear another important triad: faith, love, and hope. Neither the Thessalonians nor the missionaries live their communion with God in easy circumstances. In the midst of their affliction, they have endured in hope, a sure and strong sign of their confidence in the God who loves them. The letter-writers conclude their salutation by reminding their readers that the Gospel proclaimed by Paul came not only in Word, but also in the

power of the Holy Spirit, with much conviction. The same is true for the Gospel lived and proclaimed by the new believers in Thessalonica, and by ourselves as well.

GOSPEL　Today's Gospel is the first of four controversies in which Jesus' adversaries question him about topics of Law, belief, and behavior. After Jesus finishes his teaching in parables to some of his harshest opponents, the Pharisees initiate their plotting against him. Their plan is to entrap him; they cleverly decide to bring in the Herodians, those who

A narrative of a brief exchange in which Jesus foils the Pharisees' plan to entrap him. Don't rush and be sure the intentions and movements in this dialogue come through.

Give this narration a secretive tone; drop your voice to a whisper.

Pharisees = FAYR-uh-seez

Herodians = her-OH-dee-uhnz

Speak as if only one of them is addressing Jesus. This is supercilious flattery, of course, but make an attempt to sound sincere.

Pause at the end of the line.

They feel clever. Pause at the end of the line.

Is Jesus angry? Annoyed? Weary of them? Make a strong choice and let it come through in your proclamation.

Tentatively; they're not sure what he's getting at.

Firmly, with a tone of "Now go away and don't bother us anymore." Keep the two phrases separate.

TO KEEP IN MIND
Making eye contact with the assembly connects you with them and connects them to the reading more deeply than using your voice alone. This helps the assembly stay with the story and keeps them engaged.

GOSPEL   Matthew 22:15–21

A reading from the holy Gospel according to Matthew

The **Pharisees** went off
  and **plotted** how they might **entrap** Jesus in speech.
They sent their **disciples** to him, with the **Herodians**, saying,
  "**Teacher**, we know that you are a **truthful** man
  and that you teach the way of God in accordance
    with the **truth**.
And you are not concerned with **anyone's** opinion,
  for you do not regard a person's **status**.
Tell us, then, **what** is your opinion:
  Is it **lawful** to pay the census tax to Caesar or **not**?"
Knowing their **malice**, Jesus said,
  "**Why** are you testing me, you **hypocrites**?
Show me the coin that **pays** the census tax."
Then they **handed** him the Roman coin.
He said to them, "**Whose** image is this and whose **inscription**?"
They replied, "**Caesar's**."
At that he said to them,
  "Then **repay** to Caesar what **belongs** to Caesar
  and to **God** what belongs to **God**."

supported the Roman occupation and system of taxation, which the Pharisees themselves disputed. Jesus would be sure to offend one side or the other when the question of paying taxes to Caesar was at issue. Even more, he could be seen in opposition to Rome, getting himself in trouble as a rebel.

The plan is to so disarm Jesus with flattery so that he must either answer their question or appear untruthful and acting contrary to his own teaching, but Jesus' immediate response turns the tables. He knows their malice (*poneria*), which moti-

vates them to put on a show. Jesus rightly calls them "hypocrites," since they are playing a part in the drama they set up, pretending to ask a genuine question. When Jesus asks them to show him the coin, he forces them to acknowledge that the coin has the inscription of Caesar on it. Caesar's name on the coin means that the coin must belong to Caesar; paying the tax simply means giving back to him what already belongs to him. Although Jesus doesn't ask them, "Which things belong to God?" we can almost hear it as an unspoken query.

What is our own answer to that fundamental question? E.P.

THIRTIETH SUNDAY IN ORDINARY TIME

LECTIONARY #148

READING I Exodus 22:20–26

A reading from the Book of Exodus

Thus says the LORD:
"You shall not **molest** or **oppress** an **alien**,
  for you were once aliens **yourselves** in the land of **Egypt**.
You shall not **wrong** any **widow** or **orphan**.
If **ever** you wrong them and they **cry** out to me,
  I will **surely** hear their cry.
My wrath will **flare** up, and I will **kill** you with the sword;
  then your own wives will be **widows**, and your
    children **orphans**.

"If you lend **money** to one of your poor neighbors among
    my people,
  you shall not act like an **extortioner** toward him
  by demanding **interest** from him.
If you take your neighbor's **cloak** as a pledge,
  you shall **return** it to him before **sunset**;
  for this **cloak** of his is the **only** covering he has for his body.
What **else** has he to sleep in?
If he **cries** out to me, I will **hear** him; for I am **compassionate**."

You can see why this exhortatory reading is paired with today's Gospel. God asks us to treat others as we would like to be treated.

Exodus = EK-suh-duhs

Careful not to make this sound like a military order. Rather, God expects us to understand that relationships should be based on mutual care; this is how God relates to us. Don't swallow "alien."

God is the protector of the poor and vulnerable, and will act swiftly on their behalf.

Don't gloss over "kill you," but don't point it up either. It's the consequence of oppressing the poor.

extortioner = ek-STOHR-shuhn-*r
Adding interest will keep your neighbor poor and stuck in a cycle of borrowing, never able to get out of debt.

These admonitions may seem culturally distant; the basic message is that business pursuits must never take precedence over people's survival.

Slow down on the last phrase.

READING I In a lengthy section of the Book of Exodus (Exodus 20:19—23:33), the terms of the covenant are spelled out in detail. Included are an explanation about the proper way to worship and revere God, civil and criminal laws, and other exhortations about how to live in right covenant relationship. Fundamental to the behaviors expected of the people of Israel is the idea that as God acts toward them they are to act toward one another.

The Commandments in today's reading single out the alien, the widow, and the orphan. In ancient Israel, these groups rep-

resented the most vulnerable in society. They had no extended family to care for them, as was the custom. Similarly, those who were poor had little protection. The cloak might be the only thing left to offer in payment for a debt. The debt collector could take it as a pledge during the day, but must return it at night, since the cloak was the one covering against the chill of night. According to the practice, the poor person would return the cloak in the morning as a renewed pledge.

God's own actions, already experienced by the people of the covenant, are

the reasons for treating each of these groups with dignity and justice. When the people of Israel were aliens, God heard their cry and rescued them, and will now also hear the cry of oppressed aliens, widows, orphans, and the poor. God will hear anyone who calls out, for God is compassionate, ever acting on behalf of those in need.

READING II The faith of the Church, including that of Paul and the Thessalonian community, is based on Jesus, who died and was raised from the dead. In every aspect of his life, Paul strives

264

For meditation and context:

TO KEEP IN MIND

Be careful not to "swallow" words by mumbling. Articulate carefully so that every word is clearly heard, especially at the end of lines.

RESPONSORIAL PSALM Psalm 18:2–3, 3–4, 47, 51 (2)

R. I love you, Lord, my strength.

I love you, O LORD, my strength,
    O LORD, my rock, my fortress,
    my deliverer.

My God, my rock of refuge,
    my shield, the horn of my salvation,
    my stronghold!
Praised be the LORD, I exclaim,
    and I am safe from my enemies.

The LORD lives and blessed be my rock!
    Extolled be God my savior.
You who gave great victories to your king
    and showed kindness to your anointed.

A narrative Paul relates with great pride; a testimonial. Recall a story you've told with pride and bring that same energy and emotion to this proclamation.

Thessalonians = thes-uh-LOH-nee-uhnz

Pause at the end of the line.

The next three sentences are long, but try to keep them together, pausing only at commas. Speak directly to your assembly.

Macedonia = mas-eh-DOH-nee-uh

Achaia = uh-KAY-uh

Pause.

Their reputation precedes them.

Let your joy at their conversion show! Take a quick breath here if you need it.

READING II   1 Thessalonians 1:5c–10

A reading from the first Letter of Saint Paul to the Thessalonians

Brothers and sisters:
You **know** what sort of people we were among you for **your** sake.
And you became **imitators** of us and of the **Lord**,
    receiving the word in great **affliction**, with **joy** from the
        Holy **Spirit**,
    so that you became a **model** for all the believers
    in Macedonia and in Achaia.
For from **you** the word of the Lord has **sounded** forth
    not **only** in Macedonia and in Achaia,
    but in **every** place your faith in God has gone forth,
    so that we have no need to say **anything**.
For they themselves **openly** declare about us
    what sort of reception we had among you,
    and how you **turned** to God from **idols**
    to **serve** the living and **true** God
    and to **await** his Son from **heaven**,
    whom he **raised** from the **dead**,
    Jesus, who **delivers** us from the coming **wrath**.

to imitate the life pattern of Jesus. He rejoices that this pattern of imitation of Christ is continued in the church of Thessalonica. Their faith has gone forth, transmitted from one person to another, from Thessalonica to other cities and regions, in a process that has continued for more than two millennia. Paul and his companions, along with the Thessalonians and other believers, transmit the faith by being living examples to others, maintaining joy and hope even in the midst of suffering.

Both Paul and the believers in Thessalonica received the Word in affliction

(*thlipsis*), difficulties they believed to be the end-time tribulation. Yet those troubles have not cast them down. The joy that is characteristic of Paul in this letter is also part of the Thessalonians' faith; which Paul summarizes. They had turned to God from idols, an indication that a majority in the Thessalonian community were Gentile pagans who now serve the living and true God known to the Jews. As they do so, they are awaiting the coming again of Jesus, the Son whom God has raised from the dead. The affliction that they experience now is a prelude to divine deliverance from God's

final wrath against evil. The powerful God who raised Jesus from the dead is the one who will also rescue those who are faithful to the end.

GOSPEL In an episode between last week's Gospel and this week's, Jesus was in controversy with the Sadducees, who did not believe in resurrection. Jesus provides them with an innovative interpretation of the Torah that supports belief in the resurrection, thereby silencing them. The Pharisees, who shared Jesus' belief in the resurrection, would

A narrative, ending with a didactic passage.

Articulate carefully; the line's a bit of a tongue twister.

Pharisees = FAYR-uh-seez

Sadducees = SAD-y<u>oo</u>-seez

He's not curious or interested in justifying himself; he's "testing" Jesus, so proclaim with a tinge of suspicion in your voice. Pause. With the gentleness of a compassionate teacher

Separate these three phrases.

Take your time with this line. Pause.

Simply, but with great confidence. Here is the answer to the Pharisee's question.

TO KEEP IN MIND

In a narrative, find an emotion or point of view for each character, keeping in mind that these might change during the reading.

GOSPEL　Matthew 22:34–40

A reading from the holy Gospel according to Matthew

When the **Pharisees** heard that Jesus had **silenced** the Sadducees,
　　they **gathered** together, and **one** of them,
　　a **scholar** of the law, **tested** him by asking,
　　"**Teacher**, **which** commandment in the law is the **greatest**?"
He said to him,
　　"You shall **love** the Lord, your **God**,
　　with all your **heart**,
　　with all your **soul**,
　　and with all your **mind**.
This is the **greatest** and the **first** commandment.
The **second** is **like** it:
　　You shall **love** your **neighbor** as **yourself**.
The **whole** law and the prophets depend on **these**
　　　two commandments."

---

undoubtedly have approved of his convincing teaching. When one of them, a scholar of the Law, asks Jesus which commandment is the greatest, he could be asking a sincere question, one that was, in fact, a subject among contemporary rabbis. Those rabbis arrived at different answers; perhaps this teacher of the Law simply wanted to engage Jesus in debate.

Matthew comments, however, that by posing the question, the scholar "tested" Jesus. Testing here, like the Pharisees' query about paying taxes to Caesar, was an attempt to prove that Jesus had no author-

ity as a teacher. Jesus' answer brings together two positive commandments of the Torah that describe the right relationship with God and neighbor. The first one, which requires love of God with the entirety of one's being, is based on the Shema at Deuteronomy 6:5, to which Jesus adds "with all your mind." So important is the Shema in Judaism that it continues to be recited twice daily in our times. The second commandment is from Leviticus 19:18, commanding Israelites to love their neighbors as themselves. While the scholar had asked for only one commandment, Jesus

gives two, teaching that love of God and love of neighbor are intimately connected and embrace all the other commandments. All of the six hundred thirteen commandments of the Law are included in these two. In his test, Jesus is faithful to the tradition, and teaches with authority. E.P.

ALL SAINTS

LECTIONARY #667

READING I Revelation 7:2–4, 9–14

A reading from the Book of Revelation

I, **John**, saw another **angel** come up from the East,
　　holding the **seal** of the living **God**.
He **cried** out in a **loud** voice to the four angels
　　who were given power to **damage** the **land** and the **sea**,
　　"Do **not** damage the land or the sea or the trees
　　until we put the **seal** on the **foreheads** of the **servants**
　　　　of our God."
I heard the **number** of those who had been marked with the seal,
　　one **hundred** and forty-four **thousand** marked
　　from **every** tribe of the children of Israel.

After this I had a vision of a great **multitude**,
　　which **no one** could count,
　　from every **nation**, **race**, **people**, and **tongue**.
They stood before the **throne** and before the **Lamb**,
　　wearing **white** robes and holding palm branches in their hands.
They **cried out** in a loud voice:

　　"**Salvation** comes from our **God**, who is seated on the **throne**,
　　and from the **Lamb**."

All the angels stood around the throne
　　and around the **elders** and the four living **creatures**.
They **prostrated** themselves before the throne,
　　worshiped God, and **exclaimed**: »

An exhortatory reading telling of a fantastical vision. Don't concern yourself with the allegorical meaning; just tell the story as it is, with all its wonder and amazement. Your goal is to proclaim so that your community can see it unfolding before them.

Revelation = rev-uh-LAY-shuhn

Don't rush; there's a lot going on.

This is a scene full of power and energy. Vary your inflection and volume, but don't lose the energy. Build the intensity slowly to the end.

Raise your volume here, but not too much; you want some room to grow.

Proclaim the number as if it were the biggest number you could imagine.

See the crowd spreading out before you; imagine them filling the space you're in and spilling out of the doors!

Raise your volume and intensity a bit more here.

READING I The visions of John from the Book of Revelation are replete with imaginative sights and sounds, creating a wondrous audio-visual experience. "Experience" is the operative word, for John wants his audience to see themselves as part of his dramatic story. In order for them to interpret the visions, they must be familiar with the symbolism that John uses throughout his book: symbolic numbers, colors, animals, and other images that are common to apocalyptic writings. Much of the symbolism in Revelation has close connections with apocalyptic sec-

tions in the Old Testament, particularly Ezekiel and Daniel.

In today's reading, we see two visions: one on earth, and the second one in heaven. In the earthly vision, John sees an angel coming from the east, the direction of salvation. The angel, a divine messenger, holds a seal that is to be put on the foreheads of the servants of God. This symbolism was probably inspired by the prophet Ezekiel (9:4, 6) where an angel marks the foreheads of those who have not committed idolatry and are protected from death. In John's vision, those so marked number

one hundred and forty-four thousand who belong to and are protected by God. Not intended as a literal number, it is rather derived from the number of the twelve tribes of Israel, an identity taken on by Christians. Twelve squared and multiplied by a thousand signifies totality, a number far too large to count. Those sealed are chosen by, belong to, and are protected by God.

In the second vision, John again sees a vast multitude, this time standing before the throne of the Lamb. The Lamb has already been an important figure in Revelation, an image for Jesus, slain yet triumphant. Having

The climax of the reading; your energy should peak here.

Pause.

Drop your voice now, as if this were a more intimate conversation.

This is a rhetorical question; make sure it doesn't sound like he's asking for information.

There's a wistful joy in his voice as he recounts their suffering and perseverance.

"**Amen**. **Blessing** and **glory**, **wisdom** and **thanksgiving**,
    honor, **power**, and **might**
  be to our **God** forever and **ever**. **Amen**."

Then one of the **elders** spoke up and said to me,
    "Who **are** these wearing white robes, and where did they
        come from?"
I said to him, "My lord, **you** are the one who knows."
He said to me,
    "These are the ones who have **survived** the time
        of great **distress**;
  they have **washed** their robes
  and made them **white** in the **Blood** of the **Lamb**."

For meditation and context:

RESPONSORIAL PSALM Psalm 24:1bc–2, 3–4ab, 5–6 (6)

R. **Lord, this is the people that longs to see your face.**

The LORD's are the earth and its fullness;
    the world and those who dwell in it.
For he founded it upon the seas
    and established it upon the rivers.

Who can ascend the mountain of the LORD?
    or who may stand in his holy place?
One whose hands are sinless, whose heart
    is clean,
    who desires not what is vain.

He shall receive a blessing from the LORD,
    a reward from God his savior.
Such is the race that seeks him,
    that seeks the face of the God of Jacob.

been marked with the seal, this crowd has come through the great tribulation; their salvation has come not from their own power, but from God and from the Lamb. They sing their victory song, beginning and concluding it with a resounding "Amen!" Following their acclamation, John inserts a dialogue with the elders in which we learn the identity of those marked with the seal. They have survived the great tribulation, the end-time crisis. Their robes, washed with the Blood of the Lamb, are not blood stained with red, but radiate the white of purity and salvation.

READING II The author of the First Letter of John repeatedly addresses the recipients of his writing with terms of pastoral affection: "beloved" (*agapetoi*) and "little children" (*teknon* and *paidion*). He includes himself as part of the community, using "we" and "us," further establishing the close relationship. He sharply distinguishes this audience from other people he refers to in the letter: liars, antichrists, false prophets. At least some of these persons were former members of the community, and John writes to his beloved children to provide true teach-

ing, to offer advice and encouragement, and to issue warnings. Although he is writing about Church conflict in the first century, his instruction retains a universal appeal and significance, well-observed by St. Augustine: "This book is very sweet to every healthy Christian heart that savors the bread of God, and it should constantly be in the mind of God's holy church" (*Ten Homilies on 1 John*, Prologue). In these three verses, John focuses on the abiding relationship between God and the believing community. Because of the love (*agape*) of God, the believers are "beloved" (*agapetoi*)

An exhortatory reading, assuring us not to be concerned with the future, because God's love is destined to win and we will claim our identity as children of God.

Don't bark out "Beloved," but fill it with tenderness.
Linger over this description of God's overflowing love.

Not surprising . . . we are called what we are!

Again, use the word "Beloved" to convey your care for the community. Contrast "now" with "shall be."

This is not worrisome but exciting!

Emphasize the phrase, "we shall be like him."

he = Jesus

READING II   1 John 3:1–3

A reading from the first Letter of Saint John

Beloved:
See what **love** the Father has bestowed on **us**
    that we may be called the **children** of God.
Yet so we **are**.
The reason the world does not **know** us
    is that it did not know **him**.
Beloved, we are God's children **now**;
    what we **shall** be has not yet been **revealed**.
We **do** know that when it **is** revealed we shall be **like** him,
    for we shall **see** him as he **is**.
Everyone who has this hope based on **him** makes himself **pure**,
    as **he** is pure.

TO KEEP IN MIND
Exhortatory texts make an urgent appeal to listeners. They may encourage, warn, or challenge, and often include a call to action. You must convey the urgency and passion behind the words.

---

and are called God's own children. The relationship is so intimate that the reason the world does not know God's children is because they do not know God, nor the Son of God. This lack of knowing is much more than an intellectual failure; knowing in John's theology is close to belief and discipleship, whereas not knowing indicates hostility and willful refusal to believe. In John's Gospel the same lack of knowing is associated with rejection of Jesus. (See 1:10; 15:21; 16:3.)

The world does not know "us," John writes, and may have the same enmity toward us as it had toward Jesus. Yet, our hope is secure as God's children. John points to an eschatological fulfillment when the transformation already begun here will be revealed at the end of time. Then "we shall be like him for we shall see him as he is." We prepare for this wondrous fulfillment by making our own lives like Christ's. As he was pure (*hagnos*), so should we also be, signifying virtuous life that embraces every dimension, from ethical goodness to the purity of prayer and sacrifice, and even to thinking like Christ.

GOSPEL   The setting of today's Gospel is a mountain, the locale in Matthew's Gospel where so many significant events in Jesus' life take place: temptation, teaching, prayer, Transfiguration, Ascension. The locale immediately alerts us that something important is about to happen. On the mountain "he began to teach them," gathering his disciples for his first major discourse. He opens with a collection of beatitudes, thereby beginning his teaching the same way that the Book of Psalms begins. Both sermon and psalter set the tone for all that follows

An exhortatory teaching of Jesus. It's likely well known to your hearers. The key to keeping it fresh is not to make it about Jesus teaching the crowd, but about Jesus teaching your community. Don't let the rhythm lull you into a sleepy, singsong reading. Rather, make each verse distinct, as if each were a new idea, building up to a complete picture of the community of the faithful.

Blessed = BLES-uhd

The surprise in these verses is that the poor, the mourners, the meek, and so forth, are blessed, whereas most people would look at them and consider them cursed.

Remember, make this about your community. Speak directly to the merciful, the clean of heart, the peacemakers in your community.

Note the switch from "blessed are they" to "blessed are you."

Another surprise: we should rejoice when we're persecuted!

Slow down on this final line.

TO KEEP IN MIND
Parallelism refers to phrases or sentences that have a similar structure or express a similar idea. Use emphasis and rhythm to make sure any parallelism stands out.

GOSPEL　Matthew 5:1–12a

A reading from the holy Gospel according to Matthew

When Jesus saw the **crowds**, he went up the **mountain**,
　　and after he had sat down, his disciples came to him.
He began to **teach** them, saying:

　　"**Blessed** are the **poor** in **spirit**,
　　　　for **theirs** is the Kingdom of **heaven**.
　　Blessed are they who **mourn**,
　　　　for they will be **comforted**.
　　Blessed are the **meek**,
　　　　for they will **inherit** the **land**.
　　Blessed are they who **hunger** and **thirst** for **righteousness**,
　　　　for they will be **satisfied**.
　　Blessed are the **merciful**,
　　　　for they will be **shown mercy**.
　　Blessed are the clean of **heart**,
　　　　for they will see **God**.
　　Blessed are the **peacemakers**,
　　　　for they will be called **children** of God.
　　Blessed are they who are **persecuted** for the sake
　　　　of **righteousness**,
　　　　for theirs is the Kingdom of **heaven**.
　　Blessed are **you** when they **insult** you and **persecute** you
　　　　and utter every kind of evil **against** you **falsely** because
　　　　of **me**.
　　Rejoice and be **glad**,
　　　　for your **reward** will be **great** in heaven."

by announcing God's blessing; they intimate that every part of Jesus' teaching and every psalm gives us an insight into God's blessing. The generous and constant blessing of God underlies all of Jesus' beatitudes and all of his teaching.

　　Beatitudes are part of Wisdom literature in the Old Testament. They announce that God's blessing is assured for those who behave in particular ways deemed to be wise. They are a concise way of promoting specific actions and provide the community with a unified vision. While the beatitudes in the Old Testament generally reflect the common wisdom of the times, Jesus' beatitudes express actions and attitudes that run counter to the common norms of society, both in his own day and in our own.

　　Jesus' first beatitude can be regarded an "umbrella beatitude," one that covers all the rest. If anyone is truly poor in spirit, the rest of the beatitudes should follow. The poor in spirit rely on God for everything, placing their hope in the God who cares for them and the entirety of creation. Recognizing Jesus as the face of God, they pattern their lives on his: meek, merciful, and just, clean of heart, bringer of peace. The Kingdom of Heaven is both a present and future blessing. Even though insulted and persecuted now, God's eternal and full blessing in heaven will be their reward. E.P.

THE COMMEMORATION OF ALL THE FAITHFUL DEPARTED (ALL SOULS' DAY)

An exhortatory reading, assuring us that the dead are with God, even those who suffered in life or seemed punished by death. What does this reading want us to do or be after hearing this? Keep that intention in mind throughout your proclamation.

Imagine consoling someone who has just lost a loved one. What tone would you use?

Set this line apart.
Contrast "punished" with "hope," "chastised" with "blessed."

proved = tested. Gold is put into fire to harden it, so it will last and shine forever!

They who were thought to be punished will instead appear in glory with the power of God.

Only because of God's great mercy can we be sure of our salvation.

LECTIONARY #668

READING I   Wisdom 3:1–9

A reading from the Book of Wisdom

The souls of the **just** are in the hand of **God**,
    and no **torment** shall touch them.
They **seemed**, in the view of the **foolish**, to be **dead**;
    and their passing away was thought an **affliction**
    and their going forth from us, utter **destruction**.
But they are in **peace**.
For if before **men**, indeed, they be **punished**,
    yet is their **hope** full of **immortality**;
chastised a **little**, they shall be **greatly** blessed,
    because God **tried** them
    and found them **worthy** of himself.
As gold in the furnace, he **proved** them,
    and as sacrificial offerings he **took** them to **himself**.
In the time of their visitation they shall **shine**,
    and shall **dart** about as **sparks** through **stubble**;
they shall judge **nations** and rule over **peoples**,
    and the LORD shall be their King **forever**.
Those who **trust** in him shall understand **truth**,
    and the **faithful** shall abide with him in **love**:
because **grace** and **mercy** are with his **holy** ones,
    and his **care** is with his **elect**.

The readings given here are suggestions. Any reading from the Lectionary for the Commemoration of All the Faithful Departed (#668) or the Masses for the Dead (#1011–1015) may be used. Ask your parish staff which readings to prepare.

READING I   Most of the proverbs and poetry of Old Testament wisdom literature reflect on how to live wisely in daily life. The Book of Wisdom, written in the latter half of the first century BC, looks beyond earthly matters to consider what happens after this life and the relationship with God that transcends death.

Our reading begins, "The souls of the just are in the hand of God." From the perspective of the Book of Wisdom, those who are just or righteous live in right relationship with God and with other people. The first five chapters of Wisdom focus on such living, with the first words of the book setting forth the theme: "Love righteousness." Righteous living includes right thinking, right acting, and seeking the Lord with integrity of heart. Justice is the fundamental virtue promoted by the Wisdom writer.

The polar opposite of those who are just is those who are unrighteous people who persecute the righteous with violence and torture.

Those who are unjust are also foolish. They think that death is the end for everyone, described as an affliction and destruction. In contrast, those who are just are also wise; they believe that God's mercy and compassion will extend into a glorious future. They see God as the one who created and sustains life, and is not the God of death: "God did not make death, / nor does he rejoice in the destruction of the living"

For meditation and context:

TO KEEP IN MIND

A *didactic* text makes a point or teaches something. Help your assembly to follow the argument and understand what's being taught.

An exhortatory reminder of God's great love for us in Jesus Christ! Make sure your community knows this is good news from your voice, eyes, and face!

Start strong and full of joy and hope!

Linger over this phrase describing God's overflowing love!

"Ungodly" is a surprise; don't swallow it.

This is an aside; pick up the pace a bit.

Don't stress "proves"; here, it simply means "shows."
God's gift of love is free, for sinner and saint alike. This is indeed good news, so smile with your voice, eyes, and face!
Pause.

RESPONSORIAL PSALM   Psalm 23:1–3a, 3b–4, 5, 6 (1)

R. The Lord is my shepherd; there is nothing I shall want. or R. Though I walk in the valley of darkness, I fear no evil, for you are with me.

The LORD is my shepherd; I shall not want.
    In verdant pastures he gives me repose;
beside restful waters he leads me;
    he refreshes my soul.

He guides me in right paths
    for his name's sake.
Even though I walk in the dark valley
    I fear no evil; for you are at my side
with your rod and your staff
    that give me courage.

You spread the table before me
    in the sight of my foes;
You anoint my head with oil;
    my cup overflows.

Only goodness and kindness follow me
    all the days of my life;
and I shall dwell in the house of the LORD
    for years to come.

READING II   Romans 5:5–11

A reading from the Letter of Saint Paul to the Romans

Brothers and sisters:
Hope does not **disappoint**,
    because the **love** of God has been **poured** out into our hearts
    through the Holy Spirit that has been given to us.
For **Christ**, while we were still **helpless**,
    died at the appointed time for the **ungodly**.
Indeed, only with **difficulty** does one die for a **just** person,
    though perhaps for a **good** person
    one might even find **courage** to die.
But God **proves** his love for us
    in that while we were **still** sinners Christ **died** for us.
How much **more** then, since we are now **justified** by his Blood,
    will we be **saved** through him from the **wrath**. »

(1:13). The Lord will continue his gracious care even beyond death.

The teaching of the author of Wisdom is that *immortality*, literally "not death," is a gift from God. Because of God's grace and mercy, his holy ones (another way of referring to those who are just) will abide with God forever in love. With the gift of immortality, God transforms the pain and suffering of this life into peace, blessedness, and understanding of truth.

Neither today's reading nor the other passages in Wisdom give a precise definition of immortality. In fact, there are only hints even in the New Testament of what

life after death will be like. The fundamental teaching, however, is strong and clear: God is the God of the living, rewards the just, and will remain their loving, faithful God through all eternity.

READING II **Romans 5:5–11.** In the section of Romans from which our reading is taken, Paul describes the life of those who are justified. Seeing that believers are already justified, he develops a series of chain reactions to describe the consequences of justification, one flowing from another: affliction leads to endurance that leads to proven character, and then

leads to hope. As the final link in the chain, where today's reading picks up, hope is strong because God's love has already been poured into our hearts through the Holy Spirit. Hope doesn't disappoint; since we already have a taste of the promised fruits, we rightly expect future fulfillment.

Thus the future orientation of hope is based on what God did in the past and continues to do in the present. Paul's own hope, like our own, arises from Christ's past action of Death on the Cross, accomplished for the helpless, the ungodly, and sinners. Christ's Death *then* is the ground for hope *now*, giving assurance that he will

Raise your intensity.

Indeed, if, while we were **enemies**,
> we were **reconciled** to God through the **death** of his Son,
> how much **more**, once **reconciled**,
> will we be saved by his **life**.
Not only **that**,
> but we also **boast** of God through our Lord Jesus Christ,
> through whom we have now received **reconciliation**.

Or:

The best news yet!

We "boast" of our intimacy with God through Christ.

READING II   Romans 6:3–9

A reading from the Letter of Saint Paul to the Romans

A didactic reading, but full of good news, so proclaim with intensity.

Brothers and sisters:
Are you **unaware** that we who were **baptized** into Christ Jesus
> were baptized into his **death**?
We were indeed **buried** with him through **baptism** into **death**,
> so that, just as **Christ** was **raised** from the dead
> by the glory of the Father,
> we **too** might live in **newness** of life.

Are you unaware = Don't you know

Emphasize we were buried through Baptism.

For if we have grown into **union** with him through a **death**
> like his,
> we shall also be **united** with him in the **resurrection**.
We know that our **old** self was **crucified** with him,
> so that our **sinful** body might be done **away** with,
> that we might no longer be in **slavery** to sin.
For a dead person has been **absolved** from sin.
If, then, we have **died** with Christ,
> we believe that we shall also **live** with him.
We know that Christ, **raised** from the dead, dies no **more**;
> death no **longer** has power over him.

Unity with Christ in death also brings unity in newness of life!

Paul makes the point again. Slow down.

Our "body" represents not our physical body but our old self.

This is self-evident: the dead are no longer subject to sin!

Slow down on this final line.

---

act even more powerfully for those (including ourselves!) justified by his blood. We can see Paul's explanation as implying another chain reaction: Christ's love for sinners leads to his death, which leads to our justification, which leads us again to an abiding hope that we will be saved through him. Our salvation has already begun, and we wait in hope for its fullness.

Romans 6:3–9. At the heart of Christian belief is Christ's Death and Resurrection. In this reading Paul explains how we participate in this central mystery through Baptism. To be baptized means to be immersed, submerged, or plunged into

another place or reality. When Paul writes of Baptism, he says we have been plunged into Christ's Crucifixion, Death, and burial. In a conversation with James and John, Jesus had likewise used baptismal terminology to allude to this sharing in his Passion and Death: "Can you drink the cup that I drink or be baptized with the baptism with which I am baptized?" (Mark 10:38). He is asking two of his first disciples a question that is similar to the one that Paul asks the Roman community: "Are you unaware that we who were baptized into Christ Jesus were baptized into his death?"

As the story of Christ's Death is incomplete without inclusion of his Resurrection, so too is our participation in Christ's life through Baptism. United with Christ through a death like his, we shall also be united with him in Resurrection. Paul develops the logical conclusion: through Baptism, our old self was crucified with Christ, meaning that having been immersed into the mystery of Christ's Death, we have been absolved from, or died to, sin. Our union with the risen Christ assures us that we will live with him; our union already begun engenders hope for total union in the future.

An exhortatory reading, all good news. This is not a dry theological treatise, but assurance that we belong to Christ and so life is ours. Keep your energy up throughout.

Challenge your assembly—let us not reject anyone who comes to us!

Remember, you are speaking to a community of believers. This gift of life is for them!

How do you feel about this gift? Let your joy come through.

> TO KEEP IN MIND
> Making eye contact with the assembly connects you with them and connects them to the reading more deeply than using your voice alone. This helps the assembly stay with the story and keeps them engaged.

GOSPEL   John 6:37–40

A reading from the holy Gospel according to John

Jesus said to the crowds:
    "**Everything** that the Father **gives** me will **come** to me,
    and I will not reject **anyone** who comes to me,
    because I came down from heaven not to do my **own** will
    but the will of the one who **sent** me.
And **this** is the will of the one who sent me,
    that I should not lose **anything** of what he **gave** me,
    but that I should **raise** it on the last **day**.
For **this** is the will of my **Father**,
    that **everyone** who **sees** the Son and **believes** in him
    may have eternal **life**,
    and I shall **raise** him up on the last **day**."

GOSPEL   **John 6:37–40.** In verses before this reading begins, Jesus has fed the multitude with bread, and has begun his discourse explaining the deeper meaning of the bread that the Father gives: "I am the bread of life; whoever comes to me will never hunger." As Jesus continues his teaching, he expands on the interwoven relationships he already referred to: Jesus and his Father; Jesus and believers; the Father and believers. When Jesus says, "Everything that the Father gives me will come to me," he may be indicating all of creation; in this context, he seems to be talking about "every person" (as found, for example, in John 17:2). Jesus will not reject any person who comes to him. To come to Jesus (in John's Gospel) is equivalent to believing in him.

When Jesus welcomes anyone who comes to him in faith, he is doing the Father's will. The intimate relationship between Jesus and his Father means that he does only and always the Father's will. Jesus *knows* his Father's will, *speaks* of it to his disciples, and *does* it by his actions. His knowing, speaking, and doing the Father's will are all ways of expressing their constant union. The Father's will is that all who believe in Jesus will have eternal life; thus, that is also Jesus' will. The eternal life willed by Jesus and his Father has already begun now, and will be brought to completion when Jesus raises up those who believe in him on the last day. E.P.

THIRTY-FIRST SUNDAY IN ORDINARY TIME

LECTIONARY #151

An exhortatory warning to those who have not kept God's covenant and acted with justice. You might take your intention from the last line, "Let's not break faith with one another!"

Malachi = MAL-uh-kī

Show your disdain right way for these faithless priests.

"Listen up!" This is only the introduction to the commandment. Keep your pace up.

God has given the blessing; God can take it away as a curse. Pause.

Anger is a possible emotion for these lines, but disappointment or sadness might be a better choice.

Now, anger is an appropriate choice.

contemptible = kuhn-TEMP-tuh-b*l (worthy of scorn)

base = lowly

Here's the issue: They are not acting justly.

A long pause as the speaker shifts from God to Malachi.

Appeal directly to your assembly here. Urge them to be reconciled to God and each other. Raise the stakes. If you don't get them to do it, no one will!

Show God's frustration or regret over the community's divisions (every community has them).

READING I   Malachi 1:14b—2:2b, 8–10

A reading from the Book of the Prophet Malachi

A great **King** am I, says the LORD of **hosts**,
    and my name will be **feared** among the **nations**.
And **now**, **O** priests, this commandment is for **you**:
    If you do **not** listen,
if you do **not** lay it to **heart**,
    to give **glory** to my **name**, says the LORD of hosts,
I will send a **curse** upon you
    and of your **blessing** I will make a **curse**.
You have turned **aside** from the **way**,
    and have caused **many** to **falter** by your **instruction**;
you have made **void** the **covenant** of Levi,
    says the LORD of hosts.
I, **therefore**, have made you **contemptible**
    and **base** before **all** the people,
since you do not **keep** my ways,
    but show **partiality** in your **decisions**.
Have we not **all** the **one** father?
    Has not the **one** God created us?
Why then do we **break faith** with one another,
    violating the covenant of our fathers?

READING I   Through the prophet Malachi, the Lord of hosts (sabaoth) speaks to the priests of Israel. As great king and Lord of hosts, God is portrayed as the leader of the heavenly army as well as the armies of Israel. Commander of mighty forces, the Lord of hosts is feared among the nations. With such a self-introduction, the priests are expected to listen, or be subject to the power that God can wield; they are issued a clear warning: "If you do not listen . . . I will send a curse upon you, and your blessing I will curse."

The text of our reading today omits several verses in which God tells the priests what they should have known, but have neglected the covenant that God made with their ancestor, Levi. After these verses, our reading continues. Instead of living in keeping with the tradition begun with Levi, they have turned aside from "the way," a frequent biblical image to describe a manner of living. Not only have the priests themselves turned aside from the right way, but through their faulty instruction they have led astray the people they should have been guiding. The indictment reads literally, "you have caused many to stumble in the Torah." The core of their life and faith, the Torah, is perverted because the priests have shown partiality in their teaching, currying favor with the powerful of society.

Condemnation is not the last word of the Lord to the priests. He asks them a pointed question: "Have we not all one father?" Since God is the father and creator of all, the priests have a responsibility for leading the family in the way of the Torah. God's condemnation is for the sake of

For meditation and context:

TO KEEP IN MIND
Proclamation cannot be effective unless it is expressive. As you prepare your proclamation, make choices about emotions. Some choices are already evident in the text.

A narrative full of emotion. Recall a time in your life when you were among those you loved; perhaps you struggled and worked hard, but your love sustained you. Bring those feelings to this proclamation.

Thessalonians = thes-uh-LOH-nee-uhnz

A tender image.

Smile with your voice, eyes, and face as you recall this affection.

The Gospel was proclaimed in words as well as in the example of their lives.

Paul and his companions worked to earn a living while in Thessalonica, so as not to be a financial burden to the community.

Paul's joy is overflowing; their hard work has paid off and the Gospel is flourishing in the community!

Pleased.

RESPONSORIAL PSALM   Psalm 131:1, 2, 3

R. In you, Lord, I have found my peace.

O Lord, my heart is not proud,
    nor are my eyes haughty;
I busy not myself with great things,
    nor with things too sublime for me.

Nay rather, I have stilled and quieted
    my soul like a weaned child.
Like a weaned child on its mother's lap,
    so is my soul within me.

O Israel, hope in the Lord,
    both now and forever.

READING II   1 Thessalonians 2:7b–9, 13

A reading from the first Letter of Saint Paul to the Thessalonians

Brothers and sisters:
We were **gentle** among you, as a nursing **mother** cares
    for her **children**.
With **such** affection for you, we were **determined** to **share**
    with you
      not **only** the **gospel** of God, but our **very** selves as well,
    so **dearly** beloved had you **become** to us.
You recall, brothers and sisters, our **toil** and **drudgery**.
Working **night** and **day** in order **not** to **burden** any of you,
    we **proclaimed** to you the **gospel** of **God**.

And for **this** reason we too give **thanks** to God **unceasingly**,
    that, in receiving the word of **God** from hearing **us**,
    you received not a **human** word but, as it truly **is**,
      the word of **God**,
    which is now at **work** in you who **believe**.

---

repentance and return to the covenant of their ancestors.

READING II   In the opening chapters of Paul's First Letter to the Thessalonians, we hear about his relationship with and ministry to the young community. He gives thanks for the manifestation of their faith, hope, and love, and their reception of the Word with joy even in the midst of affliction. He has shared in their affliction, *thlipsis*, a sign of end-time suffering, yet he never lets suffering, misunderstanding, and persecution hinder his proclamation of the Good News among them. Paul's affection for this community is deepened from their common experience of suffering for the sake of the Gospel. He is as gentle among them as a nursing mother, one who looks out for the well-being of the children entrusted to her.

Paul is not alone in feeling such tenderness for the Thessalonians. Silvanus and Timothy, cowriters of the letter, have also been missionaries there, bringing the Gospel of God to them and sharing their very selves with their beloved community. Although the three missionaries had a right to expect the community to care for their physical needs while they proclaimed the Gospel, they worked at their own trades so as not to be a burden to any of them. Their ministry proved fruitful, as Paul reiterates in his thanksgiving that God's Word is working powerfully in the believing community at Thessalonica. By their lives of faith, they join with Paul, Silvanus, and Timothy in becoming transmitters of the Good News to others.

A didactic reading. Most of the specific admonitions won't be meaningful to your assembly, but the key is found in the final line.

Pause briefly after "but," then slow down.

Let your disdain for these empty works come through.

phylacteries = fih-LAK-tuh-reez (small containers with verses from the Torah, worn bound to the arms, hands, and forehead)
Pause.

Three admonitions against demanding titles which imply you are the sole arbiter of truth.

Humility is more than charity toward others or thinking less of ourselves. It means being open to learn from others, and admitting that we may not know everything.

GOSPEL   Matthew 23:1–12

A reading from the holy Gospel according to Matthew

Jesus spoke to the **crowds** and to his **disciples**, saying,
    "The **scribes** and the **Pharisees**
        have taken their **seat** on the chair of **Moses**.
Therefore, **do** and **observe** all things **whatsoever** they **tell** you,
    but do **not** follow their **example**.
For they **preach** but they do not **practice**.
They tie up heavy **burdens** hard to **carry**
    and lay them on people's shoulders,
        but **they** will not lift a **finger** to move them.
All their **works** are performed to be **seen**.
They **widen** their phylacteries and **lengthen** their tassels.
They **love** places of **honor** at **banquets**,
        seats of **honor** in **synagogues**,
    greetings in **marketplaces**, and the salutation '**Rabbi**.'
As for **you**, do **not** be called 'Rabbi.'
You have but **one** teacher, and you are all **brothers**.
Call **no one** on earth your **father**;
    you have but **one** Father in **heaven**.
Do **not** be called '**Master**';
    you have but **one** master, the **Christ**.
The **greatest** among you must be your **servant**.
Whoever **exalts** himself will be **humbled**;
    but whoever **humbles** himself will be **exalted**."

GOSPEL   In one of the most comforting passages in Matthew's Gospel, Jesus says "My yoke is easy and my burden light" (Matthew 11:30). In today's Gospel, he speaks about the burdens that the Pharisees lay upon people's shoulders, burdens that are far from easy. The Pharisees do nothing to ease the weights they impose, while they find ways to justify not taking the burdens upon their own shoulders. Seeing themselves as the authentic teachers, they expect to be treated with honor at banquets, synagogues, and even in the marketplace. They

ostentatiously widen the prayer boxes called phylacteries and lengthen the tassels on their prayer shawls so everyone will notice their devotion to the Law. They would expect also to receive honor by the respectful titles given to them: rabbi, teacher, and father. Jesus' injunction to avoid these designations is a warning to stay away from the power and status that the terms conveyed at the time.

Jesus' critique of the Pharisees in this passage is uncompromising. His harsh words here and elsewhere have sometimes led to a negative assessment of all

Pharisees. Yet Jesus' judgment is not against all Pharisees, or even against their teaching. Pharisees intended to live the Law to the fullest, and to separate themselves from everything (and everyone) unclean. Only those who took this intention to the extreme, who placed undue burdens, who expected to be revered above others, and who plotted against Jesus are the objects of his critique. E.P.

THIRTY-SECOND SUNDAY IN ORDINARY TIME

A beautiful exhortatory description of wisdom. Think of someone whose way of life makes them beautiful to you. Think of that person as you proclaim.

This reading demands that you smile as you describe wisdom. Otherwise, she will come across as a dry academic rather than a fascinating and generous woman.

This idea is repeated three times. Heighten each instance, or start high and make each more subtle.

Wisdom comes even before you desire her! Indeed, desire for wisdom is a sign that wisdom has already found you.

Note the irony that the wisdom you look for elsewhere is right outside your door!

Emphasize the action of wisdom.

Keep your tone gentle and gracious in imitation of Wisdom herself.

solicitude = suh-LIS-uh-tood (kindness)

> **TO KEEP IN MIND**
> Pay attention to the pace of your reading. Varying the pace gives listeners clues to the meaning of the text. The most common problem for proclaimers new to the ministry is going too fast to be understood.

LECTIONARY #154

READING I   Wisdom 6:12–16

A reading from the Book of Wisdom

Resplendent and **unfading** is **wisdom**,
  and she is **readily** perceived by those who **love** her,
  and **found** by those who **seek** her.
She **hastens** to make herself **known** in **anticipation**
    of their desire;
  whoever **watches** for her at **dawn** shall **not** be disappointed,
  for he shall **find** her sitting by his **gate**.
For taking thought of **wisdom** is the **perfection** of **prudence**,
  and **whoever** for **her** sake keeps **vigil**
  shall **quickly** be **free** from **care**;
because she makes her **own** rounds, **seeking** those worthy
    of her,
  and graciously **appears** to them in the **ways**,
  and **meets** them with all **solicitude**.

READING I   Today's reading from Wisdom is part of an exhortation given to kings and magistrates. The author, who is sometimes presented as the voice of King Solomon, addresses his readers as judges (1:1) and princes (6:21). Royal persons were symbols in Greek culture of the ideal human person; by addressing his audience this way, the writer intends to inspire everyone to reach for the virtues of the ideal ruler. Not only those in palaces, but every human person has an exalted, kingly dignity, and should seek wisdom. Shortly after telling his audience that he is advising them to learn wisdom, the writer describes wisdom in the lovely poetry of today's reading.

In this book, as well as other wisdom literature (Proverbs, The Song of Songs, and Sirach), wisdom is portrayed as a woman. Here, she is "resplendent [radiant] and unfading," signaling a perennial and extensive beauty. While at times she seems hidden, those who love her and seek her can readily find her. In fact, she desires to make herself known, and the task of the writer is to reveal her identity. Recognizing her requires constancy and engagement of one's whole person in the pursuit: desiring her, watching for her, setting one's heart on her, keeping vigil for her. She is sitting at the gate, but will be missed by those who are not attentive. The seeking and attention required of those who desire her is matched by Wisdom's own seeking and attentiveness.

When the many passages presenting Wisdom are brought together, her portrait comes very close to that of God. In this passage, the writer begins a sketch of her that will be more fully drawn in the subsequent chapters of the book; each added

For meditation and context:

RESPONSORIAL PSALM   Psalm 63:2, 3–4, 5–6, 7–8 (2b)

R. My soul is thirsting for you, O Lord my God.

O God, you are my God whom I seek;
    for you my flesh pines and my soul thirsts
    like the earth, parched, lifeless and
        without water.

Thus have I gazed toward you in the
        sanctuary
    to see your power and your glory,
for your kindness is a greater good than life;
    my lips shall glorify you.

Thus will I bless you while I live;
    lifting up my hands, I will call upon
        your name.
As with the riches of a banquet shall my soul
        be satisfied,
    and with exultant lips my mouth shall
        praise you.

I will remember you upon my couch,
    and through the night-watches I will
        meditate on you:
you are my help,
    and in the shadow of your wings I shout
        for joy.

A didactic reading. Paul is not so much giving a chronology of the last days, as he is emphasizing that all who love Christ will be together in the end.

Thessalonians = thes-uh-LOH-nee-uhnz

Imagine yourself consoling someone who has lost a loved one. What tone would you use?

"the rest" = those who don't believe in Christ and the Resurrection. It's not inappropriate to grieve, but we do so while holding fast to our hope in the Resurrection.

The shorter version ends here.

This is a vision of great joy, not impending doom; make that clear.

archangel = AHRK-ayn-jihl; this is the key thought. Set it apart. Pause before and after.

READING II   Thessalonians 4:13–18

A reading from the first Letter of Saint Paul to the Thessalonians

We do not want you to be **unaware**, brothers and sisters,
    about those who have fallen **asleep**,
    so that you may not **grieve** like the rest, who have **no hope**.
For if we **believe** that Jesus **died** and **rose**,
    so **too** will **God**, through **Jesus**,
    bring **with** him those who have fallen **asleep**.
Indeed, we tell you this, on the **word** of the **Lord**,
    that we who are **alive**,
    who are **left** until the **coming** of the **Lord**,
    will **surely** not precede those who have fallen **asleep**.
For the Lord **himself**, with a word of command,
    with the voice of an **archangel** and with the **trumpet** of God,
    will come **down** from **heaven**,
    and the **dead** in Christ will rise **first**.
Then **we** who are **alive**, who are left,
    will be caught up together **with** them in the clouds
    to **meet** the **Lord** in the air. »

dimension presents her as intimately connected both with God and with humanity.

READING II   Some people have no hope! In his letter to the Thessalonians, Paul explains why believers should not be counted among hopeless people who grieve over those who have fallen asleep. Paul is not referring to the natural sadness that people feel when a loved one dies; that loss is real and painful. The hopelessness that concerns Paul comes from thinking that death is the end: there is nothing beyond our earthly existence.

Hope is firmly founded on our faith in Jesus' Death and Resurrection, the source and pattern for those who die. Another affirmation that Paul emphasizes throughout this letter is that the risen Christ will come again. Paul uses the word *parousia*, ("coming" or "presence") to announce Christ's coming again, proclaimed with the voice of an archangel and sound of trumpet. In the Old Testament, this audio-visual imagery is associated with God's mysterious appearance, or theophany.

The Thessalonians were afraid that those who die before Christ's *parousia*

would be left out. Their concern is likely not only for those who have already "fallen asleep," but for themselves as well, in case they also die before his return. Paul tells them that those who die before his coming will be the first to rise at the *parousia*. And those who are still alive when the Lord comes will also be brought into his presence. Among Paul's most hope-filled words are "we shall always be with the Lord."

Paul's description of the *parousia* is not intended to describe in literal terms the future coming of Christ. There are multiple ways in which biblical writers portray God's

Make sure "these words" refer to what you've just proclaimed.

Thus we shall **always** be with the **Lord**.
Therefore, **console** one another with these words.

[Shorter Form: 1 Thessalonians 4:13–14]

GOSPEL   Matthew 25:1–13

A reading from the holy Gospel according to Matthew

A narrative, which should be great fun to proclaim. Remember Jesus' skills as a storyteller, and fill this reading with enough color and humor to attract a crowd of five thousand!

Don't lose the words "virgins" and "lamps."

What do you think about the foolish and the wise? Let your feelings about them shade your tone.

Quickly and suddenly!
A cry of joy!
Keep your pace up to convey the bustle and excitement.

A note of panic.

Is there cattiness in this reply or does it simply express a sad fact?

Jesus told his disciples this parable:
    "The kingdom of heaven will be like ten **virgins**
        who took their **lamps** and went out to meet the **bridegroom**.
Five of them were **foolish** and **five** were **wise**.
The **foolish** ones, when taking their lamps,
        brought **no oil** with them,
        but the **wise** brought **flasks** of **oil** with their lamps.
Since the bridegroom was long **delayed**,
        they all became **drowsy** and fell **asleep**.
At **midnight**, there was a **cry**,
        '**Behold**, the **bridegroom**! Come out to **meet** him!'
Then **all** those virgins got **up** and trimmed their lamps.
The **foolish** ones said to the **wise**,
        'Give us some of **your** oil,
        for **our** lamps are going **out**.'
But the **wise** ones replied,
        '**No**, for there may not be enough for us **and** you.
Go **instead** to the merchants and **buy** some for yourselves.'
While they went off to buy it,
        the **bridegroom** came
        and those who were **ready** went **into** the wedding feast
            with him.

---

final victory and Christ's *parousia*. What Paul and others assure us is that Christ *will* come again, and that we will always be with him. Paul's message is one of comfort, consolation, and abiding hope!

GOSPEL   The parable in today's Gospel is taken from Jesus' final discourse in Matthew's account. The entire discourse focuses on the last things, particularly God's final judgment, which will mean condemnation for the wicked and salvation for the just. The parable is related to apocalyptic literature: highly imaginative,

dualistic, and future oriented. There are multiple purposes in such writing. It exhorts people who are suffering to stand firm; it warns people of coming judgment; it encourages righteous living in the present; it urges vigilance, patience, and preparedness; and it engenders hope, even in face of the unknown time of God's final victory.

In this part of his long address, Jesus uses parables that explain how believers should live in the present age as they await the *parousia*. The parable of the ten virgins has some apocalyptic features, such as dualism, judgment, and separation of the

good and the bad; it does not, however, use the fantastic images that are often part of apocalyptic writing, employing instead a common experience of a wedding. The scenario comes from the first-century Palestinian custom of the bride going in procession with attendants to meet the bridegroom and share in the wedding banquet. The context of the parable gives guidance in how to interpret it. Here, as in the entire discourse, the focus is on being well prepared for the coming of the Son of Man, the bridegroom in the parable. The parable begins: "the kingdom of heaven will be like

Heighten the second "Lord." Is the tone dismayed? entitled?

Simply, without malice. It's late and dangerous to open the door.
Pause.

Here is the point. Make sure your community hears this call to steadfast awareness!

Then the door was **locked**.
Afterwards the **other** virgins came and said,
  'Lord, **Lord**, open the **door** for us!'
But he said in reply,
  '**Amen**, I **say** to you, I do not **know** you.'
Therefore, **stay awake**,
  for you **know** neither the **day** nor the **hour**."

TO KEEP IN MIND
Proclamation cannot be effective unless it is expressive. As you prepare your proclamation, make choices about emotions. Some choices are already evident in the text.

---

ten virgins." All who await the coming of the bridegroom are expected to be well prepared. They should have sufficient "oil," a symbol that can represent all the good works, such as mercy and justice and faithfulness, expected of believers. Those who do not await the bridegroom with a full supply of good works can be expected to be excluded from the great wedding banquet, symbol of the joy of the Kingdom of Heaven. E.P.

THIRTY-THIRD SUNDAY
IN ORDINARY TIME

LECTIONARY #157

An exhortation in praise of strong women. Think of a woman you know personally who inspires you with her virtue and character. Keep her in mind as you proclaim.

Take your time. Linger over the loving images in this reading, and smile as you recount them.

distaff; spindle (tools used to spin thread from wool or flax)

Heighten this line; her care extends beyond her family to the neediest in the community.

Dismiss these as worthless.

"fears the Lord" = acts as God desires, with love and justice. Pause.

With conviction; this is the conclusion. Her character is an example for all.

READING I   Proverbs 31:10–13, 19–20, 30–31

A reading from the Book of Proverbs

When one finds a **worthy wife**,
   her value is **far** beyond **pearls**.
Her **husband**, entrusting his **heart** to her,
   has an **unfailing** prize.
She brings him **good**, and not **evil**,
   all the days of her **life**.
She obtains **wool** and **flax**
   and **works** with **loving** hands.
She puts her **hands** to the **distaff**,
   and her fingers **ply** the **spindle**.
She **reaches** out her hands to the **poor**,
   and **extends** her arms to the **needy**.
Charm is **deceptive** and beauty **fleeting**;
   the woman who **fears** the LORD is to be **praised**.
Give her a **reward** for her labors,
   and let her works **praise** her at the city gates.

READING I   The reading from Proverbs is part of the instruction given to King Lemuel by his mother. She warns him about the pitfalls of strong drink, then reminds him to care for the poor and be a champion for the needy (Proverbs 31:1–9). After she cautions him about wasting his strength (*hayil*) on women, she describes the kind of woman he *should* seek: a woman of strength (*hayil*), translated in our reading as "worthy." Strength, often associated with physical or military competence, has a much broader meaning, including social, political, practical, and intellectual dimensions. Most importantly, like the king himself, his wife should be characterized by a strength that encompasses virtuous living and wisdom.

The poem is organized by the letters of the Hebrew alphabet, with each verse beginning with a consecutive letter, opening with the first (*aleph*) and concluding with the last (*tav*). Like similar structures found in the Psalms, this acrostic pattern is orderly and complete, presenting the perfect wife as a paragon of goodness worth more than rubies. To such a woman, a man entrusts his heart. Long recognized as a symbol of love, the heart (*leb*) indicates a person's innermost being, the capacities of mind and will and emotion, referring to a person in totality. The couple is thus united at the deepest level.

The worthy, strong wife exercises her skills both in the household and in the broader society. Obtaining wool and flax and plying the spindle were signs of an accomplished woman, one who would take responsibility for maintaining the home. Yet, like her husband, she looks beyond the home, reaching out to the poor and needy. The poem presents a picture of king and

For meditation and context:

TO KEEP IN MIND
What does the reading ask your assembly to do or to be after hearing your proclamation? Focus on an intention every time you proclaim.

RESPONSORIAL PSALM   Psalm 128:1–2, 3, 4–5 (1a)

R. Blessed are those who fear the Lord.

Blessed are you who fear the LORD,
    who walk in his ways!
For you shall eat the fruit of your handiwork;
    blessed shall you be, and favored.

Your wife shall be like a fruitful vine
    in the recesses of your home;
your children like olive plants
    around your table.

Behold, thus is the man blessed
    who fears the LORD.
The LORD bless you from Zion:
    may you see the prosperity of Jerusalem
    all the days of your life.

An exhortatory reading encouraging the assembly not to be concerned with the end-time, but to continue to live out of our true identity in Christ.

Thessalonians = thes-uh-LOH-nee-uhnz

This is not new information. Emphasize that your community already knows this.

These are images of things over which we have no control; emphasize the surprise more than the disaster.

Again, emphasize that your community has a different identity than those in darkness, and we need to live accordingly.

Slowly, with emphasis.

Really inspire your community: "We can do this!"

READING II   1 Thessalonians 5:1–6

A reading from the first Letter of Saint Paul to the Thessalonians

Concerning **times** and **seasons**, brothers and sisters,
    you have no **need** for anything to be written to you.
For you **yourselves** know very **well** that the day of the Lord
        will come
    like a **thief** at night.
When people are saying, "**Peace** and **security**,"
    then sudden **disaster** comes upon them,
    like **labor** pains upon a pregnant **woman**,
    and they will not **escape**.

But **you**, brothers and sisters, are not in **darkness**,
    for that day to overtake you like a **thief**.
For **all** of you are children of the **light**
    and children of the **day**.
We are **not** of the night or of darkness.
Therefore, let us not **sleep** as the rest do,
    but let us stay **alert** and **sober**.

---

queen united for the benefit of the kingdom. Accomplished as she is, the greatest praise that the worthy wife receives is that she fears the Lord. She stands in reverent awe before the God who governs all things.

Though the advice is given to a king, the portrait of the strong, ideal woman has been applied to worthy wives in general. The text is traditionally recited by Jewish men to their wives on Sabbath evenings, and is often part of funeral services for women.

READING II   Paul's Thessalonian community is awaiting the Day of the Lord. In the Jewish tradition, particularly in later prophetic literature, the Day of the Lord refers to the time of God's absolute judgment, a future event in which the power and justice of God will be revealed, with evil conquered and good rewarded. Sometimes the vision includes cosmic upheaval, and other times earthly tribulation. In common with other apocalyptic texts in the Bible, the imagery is not intended to be taken literally, but employs a variety of emotion-filled illustrations to high-

light God's power to overcome all evil. *When* this day of judgment will happen is uncertain, for it will come like an unexpected thief in the night; *that* it will happen is assured. Paul tells his new Christians that the best way to be prepared is to be children of the day, always remaining alert and sober.

Paul rarely cites Jesus' own teaching, yet when he writes here about the Day of the Lord, we hear echoes of Jesus' apocalyptic discourse. Jesus and Paul use common imagery, typical of other Jewish writings: dramatic calamities; pains like a woman in labor; contrast between darkness

A narrative. There's a lot happening here. Keep a sense of expectation and excitement for your community. At each point in the story, think to yourself, "Just wait until you hear what happens next!"

Don't swallow this line; it's important.

Pick up your pace to convey the eagerness of these two.

How do you feel about this servant? Disappointed, exasperated, embarrassed?

Proudly.

The master is impressed! Make sure his joy is evident (see below).

Keep the excitement up!

Pause.

Remember, this servant was judged to have lesser ability, so the fact that he made two talents is still a good outcome.

This is the same response as before. Slow down, and raise your energy, as if this accomplishment is even more impressive!

GOSPEL   Matthew 25:14–30

A reading from the holy Gospel according to Matthew

[**Jesus** told his disciples this parable:
    "A man going on a **journey**
        called in his servants and **entrusted** his possessions to them.
To one he gave **five** talents; to another, **two**; to a third, **one**—
    to **each** according to his **ability**.
Then he went away.]
Immediately the one who received **five** talents went and **traded**
        with them,
    and made **another** five.
Likewise, the one who received **two** made **another** two.
But the man who received **one** went off and dug a **hole**
        in the ground
    and **buried** his master's money.

["After a **long** time
    the master of those servants came back
    and settled accounts with them.
The one who had received five talents came forward
    bringing the **additional** five.
He said, 'Master, you gave me **five** talents.
See, I have made five **more**.'
His master said to him, 'Well **done**, my good and
        faithful servant.
Since you were faithful in **small** matters,
    I will give you **great** responsibilities.
Come, share your master's **joy**.']
Then the one who had received two talents **also** came forward
        and said,
    'Master, you gave me **two** talents.
See, I have made two **more**.'
His master said to him, 'Well **done**, my good and
        faithful servant. »

---

and light; an unknown day and hour. The language is sharp and readily draws us into the scenes. Though the images are frightening, both Jesus and Paul use them to encourage disciples to remain faithful until the end.

Paul had good reason to write about the Day of the Lord, and the expectation of Jesus' return (*parousia*). The Thessalonians offer us the earliest picture of the problems associated with misguided understanding and excessive focus on God's future coming as judge and redeemer. The community was more anxious than joyful, more fearful

than hopeful. A similar misunderstanding has led repeatedly to dire predictions, judgments regarding who will be saved, and calculating the precise date of the end of this world. Paul's exhortation to the community states clearly that we do not know when Christ will come again, and that here and now we should comfort one another, living in steadfast and sure hope.

GOSPEL   In Thessalonians, Paul exhorts the community to be prepared for the Day of the Lord by remaining alert and sober. Paired with the

parable in today's Gospel, we learn that being alert and sober is not a passive stance of simply waiting patiently for the Lord's coming. Preparedness involves working according to one's capability, faithfulness, and taking responsibility.

Jesus introduces the parable simply: a man going on a journey calls his servants together before departing. He entrusts his possessions to them and gives each talents based on their abilities. A talent, in the Judaism of Jesus' day, is a monetary unit of high value, variable depending on the metal used as well as its place of origin. Even one

Since you were faithful in **small** matters,
    I will give you **great** responsibilities.
Come, **share** your master's **joy**.'
Then the one who had received the **one** talent came forward
    and said,
    'Master, I knew you were a **demanding** person,
    harvesting where you did not **plant**
    and **gathering** where you did not **scatter**;
    so out of **fear** I went off and **buried** your talent in the ground.
Here it is **back**.'
His master said to him in reply, 'You **wicked**, **lazy** servant!
So you **knew** that I **harvest** where I did not plant
    and **gather** where I did not scatter?
Should you not then have put my money in the **bank**
    so that I could have got it back with **interest** on my return?
Now then! **Take** the talent from him and give it to the one
    with **ten**.
For to everyone who **has**,
    more will be given and he will grow **rich**;
    but from the one who has **not**,
    even what he **has** will be taken **away**.
And **throw** this **useless** servant into the **darkness** outside,
    where there will be **wailing** and **grinding** of teeth.'"

[Shorter: Matthew 25:14–15, 19–21 (see brackets)]

Side notes (left column):

Pause.

The servant's fear should be evident in his voice.

Don't lose "out of fear."

The anger in this response comes suddenly. Quicken your pace and raise your intensity.

TO KEEP IN MIND
In a narrative, find an emotion or point of view for each character, keeping in mind that these might change during the reading.

---

talent gives the servant a significant amount of money, and the master rightfully expects a return on his investment.

It is easy to see that the master (*kyrios*) represents the Lord who will return and judge the actions of his servants. The first two have increased the original talents, and earn the master's praise, first with an exclamation: "Well done!" They are good and faithful. The first term affirms that the servants have acted responsibly in accordance with the master's will; the second that they have been dependable and trustworthy. The master refers to each of them as *my* good and faithful servant, highlighting his personal relationship with them. It is his own joy that they will share.

What a strong contrast with the terms he uses to describe the third servant! He is wicked, lazy, and useless. The three words together paint a picture of one whose lack of action squanders the master's gift and is contrary to the master's intentions. The relationship is severed, "you" wicked servant, not "my" servant. The servant himself uses a word that sums up the reason for his failure: fear. His fear has led him to view the master only as harsh, and to hide all that he received.

Both the positive and negative portraits can act as incentives to be always prepared for the Lord's coming, whether that be in the here and now or at his final appearance. E.P.

OUR LORD JESUS CHRIST, KING OF THE UNIVERSE

LECTIONARY #160

An exhortatory description of God's loving care for us. The reading is in God's voice. How does God sound describing this tender care for us?

Ezekiel = ee-ZEE-kee-uhl

The first time you practice this reading, try substituting the word "you" for "my sheep" or "them." (Do this only in practice, of course!) What intention and emotions come up for you? Then practice the reading as written, with the same intention and emotions.

Keep your tone gentle and full of compassion.

These sheep are too important to hire someone to shepherd them.

Slow down; make each of these five actions distinct. Raise your intensity slightly on each of the first four.

Now drop your tone. This action is also part of how God cares for the sheep. The unspoken assumption is that the sleek and strong have gotten so by preying on the weak.

This judgment is still an expression of God's care.

READING I   Ezekiel 34:11–12, 15–17

A reading from the Book of the Prophet Ezekiel

Thus says the Lord GOD:
   I **myself** will look after and **tend** my sheep.
As a **shepherd** tends his flock
   when he finds himself among his **scattered** sheep,
   so will **I** tend my sheep.
I will **rescue** them from every place where they were **scattered**
   when it was **cloudy** and **dark**.
I **myself** will **pasture** my sheep;
   I **myself** will give them **rest**, says the Lord GOD.
The **lost** I will **seek** out,
   the **strayed** I will bring **back**,
   the **injured** I will **bind** up,
   the **sick** I will **heal**,
   but the **sleek** and the **strong** I will **destroy**,
   shepherding them **rightly**.

As for **you**, my sheep, says the Lord GOD,
   I will **judge** between **one** sheep and **another**,
   between **rams** and **goats**.

READING I   The God who speaks to Ezekiel announces both comfort and judgment. In the verses just before today's reading, God tells Ezekiel to prophesy against the shepherds, or leaders, of Israel, particularly the kings who have responsibility for the flock. Because they have not cared for their subjects, God declares, "Woe to the shepherds of Israel who have been pasturing themselves!" God says that his flock has become food for wild beasts because their shepherds looked out only for themselves.

Concerned for these abandoned sheep, God promises to become their shepherd, saying "I myself will look after and tend my sheep." Unlike the lax and self-centered leaders of Israel, God's shepherding will be energetic and attentive. God will look after and tend the flock; both verbs indicate active searching, necessary because so many sheep have been scattered due to the neglect of kingly shepherds. God will rescue these scattered sheep; here God's action is forceful, snatching them away from predators. The flock belongs to God, who refers to them as "my

sheep," the sheep are God's own, and God takes on all the responsibility for them: pasturing (feeding), giving them rest (letting them lie down). God announces that the lost, strayed, injured, and sick will receive special attention.

After describing God's compassionate shepherding, the prophecy returns briefly to the condemnation of those who grow sleek and strong while ignoring their flock. God will shepherd them rightly, literally, "will make them feed upon justice." Hearing this reading on the last Sunday of the liturgical year, we look ahead to God's final

For meditation and context:

RESPONSORIAL PSALM   Psalm 23:1–2, 2–3, 5–6 (1)

R. The Lord is my shepherd; there is nothing I shall want.

The LORD is my shepherd; I shall not want.
    In verdant pastures he gives me repose.

Beside restful waters he leads me;
    he refreshes my soul.
He guides me in right paths
    for his name's sake.

You spread the table before me
    in the sight of my foes;
you anoint my head with oil;
    my cup overflows.

Only goodness and kindness follow me
    all the days of my life;
and I shall dwell in the house of the LORD
    for years to come.

A didactic reading about Resurrection; there's great joy in this teaching. Let that come through in your proclamation.

Corinthians = kohr-IN-thee-uhnz

Paul repeats the same point (that Christ's Resurrection prefigures our own) in different ways.

This should sound self-evident.

What follows is a list of three events.

This is good news! The world will be freed from every oppression and evil. Don't make it sound terrible.

A complex construction. Take your time.

No pause after "subjected."

"The one" is God the Father.

This is the point. Slowly and deliberately.

READING II   1 Corinthians 15:20–26, 28

A reading from the first Letter of Saint Paul to the Corinthians

Brothers and sisters:
Christ has been **raised** from the dead,
    the **firstfruits** of those who have fallen asleep.
For since **death** came through **man**,
    the **resurrection** of the dead came **also** through man.
For just as in **Adam** all **die**,
    so too in **Christ** shall all be brought to **life**,
    but each one in proper **order**:
    Christ the **firstfruits**;
    then, at his coming, those who **belong** to Christ;
    then comes the **end**,
    when he **hands over** the kingdom to his **God** and Father,
    when he has **destroyed** every **sovereignty**
    and every **authority** and **power**.
For he must **reign** until he has put **all** his enemies under his **feet**.
The **last** enemy to be destroyed is **death**.
When **everything** is **subjected** to him,
    then the Son **himself** will **also** be subjected
    to the one who subjected everything to **him**,
    so that **God** may be **all** in **all**.

---

accounting of all in the flock, from the lost to the leaders. It is reassuring that the God who will judge is the same God who is the benevolent shepherd, the one to whom the flock belongs.

READING II The Death and Resurrection of Jesus is at the heart of Paul's faith. When he writes about what God will do in the future, Paul bases his confidence on what God has already done: "Christ has been raised from the dead." Referred to as the kerygma (the earliest Christian proclamation and preaching), the

Death and Resurrection of Christ is the foundational belief of the whole Church, past and present.

The kerygma affirms that Christ has been raised (more literally) "from among those who have died." Paul does not use the word *thanatos*, indicating resurrection from a "state of death" (even though that is also true), but *nekroi*, "those who have died." He thereby emphasizes that Christ has a bond with those who have died. Like others who have died, Christ has run the whole course of human life, and experiences with all humanity the reality of

death. He is the "firstfruits of those who have fallen asleep." Paul's use of the terminology "firstfruits" and "falling asleep" points to the future. Since Christ is the "firstfruits," we can look forward to a full harvest of all the *nekroi*. Those who have fallen asleep, like Christ, will be awakened.

In Christ's Resurrection, Paul envisions Christ as the second Adam. The first Adam brought death into the world; the second Adam brought life—a life that stretches beyond our mortal existence, and will be given to those who have fallen asleep in death. Not only is Christ the life-giver, he

A narrative. The story is simple yet powerful.

See this awesome scene unfold before you as you proclaim. Keep your energy up.

The act would have been very familiar to Jesus' listeners.
Rather than divide the assembly into "right" and "left," vary eye contact throughout the assembly during the whole reading.

Note that Jesus speaks of himself in the third person (as the "king").

With loving invitation.

Slowly. Give each action its due. Imagine yourself as the recipient of these acts of kindness. How do you feel as you express your gratitude?

Their response becomes more confused (and curious) with each question.

Note that how we care for the least is the single criterion for entrance to the Kingdom. Simply; this is not a new insight you're teaching. Rather, you're saying, "Didn't you know this?"
Pause.

GOSPEL   Matthew 25:31–46

A reading from the holy Gospel according to Matthew

Jesus said to his **disciples**:
   "When the Son of Man comes in his **glory**,
      and all the angels with him,
      he will sit upon his glorious **throne**,
      and **all** the nations will be **assembled** before him.
And he will **separate** them **one** from **another**,
      as a **shepherd** separates the **sheep** from the **goats**.
He will place the **sheep** on his **right** and the **goats** on his **left**.
Then the king will say to those on his **right**,
      '**Come**, you who are **blessed** by my Father.
Inherit the kingdom **prepared** for you from the **foundation**
            of the world.
For I was **hungry** and you gave me **food**,
      I was **thirsty** and you gave me **drink**,
      a **stranger** and you **welcomed** me,
      naked and you **clothed** me,
      ill and you **cared** for me,
      in **prison** and you **visited** me.'
Then the righteous will answer him and say,
      'Lord, **when** did we see you hungry and **feed** you,
      or **thirsty** and give you **drink**?
When did we see you a **stranger** and **welcome** you,
      or **naked** and **clothe** you?
When did we see you **ill** or in **prison**, and **visit** you?'
And the king will say to them in reply,
      '**Amen**, I say to you, **whatever** you did
      for one of the **least** brothers of mine, you did for **me**.'

---

will even destroy death. When he comes again, he will overcome every enemy, death being the last, and will subject everything to himself.

   Paul's proclamation of Christ's Death, Resurrection, and coming again is a hope-filled harbinger of the future. We end the liturgical year looking ahead to more than another year, to God's final victory, and to God being all in all. So inclusive is the final portion of our reading that it can be understood as God being everything to everyone, expressing the ultimate purpose of God's saving plan.

GOSPEL The Gospel parables from the past two Sundays focus on preparedness for Christ's coming again, with images of the coming of the bridegroom and return of the master. The virgins who were prepared enjoyed the marriage feast and the faithful servants received the master's generosity, while unprepared bridal attendants were shut out of the marriage feast and a fearful servant cast into darkness. Today's Gospel follows these two parables in Matthew's account, this time speaking of the coming of the Son of Man. The scene is the Last Judgment where we

see people who prepared well for the coming of the Son of Man, and those who did not. The criterion for judgment comes as a surprise to the people in the narrative, as well as to audiences who hear it.

   The judge is the Son of Man, coming in glory. He separates sheep and goats, an action easily understood by a first-century audience, with the more valuable sheep given a privileged position on the right. Like the wise virgins and the faithful servants, those placed on the right are well prepared for the coming of the Son of Man. They are blessed because of what is traditionally

Don't lose "accursed" (= uh-KERST).

Keep your pace up; the point is evident.

This list is more easily proclaimed with very short pauses after "thirsty," "naked," and "prison."

They are incredulous! "We would never do such a thing!"

Firmly.

The last proclaimed word of the year is one of good news! Make sure you proclaim with a smile in your voice, eyes, and face.

TO KEEP IN MIND
Making eye contact with the assembly connects you with them and connects them to the reading more deeply than using your voice alone. This helps the assembly stay with the story and keeps them engaged.

Then he will say to those on his **left**,
    '**Depart** from me, you **accursed**,
    into the eternal **fire** prepared for the **devil** and his angels.
For I was **hungry** and you gave me **no** food,
    I was **thirsty** and you gave me no **drink**,
    a **stranger** and you gave me no **welcome**,
    naked and you gave me no **clothing**,
    ill and in **prison**, and you did not **care** for me.'
Then they will answer and say,
    'Lord, **when** did we see you **hungry** or **thirsty**
    or a **stranger** or **naked** or **ill** or in **prison**,
    and not **minister** to your needs?'
He will answer them, '**Amen**, I say to you,
    what you did not do for one of these **least** ones,
    you did **not** do for **me**.'
And **these** will go off to eternal **punishment**,
    but the **righteous** to eternal **life**."

---

called "the works of mercy": feeding the hungry, giving drink to the thirsty, and so forth. While apparently the blessed ones performed these works for "the least brothers of mine," they in fact did it for the king. Those who did not perform any of the works of mercy are comparable to the unprepared virgins and the fearful servant, and receive a similar harsh punishment.

"The least ones" has been interpreted in a variety of ways. Because the Son of Man refers to them as "least brothers *of mine*," "least of these brothers and sisters of mine," some scholars see them as Jesus'

own disciples, or more narrowly, as Christian missionaries. Thus, the way people treat Jesus' disciples is the basis for judgment. A broader interpretation regards the least ones as any disadvantaged members of society. All people will be judged on the mercy they show to the hungry, thirsty, naked, and so on, whether they are Jesus' disciples or not. Whatever the original intent of the judgment scene may have been, the broader, universalist understanding offers an important challenge to all of us who hear this Gospel. The little ones of our world all belong to Christ, and in show-

ing mercy to them, we meet the Christ who will also come as judge. E.P.